Political Participation in the Middle East

POLITICAL

PARTICIPATION

IN THE

MIDDLE EAST

EDITED BY
Ellen Lust-Okar
Saloua Zerhouni

LYNNE
RIENNER
PUBLISHERS

BOULDER
LONDON

Published in the United States of America in 2008 by
Lynne Rienner Publishers, Inc.
1800 30th Street, Boulder, Colorado 80301
www.rienner.com

and in the United Kingdom by
Lynne Rienner Publishers, Inc.
3 Henrietta Street, Covent Garden, London WC2E 8LU

Library of Congress Cataloging-in-Publication Data
Political participation in the Middle East / edited by Ellen Lust-Okar and
Saloua Zerhouni.
    p. cm.
  Includes bibliographical references and index.
  ISBN 978-1-58826-626-2 (hardcover : alk. paper) — ISBN 978-1-58826-602-6
(pbk. : alk. paper)
  1. Political participation—Middle East. 2. Political
participation—Africa, North. 3. Elections—Middle East.
4. Elections—Africa, North. I. Lust-Okar, Ellen, 1966– II. Zerhouni, Saloua,
1973–
  JQ1758.A91P65 2008
  323'.0420956—dc22

                                                        2008006783

British Cataloguing in Publication Data
A Cataloguing in Publication record for this book
is available from the British Library.

Printed and bound in the United States of America

The paper used in this publication meets the requirements
of the American National Standard for Permanence of
Paper for Printed Library Materials Z39.48-1992.

5   4   3   2   1

Contents

Acknowledgments   vii

1   Taking Political Participation Seriously
    Ellen Lust-Okar   1

Part 1 Participation Under Authoritarian Rule

2   The Nature of Political Participation
    Holger Albrecht   15

3   Formal and Informal Venues of Engagement
    Laila Alhamad   33

Part 2 Negotiating the Electoral Arena

4   Intra-Elite Struggles in Iranian Elections
    Güneş Murat Tezcür   51

5   Competitive Clientelism in Jordanian Elections
    Ellen Lust-Okar   75

6   Inside an Egyptian Parliamentary Campaign
    Samer Shehata   95

7   Local Elections in Gaza
    Dag Tuastad   121

Part 3 Beyond Electoral Politics

8   Opposition Groups in Bahrain
    Katja Niethammer   143

9   Mapping Participation in Egypt
    Nihad Gohar   171

10   The Dynamics of Civil Society in Morocco
     Driss Maghraoui   193

11   The Moroccan Parliament
     Saloua Zerhouni   217

12   Trade Unions in Tunisia
     Delphine Cavallo   239

Part 4 Conclusion

13   Looking Forward
     Saloua Zerhouni   259

Bibliography   267
The Contributors   285
Index   287
About the Book   301

Acknowledgments

This book is the outcome of a long, collaborative, and enormously enjoyable journey, for which there are many to thank. It began in a workshop on political participation under authoritarianism in the Middle East and North Africa at the seventh Mediterranean Social and Political Research Meeting, organized by the Robert Schuman Center for Advanced Studies of the European University Institute (EUI). Convened in Montecatini Terme, Italy, the intensive workshop brought together scholars from Europe, the Middle East, and the United States, providing a wonderful atmosphere not only for serious reflection, but also for establishing and strengthening friendships that sustained our collaboration and made work on this volume a pleasure. To the EUI staff and, in particular, Imco Brouwer, whose enthusiastic and friendly coordination makes these meetings such a success, we give our thanks.

We are also grateful to our contributors, who encouraged us to undertake this volume, and we thank them for their patience and hard work. In addition, we thank Brian Calfano, Samir Fayyaz, Emile Sahliyeh, and Jillian Schwedler for their constructive feedback.

We also wish to acknowledge those whose cheerful assistance in editing have made this project much more fun than it otherwise would have been: we thank Lydia Lundgren, Elise Pfeiffer, and Hannah Wallerstein for their work. We are also grateful for support provided by the MacMillan Center for International and Area Studies, which has made this project possible. And last, we thank Lynne Rienner Publishers and two reviewers for invaluable input into the project. We are particularly grateful to Marilyn Grobschmidt for her seemingly unlimited patience and wonderful guidance. Without the assistance, encouragement, and enthusiasm of so many, this project simply would not have been realized.

—Ellen Lust-Okar
Saloua Zerhouni

1

Taking Political Participation Seriously

Ellen Lust-Okar

Since the 1980s, we have seen renewed political participation in the Middle East and North Africa (MENA), and in authoritarian regimes more generally. Voters went to the polls, political parties (re)opened their offices, nongovernmental organizations (NGOs) mushroomed, and vigorous debates over political and economic reform were published in newly founded and independent media. Political activity has often coincided with, and in some cases was stimulated by, Western policies focused on democracy promotion. Funding for NGOs, election promotion, parliamentary strengthening, and other projects poured into the region, and "democratization" became the buzzword, though not the reality.

Scholars and policymakers tried to make sense of the changes in the context of democratization. Studies of elections, political parties, and other civil society actors questioned whether, and how, such political participation could promote democracy. Later, as the prospects for democracy went unmet, attention turned toward studies focusing on the endurance of authoritarianism.[1]

Whether viewed with optimism or despair, examining participation in elections, political parties, and other "democratically oriented" institutions through the lens of democratization is problematic. Scholars have tended to disregard the reforms that have taken place, largely ignoring important changes that permit political participation. The tendency to dismiss these venues as meaningless charades, often played for the pleasure of international forces, is also particularly disturbing. While this approach may indicate why regimes provide these institutions, it underestimates the agency of citizens within these states: Why do candidates and voters participate in such vacuous exercises? And how can such frameworks help to explain who participates, when, and how?

This volume aims to shift attention away from questions of democratization and enduring authoritarianism, toward the politics of participation in nondemocratic regimes. It seeks to move away from the state-centered approach, which has been the fundamental basis of a range of studies— from those that distinguish different types of authoritarianism and foundations of its stability,[2] to those that examine civil society and political liberalization—in order to discern the potential for democracy.[3] The chapters in this volume continue to recognize the importance of state institutions, but in addition they focus heavily on societal factors.

The volume seeks to bridge the gap between studies of authoritarian politics that view participation largely through formal, "democratic" institutions (e.g., elections, political parties, parliaments) and those that focus on informal institutions (e.g., kinship networks, informal mediation mechanisms). There is a tension between scholarship that essentially dismisses participation through formal venues, and scholarship that focuses on these institutions (particularly on their potentially democratizing effects); scant attention is paid to the informal institutions and coalition politics within which these formal venues are embedded. As Laila Alhamad and Holger Albrecht discuss herein, the debate over whether important political participation takes place within formal *or* informal venues is likely misguided. Political participation is best understood through the interface of informal and formal politics.

This volume seeks to expand our understanding of political participation *as it exists* under authoritarian regimes of the MENA region. It addresses three questions: How do we define and determine the venues of formal and informal political participation in these authoritarian regimes? How do we understand actions and strategies that different actors take within these venues? To what extent does the nature of participation in these venues vary across time and space? We aim to provide a catalyst for an important shift in the prevailing work on the region, which has tended to focus on the possibilities for democratization of these regimes, rather than on the politics of authoritarianism. We also hope to challenge the tendency to dismiss participation within formal arenas—whether in elections, parliaments, political parties, or trade unions—and the tendency to underestimate the importance of informal mechanisms of rule, seeking instead to explore the important intersections of these forces.

■ Outline of the Volume

The authors of this volume turn our attention to recognizing the various forms of political participation in the MENA region, and to how new and existing spaces for political participation affect both the strategies and the venues through which actors attempt to influence decisionmaking in nondemocratic regimes. The authors bring diverse analytical perspectives to the table—including anthropology, history, and political science—in their examination of a wide range of cases, from Bahrain to Palestine.

Part 1 provides a conceptual framework for studying political participation in the Middle East and North Africa. In Chapter 2, Holger Albrecht asks a fundamental question: How should we conceptualize "political participation" in nondemocratic regimes? He argues that understanding political participation is "not only *applicable* in authoritarian states of the Middle East and North Africa . . . but also *critical* to a comprehensive understanding of state-society relationships in this region." Yet he notes that several distinctions must be recognized when applying this concept to MENA states. Perhaps most important, in authoritarian regimes, the "political" sphere frequently overlaps with other spheres, such as the social and economic. Thus the salient issue is whether participation is intended to influence the state, not whether it takes place in ostensibly "political" venues. In addition, Albrecht suggests that analyses need to be cognizant of the various venues of participation (e.g., "classical channels" of political parties and NGOs, state-mobilized participation in corporatist arrangements, and informal social networks), of whether participation occurs through formal or informal channels, of whether it is initiated from above or below, and of whether it is "high intensity" or "low intensity."

In Chapter 3, Laila Alhamad focuses our attention further on the various mechanisms and forms through which the population expresses itself in the public arena. The chapter juxtaposes participation through civil society (i.e., organizations that fill the space between the citizen and the state) and participation through informal venues (i.e., the networks, assemblies, and various other vehicles that prevail throughout society but are not always within purview of the state). Alhamad argues that the objectives of participation in these channels are manifold, and include sharing information, having a voice in political, economic, and social affairs, and finding mechanisms through which to access services and public resources. While this participation is more difficult to see and certainly more difficult to measure, recognizing the various forms of political participation is critical if we are to dispel the myth that MENA states are culturally indisposed to participation, ascertain the deficiencies of formal institutions, and propose ways to enhance participation to achieve better governance.

Part 2 explores electoral participation in Iran, Jordan, Egypt, and Palestine. Elections are particularly interesting, for they are overt opportunities for political participation, and yet many of the incentives that apparently drive candidates and voters to participate in democratic elections (namely policymaking and elite turnover) are arguably less important in nondemocratic regimes. What is it, then, that drives participation, and how does it play out in the MENA states?

The first two chapters in Part 2 explicitly explore the role that elections play in authoritarian regimes. In Chapter 4, Güneş Murat Tezcür examines the 2004 parliamentary and 2005 presidential elections in the Islamic Republic of Iran. He argues that Iranian elections provide a mechanism to resolve intra-elite conflict. They are neither catalysts of democratization nor mechanisms that solidify and consolidate the regime's control over society; rather they serve to perpetuate pluralistic authoritarianism. Ultimately, elections provide formal channels of sustainable political participation that regulate limited competition and pluralism within the boundaries set by the guardians.

In Chapter 5, in contrast, I show how elections under Jordan's authoritarian regime provide an arena for significant competition over access to state resources. This "competitive clientelism" is both systematic and shaped by institutions, although in ways that are fundamentally different from electoral politics in democratic regimes. Most important, voters and candidates behave in ways that are both systematic and strategic, but also that tend to shore up the regime.

In Chapter 6, based on a very similar view of elections, Samer Shehata provides fascinating insights into electoral politics through an ethnographic study of the reelection campaign of a sitting Egyptian parliamentarian, Mounir Fakhry Abdelnour. Shehata demonstrates that candidates attempt to gain support, and citizens understand the role and function of parliamentarians, largely within a "service" framework. Parliamentarians are expected to deliver selected goods and services rather than large-scale public policies. Moreover, he shows how the Egyptian "election season" provides temporary economic relief for coffeehouse owners, potential voters, and others.

Chapter 7 focuses on the politics of local elections in Palestine, another case where elections play a more important role in elite turnover. Dag Tuastad analyzes local elections in Gaza as a space for competition over political authority among different factions whose main motive is to preserve their position. He demonstrates how the elections increase intra-elite conflicts as the power of incumbents becomes threatened. Indeed, the recent violence following the annulment of municipal election results in Gaza demonstrates the alliance of two sets of antidemocratic elites: Fatah, which controlled the formal authority in the area, and the traditional elite, the large families. In the face of a potential Hamas victory, these forces allied to undermine the electoral results, even using violence to undermine the ballot box. In a context characterized by violence, neopatrimonial rule in Palestine constitutes a major handicap to efficient participation.

Part 3 examines the multiple venues of political participation through case studies of Bahrain, Egypt, Morocco, and Tunisia. In Chapter 8, Katja Niethammer further demonstrates how the formal and informal arenas of political participation overlap in sometimes surprising ways. In her study of

Bahrain, Niethammer outlines various arenas of participation, varying in degrees of formality, and then focuses on three groups of actors that have different positions toward state institutions, ranging from adoption to rejection. She demonstrates that these groups have developed divergent strategies directed both toward exerting pressure on the government and toward competition with other oppositional groups. Indeed, the fragmentation of Bahrain's society and the resulting high level of distrust between the participants and boycotters, and more fundamentally between the various religious and ethnic groups, has severely constrained most political actors and reshaped political participation.

In Chapter 9, Nihad Gohar maps the most important channels of participation in Egypt, such as political parties, syndicates, and civil society organizations, both secular and religious, and explores the intersections between official and parallel venues of participation. She analyzes the relative weaknesses and strengths of the various channels of participation, as well as their boundaries and restrictions.

In Chapter 10, Driss Maghraoui examines the political significance of civil society organizations in Morocco, specifically the Equity and Reconciliation Commission and the Royal Institute for Amazigh Culture. He demonstrates that NGOs not only offer space for political activity, but also serve as mechanisms by which the Moroccan monarchy can ease social tensions. On the one hand, these organizations represent the monarchy's specific response to major social and political problems. At the same time, the palace uses them to mobilize, divide, and balance various tendencies within society, thereby helping to ensure its survival. The chapter therefore demonstrates how NGOs, and other venues of participation, should not be seen as exogenously created institutions through which citizens participate, but rather as institutions created in response to—and that also shape—the dynamics of state-society relations.

In Chapter 11, Saloua Zerhouni examines political participation in the Moroccan parliament. The inclusion of parliamentary activity in a study of political participation may at first seem curious; however, as Holger Albrecht notes, given the permeable nature of the boundary between politicians and participants, aimed at influencing the political process, the activities of parliamentarians are perhaps best thought of as political participation. Zerhouni therefore considers the incentives behind parliamentarians' participation in the legislation process and in government oversight.

In Chapter 12, Delphine Cavallo explores the General Labor Union of Tunisia as an arena of both legal and illegal political expression. As a national organization, this union participates in decisions concerning labor rights and laws. At the same time, however, the union sometimes engages in struggling against political and social decisions. Like many other state-created institutions in authoritarian regimes, it plays an ambivalent role, providing a site of activity for supporting the state, but also a space for contestation between actors more and less concerned with political and economic issues, and with supporting or undermining state authority.

▓ Preliminary Insights and Implicit Debates

This volume presents a number of lessons and underlying debates. All contributors generally agree that political participation in the MENA region must be taken seriously. However, they disagree on a number of major issues: the nature of participation—who participates, where and how, and whether the significance of participation lies in the behavior of elites or average citizens; how to characterize the boundaries between informal or formal institutions, the extent to which these venues are integrated, and the degree to which each should be emphasized; the role that international forces play in shaping participation; and finally, the ways in which participation varies across regime types and the availability of other arenas of participation.

There is some debate over the very definition of participation. For instance, the question of intent lies at the heart of a debate between Holger Albrecht and Laila Alhamad. For Albrecht, political participation must be intentionally aimed at influencing public policy. In contrast, Alhamad takes a much broader view, adopting the position of scholars who have defined participation more broadly, not limited to an intentional action aimed at influencing decisionmaking.

The authors also take different approaches to the questions of who participates, and whether participation of average citizens or elites should be studied seriously. Laila Alhamad emphasizes the ways in which a broad public engages in politics, from the man on the street growing a beard in Algeria to the shaikh acting as an intermediary between state and society. Dag Tuastad and Samer Shehata demonstrate a similar breadth of focus. Exploring the politics surrounding elections, they highlight the wide range of actors who engage in politics—from the average citizen mobilizing in support of candidates or exerting pressure on local elites, to local and national party elites attempting to shore up their power. Similarly, I too emphasize the participation of a range of actors, arguing that rural, less educated actors are actually more likely to participate in the case of Jordanian elections.

Other contributors focus their attention primarily on existing and rising elites. For instance, although Holger Albrecht argues convincingly for broadening the notion of participation, he nevertheless pays most attention to the predominantly urban, educated sectors of society. Similarly, Güneş Murat Tezcür and Katja Niethammer focus their efforts on examining how contending elites, at times strengthened by popular mobilization, use various institutions in struggles over political power in Iran and Bahrain. Examining very different venues, Delphine Cavallo and Saloua Zerhouni emphasize how Tunisian trade unions and the Moroccan parliament provide spaces for elite conflict.

Even when examining the same actors, the authors differ in the motivations they attribute to participation. The chapters on elections present very different perspectives on the motivations driving voters. In both Samer Shehata's study of Egypt and my study of Jordan, the prospect of obtaining services and access to state patronage through winning candidates lures voters to the polls. Alternately, in Tezcür's study of Iran, voters are brought to the polls by the need to obtain a stamp on their identification card, without which their access to state services is impeded. This has important implications, for it is not the specific candidate who wins that will determine whether or not voters benefit from turning out at the polls, but the general act of voting that matters. Finally, although Dag Tuastad's study of Palestinian elections is not focused on the motivations of voters, he portrays a society in which both voters and party elites appear to believe that elections can provide a vehicle for fundamental change in the ruling elite—as indeed they did—and in essence change their lives. Such change, particularly at the top levels, is unthinkable in Egypt and Jordan.

Indeed, to some extent, fundamental differences in regime types may be responsible for variations in both the motivations of actors and the range of actors who participate politically. There are enormous distinctions between the nondemocratic regimes in the MENA region: the monarchies of Bahrain, Jordan, and Morocco function very differently than the dominant party states of Egypt and Tunisia, for instance. Even within these broad regime types, there are stark contrasts in the level of contestation within the public sphere, socioeconomic structures, and the nature of the regime. Jordan is not Bahrain, and Tunisia is not Egypt. Consequently, differences in regime type may explain the apparently conflicting interpretations of voters' motivations. The same venue of participation—such as elections—may play a very different role in Palestine, where the distribution of decision-making power among competing elites is at stake, than it does in Jordan, where elections may be better understood as a competition over access to state patronage.

As well, the extent to which high turnout and an appearance of "democracy" is evident may vary, across both regimes and time. At a time when Iran is under enormous pressure from Western, democratic nations, Tezcür is likely correct when he argues that "the regime perceives high turnout rates as a confirmation of the Islamic Republic's public legitimacy and portrays voting in the elections as a national, patriotic duty." Moreover, in a system with large blocs of competing elites in the innermost circles of the regime, elections can become a mechanism of managing factional conflict that is not necessary for the maintenance of the contemporary Egyptian or Tunisian regimes, or the Iranian regime under the Shah.

More generally, the role and impact that various venues for participation play in the distribution of resources and policymaking in authoritarian regimes depend not only on the legal framework that regulates an institution (be it parliament, civil society, etc.), but also on frameworks that regulate other venues. For instance, Nihad Gohar points out that in Egypt the role of political parties is determined not only by laws governing political parties and elections, but also by laws restricting the judiciary, civil society, and other possible sites of participation. The decision to turn to different institutions to voice demands, and the ways in which other institutions are used, can only be understood as part of a larger, interconnected whole.

Thus, how important one institution, whether formal or informal, is as a venue for raising political demands depends in part on the availability of alternative sites. Delphine Cavallo argues that tight restrictions on formal political institutions led Tunisians to use the labor union as a site to make political, as well as economic, demands: it "is an arena that offers competing actors a means to express themselves, to organize themselves, and to be heard." As such, "the UGTT [General Labor Union of Tunisia] remains an important arena for contestation over the balance of power among actors, and indeed for contestation over the boundaries of the state."

For some contributors, the formal political arena has become so restricted as to be rendered nearly meaningless. In this vein, Laila Alhamad argues, "probably the most ubiquitous forms of participation in the MENA region are those of the informal realm, many of which are perpetuated by the rigidity of the formal political sphere. When the state, through its formal institutions, represses, excludes, or fails to listen or respond to people's needs, people resort to the informal realm." The political space within which actors participate has important implications, however. Strengthening participation in the informal realm undermines formal institutions, influences society, and ultimately shapes participation. As Alhamad continues, "This underworld of participation perpetuates a short-term and individualistic vision of society. Promoting ties of patronage, distorting incentives, eluding the rule of law, and evading accountability, these networks do not measure up to the 'good governance' criteria for sustainable political and economic development."

Other contributors present a more complex picture of interactions between formal and informal participation. For example, Katja Niethammer, in her chapter on Bahrain, illustrates how parliamentarians, boycotters, and the more radical opposition, who are engaged in competition with each other as well as with state elite, use both formal and informal participation channels mobilization mechanisms depending in part on the relationship between these actors and the state. The most obvious example is that parliamentarians can use the Shura Council to voice demands, while boycotters and radical opponents cannot. Niethammer also demonstrates, however, the complex relationships between these arenas, which, while distinct, are not entirely divorced from each other. Thus, for instance, a deputy chairman of the elected parliamentary chamber attempted to negotiate with boycotters not by addressing them through political parties, but rather by first informally approaching a leading Shiite cleric. Dag Tuastad's discussion of negotiations over the 2005 local elections in Gaza demonstrates similarly fluid maneuvering between formal and informal political institutions. There, not only did Fatah try to shore up power by reinstituting the role of the mukhtar, which itself reinforced and politicized family structures, but negotiations over the violence that followed the elections also took place through both formal and informal political channels. Boundaries between formal and informal arenas are porous, bringing into question the extent to which primacy should be given to either formal or informal channels of participation.

A third approach focuses on participation in formal arenas but recognizes that social structures and informal political institutions affect participation in these channels. From this perspective, elections, parliaments, and other formal venues are given primary attention, and the institutions within them shape participation. Thus, for instance, Tuastad's chapter on Palestine and my own chapter on Jordan both demonstrate how election laws, districting, and institutions affect political participation and representation. Yet kinship networks and sectarian relations also play major roles in the elections in Egypt, Jordan, Palestine, and Bahrain. Indeed, formal institutions may have very different implications where these social networks are salient than they do elsewhere. Thus the majoritarian electoral laws put in place in Jordan, where tribal networks are salient, acted to fragment the political system rather than to strengthen a small number of political parties, as they do in most established, Western democracies. Social structures and informal mechanisms of obtaining resources significantly shape participation in formal political arenas. From this perspective, formal political arenas and institutional structures within them matter; however, participation in these arenas cannot be understood independently of social identities and informal venues (e.g., tribe, sects, gatherings, and weddings).

A final point of some debate concerns the role that international forces play in promoting and influencing political participation in the MENA region. All contributors agree that international forces have played a major role in the region's domestic politics, although some have addressed this issue more directly than others. There is some disagreement over the impact these forces have had. For Katja Niethammer, international actors—and particularly the National Democratic Institute (NDI)—have played a positive role in mediating between competing elites, bringing them to the negotiating table to resolve differences when all else fails. In a similar respect, Nihad Gohar suggests that, in Egypt, international pressures have combined with internal pressures in "forcing the government to (somewhat) succumb to vocal opposition in the media." The United States and other governments, global civil society organizations, intergovernmental organizations, and international donors voicing concerns about freedom, good governance, and democratization have all provided catalysts for change in Egypt.

Others contributors are much more critical. Laila Alhamad most directly voices this alternative view, arguing that the efforts of international organizations tend to foster an appearance of political reform and democratization while simultaneously shoring up the authoritarian regime:

> Quick and simplistic recipes for political reform, such as those that are put forward by a number of Western governments and scholars, and that figure so prominently in the media and policy debate, provide as cosmetic an attempt at reform as that which MENA governments wish to undertake. Indeed, these have helped to somewhat reduce popular frustration, served to make the West feel good about its efforts, and shed a positive light on MENA governments' perfunctory attempts at political reform.

Other chapters reveal similar perspectives, including my own analysis of Jordan, which suggests that elections (often the centerpiece of international democratization efforts) help sustain the Jordanian monarchy, and Holger Albrecht's analysis of Egypt, which suggests that only a small segment of the population shows interest and confidence in political parties and electoral politics.

However, despite disagreements on the role of international forces, all contributors would agree with Alhamad's recommendation: "To remedy this situation, the debate on democratization in the region needs to move away from its focus on funding and quick fixes, to consider options for political change based on the reality on the ground." Both the more optimistic scholarly works on democratization and democratization programs, and the fairly pessimistic writings on enduring authoritarianism, have more frequently focused on the nature of political participation in democracies than on the reality of participation in nondemocratic regimes. Mapping a strategy to achieve democracy without first taking careful account of where nondemocratic regimes currently are is almost bound to fail. The chapters that follow aim not only to provide readers with a better understanding of the many venues of political participation in a diverse set of nondemocratic regimes in the MENA region, but also to turn our attention back to "what is." Doing so sheds much-needed light on the politics of nondemocratic regimes in the MENA region, specifically, and grants invaluable perspective to those engaged in democracy promotion more broadly.

▧ Notes

1. See, for example, essays in Posusney and Angrist 2005 and Schlumberger 2007.

2. This large literature, which spans decades and a diverse set of approaches, cannot be cited fully here. It includes such works as Hudson 1977; Hinnebusch 1985; Sharabi 1988; and Wedeen 1999.

3. Most notably, see contributions in Norton 1995, 1996; and Brynen, Korany, and Noble 1995, 1998.

PART 1

Participation Under Authoritarian Rule

2

The Nature of Political Participation

Holger Albrecht

Many argue that it is a difficult task to identify and explore political participation in an authoritarian environment. This is because political participation is a concept primarily used to analyze activism within democracies. If political participation has been explored within authoritarian governments, it has been with a focus on real or supposed democratization processes.

A core argument of this chapter is that this focus is too narrow. Broadening the perspective reveals that political participation exists in *every* political system, irrespective of whether it is democratic or authoritarian, or whether it is experiencing fundamental changes or not. Moreover, this chapter maintains that the concept of participation is not only *applicable* in the authoritarian states of the Middle East and North Africa (MENA), but also *critical* to a comprehensive understanding of state-society relationships in this region.

Taking into consideration the often emphasized link between participation and democratic rule, it is essential to explore the concept of political participation and the possibility of applying this concept to authoritarian systems. The first section of this chapter works to define these concepts. In addition, defining political participation broadly, as a social activity to influence governmental decisionmaking, raises some questions that deserve special consideration: What constitutes an "activity"? What participation is "political"? Is the participation mobilized by or autonomous from the state?

The latter question is particularly important, as it is key to understanding and debating the role of political participation in authoritarian settings. Thus this chapter identifies and discusses various channels of political participation. The first is a "classical" channel of political participation (e.g., political parties and civil society organizations), many of which do exist in the Middle East but are not necessarily of prime importance. The second is state-mobilized participation (during populist experiments and corporatist arrangements), and a third is participation through informal social networks. These latter channels are particularly important to understanding political participation and the politics of liberalization and deliberalization in the MENA region.

Political Participation and Authoritarianism

Initially, it may seem that the idea of political participation does not travel easily to authoritarian grounds. In most classical readings, political participation is somehow "naturally" linked to the notion of democratic rule.[1] Political participation appears as a sine qua non condition for the existence and the persistence of democracy, but this does not hold true for authoritarian rule. Here, the power to rule is not put at stake in regular intervals, and the populace cannot hold incumbents universally accountable for their decisionmaking. Thus, one may well imagine that authoritarian rulers would need to confine the active political involvement of their populace in order to secure their power and control. In short, the argument holds that autocrats do not want to be held accountable by the people; therefore, they do not welcome political participation that is autonomous from their own control mechanisms. Accordingly, most of the early works on political participation within nondemocracies focus on the degree of political participation present and the potential it might have to challenge authoritarianism and trigger democratization processes.[2] Past studies have paid little attention to the diverse forms of political participation taking place in authoritarian regimes, or the roles that such participation may play apart from democratization.

The (presumed) fact that authoritarian incumbents do not like political participation does not alone warrant assuming that participation is absent. Rather, the active involvement in politics, at least of a substantial proportion of the populace, is a phenomenon with which every political ruler in any political system, democratic or authoritarian, has to cope. That autocrats perceive political participation as a potential constraint to their hold on power seems evident. However, it is important to bear in mind that democratic politicians do not always praise political participation too, because in the end the outcome of democratic participation may trigger their departure from decisionmaking circles just as often as it may reinstitute them. Thus, political participation presents a potential challenge for governing elites, irrespective of the regime within which they operate.

The nature of political participation depends highly on the notion of authority. "The attitude of the political elites towards political participation is, in any society, probably the single most decisive factor influencing the nature of participation in that society" (Huntington and Nelson 1976: 28).

That is, generally speaking, different types of political regimes shape the attitudes of rulers toward political participation—and subsequently the forms, channels, and outcomes of political participation as well. When analyzing political participation in authoritarian settings, the question is not whether political participation exists; more relevant are the nature, form, and implications regarding state-society relations.

A broad, yet simple, definition by Samuel Huntington and Joan Nelson provides a helpful starting point. In their view, political participation is an "activity by private citizens designed to influence governmental decision-making" (1976: 4).[3] There are several implications to this approach: First, the term "activity" implies that personal attitudes and orientations, be they political or not, are not sufficient to be defined as political participation. Rather, participation implies either direct political action (e.g., to cast a vote at elections, join politically relevant organizations, or attend a demonstration) or, in its most simple form, the *public formulation* of political opinions. Regarding the Middle East and North Africa, Nazih Ayubi has made the important observation that activism often takes on a decisively "defensive" nature: "Urban collective action in the traditional Middle East was usually distinctively reactive. Its purpose was not to advance new claims, but to resist the perceived or real new claims of others: the state, foreign powers, or members of the religious minority" (1995: 165).[4] This "reactive activism," however, should not be equated with political apathy, or abstention. True, apathy might contain a potential political impact: low turnout rates at elections can have strong political implications in both democratic and authoritarian regimes.[5] However, while political apathy can be, and often is, politically relevant, it cannot be perceived as a participatory act of a "silent majority." In other words, the political relevance of an action does not necessitate the naming of such an action as "political participation."

Furthermore, the *quality* of a participatory activity may vary from one case to another, even when the venue is the same. A clear example is membership in labor unions. In Egypt, labor unions are incorporated within the system of state corporatism. By contrast, in Morocco, labor unions are associated with different political parties, both in government and in opposition. Consequently, unionism is embedded there in a comparatively competitive political system (see Dillman 2000) that ascribes a very different quality to activism in labor unions of Morocco than in those of Egypt (see el-Mikawy and Posusney 2000). Tunisia and Algeria further illustrate the complex nature of political participation through labor unions. In both countries, since the 1980s, the unions have been subject to substantial Islamist penetration, rendering activism in this field clearly oppositional and sometimes antisystemic. Certain similarities notwithstanding (for instance, that Islamists have played some role in labor unions in all the concerned countries), the *quality* of political participation in the unions differs tremendously between Tunisia, Algeria, Egypt, and Morocco (see Alexander 2000), mainly because of the different role of the unions in the respective political systems and in state-society relations.

It is not only the *quality* of participation that requires attention, but also the more general question of what renders participation "political." As Myron Weiner has argued, this question does not elicit an easy answer: "What constitutes a political act in one society may be nonpolitical in another; similarly an identical action may be defined by most people in a society as nonpolitical at one point in time, but as political at another" (1971: 163). Empirically, the distinction between the "political" and the "nonpolitical" can be difficult to measure, but it must be kept in mind to avoid a "conceptual stretching" of the notion of political participation. Moreover, the political nature of participation must be immediate. Rather than adopt a "chaos theory" of political participation, in which any word or action of a private individual might, in a long chain of reactions, have political implications, we need to identify whether the activist *intended* to influence governmental decisionmaking.[6] Only in these cases are the actions "political participation."

In defining the "political," we should also restrict our attention to the actions of individuals participating as private citizens, not as professional politicians. This point may seem evident within democracies where the distinction between "political men," on the one hand, and citizens, on the other, can be more easily made than in authoritarian settings. In authoritarian regimes, a distinction may be drawn only between the state incumbents and the rest of society. However, in these cases there may arise some difficulties when categorizing in such a way. Take, for instance, militaries in many Arab countries, particularly those with a sociorevolutionary history, such as in Syria, Egypt, Tunisia, and Algeria. One cannot deny that these groups may exert a strong impact on politics.[7] On the other hand, some may argue against identifying the militaries, not to mention the *mukhabarat* (intelligence services) and security apparatus, as political professionals.

It is an even more difficult task to distinguish the "political man" from the citizen when we consider the role of political activists working against authoritarian states. As a rule of thumb, opposition in Middle Eastern political systems is often not institutionalized, as it is in democracies. Thus, while opposition politicians are potential stakeholders in democracies, this rarely defines their position in authoritarian regimes. Consequently, one may reasonably speak of opposition members as citizens, not professionals, in politics. The members of Islamist, liberal, and socialist movements will in many cases refer to themselves as doctors, engineers, and university professors rather than as politicians. Therefore, in their own self-image, as well as the views of others, they are seen as attempting to *influence* politics, but not *make* politics. In order to distinguish between political *professionals* and political *participants,* I propose a rather inclusive approach: identifying the inner circle of political decisionmakers (including political advisers and the top ranks of the military, security, and bureaucratic apparatus)[8] as political practitioners and professionals, and the remaining (including both intra-regime circles and counter-elites) as political *participants.* In this view, most parliamentarians are political participants, an approach that Katja Niethammer and Saloua Zerhouni also take in this volume (see Chapters 8 and 11) in their analyses of Bahrain and Morocco, respectively.

It is also important to recognize how the intersection of politics and economics affects the determination of political participation in the Middle East and North Africa. Generally, the notion of the "political" in political participation contends that such participation will be directed toward influencing governmental decisionmaking, but not decisionmaking in other spheres of society, such as the economic realm. In the MENA region, however, these boundaries are often blurred. First, it has been shown that economic structures significantly resemble political structures.[9]

Second, and more important, economic activism can, and often does have in the Middle East, strong political implications. In the wealthier economies of the Arab Gulf states, and also in the (neo)liberalizing systems of "crony capitalism," control over economic resources is intertwined with control over political resources and power (see Henry and Springborg 2001; Richards and Waterbury 1998). Thus, economic activism does have, in many cases, strong political implications, often to a greater extent than in democracies. One possible solution to the conceptual problem of grasping the "political" in this case, then, is to define economic (or social) activism as political participation if it meets two conditions: first, if the activism is intended to reach beyond the pure economic self-interest of an individual, and second, if it has palpable implications (demanding or supportive) for the choices of political decisionmakers, irrespective of whether these implications are transformed into an observable and relevant action on behalf of political decisionmakers.[10] Someone's struggle for a higher personal salary cannot be identified as an act of political participation, but union strikes or enrollment in labor unions and professional associations may. Of course, to distinguish between individual self-interest and collective action is often difficult. In their contributions in this volume, Ellen Lust-Okar and Samer Shehata (see Chapters 5 and 6) stress the extent to which it is individuals' access to state resources, or at least the proximity to those distributing state resources, that helps explain the behavior of both voters and candidates.

Another important distinction is between political participation that is *mobilized* and political participation that is *autonomous.* Many scholars of democratization focus on autonomous forms of political participation, because they consider these forms of participation to be decisive politico-cultural prerequisites for the establishment of democracy.[11] On the other hand, scholars of authoritarianism have predominantly focused on state-mobilized participation, under the assumption that this is the most prevalent form of participation in these regimes. As Huntington and Nelson argued, "Mobilized participation occurs only when political elites make efforts to involve masses of the population in politics. Autonomous participation can occur at reasonable costs only if political elites encourage it, permit it, or are unable or unwilling to suppress it" (1976: 28). The early works on corporatism and populism are prominent examples of this approach (see Ayubi 1995: 183–223). Populism has been a widespread phenomenon, particularly in newly established authoritarian regimes during postrevolutionary, nation-building adventures.

Importantly, populism presents a strong—albeit somewhat ambiguous—picture of participation in authoritarian regimes. It entails the vision of controlling society and propping up authoritarian rule, but it also implies the mobilization and politicization of larger parts of society than only the small group of a politicized revolutionary elite. Thus inherent to populism is a strong, naturally embedded sense of political participation. From this viewpoint, the populist is passive, merely adapting his or her actions and discourses according to a certain sociopolitical environment. Simply speaking, the populist does not tell people how to act and speak, but the other way around (see Soeffner 1992: 177–202). Thus the channels that populists use to discover the "public soul" are not obviously apparent in authoritarian regimes. Yet they are also not necessarily inoperative or ineffective.[12]

Corporatism under authoritarian auspices is usually seen as a prominent strategy that authoritarian incumbents use to control participation through modern institutions. However, recalling a classical definition of corporatism as a "system of organized interest representation,"[13] it would be naive to assume that corporatist institutions would remain unidirectional, one-dimensional channels of statist control. Rather, the term "corporatism" implies that usually only parts of society are *incorporated* into the realm of authoritarian regimes. This necessarily implies that those who are incorporated will be empowered as political participants with access to approved channels of participation. The major difference between these mobilized and state-controlled forms of political participation versus autonomous participation in a pluralist-democratic setting is that, for society, the latter is an integrative, all-encompassing model, while the former is highly discriminative and, in a normative perspective, unjust or "unruly" (Bianchi 1989).

The distinction between *mobilized* and *autonomous* forms of participation[14] is often implicitly equated with a distinction between *state-driven* participation (i.e., corporatist, populist) and *society-driven* participation (i.e., social movements, civil society), respectively. From this perspective, "autonomous political participation" reads *autonomous from state control*. However, from a perspective focusing on the relationship between a political organization and individuals in the society, the distinction between autonomous and mobilized participation may take on a different meaning. Clearly, both statist and societal organizations can mobilize political activity. Yet this does not necessarily determine whether political participation is initiated by a political actor or is the result of an individual decision of the participant. That requires a careful analysis of the individual's decision to participate.[15]

The demonstrations against the Muhammad cartoons, published in late 2005 and early 2006 in several European newspapers, serve as an example. The demonstrators' participation can be viewed from different perspectives. First, it may represent an Islamist organization's ability to mobilize support, which will in turn become an asset in its relationship with the respective political regime. However, this view of mobilization can be misleading. The fact that a Middle Eastern regime or its Islamist counterpart has mobilized support does not necessarily affect the decision of an individual to participate. The individual may respond to the cartoons, whether or not he or she was mobilized by a state or an Islamist group. His or her decision to demonstrate, then, may have been made irrespective of the fact that the individual act of participation might be used in the political struggle between an authoritarian state and an Islamist opposition.[16] Thus, political participation within the realm of Islamic activism can be understood as "autonomous" only when it has been acknowledged as separate from the authoritarian, statist capabilities to control society (and participation). To summarize, when distinguishing between autonomous and mobilized participation, one will have to distinguish between individual action and group action.[17]

■ Channels of Political Participation in the Middle East

The *means* of political participation must be distinguished from the *content* of political participation. Examining the content of participation is important, of course, leading to studies on support and opposition within authoritarian regimes. Yet the means of political participation also require attention, leading to an inquiry about the channels through which political participation can be organized, performed, and voiced.

Some political institutions are routinely identified as the "natural" sites of political participation. These would include political parties and all those societal institutions that can be included under the "civil society" label: nongovernmental organizations (NGOs), private voluntary associations (PVAs), rural self-help organizations, and the like. The recent histories of many Middle Eastern countries have witnessed phases of institution building during which such organizational structures developed. For example, Egypt developed a multiparty system in the late 1970s, followed by the rise of "civil society" from the late 1980s onward. Other states in North Africa (except Libya), the Levant (with considerably higher restrictions in Syria), and the Gulf saw similar developments, although not necessarily simultaneously. Kuwait operates as the most liberal of the oil-rich Gulf monarchies (see Tétreault 2000).

While significant, the importance of these institutions should not be overstated. In democracies, these organizations constitute the nucleus of political participation and are, as such, built very much according to that principle and objective. In the authoritarian Middle East, these institutions exist, often as part of, and an expression of, a larger landscape of societal challenge and opposition (Langohr 2004).[18] However, the objectives and functions of these institutions are not as significant an influence on political participation in these regimes as they are in democracies.

Generally speaking, the majority of citizens in the Middle East do not express themselves politically through these institutions of political participation. Rather, these organizations are limited to certain strata of society, particularly the urban, politicized, and educated middle classes and upper-middle classes.[19] Thus they play a very limited role in political participation compared to democratic countries. However, they are important channels for the *politicized* parts of society, which should not be underestimated. Indeed, the middle and upper-middle classes offer "high-intensity" political participation in that they constitute a significantly high "amount of time, effort, and emotional involvement" to politically relevant activism (Baylis 1978: 35). This means that these institutions become more important when the *intensity* of political participation escalates, usually at specific limited but significant periods in a country's history (for example, in revolutions "from above"). Their significance decreases when the *quantity* of political participation is important—that is, when larger parts of society are involved. For instance, populist phases have seen the decrease in importance of such institutions, while eras that have witnessed a "depoliticization" of society have seen the rise of such institutions in the political landscape.

The impact of such formal institutions (e.g., parties, parliaments, civil society organizations) certainly depends on the historical situation in any given country. However, it does not mean that other strata, in particular the urban and rural poor, whom these institutions do not represent, are excluded from political participation altogether. Rather, they participate through other channels. Diane Singerman (1997a) shows in her study of the urban poor in Cairo that informal institutions and social networks—based on kinship rather than class—are the key to understanding the participation of the urban poor and lower-income classes.[20] Others have examined informal mechanisms of societal organization, and particularly the importance of *wasta,* or mechanisms of intermediation, on formal institutions (see Cunningham and Sarayrah 1993). Thus, for instance, as Ellen Lust-Okar stresses in this volume (see Chapter 5), *wasta* mechanisms not only determine the interrelationship between the voter and the elected, but also undermine the formal institutions (elections, parliaments) of participation.[21] Indeed, Laila Alhamad argues in this volume (see Chapter 3) that informality is the key to understanding political participation in the MENA region. Certainly, incorporating attention to these mechanisms into studies of participation allows for a broader, more comprehensive account of the "political" within authoritarian regimes.

For example, in heterogeneous and fragmented societies, the primordial cleavages along which political participation occurs (along religious lines, such as in Lebanon or Iraq, and along tribal lines, such as in Yemen and Jordan) are particularly apparent. In Lebanon and Iraq, consociational arrangements of power-sharing (or struggle) among ethnic and religious strata increase the probability of mobilization of political participation along the respective ethnic and religious channels. The cases of the particularly crisis-ridden Lebanon and Iraq also show that political participation through these mechanisms does not always produce positive results. Rather, mobilized political participation within informal ethnic and religious channels can fuel political crises to such an extent that they trigger civil war.

Apart from the often hidden networks of families, tribes, and ethnic cleavages, there are more visible manifestations of political participation that are still informal in the sense that they operate underground. Social movement theory deserves credit for identifying the power of mobilization that Islamist groups have at their disposal in many countries of the Middle East (see, among others, Wiktorowicz 2004; Wickham 2002; Hafez 2003). Throughout the region, Islamist groups have taken over social, charitable, and cultural tasks that many states in the Middle East could no longer maintain in times of economic crises (see Clark 2003). As a result, these groups received high levels of support among the populace, and this support provided a basis for mass public support of political organizations of the Islamist movement. Since the electoral victory of Hamas in the occupied Palestinian Territories and of the Muslim Brotherhood in the Egyptian 2005 elections, many observers agree that the Islamist movement has been the most powerful and vivid expression of political participation in the region. Their success is the reason that Islamist social movement organizations that rely on a mass social basis are, more often than not, oppressed by many Middle Eastern regimes to a higher extent than are legalized political parties and other, nonreligious civil society organizations. Thus, political activism and participation within the Islamist movement often entail the danger of becoming the subject of statist repression.

There are a number of important suppositions regarding characteristics of Middle Eastern political participation that may be drawn from such analysis of formal and informal dynamics. First, those channels of political participation, that employ formal institutions (political parties, NGOs, PVAs) lack a mass social basis but encapsulate "high-intensity" political participation from the politicized, urban-based social strata of society. Second, the more that political participation takes on an informal nature, the more it may be assumed to be rooted within society. Third, due to statist repression, greater inclusiveness or involvement does not necessarily guarantee a stronger political impact or response. Yet greater liberalization within authoritarian systems does not necessarily guarantee greater political participation.

A formal system of electoral representation, NGOs, and media discourse may appear well developed within a given Middle Eastern country (according to the Western image of these organizations). However, the lack of mass societal support for these organizations, and the lack of meaningful participation within the corresponding institutional arrangements (e.g., political parties, elections, or parliaments) is reflected in the low voter turnout that often afflicts elections in Middle Eastern states.[22] This does not mean that these institutions do not matter in politics.[23] However, given that states tightly control and contain these formal institutions, they cannot perform as channels of meaningful *mass* participation but rather remain the vehicles for political expression for those few who compose them. Therefore, they will not come close to achieving the *potential* for political participation, whether materialized or not, as support or objection vis-à-vis incumbents, that the socially rooted *qat* sessions in the Yemeni *mafraj*,[24] the Syrian *diwaniyya,* or the Bahraini *majalis* embody (see Chapters 3 and 8).

These propositions lead us to recognize why the phases of political liberalization in the Middle East do not necessarily result in the expansion of political participation among the broader public. Efforts toward political liberalization have been observed in almost every country in the MENA region during roughly the past three decades, even though they have not been uniform across the region. What is common to all liberalization efforts in post-Khomeini Iran, in reunified Yemen (1991–1995), in Egypt during the 1980s, in Bahrain since 2001, and at the recent "springs" in Damascus, Beirut, and Cairo (to indicate only a few liberal moments in the recent history of the Middle East)[25] is that they resulted in the lifting of restrictions on the media, in legal reforms, in the proliferation of NGOs and PVAs, and in heydays of election politics, without altering the authoritarian nature of the regimes concerned (see Albrecht and Schlumberger 2004; Brumberg 2005). The common denominator of all these measures is that they did not substantially affect the political, economic, and social life of the ordinary citizen. Rather, these reforms have widened the space (or contracted it during times of deliberalization) for those formal institutions described above, which are limited to a very small proportion of the populace in the region. Thus, measures such as these may not even change the incentive structure concerning political participation of the mass public in these countries.

However, extrapolating from this perspective, one should not dismiss the possibility of higher degrees of mass participation in a country in times that are perceived by outside observers as phases of political deliberalization.

This chapter maintains that life for the people in the Middle East has changed tremendously during the past three decades, but not so much as a result of the politics of liberalization described above. Rather, cultural changes, questions of war and peace, or changes in the politics of economic distribution have been perceived as much more influential by the citizens in the Arab countries than changes on the institutional political landscapes in their countries.[26] However, the conclusion ought not be drawn that people are depoliticized because they do not care very much about formal political-institutional arrangements or changes within them. A decision not to vote at elections or engage in the Middle Eastern "civil society" (and the organizations associated with this label) does not consequently rule out an individual's deep concern about politics. As described above, the method of political participation may be informal rather than formal, and thus culturally embedded rather than politically apparent.

Importantly, Middle Eastern state elites themselves play an important role in the game of political participation. Authoritarian elites in the Middle East are usually not particularly motivated to establish channels of political participation that mobilize autonomous societal demands. Yet state elites have developed institutions that have inadvertently become channels for political participation even though they were crafted for entirely different purposes—for example, the militaries, security apparatus, trade unions and professional associations, as well as the judicial systems and, at least in some countries, such as in Saudi Arabia and Egypt, the official clerical institutions. Initially, one may not expect these institutions to play a major role as channels of political participation. Rather, one would assume, the military should defend the nation in the face of external threats; the judiciary's task is to administer law and order, while the security apparatus's is to implement it.

The history of the Middle East, however, shows that such a view of state institutions underestimates their potential or real impact on politics. Militaries in the region were the vehicles of political participation for the urban middle classes of society during the revolutionary movements of the 1950s–1970s. States that came into being through revolutions underwent a process of "civilianization" shortly after a military takeover of power (Halpern 1962; Ben-Dor 1975), but despite this "return to the barracks," one should not underestimate the strong potential that militaries still have to influence politics (see Rubin 2001).

Whereas militaries have always been rather closed circles, judiciaries can play a different role in promoting political participation. In countries where judicial systems are well developed and enjoy some degree of independence, people can use the courts in an attempt to hold state incumbents accountable (if they accept court rulings) or detect illegitimate behavior (if they circumvent court rulings) (see Brown 1997). Thus the judiciary in a given country can turn into a platform for contentious action against the regime, becoming a channel for vocal political participation.[27]

Religious institutions also can play a significant role in channeling political participation. For example, Al-Azhar, the most recognized institution of religious (Sunni) guidance and higher education in the Muslim world, has been co-opted by the authoritarian regime in Egypt since Gamal Abdul Nasser took power. Yet while Al-Azhar has always been an important source of legitimacy for the regime, it has also become an advocate of Islamism, at times in a rather radical voice, and thus the most outspoken social movement autonomous from state control (see Zeghal 1999).[28]

Labor unions and professional syndicates are also state-fostered institutions that have become important channels of political participation. State elites originally created these institutions in an attempt to control society through corporatist means, but they have also at times served as important institutions for societal contention. This was the case for labor unions in Morocco and Tunisia, the revolutionary movements of South Yemen, and in the Iraqi communist movement. Professional syndicates became a scourge, particularly for the authoritarian regime in Egypt (see el-Mikawy and Posusney 2000; Chapter 12 in this volume; Carapico 1998: 84–106; Farouk-Sluglett and Sluglett 1987: 38–45; Bianchi 1989).

Thus, where political participation is restricted and controlled, statist institutions, designed for different purposes, are vulnerable to being seized as platforms for political participation, both elitist and societal. Delphine Cavallo, in this volume (see Chapter 12), has most clearly demonstrated this process focusing on the labor unions in Tunisia. Clearly, this form of political participation via statist channels is "participation by default," unintended by state elites who created or attempted to co-opt these institutions.

However, there are also "genuine" forms of state-induced political participation: state corporatism and populist experiments. Middle Eastern populism has been limited to certain historical moments, in particular in the immediate aftermath of sociorevolutionary changes. The early period of Nasser in Egypt reminds us of the fact that populist experiments are a strategy of limited avail, because one needs sufficient charisma to deploy them successfully as a strategy of power maintenance. Moreover, authoritarian leaders will find populism a double-edged sword in that it activates and politicizes a mass public who may turn, under changing circumstances, against the one who triggered their activism. Thus, with the demise of Nasserism and other "indigenous" ideologies (pan-Arabism, Baathism), larger populist projects have been almost entirely renounced in Middle Eastern politics (Hinnebusch 1985).

Corporatism, in turn, has been the rule of the game in the statist economic structures in the Middle East, and is the basis of state-sponsored and state-controlled political participation in professional syndicates, labor unions, and also political parties. Similar to populist experiments, corporatism as a channel of political participation has declined since the 1980s, except in the oil-rich Gulf states that can still "afford" corporatist arrangements at a high degree (Ehteshami and Murphy 1996).[29] This is mainly due to the deep financial crisis of the statist economic structures that have been broken up by economic liberalization strategies under neoliberal auspices.

The Middle East has generally witnessed the decline of state-mobilized political participation, although there are still some pockets left in which state authorities espouse participation. Iran is the most notable case where the employment of Islam as a state ideology increases the prevalence of state-sponsored political mobilization.[30] The anti-Western discourses that have been launched by the government under President Mahmoud Ahmadinejad are a current populist endeavor. Libya is another example where the ideological foundations of the state encourage political participation. Based on a rather bizarre mixture of socialist and Islamic principles, Muammar Qaddafi implemented his ideas of a people's republic (*jamahiriyya*) in a claim to encourage the participation of its citizens in so-called general people's congresses and committees, at least in principle (see Vandewalle 1998).[31]

In sum, authoritarian regimes do not actively encourage political participation. The exceptions of populist experiments and corporatist arrangements are, for the most part, temporary. Corporatism and populism attempt to exclude political participation that is autonomous from state control, which is carried out more often than not in an oppositional manner. Thus, authoritarian rulers often find themselves in a defensive position toward the phenomenon of political participation. They like participation only if it is state-sponsored, if it occurs at certain points or during limited periods of time, and if they can control and possibly reverse it. While political participation is an unavoidable phenomenon that authoritarian incumbents must deal with, they put it "under siege" and control, in particular when they realize that the content of political participation is one of opposition and resistance.

Conclusion

It is a widely held misconception of political participation in the Middle East, and maybe of authoritarian regimes in general, that the institutions allegedly designed for political participation exist as the main channels of political participation. Rather, in the Middle East, political parties and civil society organizations play only a very limited role as channels of mass participation compared to informal channels and even state-sponsored or state-related participation. The former institutions of political participation can better be understood as "imitative institutions" in that they resemble the picture of a democratic archetype but do not exert the same functions in an authoritarian context (Albrecht and Schlumberger 2004).

Apart from the middle classes and upper-middle classes of Middle Eastern societies who have ample means at their disposal (particularly those within the realm of formal institutions), three ways to express effective and meaningful political participation are open to larger parts of societies. The first is political participation within the confinements of the authoritarian state, usually through populist or corporatist endeavors. This form of political participation contains an open, "visible" political agenda. It is, in its societal outreach, far-reaching but not all-inclusive, and remains subject to an authoritarian regime's claim to keep society under control and, ultimately, its own hold on power alive. If it does not contribute to that very aim, state-sponsored participation will be revoked. Political participation under such circumstances can be "rewarding" for an individual participant in that he or she will have the impression that participation is meaningful without bearing the consequences of repressive responses.[32]

The second venue for political participation is informal social networks. This is largely considered by majorities within society to be the most efficient means of political participation with respect to realizing participants' aims. In contrast to the first form of political participation, informality often incorporates only a "hidden" political agenda, and sometimes it is difficult to distinguish political participation from the pursuit of purely individual self-interest. The latter holds particularly true when the more primordial social bonds of kinship, family, tribe, or *shilla* (peer group) are involved. Concerning the content of informal social networking, it can be supportive of, or challenging toward, political decisionmakers.

The third framework for political participation is offered by oppositional political institutions autonomous from state control. Participation under such circumstances has (like the first venue) an outright political agenda. It will be performed by larger parts of society primarily within channels of political participation perceived as "autochthonous," such as Islamist movements, but not within those perceived as "alien" (parties, "civil society" organizations, etc.). In this third framework, however, compared to the first and the second, the potential for frustration of the participator is high, given an authoritarian regime's readiness to use repression at a substantial level in order to contain opposition. "Successful"—that is, efficient—participation under this domain elicits repression, which in turn increases the likelihood that opposition will be crushed or transformed into resistance.

When it comes to transcending a rather simplified division between democracy and authoritarianism, regime type is an important aspect that needs to be taken into account more often in order to identify the peculiarities of sources, channels, aims, and effectiveness of political participation and the differences that distinguish one case from the other. In order to examine political participation in the Middle East in greater depth, we need to distinguish between different types of authoritarian rule (monarchies versus republics, bureaucratic versus patrimonial and sultanistic), and between different strategies of legitimation and degrees of statist repression. One must also take into account differences in institutional arrangements and in the "structures of contestation" between authoritarian incumbents and opposition forces (Lust-Okar 2005b).

Further research on political participation in the MENA region may help overcome an exclusive focus on the "society perspective" in studies of democracies and democratizations, and widen the debate to include studies of authoritarian political environments, whether stable or changing. At the same time, a focus on political participation in the MENA region will certainly enrich our empirical and conceptual knowledge of state-society relations under authoritarianism.

■ Notes

This chapter is part of a research project on political opposition under authoritarian rule in Egypt. I am indebted for insightful comments on a previous draft to the members of the Middle East Research Forum at Tübingen University, to the contributors to this volume, and particularly to the two editors of this volume.

1. Among many books and articles on democracy and democratization, Robert Dahl's *Polyarchy* (1971) stands out as a modern classic. Its subtitle, *Participation and Opposition,* hints at the importance of the concept of political participation for theories of democracy. Among those works on democracy that identified participation at the very center of their scholarship, see Sidney Verba and Norman Nie's *Participation in America* (1972). Analyses on political participation in nondemocratic settings date back to the 1970s and have been particularly inspired by modernization theories (see Huntington and Nelson 1976; Weiner 1971). For an overview of the early works on the concept, see Conge (1988).

2. See, for instance, Huntington (1968); Bienen and Morell (1976); Schulz and Adams (1981); and *Political Participation in Latin America* by John Booth and Mitchell Seligson (1978b). In the latter volume, the chapters by Booth and Seligson, Thomas Baylis, and Lawrence Scaff and Edward Williams contributed to an early effort to conceptualize political participation under authoritarianism.

3. This understanding of political participation comes very close to what Albert Hirschman (1970) called the "voice option" of individuals in a society—that is, the direct expression of dissatisfaction with the authorities. John Booth and Mitchell Seligson (1978a) replaced "governmental decisionmaking" with the notion of "public goods."

4. Asef Bayat has observed six types of activism in the Middle East: "urban mass protest, trade unionism, community activism, social Islamism, nongovernmental organizations (NGOs), and quiet encroachment" (2002: 3).

5. A recent example for the relevance of voter numbers is the referendum on the amendment of the constitution in Egypt, on May 25, 2005. In an attempt to draw

some "democratic" legitimacy from these reform measures, the Egyptian authorities tried hard to secure a high voter turnout. The officially claimed figure of 53.6 percent was severely challenged by numerous opposition groups (el-Nahhas 2005b).

6. There is no agreement on this point. Laila Alhamad (see Chapter 3) is among those who dismiss the notion of *intention* (to influence politics) as a necessary precondition to define an action as political participation (see also Booth and Seligson 1978a: 8). In contrast to such approaches, I hold that the very fact that the issue of political participation under authoritarianism is understudied (and presumably more difficult to study than under democracy) should not lead us to abolish definitional boundaries altogether and, as a consequence, establish a notion of "political participation" as a catch-all category that explains basically every kind of action of men and women, which would lose its explanatory power.

7. This is confirmed both by those who highlight the active role of the militaries in revolutionary movements (Trimberger 1978) as well as those who observe a disengagement of the militaries from Middle Eastern politics (Harb 2003).

8. A good point of departure is Volker Perthes's (2004) work on political elites.

9. Samer Shehata's field research (2003) shows that authoritarian structures are well developed in Egyptian firms and enterprises.

10. The question of efficacy of acts of political participation is also critical (Weiner 1971: 161). I follow Booth and Seligson, who argued that "whether an effort to influence the distribution of a particular public good succeeds is immaterial. . . . If one votes for a candidate but he loses, voting participation has nevertheless occurred" (1978a: 8). While the efficacy of political participation certainly remains an interesting topic in its own, I will not focus on it here, in the interest of keeping my arguments concise.

11. This is the point of departure for theories of democracy focusing on the role of civil society and social capital.

12. Raymond Hinnebusch (1985) has shown that populist experiments are often short-lived and particularly vulnerable to transformations, in the case of post-Nasser Egypt, *within* an authoritarian regime.

13. It is interesting that corporatism is among the very few concepts that have been developed concurrently in studies on democracies and authoritarianism. Important distinctions between the political systems notwithstanding, Philippe Schmitter provided a largely accepted definition that included authoritarian state corporatism and democratic understanding of organized (in contrast to "pluralist") interest representation: "Corporatism can be defined as a system of interest representation in which the constituent units are organized into a limited number of singular, compulsory, noncompetitive, hierarchically ordered and functionally differentiated categories, recognized or licensed (if not created) by the state" (1979: 13). On development of the concept of corporatism, see Williamson (1989).

14. Thomas Baylis distinguishes between "manipulated" and "influential" participation (1978: 37).

15. For a behaviorist approach on political participation, see Milbrath (1971).

16. On the other hand, one can also imagine a "two-level game" of the political activism of an individual: here the intention is to express both criticism of the Muhammad cartoons *and* support for an Islamist opposition organization. The same logic may hold true for the participation in (or the support of) an independent labor union, a political party, or a rural self-help organization. Accordingly, the participation in a state-organized venture may also embrace an expression of support for the state—an "act of submission," as Jillian Schwedler and Samir Fayyaz (2006) put it.

17. I am grateful to Ellen Lust-Okar for clarifying this point.

18. A clear classification as societal organizations (vis-à-vis authoritarian incumbents) is not always easy to draw. In Egypt, for instance, opposition parties were created in the late 1970s as platforms of the former and single statist party, the Arab Socialist Union, while others were established and work under tight confinements of the regime. If we look at the biographies of the founders or elder party leaders of the Tagammu, Nasserist, or Labor Parties, respectively, we recognize that they played important roles in the Nasserist regime. The Wafd Party, revitalized in 1983, is an old party that led the nationalist struggle in the pre-Nasserist period. Younger groups, such as the Ghad Party or the Karama (Dignity) Movement, are breakaway factions of the Wafd and the Nasserists, respectively (see Chapter 9). Concerning the "civil society" institutions that mushroomed in several countries in the Middle East, Sheila Carapico (2000) has convincingly argued that they are, more often than not, closely observed, and even established by the states. For a discussion on the relationship between authoritarian incumbents and opposition in the Middle East, see Lust-Okar (2005b) and Albrecht (2005).

19. Exceptions from this general rule are the labor unions. Wherever they exist, and whatever political impact they might have in a country, they do represent urban, lower-income strata of society. As for the political parties, they can be effective and genuine channels of political participation, mainly when they represent specific social formations, such as tribes and religions (Abukhalil 1997: 152). This can be seen with the political parties in Lebanon and Morocco, and with the legalized Islamist parties in Yemen (Hizb al-Islah) and Jordan (Islamic Action Front).

20. Diane Singerman's work (1997a) is a brilliant account of informal societal organization; for a similar account on Iran, see Asef Bayat's *Street Politics* (Bayat 1997). However, I challenge Singerman's understanding of "political" participation (see Singerman 1997a: 6–10). By highlighting the economic self-interest of the people as the ultimate impetus, Singerman may have stretched the idea (what is political and what is not) and employed a notion of political participation far too broad to guarantee its general explanatory power.

21. Interestingly, *wasta* (meaning "intermediation" or "go-between") finds its expression in other societies that are also heavily affected by clientelism; compare the approaches of *blat* (Russian) or *guanxi* (Chinese).

22. There are exceptions to this rule. People do matter in formal politics, particularly when elections are indeed meaningful concerning access to, and composition of, political power. Examples include the first Yemeni parliamentary elections after unification in 1993, which prompted the turnout of 85 percent of registered voters, and the 2006 parliamentary elections in the Palestinian Territories, which resulted in 78 percent voter turnout (see, respectively, Glosemeyer 1993: 447; and Baumgarten 2006: 178). In general, however, voter apathy is not surprising, given the tight restrictions to which "authoritarian elections" in the Middle East are usually subject (see Schwedler and Chomiak 2006).

23. Laila Alhamad argues convincingly in Chapter 3 that it is the interplay of formal rules and institutions with informal mechanisms that best explains the phenomenon of political participation in the MENA region. Much of the current work on political participation in the Middle East concentrates on politics in elections and parliaments. At the core of most research are questions concerning statist capabilities to manage, manipulate, and control societal forces, and the opposition's quest for participation in the attempt to keep alive the incumbents' control over political power and the distribution of economic resources. On Iran, Jordan, Egypt, and Morocco, see Chapters 4, 5, 6, and 10–11, respectively. For a recent theoretical account, see Schedler (2006).

24. Yemen is an interesting case where statebuilding (and statist control over

society) is relatively underdeveloped, which has opened the space for an unparalleled degree of popular activism (see Carapico 1998; Wedeen 2003). On the political role of Yemeni *qat* sessions, see Lisa Wedeen's forthcoming *Peripheral Visions: Political Identifications in Unified Yemen.*

25. Even the oil-rich Gulf states have embarked on political liberalization efforts, albeit carefully controlled (see Herb 2004; Ehteshami 2003). For the case of Bahrain, see Chapter 8 in this volume.

26. For an insightful account on what kind of changes in daily life Arab people care about, see Amin (2001).

27. Under other conditions, judiciaries can be an important source of support for an authoritarian regime, such as in Turkey, where the judiciary played a crucial role in preserving Kemalist principles before the advent of a more liberal political realm (personal communication with Peter Pawelka, Tübingen, January 2006).

28. In countries where theocratic arrangements play an even more prominent role for the fundamental modes of the political systems (such as in Saudi Arabia and Iran), religious institutions are even more important channels of political participation than in Egypt.

29. Steffen Hertog (2006) has used the concept of corporatism to explain the recent reshaping of political institutions and debates in Saudi Arabia from above.

30. This may explain the relatively high degree of political pluralism and competition that—as is shown in Chapter 4—distinguishes political arrangements in contemporary Iran.

31. In reality, the vast majority of the people are deprived of the right and ability to affect political decisionmaking directly. That remains solidly in the hands of Qaddafi and a small clique of relatives and close aides.

32. Speculating about the motivations and aims of individuals who engage in political participation—particularly contentious political participation—is not the center of inquiry in this chapter. Interesting insights on Egypt and Morocco can be drawn from Chapters 6 and 11, respectively.

3

Formal and Informal Venues of Engagement

Laila Alhamad

Since the events of September 11, 2001, the West—through governments, nongovernmental organizations (NGOs), and scholars—has paid a great deal of attention to the development of democracy in the Middle East and North Africa (MENA).[1] Scholarly articles and publications have mushroomed, northern NGOs have expanded their programs into the region, and European and US funding has multiplied into the hundreds of millions of dollars to bolster this commitment. In good part, scholarly debate, policy prescription, and on-the-ground action have revolved around support for civil society groups as a bulwark against the authoritarian state and as a force for democratization. The conventional wisdom that prevails in this viewpoint pertains to the neo-Tocquevillian idea that a strong civil society can slowly challenge authoritarian governments as it is able to empower and mobilize disillusioned populations to demand greater democracy and freedom.

To this end, attempts have been made to strengthen mainly formal civil society groups—for example, women's organizations, human rights groups, and organizations supporting media freedoms—in exacting democratic reforms from their governments. These groups' efforts are indeed noteworthy, and have included activities involving government advocacy and monitoring, civic education, and human rights awareness. Through these activities, these groups and their leaders, who are usually reform-minded Arabs, seek to put pressure on authoritarian MENA governments to introduce reforms and greater political and civil liberties while at the same time familiarizing citizens of the region with concepts of democracy, pluralism, and citizenship.

These groups sustain considerable pressures and run severe risks on a day-to-day basis. Despite their commendable efforts, it is difficult to draw a causal relationship between these organizations and the recent top-down reforms (cosmetic as they may be) initiated by some Arab governments. Indeed, many of the reforms that have been introduced in recent years owe more to pressure exerted by Western governments than to local civil society groups. Focusing much of the debate on these groups and placing unrealistic expectations on them underestimates the impervious nature of authoritarian governments, their tactics of survival, and their ability to preserve power and maintain a tight grip on the political arena.

At the same time, understanding the sources of political change in the region, particularly under authoritarian rule, requires widening the lens to capture other avenues of popular political participation that are within the reach of the masses and often escape state control. While democracy is a greater goal to which many in the Middle East aspire, political participation—through its various forms—is a reality for many Middle Easterners, not simply for the elite. Exploring these forms of participation, and the vehicles through which people in the region participate in political life, might give a more complete view of how both the elite and the masses have, for decades, confronted, resisted, cooperated, and coexisted with authoritarian governments. In essence:

> The success of narrow-based regimes to control political participation should not blind scholars to the strength of people's ability to adapt, resist, and even prevail. If opposition to a regime is too risky and dangerous, and therefore not publicly articulated, it does not mean that political activity has disappeared or that people are apathetic or apolitical. Rather, it presents a challenge to look harder, and certainly to look outside of conventional political venues and historical accounts. (Singerman 1997b: 81)

Using a broad definition of political participation, this chapter seeks to enlarge the lens through which political participation in the MENA region is considered and analyzed. It attempts to cast light on some of the formal organizations that citizens use to mobilize and participate, as well as on some of the informal modes of participation that are pervasive in the region. In the first case, the chapter highlights the formal civil society organizations that exist in the region as well as the challenges they face. In the latter, the chapter explores the informal modes of participation that the political literature has captured in recent years, and that, to date, do not seem to have received adequate analysis from a political participation perspective. This exploration does not seek to be complete or exhaustive but rather tries to illustrate the existence of a range of modes that defy the conventional meaning of political participation and that provide a better understanding of the meaning and sources of political change as well as the various consequences and objectives intended.

■ Political Participation in MENA: Broadening the Discourse

In countries where political space exists—where participation can affect outcomes and actions carry minor or limited personal risks—participation mainly occurs through formal channels. This is the case in most developed democracies, where a relatively functioning system of checks and balances is set in place through legally recognized and formal institutions and groups, and the law protects citizens from potential state abuses.[2] On the other hand, in environments where the political space is circumspect and citizens face the risk of repression, the populace often resorts to alternate channels, such as informal networks that arise in lieu of, or alongside, the formal institutions.

In most MENA countries, political participation remains constricted by the tight political space that is imposed by authoritarian governments. Therefore, the traditional definitions of political participation, as understood in democratic systems, are insufficient to capture the panoply of methods of political participation to which people resort. For instance, the growing of a beard in Algeria carries political meaning and can be seen not only as subversive, but as overtly defying the state. Such an action might escape conventional understandings of political participation, but both the Islamists and the government in Algeria are well aware of its political meaning. Similarly meaningful is the act of not participating in elections, which can be viewed as a political statement in rejection of rubber-stamp elections, impotent political parties, and the absence of competition that has been customary in the region. The act of creating "a state within a state," as witnessed by many Islamic organizations that set up a parallel system of services and values alongside the state, can also be seen as an act of political participation:

> Mosque-based medical clinics, for example, become independent institutions with their own distinct aims and strategies, having connections to other Islamic institutions—day care centers, schools—usually via common friends, applying Islam to the public sphere and consciously or unconsciously engaging in a larger symbolic political protest against the ruling secular state in support of the implementation of an Islamic state based on Islamic law *(shari'a).* (Clark 2004: 943)

In this light, the concept of political participation used in this chapter is based on attempts to "survey the subject in question, not the concept itself."[3] Indeed, the most creative and groundbreaking accounts of political participation in the MENA region in recent years are those that have sought to prioritize the reality on the ground rather than to find a fit for existing definitions and theories of political participation, most of which tend to underestimate the specificities of the region or the constraints imposed by authoritarian governments.

There is a growing literature that casts political participation under authoritarianism more broadly, one that is not constrained by the intent to primarily or ultimately "influence government decision-making" (Huntington and Nelson 1976: 3). Works by Mounia Bennani-Chraibi, Diane Singerman, Quintan Wiktorowicz, and Asef Bayat, among others, have started to defy the conventional boundaries of definitions of political participation, widening the discourse and demonstrating that political participation goes beyond the formal realm and that subtle, seemingly nonpolitical actions by citizens carry considerable political meaning. Such participation often takes place through loosely based, informal vehicles, many of which serve multiple purposes—social, political, occupational—and are often indigenous to the region. These informal vehicles can be traced back through Middle Eastern social history. Their versatile and polyvalent nature has been key to the survival of many. Citizens tend to use these vehicles for purposes of patronage, to extract resources from the state, to further personal interests, to voice and mobilize public opinion, to resist and oppose the political status quo, to exchange ideas on political, economic, and social issues, and to challenge and threaten the state's grip on values, religion, and cultural codes.

■ Limits of the Formal Realm: MENA Civil Society Organizations

In recent years, increasing amounts of financial and political support by Western countries have been channeled to strengthen democratic institutions in the MENA region.[4] In practical terms, this has entailed funding for election monitoring, political-party training, parliamentary capacity building, supporting independent media, promoting the rule of law, strengthening business associations and trade unions, and fostering a strong civil society. While many donors espouse the idea that democracy is best developed within local contexts through indigenous vehicles, the kinds of activities and organizations that ultimately have gained support tend to fit a Western model of democracy and political participation.

Within this framework, formally registered and secular civil society organizations have been considered one of the primary means to enlarge the space for political participation in the region. While there is little consensus on the meaning of civil society in the MENA context, there is an active policy debate that has tended to revolve around the mainly secular, nongovernmental organizations that "seem to resemble those with which [donors] are most familiar in their own countries" (Hawthorne 2004: 14). These groups include professional associations, human rights groups, trade unions, community-based organizations, cultural and research centers, women's organizations, and media groups.

A number of these groups are newly established, while others have been around for decades. For instance, numerous organizations go as far back as the colonial period and emerged in support of the anticolonial struggle. In the 1920s in Syria, organizations were established to protect the vulnerable populations against the massive inflow of European goods. This inflow had destabilized the local economy and created hardship for the local populations (Khouri 1984). Headed by artisans and merchants, these organizations were used as platforms to make demands on the government, attempting to create alternate ways of pursuing personal and community interests for those associated with the political notables upon whom the people had traditionally relied (Ben Nefissa 2002: 79).

Other organizations, formed in the era following independence, have their roots in leftist movements. With the rise in education, economic status, and an urban middle class, formal groups, particularly trade unions, political parties, and professional syndicates, began to form more systematically. The development of these organizations came in conjunction with the formation of modern nation-states and polities in the region, which was accompanied by the rise of modern constitutions and political institutions mainly fashioned along the lines of those adopted in European countries. Seeking to break away from the system of informal networks, clientelism, and patronage through which politics in the region had been played in the past, the modern and educated adopted these formal organizations as the primary vehicles for political participation and mobilization.

Prior to the 1980s, there was a period during which a number of the region's governments amplified their authoritarian tendencies and tactics by introducing measures of state repression against any potential opposition, emergency rule, the suspension of political liberties, the dissolution of parliaments, and the consolidation of power through one-party rule. Following this era was a resurgence of civil society groups in the late 1980s and early 1990s in countries like Morocco, Jordan, Palestine, and Yemen. From fewer than 20,000 in the mid-1960s, the number of civil society organizations in the region rose to about 70,000 in the late 1980s (Norton 1996: 39).

To a certain extent, this phenomenon was driven by the economic pressures confronting many of the governments in the region. The period before the 1991 Gulf War can be illustrated as a time when popular disaffection associated with measures of economic austerity translated into popular strikes and street protests, and gave rise to support for political Islam (Norton 1996: 45). For purposes of regime preservation and survival, a number of governments in the region had little choice but to grant political concessions in the form of mild liberalization measures. As such, Algeria transitioned from a one-party to a multiparty state system, Morocco freed hundreds of political prisoners, and Jordan reinstated its parliament.

Two kinds of groups emerged during this period: those that focused on service delivery, relieving populations from difficult economic conditions at a time of subsidy cuts and austerity measures, and others that focused on encouraging political participation and accountability through advocating for human rights, promoting civic education, or carrying out research and public opinion polls on politically related issues (Ben Nefissa 2002). Captivated and lured by the positive experiences of civil society groups in other parts of the world, particularly in Eastern Europe, that weakened and helped unseat authoritarian regimes, many Arab reformers saw civil society as providing new opportunities to mobilize populations, shape public opinion, and apply pressure on the state.

At the same time, many groups viewed themselves as alternatives to political parties, which have generally had a weak record of credibility and performance in the region. Historically, a number of political parties were created by governments to display a semblance of democracy, *dimokratiyah shikliyah,* to crowd out the political space, and to undermine any potential opposition. This weakness goes hand in hand with the supreme role ascribed to the executive branch in most Arab countries, well illustrated in the example of the Egyptian constitution, which "devotes 30 articles making up almost 15 percent of the whole Constitution to Presidential prerogatives, while only one article discusses the Presidential accountability" (Saeed Ali 2003: 5).

Through these groups, civic education curricula and textbooks were developed in Palestine, dozens of new publications saw the light of day in Morocco and Yemen, and advocacy campaigns on sensitive and taboo issues such as street children, prostitution, female genital mutilation, corruption, and violence against women were launched throughout the region. The presence of women in civil society was also felt, with women taking on leadership positions and vocal stances on democratization and reform. Networks of women's organizations began forming and expanding throughout the MENA region, benefiting from the exchange of relevant experiences and the search for common solutions to issues of personal status. From Lebanon to Morocco, networks of pro-democracy, anticorruption, and human rights activists also emerged.

Though tolerated to a certain extent, civil society groups were, by and large, treated with suspicion by governments in the region. Over the years, MENA governments have perfected a repertoire of tactics that effectively tie the hands of these organizations and prevent them from posing any important threat to the state. Several of these tactics, such as intimidation, co-optation, the creation of parallel governmental organizations with greater resources, and bureaucratic requirements, have been refined to exert tight control over civil society while at the same time giving outsiders the appearance of a reformist and tolerant attitude.

The introduction of strict regulatory frameworks governing associations and the media is seen as one of the main tools to control these groups and curtail their maneuverability margin. Quintan Wiktorowicz explains that the government does this by "embedding [them] in a web of bureaucratic practices and legal codes which allow those in power to monitor and regulate collective activities. This web reduces the possibility of a challenge to the state from civil society by rendering much of collective action visible to the administrative apparatus. Under such circumstances, civil society institutions are more an instrument of state social control than a mechanism of collective empowerment" (Wiktorowicz 2000a: 43). Occasionally, activists who are seen as crossing the line of acceptability in posing a challenge to the state are arrested, though on a limited scale because foreign media and governments often give them support and attention.

Civil society groups not only face challenges from the state and its methods of authoritarian control, but also meet resistance from conservative elements in society, such as Islamist groups, and have a limited ability to empower and mobilize populations on a large scale. Many of these groups are urban-based, with limited reach to the masses. Their ability to attract only a limited constituency is in contrast to many of the Islamist networks and groups whose popularity extends throughout the poorest and most populated urban areas, often managing to transform into social movements.

Moreover, the elite nature of these groups, their members, and often the subject matter they focus on affects their support base, making it more difficult for them to appeal to and mobilize large populations in support of such issues as human rights or women's rights. The issue of women's rights in particular has put many of these groups at loggerheads with conservative elements of society. For example, in Morocco in 2000, secularists and women's groups participated in massive demonstrations, demanding reform of the *moudawana,* the Moroccan personal status code, and a gender action plan. At the same time, conservative Islamist groups often challenge the message and mission of these organizations by denouncing their association with Western governments.

For these reasons, establishing the necessary level of linkages and trust has been a challenge for many of these groups. This has been complicated by issues of foreign funding, upon which they rely heavily, but which is viewed with suspicion by the populace. Dependence on foreign sources of funding also raises the issue of accountability and representation, rendering these organizations more accountable to external donors than to local constituencies, and weakening their support base. For instance, in the case of post-1987 intifada Palestine, this shift in accountability transformed a mass movement that had acted collectively and had successfully stood up to

Israeli occupation "into an NGO community of elite, professional and politically autonomous institutions," with the activities of these groups being altered in order to "meet developmental, rather than political, goals" (Hammami 2000: 17).

■ Revisiting the Past: Informal Participation in Historical Context

Probably the most ubiquitous forms of participation in the MENA region are those of the informal realm, many of which are perpetuated by the rigidity of the formal political sphere. When the state, through its institutions, represses, excludes, or fails to listen or respond to people's needs, people resort to the informal realm. From the Jmaas in Morocco to neighborhood networks in Cairo, the informal sphere has existed in the region throughout the ages, facilitated by a strong family ethos and a feeling of community, solidarity, and kinship. While the decades following independence saw the rise of formal institutions and organizations, none has been able to challenge the strength and pervasiveness of these informal channels in Middle Eastern life. Indeed, many of the formal institutions have been suffused by patterns characteristic of the informal realm.

The region's history (post-Islam) is rich with examples of informal forms of participation. Historically, the region was part of an expansive Islamic *ummah,* spanning several continents and ruled over by numerous, often non-Arabic-speaking dynasties. From the Seljuks in the eleventh century to the Ottomans in the sixteenth, these dynasties shared little with the local communities (Denœux 1993), a condition that Mohamed Bamyeh describes as "incomplete state diffusion into society" (2005: 40). In this regard, large as the *ummah* was, communities had limited contact with the ruling authorities and were largely self-managed.[5] Peoples' expectations of the authorities pertained to protection against external threats and the provision of food, public order, and to a certain extent infrastructure (Denœux 1993). Rulers were also expected to uphold Islamic principles and behaviors.

Interactions between rulers and the people were indirect, carried out through intermediaries who were informally appointed by the authorities. Local leaders and notables known as *ulama, shyukh, shurafa,* and *ruasa,* as well as merchants, acted like quasi-governmental agents and informants, collecting taxes, settling disputes, and executing government orders (Denœux 1993). In this respect, the de facto governing of the *ummah* was highly decentralized and was instead carried out locally. Several outcomes resulted from this type of arrangement. The first was the instilling of clientelistic relations between the people and their intermediaries, heavily favoring personalized relations and contacts; the second was the self-contained nature of localities in terms of providing residents with support networks for religious, professional, and other needs; and the third was the limited growth of institutions.

The dearth of institutions and the limited role of the state spurred the growth of informal self-help networks throughout the region. Principally an urban phenomenon, networks constituted sources of solidarity, information, assistance, and protection as well as channels to oppose the authorities. These networks were vigorous, and "suggest an image that differs significantly from the lingering and simplistic view of a Middle East despotism, in which a leviathan-type state rules over the apathetic, atomized, and powerless society deprived of a collective will, and of any ability to resist the exactions of predatory governments" (Denœux 1993: 34). Based mainly on kin, religion, neighborhood, occupation, and commercial interests, these networks provided communities with a sense of collective identity and a vehicle for collective action. Indeed, they were often used to resist and oppose certain state measures, particularly those intended to exploit or extract resources from communities.

Commercial networks, for example, were useful in passing on sensitive political and economic information across the *ummah,* and were used to coordinate political insurgents (Denœux 1993: 48). Other networks, such as mosques or *zawaya,* revolved around religion, providing a channel for popular disaffection and furnishing people with the resources and space for collective action. Similarly, networks of Sufi brotherhoods spanned an impressive network of contacts and information across the *ummah,* and were often considered a threat to the authorities. Indeed, Islam-based networks played an integral part in the everyday lives of people, holding "Middle Eastern urban society together by providing spiritual guidance, accepted norms of behavior and ways of conducting private and commercial transactions" (Denœux 1993: 39).

Collective action was also reflected in urban living quarters, or *harat,* prevalent throughout the region. Arab cities were historically divided into living quarters, which operated as self-contained organizations, with their own sense of identity, and "an almost unique culture of neighborliness . . . among the residents" (Sato 1997: 23). The quarter prompted a strong sense of loyalty and belonging among residents, as is illustrated by the Iraqi quarter of Buraq in Najaf, which upon the expulsion of the Turks in 1915 declared independence and wrote its own constitution. Mandating the quarter to behave like a tribe, the constitution called for solidarity among, and the protection of, Buraq's residents (Batatu 1993).

Each quarter behaved similarly to an association or a local government, providing such services as water distribution, street cleaning, lighting, and maintaining order. During the French mandate in Syria, for example, the old quarters of Damascus were centers of political and social organization with their own *majlis* (local council), "which acted as a mini-government to protect quarter residents from excessive state interference, to represent the quarter in disputes with other quarters, and to mediate internal conflicts" (Khouri 1984: 514). Meetings between the local leaders and the community took the form of informal *diwaniyya,* or gatherings, held in important homes to discuss issues of concern, contributing "far more than newspapers and other media to the formation and reinforcement of public opinion. Since the mandate authorities frequently censored or suspended publication of newspapers and magazines, the *diwan* served as a great storehouse of much fresher and more confidential information" (Khouri 1984: 515).

Other forms of participation related to occupational and commercial interests, represented by guilds. Under Ottoman rule in Syria, for instance, guilds (also referred to as *tawa'if)* constituted "the backbone of the traditional society and economy" (Sato 1997: 22). These guilds spontaneously developed "from below, created, not in response to a state need, but to the societal requirements of the laboring masses themselves" (Bill and Springborg 1990: 91). Guilds, brotherhoods, and quarters were some of the forms of participation concentrated in urban areas. In rural areas, the primary form of participation was the tribe, which performed the functions of a ministate within its territory, providing its members with a code of existence and conduct, mechanisms for defense and collective action, and a system of justice and security.

■ Widening the Discourse: Today's World of Informal Participation

Despite massive changes in the 1970s and 1980s—including urbanization, which has broken down formerly close-knit neighborhoods and bloated public sectors and bureaucratic red tape, which in turn have crowded out the private sector guilds—informal modes of political participation continue to reign throughout the Middle East and North Africa. Indeed, as much as the state has perfected its repressive tactics on the formal realm of political participation, the informal realm has been the arena where the alternate expressions of participation have been played out. With the overwhelming grip of the state on political life, and the increasing economic needs that have gone unmet, people have resorted to the traditional informal modes of participation to access resources, curry favors, and have a voice in everyday political, economic, and social matters. As Nazih Ayubi notes:

> Since the state has managed to encircle the society to this extent, the only way to go around the encirclements is to revive and re-engage all sub-political structures of the civil society by way of pumping in new blood and reviving the various social forces so that they can participate in due course in the process of political change. These include the mosques, *zawaya,* religious orders and brotherly solidarities that have been re-

embraced by the popular forces, at a time when nationalist and leftist elites
are still struggling to turn their civil associations and societies into viable
structures for rejuvenating the civil society. (1995: 445)

Because of their fluidity and inconspicuous nature, informal networks
are by far the most widespread vehicles of participation in the MENA region.
Tapping into the layers of social ties and mutual trust that thrive in the
region, these networks fulfill a multitude of purposes and as such create positive and less risky incentives for participation. These incentives, both material and nonmaterial, include furthering personal interests usually related to
tapping into state resources, providing a conduit of information, building key
alliances, and challenging the state's monopoly on reigning ideologies.

Although the bulk of literature related to networks in the region tends
to concentrate on extremist Islamist networks, there is a small but growing
field of research and analysis that has widened the prism through which we
view them in the context of political participation and resistance. This field
has brought to the surface the everyday networks that people tap into for
purposes of survival and protest, networks that are rich with political significance. These examples are peeling away the layers of misconceptions surrounding the apathy of the "Arab street" while at the same time reminding
us of the challenges associated with bringing about reform and democracy
in authoritarian systems.

Drawing examples from the mosques of Morocco to the Islamist networks of Cairo, Mounia Bennani-Chraibi and Olivier Fillieule (2003) give a
taste of the various modes of resistance and participation in the region that
are based on operational rather than theoretical definitions of political participation, the latter being based on Western political theory. Similarly,
demonstrating that political participation extends beyond participating in
formal organizations, Diane Singerman skillfully documents the various
avenues of informal participation taken by the Egyptian populace, *sha'ab,*
to "create public space and invade what is conventionally considered the
public arena as they connect individuals, households, and communities to
state bureaucracies, public institutions, and formal political institutions . . .
to fulfill individual and collective needs" (1995: 87). And Asef Bayat
reveals a world of subtle forms of political protest and mobilization among
the popular Egyptian classes. Among those that have yielded results and
escaped state control, he cites the rise of informal market shaikhs in Cairo
to mediate between the thousands of small street vendors who have
emerged spontaneously and informally, and the state. Effective at negotiating on behalf of the vendors, these "surrogate" union leaders have gained
clout and respect through their informal yet effective "quiet diplomacy"
(1997: 12).

Quintan Wiktorowicz widens the meaning of political participation by
examining that which involves the "symbiotic struggles over the rules that

guide everyday life" and makes "politics and governance much broader than the State" (Wiktorowicz and Farouki 2000: 688). To this end, he illustrates the strategy of the Salafis in Jordan, a powerful Islamist network whose main objective is not to confront the state openly but rather to trespass on and reduce its monopoly over cultural codes. In contrast to the Muslim Brotherhood, which contests politics through the formal realm, Wiktorowicz argues that the Salafis spread their ideology and cultural vision through subtle mobilization patterns in the informal nonpolitical realm: "Because they embed collective action in everyday interactions, [their strategy] eludes the state's repressive tendencies, [making them the] leaders [that] dominate the *ulama* of Jordan. They are the shaykhs of religious knowledge and attract the vast majority of students of Islamic learning in traditional lessons and study circles" (Wiktorowicz 2000b: 220–221).

In closed societies, informal gatherings and assemblies have also provided a venue through which the political pulse is taken, where public opinion is indirectly measured by the authorities without their having to widen or institutionalize the formal political space or go through a formal political process. Sadik al-Azm highlights these in the context of Syrian politics:

> Through a series of informal, private, and overwhelming circles, people discuss and re-discuss, hash and rehash, spoof and re-spoof the affairs of the world big and small, internal and external, Pan-Arab and local, regional and international. Through these personalized, highly efficient and always active informal networks and face-to-face encounters, an informal public opinion is created and crystallizes on the issues, anomalies and problems of the day. The result is a public opinion which the power centers take into account without ever formally admitting it. (2000: 2)

Numerous works have documented the *diwaniyya,* a frequent informal gathering that brings together adult males and which has been a pillar of participatory politics in the Gulf countries. Usually shielded from the watchful eye of the state, the *diwaniyya* is an indigenous social institution that plays a critical political and social role in traditional Gulf societies, providing citizens with a forum for political debate. As in Syria, however, the *diwaniyya* also serves as an informal conduit of information between the governed and the governing. The modern council-type institutions, *majalis,* that many Gulf states like Saudi Arabia and Oman have created, are fashioned along the lines of informal assemblies. Historically, these *majalis* were a means through which individuals, rich and poor, accessed their leaders and requested assistance (Bill and Springborg 1990).

In several countries in the MENA region, tribes serve as informal vehicles for participation and mobilization. Their methods of resistance and political negotiation are well documented in countries such as Yemen. For instance, in cases of conflict between the government and tribes, "road blocks are put up *(qata')*, access to territory is denied by men 'guarding the borders' *(zabinin al hudud)*, delegations are formed to provide mediation *(wasta)*, rifles are proffered, guarantors appointed, and arbitration pursued by the same means as were used before the new economy came to Yemen" (Dresch 1989: 312). In many such cases, the shaikh (tribal chief) serves as the intermediary between the tribe and government. In Algeria, traditional tribal institutions known as *arsh* or *aroush* led a social movement that in 2001 erupted in protests by thousands of Algerians in the Kabilye region (Layachi 2001). Contesting the government's marginalization of Berber culture, the protests forced several concessions by the state, including recognizing Tamazight, the Berber language, as an official language.

The informal modes of participation described above are far from being unique to the MENA region. Indeed, these informal vehicles are widespread throughout most regions of the world, and have received a great deal of attention, research, and analysis in the context of South Asia and Latin America. In authoritarian contexts such as MENA, they offer great appeal to the population because of their more risk-free and incentive-based track record. The fact that these modes and vehicles are based on familiar structures and mutual trust provides a layer of comfort and a sense of protection from the claws of the state. Moreover, the effectiveness of these modes in exacting results—as wide-ranging as these might be—also reinforces this appeal.

At the same time, however, this underworld of participation perpetuates a short-term and individualistic vision of society. Promoting ties of patronage, distorting incentives, eluding the rule of law, and evading accountability, these networks do not measure up to the "good governance" criteria for sustainable political and economic development. Usually benefiting individualistic or interest group needs, these forms of participation tackle problems through individual favors rather than overarching policies. Asef Bayat notes that, "as fluid and unstructured forms of activism, these largely atomistic strategies have the advantages of flexibility and versatility, but they fall short of developing legal, technical and organizational support needed to advance the search for social justice on the broader, national level" (1997: 12).

Moreover, as much as these forms are effective and lasting because they are based on social institutions with deep roots, it is their rootedness that often makes them resistant to change. The *diwaniyya,* for instance, is an all-male institution. While women in the Gulf have recourse to other social institutions through which they negotiate to further their interests, such as the role they play in arranging strategic marriages, they remain excluded from many of the key institutions of political life. As such, many of these institutions tend to reflect the traditional structures of society, like patriarchy, resisting the natural course of social change that every society undergoes.

▨ Revisiting the Paradigm:
Pursuing the Road Less Traveled?

It is important to recognize that weak formal institutions in an environment of authoritarianism are vulnerable to infiltration by informal networks, with the end result being that informal structures get reproduced within these institutions. Robert Springborg illustrates this point through his study of Egyptian professional syndicates under Gamal Abdul Nasser: "The informal authority structure within syndicates is in most cases not coincidental with the organizational mode. Syndicates are typically governed by a 'nuclear' group, or small handful of activists who are themselves perennial board members." He goes on to note that "the lack of sustained organizational activity by the bulk of the members enables small groups to dominate syndicates" (1978: 280–281). To this end, the various efforts to strengthen democratic institutions, which usually take the form of capacity-building exercises, are unlikely to change the internal power dynamics of these institutions and truly transform them into institutions of empowerment and political voice.

The permeability of formal institutions by informal networks can distort the nature of these institutions, transforming them into agents of patronage and kinship and detracting them from their public service role. Indeed, this weakness has often been instrumental in the actions of governments to curb the influence of formal institutions. For instance, governments in Jordan, Kuwait, and Yemen have all tried to incorporate tribal members into parliamentary life, ensuring that structures of kinship are perpetuated within their parliaments. As such, parliamentarians see their role as one of an "intermediary between their constituents and the State, interceding frequently to generate jobs, contracts, development projects, and other state resources for their districts" (Khouri 2003: 6).

It is this complex reality that one must be aware of when addressing the issue of reform and political change in the MENA region. Quick and simplistic recipes for political reform, such as those that are put forward by a number of Western governments and scholars, and that figure so prominently in the media and policy debate, provide as cosmetic an attempt at reform as that which MENA governments wish to undertake. Indeed, these have helped somewhat to reduce popular frustration, served to make the West feel good about its efforts, and shed a positive light on MENA governments' perfunctory attempts at political reform.

To remedy this situation, the debate on democratization in the region needs to move away from its focus on funding and quick fixes, to consider options for political change based on the reality on the ground. Indeed, as long as misconceptions of the Arab street, ranging from apathy to incivility, continue to dominate the debate, there is little hope for the debate to be enriched by gaining a better understanding of how the Arab street mobilizes. The issue at hand is not about preserving and perpetuating informal networks but about understanding these in order to gain insights into how political change can happen. It is about understanding how an effective social movement can turn into a political party and gain popular support. Certainly, such a shift requires a greater disposition to pose difficult questions and undertake the necessary research and thinking that a task as massive as bringing democratization into the Middle East and North Africa necessitates.

▓ Notes

1. In this chapter, "the Middle East and North Africa" refers only to the predominantly Arabic-speaking countries of the region.

2. This is not to say that informal networks and institutions are absent in developed democracies. On the contrary, these do exist and play an important role in their countries. However, because of the relative effectiveness and credibility of formal networks, the core of political participation tends to take place through these channels.

3. This approach is borrowed from that of Mohamed Bamyeh (2005), which seeks to redefine the concept of civil society in the Islamic experience in this manner.

4. Between 1991 and 2001, the United States provided approximately $150 million for projects related to civil society strengthening. For more information, see Hawthorne 2004.

5. As Nazih Ayubi notes: "Until the beginning of the Nineteenth Century, Muslims had thought of politics in terms of the *umma* . . . and of *khilafa* or sultan. . . . A concept of the "state" that may link the . . . community and the government, was not to be developed until later on" (1995: 21).

PART 2

Negotiating the Electoral Arena

4

Intra-Elite Struggles in Iranian Elections

Güneş Murat Tezcür

In the early twenty-first century, explicit justifications for guardianship within regimes have lost their appeal. Based on the notion that a group of elites should govern by reason of their superior political skills, guardianship was thought to be a lasting alternative to democratic rule until recently (Dahl 1989: 52). Vanguard politics and the pursuit of ideological utopias, which had been prevalent throughout the twentieth century, became remnants of a past era after the fall of the Soviet Union. Since then, surviving dictators have been at pains to highlight their "democratic" credentials.

In this context, the Islamic Republic of Iran stands as a unique case where guardianship is explicitly justified in the constitution and coexists with popular sovereignty. In fact, the Islamic Republic epitomizes the fundamental contradiction between guardianship and popular rule. On the one hand, ultimate power lies in the hands of a group of clerics who are not popularly accountable and have veto power over elected officials. On the other hand, regular and relatively competitive elections take place for the presidency, the parliament, and the municipalities. While the guardians strictly supervise these elections, these political processes nonetheless introduce a degree of uncertainty, pluralism, and public participation into Iranian politics unprecedented in the authoritarian regimes of the Middle East. This chapter offers an analytical survey of the elections in the Islamic Republic with a focus on two interrelated questions: What are the major characteristics of, and the nature of political participation within, the elections in the Islamic Republic? And how do elections affect the evolution of factional politics?

Currently, the Islamic Republic has four types of popular elections: presidential, parliamentary, municipal, and the selection of the eighty-six members of the Assembly of Experts. Both the presidential and parliamen-

51

tary elections take place every four years. The municipal elections were first organized in 1999 and are also scheduled to take place every four years. The elections for the Assembly of Experts, a body that is constitutionally empowered to supervise and select the most powerful man in the regime *(faqih)*, take place every eight years. This chapter, however, focuses on the presidential and parliamentary elections, as they have been central to the evolution of Iranian politics. A main argument of this chapter is that elections primarily serve to perpetuate pluralist authoritarianism in the Islamic Republic. Rather than being a catalyst for democratization or simply solidifying the regime's control over society, elections manage interfactional conflict and introduce an element of uncertainty and dynamism to Iranian politics unparalleled in many other authoritarian regimes.

The chapter first places current politics within a historical context by providing an overview of elections under the Pahlavi monarchy (1925–1979). Unlike in the Islamic Republic, elections were never critical to the political legitimacy of the sultanistic Pahlavi regime. Nonetheless, the Islamic Republic adopted many characteristics of the Pahlavi-era elections. Next the chapter examines current politics, summarizing the evolution and primary characteristics of elections in the Islamic Republic, and analyzes the rise of the reform movement (Dovom Khordad), its electoral victories in the 1997 and 2001 presidential and 2000 parliamentary elections, and finally the factors that contributed to its demise in the 2004 parliamentary and 2005 presidential elections. Electoral competition enhances pluralistic authoritarianism of the Islamic Republic. It does not invite political participation in the form of opposition to the authoritarian nature of the regime. The chapter is based on my study of the 2005 presidential elections as a participant-observer, systematic analysis of electoral data, and a compilation of printed and electronic news in Persian, especially during the electoral periods. My 2005 fieldwork involved observing campaigns of the presidential candidates, interviewing campaign managers, workers, journalists, and voters.

■ Iranian Elections Before the Revolution

Elections in Iran date back to the Constitutional Revolution of 1906.[1] The driving force of the constitutionalist movement was the hope that a constitutional monarchy would create a centralized state with the capacity to modernize the country (Arjomand 1988: 35; Baktiari 1996: 13–14; Gheissari and Nasr 2006: 24). The first Iranian parliament *(majles-e shura-ye melli)* was convened in October 1906 after the Qajar shah was forced to accept a constitution that limited his absolute authority. The constitution of 1906 and the supplementary fundamental law of 1907 remained intact until the 1979 revolution and formed the legal basis of electoral politics under monarchical rule. The power of the parliament basically depended on the effectiveness of the ruling shah. As long as the shah was a weak figure, the parliament was able to successfully challenge the government's unilateral decisions. For example, the parliament that was elected in 1921 repudiated the government's agreement that gave Great Britain significant influence in Iran (Baktiari 1996: 19). However, with the rise of Reza Pahlavi, who deposed the Qajar dynasty (1796–1925) and was crowned as Shah in 1926, the parliament gradually lost its autonomy and influence.

After the forced abdication of Reza Shah in 1941, the parliament reasserted its prerogatives and Iranian politics were characterized by an unprecedented level of pluralism. Mohammed Reza, who replaced his father as shah at the request of the British, was too insecure to impose his will on the parliament. Thus, from 1941 until the coup d'état of 1953, the parliament became increasingly more assertive. A central figure in this period was Mohammed Mosaddeq, who became the prime minister in 1951 and nationalized the oil industry the same year after securing the approval of the parliament. However, Mosaddeq did not last in power and was overthrown by a pro-Shah coup backed by the United States and Britain (Gasiorowski 1987). Subsequently, the Shah gradually consolidated his power and created a typical "sultanistic" regime in which power emanated from the ruler. Sultanistic regimes are characterized by very low institutionalization and a lack of rule of law. All citizens, including high-ranking civil servants, are ultimately subject to unpredictable and despotic intervention of the ruler. In these types of regimes, nonviolent paths to regime change are, for the most part, precluded (Linz and Stepan 1996).

Despite the concentration of power in the hands of the Shah, the parliamentary elections continued to take place with some regularity after 1953. However, by 1961, the Shah had no qualms over dissolving the parliament, which was transformed into a subservient body. Moreover, the establishment of a senate, a body superior to the parliament, sharply curtailed the authority of the latter. Elections for the senate took place for the first time in 1950. It consisted of sixty members, thirty of them directly appointed by the Shah himself. Half of the elected seats were assigned to Tehran. After entirely pacifying the parliamentary opposition to his rule, the Shah used parliamentary elections to deflect criticism of his regime and encouraged competition among his loyal servants. An "official opposition party," the People's Party, was established in 1957 under the chairmanship of one of the Shah's trusted aides. A year later, the National Party was formed as the "party of the government," and in 1963 the New Iran Party was established. By 1975, four regime-sanctioned parties were participating in the parliamentary elections.

This multiple-party system under monarchical tutelage ended in 1975 when the Shah decided to create a one-party system with the capacity for mass mobilization. All four parties were closed and were replaced by a single party, the National Resurrection Party (Hezb-e Rastakhiz-e Mellat-e Iran). Then–prime minister Amir Abbas Hoveyda became its chairman, and the party rapidly organized itself throughout the country while the regime urged citizens to join it.

The 1975 elections deserve some attention, as they typified some of the practices later adopted by the Islamic Republic. This time, the regime exhorted participation in this year and initiated a campaign of voter registration. Eventually, nearly 7 million registration cards were issued out of a pool of 14 million, and approximately 5 million people voted. Candidates who wished to run under the party ticket were selected after rigorous monitoring. The practices of prescreening candidates and exhorting people to vote in the elections were later copied by the Islamic Republic.

The monitoring process involved two stages. Local councils formed by regime loyalists evaluated the credentials of the candidates and suggested names to the executive board of the party. As a result of this process, 861 candidates out of 7,000 applicants were allowed to represent the party. As the parliament had 268 seats in 175 constituencies, the party put forward three or four candidates for each seat. However, one peculiar aspect of the elections was the lack of official ballots. Voters had to write their choices on pieces of paper, or had to bring lists with them. Voters were allowed to vote for as many candidates as there were seats in their constituency. For example, the Tehran constituency had 27 parliamentary seats, so voters chose 27 names from a list of 109 candidates (Mohammadi-Nejad 1977). Inevitably, the structure of voting undermined the formation of strong party alliances and contributed to the individualization of political competition. Candidates formed informal coalitions and disseminated lists to voters. It was possible for a candidate to be on multiple lists. All of these practices have continued into the current elections of the Islamic Republic.

To the lament of the Shah, this rather perplexing attempt at combining one-party rule with absolute monarchism did not succeed. Traditional monarchical institutions, unlike modern one-party regimes, may not be in a position to channel and structure rising demands for political participation (Huntington 1968: 153–191). As the monarch does not derive his power from popular sovereignty, extensive political participation is likely to undermine his legitimacy. The National Resurrection Party did not succeed in gaining the allegiance of the citizens and did not form an institutionalized and autonomous channel of communication between the ruler and the people. For instance, according to a youth survey conducted before the elections, only 13 percent of respondents expressed that they had a reason to vote (Mohammadi-Nejad 1977). Ultimately, the Shah failed to extend his support base beyond the court, the bureaucracy, and the army. Overall, the elections neither helped the Shah to prolong his rule nor contributed to peaceful transition of power (Razi 1987).

■ Elections and the Distribution of Power in the Islamic Republic of Iran

In contrast to the previous era, elections in postrevolutionary Iran have been central to the politics of the Islamic Republic. The constitution of the new regime was drafted by a popularly elected assembly and was approved by a referendum in December 1979. The nomination process in the formation of the assembly was far from being democratic (Saffari 1993). The Islamic radicals who crafted the constitution had several priorities. Their political visions were informed by Ayatollah Khomeini's theocratic revision of Shi'i thought and popular struggle against the monarchical regime. Primarily, they were concerned with the retention of ultimate power within the hands of the Revolutionary Guard, who were not subject to the whims of public opinion (Samii 2001). Hence the institution of *faqih,* which was first described in Khomeini's 1971 lectures on Islamic governance, was created and given extraordinary veto powers. The powers of the *faqih,* which are defined in Articles 2 and 110 of the constitution, include control of the Revolutionary Guard, dismissal of the president, and appointment of key members of office, such as half the members of the Guardian Council (Shura-ye Negahban), all members of the Expediency Council (Shura-ye Tahsis-e Maslehat-e Nezam), and the head of the judiciary. The Guardian Council is a body of twelve jurists and is entitled to review all parliamentary laws to decide whether they violate the Islamic principles and the constitution (Articles 91, 98, 99). It is also given the power to interpret the constitution and has gradually taken over the task of monitoring the candidates for popular elections. The consolidation of the clerical rule has inverted the Shi'i religious hierarchy and generated discontent among some senior clerics who were excluded from power (Roy 1999; Arjomand 2002). In essence, this institutional structure created a regime that glorified a statist understanding of Islam at the expense of traditional Shi'i clergy and popular religion (Schirazi 1998: 64; Tamadonfar 2001). As an unintended consequence, rates of attendance in mosques and Friday congregations are very low under the Islamic Republic (Tezcür, Azadarmaki, and Mehri 2006).

Another priority of the revolutionaries was the popular legitimacy of the new regime. They thought of elections as institutional means to ensure that the regime was *perceived* to be based on popular consent and appeals to the people. After all, the Islamic Republic came into existence as a result of popular uprising, and the monarchical regime was overthrown only through mass mobilization. Furthermore, the new regime has been characterized by open conflict among factions since its early days (Chebabi 2001; Moslem 2002). Elections provide a mechanism to publicly mediate this conflict.

A final priority of the revolutionaries was the creation of a relatively weak presidency (Milani 1993). Hence the executive power was divided between a president and a prime minister. The prime minister and the cabinet were required to receive a vote of confidence from the parliament. The parliament was also given the right to form investigatory commissions and hold the executive accountable for any misdeeds (Articles 76, 85, 89). This institutional configuration lasted until 1989, when Khomeini, several months before his death, ordered the formation of an assembly to revise the constitution. The constitutional amendments abolished the office of prime minister, and the *faqih* was no longer required to be one of the most learned religious scholars *(marja-ye taqlid)*. The president was defined as the head of the executive (Article 113). Meanwhile, the Expediency Council was created to arbitrate between the parliament and the Guardian Council. Since then, the Expediency Council has often sided with the Guardian Council at the expense of the parliament (Samii 2004).

The revolutionaries have built a complex and elaborate power structure with a myriad of veto holders and the diffusion of power among a group of elites (Buchta 2000). While the insulation of the most powerful political offices from popular accountability ensures that ultimate power lies in the hands of clerical guardians and their associates, elections institutionalize limited pluralism. Most important, the parliamentary and later the presidential elections enable factions to participate politically and to nonviolently compete against each other while seeking public approval. Consequently, elections determine the balance of power among factions. Meanwhile, elections do not undermine the continuity of the clerical rule, as the guardians decide who can be included in the electoral competition. Only the "loyal opposition" is permitted to participate in the electoral process. The regime regularly encourages the public to participate in the elections, and portrays public potential participation as a sign of its strength and stability. In the Islamic Republic, the parliamentary and presidential elections, by their very nature, are extensions of factional conflicts and did not facilitate the formation of effective mass parties. The system worked without a major crisis, despite the intensity of factional conflict, as long as Khomeini was alive and able to balance factions against each other. After his death in 1989, there was no authority to restrain factions from excluding each other from the political scene. The leftists were forced to the fringes of power following the 1992 parliamentary elections. During the 1990s, they reinvented themselves as reformists and successfully swept the 1997 presidential and 2000 parliamentary elections.

However, electoral victories did not translate into any organized mass mobilization capacity on the part of the reformists. Public support for the reformists was not sustainable and faded quickly after the 2000 parliamentary elections. As long as the reformists participated in the elections, they did not pursue any alternative oppositional strategies. When they challenged the supremacy of the guardians, the latter ceased to perceive them as the "loyal opposition." Consequently, the guardians obstructed the reformists' access to the electoral process and the latter did not have the organizational capacity and public support to resist. The factional nature of electoral competition precluded any significant change to the fundamental nature of the regime.

■ Election Characteristics in the Islamic Republic of Iran

There have been eight parliamentary elections since the establishment of the Islamic Republic in 1980, and the parliament has grown from 270 members to 290 in 2000. Several of the electoral practices have exhibited continuity with the 1975 elections of the Pahlavi monarchy. Voters express their choices by writing their favored candidates on a piece of paper. As previously explained, they may vote for as many candidates as there are seats in their districts. Parties often circulate lists of candidates and distribute these to voters before the elections. However, a candidate's name may appear on multiple party lists.

Some new characteristics exist, as well. According to the electoral law of 1980, elections are to take place in two rounds. Initially, a candidate had been required to acquire more than 50 percent of all valid votes to be elected in the first round. Later this threshold was reduced to 33 percent, and then to 25 percent by the time of the 2000 elections. In runoffs, the two candidates with the most votes vie for each remaining seat. All candidates have to apply to the Ministry of Interior, which sends their files to the provinces. In the provinces, these files are investigated by district committees, which communicate their decisions to the central committee. Final decisions are made by the Guardian Council, which has the authority to disqualify any candidate. The Guardian Council does not provide a public rationale for its decisions. Usually, the rate of disqualified applicants reflects the nature of existing political conflicts within the system.

When the factional conflicts intensified after the death of Khomeini, the Guardian Council, which had been controlled by the hard-liner faction,[2] intervened in critical junctures to ensure that rightist candidates ran almost unopposed in the parliamentary elections. Figure 4.1 shows the disqualification rate from the 1984 elections, when the Guardian Council was first involved in the screening process, to the 2004 elections. In the elections for the second and the third parliament, the disqualification rate was low: in 1984, 271 of 1,854 applicants, and in 1988, 386 of 1,615 applicants, were blocked from running in the elections. This pattern was reversed with the 1992 elections, when the Guardian Council applied more rigid criteria to disqualify members of the leftist faction who had dominated the third parliament. Overall, 34 percent of all applicants, including 40 incumbents, were disqualified. A similar pattern was observed in 2004, when the

Figure 4.1   Ratio of Disqualifications by Iran's Guardian Council in Parliamentary Elections, 1984–2004

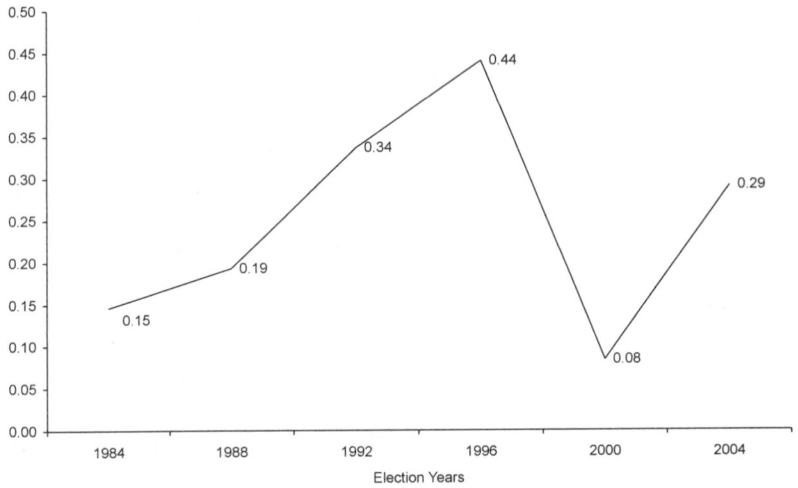

Sources: 1984–1992, B. Baktiari, *Parliamentary Politics in Revolutionary Iran: The Institutionalization of Factional Politics* (Gainesville: University of Florida Press, 1996); 1996, Human Rights Watch 2000; 2000, A. W. Samii, "Iran's 2000 Elections," *Middle East Review of International Affairs* 4 (2000): 1–15; 2004, Iranian newspapers.

Guardian Council disqualified about 2,300 applicants, including 83 incumbents, out of more than 8,000. As a result of this monitoring and the weakness of parties, membership in the parliament has been very volatile and incumbents do not enjoy strong advantages against challengers. The turnover rate between the parliaments has consistently been more than 50 percent. For example, 105 incumbents retained their seats in the second parliament in 1984, 66 in the third parliament in 1988, 83 in the fourth parliament in 1992, and fewer than 60 in the sixth parliament in 2000.[3]

While turnout for the parliamentary elections has been characterized by large fluctuations, it has never exceeded 75 percent. Currently, all citizens who are eighteen years of age are eligible to vote in both the parliamentary and the presidential elections. Figure 4.2 shows turnout rates for all the parliamentary and presidential elections from 1980 until 2005. The significant increase in voter turnout in the 1996 and 2000 elections was not sustained in the 2004 elections. Turnout in 2004 dropped to 51 percent, which was as low as in 1980 when elections for many districts, especially in the Arab, Azeri Turk, and Kurdish regions, could not be completed because of the ensuing political instability. In general, voter turnout tends to be higher in

Figure 4.2   Turnout in Iranian Parliamentary and Presidential Elections, 1980–2005

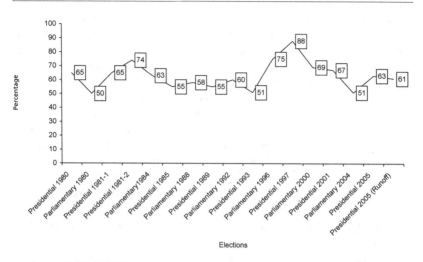

Sources: 1980–1997, *Resalat,* May 29, 1997; 2000–2005, Iranian and Western newspapers.

provincial towns and small districts, where personal connections and patronage promises are decisive, and lower in big cities. For example, turnout in Tehran in 2004 was around 33 percent, well below the national average. There might be several factors that cause fluctuations in voter turnout. It has been suggested that there may be a negative relationship between the Guardian Council's disqualification ratio and voting turnout (Samii 2004). However, available evidence does not necessarily support this claim. For example, turnout in the 1996 elections was 75 percent, despite the fact that the Guardian Council disqualified 44 percent of the applicants. Another possible factor that influences turnout is variation in the intensity of competition. Some parliamentary elections, such as the one in 2000, are characterized with relatively high levels of competition and vote-gathering efforts. In contrast, many reformist parties boycotted the 2004 elections. In any case, the campaigns for parliamentary elections are typically short (just one week) and do not involve systematic canvassing. Furthermore, the Iranian political parties have, for the most part, comprised loose collections of individuals, lacked extensive organization among the public, and represented factional interests (Fairbanks 1998). Most groups that field candidates in the elections do not even register as political parties with the Ministry of Interior. In most cases, candidates have to rely on personal funds to sponsor their campaigns. In addition, they are not permitted to run advertisements on state-controlled television and radio stations.

Although nine presidential elections took place in Iran between 1980 and 2005, only two of those races were truly competitive—the 1980 and 2005 elections themselves. In 1980, the first presidential election, ten candidates participated. The winner, Abdolhasan Banisadr, was not affiliated with the Islamic radicals and was elected with 76 percent of the vote. He was impeached in 1981 after his fallout with Khomeini. From that point, until the 2005 elections, favored candidates easily secured landslide victories. Ali Khamenei, who was elected the *faqih* in 1989, gathered 95 percent of the vote in 1981 and 85 percent in 1985. His successor, Ali Akbar Rafsanjani, won two easy victories in 1989 and 1993. However, turnout in the 1993 elections dropped to the dismal rate of 51 percent, reflecting the rise in public apathy. The trend was sharply reversed in the 1997 elections, when the former minister of guidance, Mohammed Khatami, beat the regime's favored candidate by capturing 69 percent of the vote. While Khatami easily won a second election in 2001, the 2005 elections turned out to be the most unexpected and competitive.

As Figure 4.2 demonstrates, turnout in the 1980–2005 presidential elections had three phases. In the first three elections, which took place during the revolutionary years, public interest in the elections was relatively high. After the consolidation of the regime, the presidential elections were characterized by public disinterest and apathy. Turnout dropped from 74 percent in 1981 to 51 percent in Rafsanjani's second election in 1993. Meanwhile, the Guardian Council continued to approve only a few candidates. In 1985 only three, in 1989 just two, and in 1993 only four candidates were approved by the Guardian Council. This increasing insignificance of the presidential elections to the public was sharply reversed by the 1997 elections, which delivered one of the most unexpected electoral results in Islamic Republic history, with turnout skyrocketing to an impressive 88 percent. However, turnout dropped to 67 percent in 2001 and to 63 percent in 2005.

An overview of the parliamentary and presidential elections in Iran warrants four generalizations. First, the unelected Guardian Council acts as the ultimate gatekeeper, deciding who is eligible to run in the elections. In a sense, the Guardian Council confers political legality to the actors who are allowed to run in the elections. This severely restricts the scope of political competition and pluralism, as many potential candidates are disqualified on the grounds that they are not committed to the Islamic Republic and the institution of *faqih* (Article 28 of the electoral law). Iranians who served under the monarchy in various political and administrative capacities are also barred from participating in elections (Article 30) (Samii 2000). Additionally, the Guardian Council has the authority to invalidate electoral results. Thus, usually, only figures whose loyalty to the clerical system is beyond any doubt in the eyes of the Guardian Council can compete in and win the elections. Second, while the guardians manipulate the elections by disqualifying many candidates, they simultaneously perceive elections as means to legitimize their rule and hence strongly encourage and rouse public participation. This exhortation of participation also involves intimidation, however. Citizens receive a stamp on their identity cards when they vote and citizens without a stamp are likely to experience various degrees of discrimination in their dealings with the state authorities.[4] The regime perceives high turnout rates as a confirmation of the Islamic Republic's public legitimacy and portrays voting in the elections as a national, patriotic duty. Third, and equally important, elections ensure that factional conflict remains within the boundaries of the rule of law and does not spill over into the streets. Hence the elections can be best understood as an extension of factional conflict that meanwhile introduces an element of limited pluralism, dynamism, and stability to the Islamic regime. Finally, the structure of the elections does not contribute to the formation of mass-based party organizations with extensive grassroots. Both the parliamentary and the presidential elections are completely based on individualistic competition and the existing parties are basically amalgams of individuals with similar political orientations and priorities. They lack name recognition, coherence, and discipline. The Islamic Iran Participation Front (Jebhe-ye Moshakerat-e Iran-e Eslami) is a partial exception to this rule, but still lacks mass-mobilization capacity.

■ The Rise and Fall of the Reform Movement

Although factional conflict had been fairly well controlled by the regime through the use of elections, the development of the reform movement (Jebhe-ye Eslahat or Dovom Khordad) provides an example of factional conflict that ultimately stretched beyond the boundaries set by the regime. The movement attempted to transform the elections from an avenue of factional conflict to democratization. The origins of the movements date back to the 1992 parliamentary elections. Before those elections, the Iranian political scene had been characterized by constant jockeying among several factions for influence and power (Akhavi 1987; Baktiari 1996). The leftists demanded heavy state involvement in the economy, espoused distributive policies, and advocated radical foreign policy initiatives. They controlled the parliament after the 1988 elections and maintained strong influence in the government of Prime Minister Mir Hossein Musavi. The rightist hardliners favored restrictive social and cultural policies, supported private enterprises, and were in favor of a more realistic foreign policy. They dominated the Guardian Council and retained the backing of Khamenei, who became the *faqih* after Khomeini's death in 1989. Individuals who rallied behind Rafsanjani, who had been the speaker of the parliament before becoming the president in 1989, formed another faction. Rafsanjani was a

pragmatist who avoided identification with any factions and pursued economic policies favoring private ownership and investment. In 1992 he
formed a strategic alliance with the rightist faction. The Guardian Council
disqualified many leftist candidates who failed to mobilize public support.
Consequently, the leftist faction suffered a huge electoral defeat in the 1992
elections.

Persecuted by the rightists and subsequently marginalized in the politics, the leftists reconsidered their position and became increasingly critical
of the authoritarian tendencies of the theocratic rule. Gradually, this leftist
faction developed a discourse that emphasized the rule of law, development
of civil society, protection of human rights, détente in foreign policy, and
limits on arbitrary state power. In a sense, the leftists experienced an ideological metamorphosis throughout the 1990s and became advocates of democratic reforms as a result of soul-searching. Many prominent reformist figures of the late 1990s and early 2000s had been followers of radical
Islamism in the 1980s. Their transformation points to the multiplicity of
Islamic political identities and the potential for the development of Muslim
democratic stances.

Mohammed Khatami, president from 1997 to 2005, had been the minister of Islamic guidance in two cabinets, from 1982 to 1986 and from 1989
to 1992. Ata'ollah Mohajerani, who served as Khatami's minister of culture
and Islamic guidance and was renowned for his liberal press policies during
his tenure, was elected to the first parliament and served as the parliament
deputy to Musavi. Abdollah Nouri, who was Khatami's interior minister
before being impeached and sentenced, had previously served as the interior
minister in Rafsanjani's first cabinet and had been Khomeini's representative in the army. Journalist Abbas Abdi, who was a leading figure in the
Islamic Iran Participation Front (Jebhe-ye Moshekerat-e Iran-e Eslami), had
been one of the leaders of the students who stormed the US embassy in
November 1979. Saeed Hajjarian, who was considered the architect of the
reformist electoral victories, had been one of the founders of the Islamic
Republic's Ministry of Intelligence. Abdolkerim Soroush, the leading intellectual of Iran since the early 1990s, had been a member of the committee
tasked with restructuring higher education according to "Islamist" standards. Mehdi Karroubi, who in 2000 was elected as speaker by the
reformist-controlled parliament, had also been speaker of the leftist-dominated third parliament. Bahzad Nabavi, who was deputy speaker of that
same reformist parliament, had been chief negotiator with the United States
during the hostage crisis of 1979–1980, and had been minister of industry
under Musavi. Mohammed Musavi-Khoeniha, who was the publisher of one
of the most important reformist newspapers, *Salaam,* had been deputy
speaker of the first parliament and served as a liaison between Khomeini
and the students who occupied the US embassy. Hadi Khamenei, who is the

brother of the current *faqih* and was elected to the sixth parliament under a reformist ticket, had been an influential member of the leftist-dominated third parliament. Evidently, the reform movement sprang from the revolutionary cadres themselves.

The central idea that drove the reform movement was recovery of the democratic spirit of the revolution. The leftists accused the hard-liner rightists of abandoning the revolutionary heritage in order to establish an autocratic regime. In a manifesto before the 2000 elections, the Islamic Iran Participation Front declared that it was following Khomeini's path and would revive the democratic promise of the 1979 revolution. It announced that the special courts for the clerics would be abolished, the press law would be amended to protect the freedom of expression, and censorship would be eliminated.[5] In a press conference immediately before his reelection, Khatami defined the reform movement as a force that embodied the Constitutional Revolution of 1906, the nationalization of the oil industry in 1951, and the Islamic Revolution of 1979.[6] According to him, the main goal of the Islamic revolution was to establish the rule of the people.[7] In a speech addressed to a youth organization in the aftermath of the 2004 elections, he emphasized the importance of the republican nature of the regime, advocated by Khomeini. Khatami defined republicanism as the supremacy of people's will in politics and implicitly criticized the Guardian Council's decision to prevent the reformists from participating in the elections.[8] Similarly, Karroubi criticized the Guardian Council's acts of disqualification as defying Khomeini's insistence on the Islamic Republic.[9] In general, the reformists defined their movement as the true expression of the 1979 revolution and promoted a platform that synthesized democratic ideals with the revolutionary tradition (Brumberg 2001).

However, the differences between the revolutionary ideals and the democratic ideas advocated by the reformists were difficult to resolve. While Khatami perceived liberal democracy as one of the finest achievements of Western civilization (Milani 2001), his mentor Khomeini dismissed "Islamic democracy" as being irrelevant.[10] Furthermore, the hard-liners effectively challenged this democratic interpretation of the revolutionary heritage by denouncing the reforms as anti-Islamic and anti-regime. For instance, in an address in April 2000, the *faqih* made a distinction between "Islamic" and "American" types of reforms and accused the liberal press of espousing the latter, which he considered detrimental to Islam and to the regime.[11] He repeatedly warned the reformists against serving the interests of the regime's enemies (e.g., the United States, exile groups).[12] Simultaneously, Ayatollah Mohammed Mesbah Yazdi, who was one of the most influential hard-liners, characterized freedom of press as a conspiracy against the Islamic system and implicitly accused the reformists of "trampling upon the blood of hundreds of thousands of martyrs."[13] The same ayatollah later accused the reformists of sponsoring cultural centers where girls and boys engaged in immoral relationships in the name of cultural freedom.[14] After the 2000 elections, the Revolutionary Guard issued a statement that denounced "the champions of American-style reforms in Iran."[15] During the political crisis preceding the 2004 parliamentary elections, an editor of the hard-liner newspaper *Resalat,* Mohammed Anbarloui, accused incumbent parliamentarians who had organized a sit-in of being spies for the United States and violating the Islamic rules.[16] These examples point out that the hard-liners vehemently opposed the reformists' interpretations of the Islamic revolution and attempted to portray them as being naive or even subversive, and in service of the regime's enemies. This counterstrategy might not be effective among the public, but it is nonetheless clear that the hard-liners defended the legitimacy of their authoritarian practices on the basis of Islam and revolutionary traditions.

Despite its limits, the reformist discourse introduced democratic concepts into the mainstream Iranian politics. Khatami's candidacy in the 1997 elections generated substantial public interest, and his campaign revolved around the promises of civil society *(jamiyya-e madani)* and the rule of law *(hokumat-e qanuni).* The reformists entered into a tactical alliance with the economic pragmatists, led by Rafsanjani, before the elections (Seifzadeh 2003). Subsequently, Khatami won the elections by a wide margin.[17] He drew support from all regions of the country. His hard-liner opponent and then–speaker of parliament, Nateq Nouri, was victorious only in two provinces, Lorestan and Mazandaran. Three years later, the reform movement, which loosely organized under the rubric of Dovom Khordad (the date of Khatami's 1997 victory on the Persian calendar), secured an impressive victory in the parliamentary elections. Eighteen groups, including the Islamic Iran Participation Front, the pro-Rafsanjani and pro-capitalist Executives of the Construction Party (Hezb-e Kargozaran-e Sazandegi), the Organization of Endeavorers of Islamic Revolution (Sazeman-e Mojahedin-e Enghelab Eslami), and the chairman of Khatami's party, the Militant Clerics Association (Majma-ye Ruhaniyun-e Mobarez), formed Dovom Khordad.

While these groups could not produce a unified list of candidates, there was considerable overlap between their lists in some districts. The fact that the Guardian Council disqualified only about 8 percent of all applicants (out of 6,856 applicants), combined with a relatively high turnout of 69 percent, positively affected the outcome for the reformists. They captured a majority of the seats in the first round. The Islamic Iran Participation Front alone gained control of 98 parliamentary seats.[18] In Tehran, the reformists won 29 of 30 seats. The reformists won in every district with the exception of Qom and western Lorestan electoral districts. The pattern continued in the second round, when the reformists secured 40 out of 65 seats. As a result, Dovom

Khordad controlled a majority of the 290 seats in the sixth parliament (2000–2004).[19] A year later, in 2001, Khatami easily secured his position by gathering 77 percent of the vote. However, the turnout rate dropped to 67 percent that same year, reflecting the growing public disenchantment with Khatami. Abstention was particularly acute in peripheral regions inhabited by ethnic and religious minorities. In Kordestan and Zanjan, the difference in turnout rates between the 1997 and 2001 presidential elections was 25 percent; in Chaharmabal and Bakhtiari it was 20 percent.

In retrospect, it is not hard to understand why the reformist electoral victories did not translate into substantial changes in the Islamic Republic. The euphoria generated by Khatami's victory in 1997 was rapidly overshadowed by a hard-liner backlash. The serial killings of intellectuals, the brutal suppression of the student demonstrations, the judicial harassment (Tabari 2003), and the crackdown on the media exposed the powerlessness of Khatami and gravely undermined his ability to pursue his reformist agenda. A similar pattern was repeated after the reformist victory in the 2000 parliamentary elections. Less than a month after the elections, the main strategist of the reformists became the victim of an assassination attempt, and later the judiciary imposed bans on almost two dozen reformist publications. Furthermore, the Guardian Council annulled the results of more than a dozen elections won by the reformists. The distribution of power clearly favored the hard-liners, who were well positioned to block any legal attempt to democratize the regime. A central strategy of the reform movement was the introduction of two bills that would reduce the Guardian Council's "approbatory supervision" over the electoral process and augment the powers of the president vis-à-vis the Guardian Council, the bureaucracy, the legislative, and the judiciary. Not surprisingly, the Guardian Council rejected these two bills in 2003 and Khatami eventually withdrew them in March 2004.[20]

Despite his inability to change the basic parameters of the regime, Khatami did not resign. Even after the Guardian Council disqualified an unusually high number of reformist candidates on the eve of the 2004 parliamentary elections, he still encouraged the public to vote in the elections.[21] He considered the development of an atmosphere fostering criticism of the second highest authority, namely himself, one of his greatest achievements.[22] Although Khatami and his reformist allies occasionally openly defied the political system,[23] they were mostly isolated and were under constant pressure from the guardians.

Additionally, the reformists could not overcome the widespread belief that they were simply yet another faction fighting for the control of state resources. Consequently, the public remained largely aloof when the reformists were crying foul and trying to rally support during the 2004 parliamentary and the 2005 presidential elections. A survey conducted in Tehran in August 2003 on religiosity and political attitudes provides some valuable information on public opinion.[24] In general, survey results reflected widespread dissatisfaction with how the political system worked. Over 50 percent of respondents perceived the political system to be either rarely or never responsive to their needs. About 45 percent of them believed that the state had completely failed to achieve the goals that they considered important, and almost 70 percent claimed that they had been occasionally mistreated by the state. Yet survey results also revealed high levels of disillusionment with the reformists. When respondents were asked to identify the groups that were capable of solving political problems, only one-third of them mentioned groups associated with the reformist current. About 25 percent of the respondents did not perceive any group as capable of solving the country's problems.

The demise of the reform movement in Iran exemplifies the dilemmas confronting "legal oppositions" in pluralistic authoritarian countries. Once the reformists decided to challenge the ruling regime by participating in the regime-controlled elections and institutions, they institutionally became prisoners of this choice. They committed themselves to a legally guided, nonconfrontational strategy,[25] and pursued reforms within the existing constitutional framework.[26] They perceived elections as an extension of factional politics, but also a means for rulers to return to power. This was not surprising, as many of the reformists belonged to the revolutionary generation and had been active in the first decade of the revolutionary government. Meanwhile, the reformists remained oblivious to nonelectoral oppositional strategies. When the guardians blocked the legal ways of reform and eliminated the reformists from the parliament, the reformists became organizationally and ideologically incapable of pursuing alternative strategies such as mass civil disobedience or continuous street demonstrations.

■ Factional Politics Redux: The Hard-Liner Victories

By 2004, public enthusiasm for the reformists had been replaced by widespread public apathy. Khatami had failed to empower the parliament and presidency vis-à-vis the unelected Council of Guardians and the *faqih*. Furthermore, bastions of the hard-liners, including the judiciary, huge economic conglomerates *(bonyads)*, paramilitary forces *(basij)*, the Revolutionary Guard, and religious associations with extensive influence, remained hostile to the reformist agenda. Meanwhile, growing public frustration with the reform movement had translated into low voter participation. Participation in the second municipal elections in 2003 was only 39 percent, compared to 64 percent in 1999. In Tehran, turnout reached a nadir of 13 percent. Turnout also remained low in the 2004 parliamentary elections, following the Guardian Council's mass disqualification of the reformist candidates, including about eighty incumbents,[27] and calls for boycotting the elections. The reformist parliamentarians protested the Guardian Council by staging a sit-in for twenty-six days. Still, the reformists failed to pursue a common strategy. While several parties boycotted the elections, several others participated to prevent a complete hardliner domination of the parliament.[28] Turnout dropped to 51 percent nationwide and to 33 percent in Tehran. About 23 million of 46 million eligible voters did not participate in the 2004 elections.[29]

The winner of the 2003 municipal and 2004 parliamentary elections was a group of hard-liners who were organized under the rubric of the Developers Council (Etelaf-e Abadgaran). This group won fourteen of fifteen council seats and all thirty parliamentary seats in Tehran in 2003 and in 2004, respectively, and gained the control of the parliament. Another recently formed hard-liner group was the Devotees Society (Jameyat-e Esargaran), which represented a younger generation of hard-liners who were veterans of the Iran-Iraq War.[30] The group repeatedly attacked President Khatami for his failure to address unemployment, inflation, and corruption (Samii 2005). Correspondingly, the hard-liner candidates in the 2004 elections campaigned on a theme of economic reform and avoided radical discourse on cultural issues.[31] This was also the strategy of Mahmoud Ahmadinejad, who eventually won the 2005 presidential elections.

The 2005 presidential elections were unprecedented with regard to the scope of competition and the diversity of candidates. Initially, 1,014 people applied to the Guardian Council to run in the elections. The council approved only six of these candidates. Not only had reformist candidates been disqualified, but so too had several well-known hard-liners. For instance, Reza Zavarei, who had served in the Guardian Council for over a decade and was strongly affiliated with the powerful *bazaari* interests, was among the disqualified.[32] Reformist Mostafa Moin, who was backed by the Islamic Iran Participation Front, was also disqualified. However, the Guardian Council later reinstated Moin and another reformist candidate after the intervention of Khamenei. As a result, reformist candidates were eligible to run only at the discretion of the *faqih* (leader's decree; *hokm-e hokoumati*), whose unilateral action was without any legislative or judicial sanctioning. The irony of this outcome is difficult to ignore: the reformists benefited from an authoritarian practice they would have liked to eliminate. Ultimately, eight candidates entered the race; however, one of these, hardliner Mohsen Rezai, later withdrew. Among the remaining seven candidates, former president Rafsanjani, former police chief Mohammed Qalibaf, who was supported by the hard-liner Devotees Society, and former vice president Moin received the greatest media coverage.

During the campaign period, which lasted three weeks, candidates employed some novel tactics to attract voters. Rafsanjani's and Qalibaf's

The contrast between the unpretentious and man-of-the-people image of Ahmadinejad (*right*) and the aloof and haughty image of his rival, Rafsanjani (*left*), turned out to be decisive in the 2005 presidential elections. Ahmadinejad's banner reads: "We can do it." Rafsanjani used the slogan: "The essence of Iranians is like jewels."

campaigns were most visible and lavishly funded (Nourbakhsh 2005). As a testimony to the lasting legacy of Khatami and the reform movement in Iranian politics, most of the candidates adopted reformist cum pragmatist slogans and eschewed radical platforms. In general, candidates strove to portray themselves as advocates for change and catered their platforms to the aspirations of the youth. Even the hard-liner candidates adopted and embraced reformist themes such as cultural freedom and public accountability, given the appeal of Khatami's moderate discourse and platforms in the 1997 and 2001 elections. A notable exception was Tehran mayor Mahmoud Ahmadinejad, who appealed to the working poor and combined explicitly populist rhetoric with promises of crusades against rampant corruption, nepotism, and "mafia"-type groups that were choking the Iranian economy.[33] Dismissing accusations of fanaticism, he portrayed himself as a modest man who best represented the "authenticity" of the Iranian Revolution and its commitment to the working poor.[34] He highlighted the problems of growing socioeconomic inequality and financial hardship experienced by vast segments of the population, despite the windfall from the rising oil prices. In fact, socioeconomic issues, rather than issues of political and cultural freedom, turned out to be more relevant for voters. Consequently, candidates with populist platforms performed well. Karroubi, who promised to pay around US$55 (500,000 rials) a month to every Iranian citizen older than eighteen, gathered more votes than the favored reformist candidate Moin.

While émigré groups and intellectuals called for a boycott of the elections, main reformist groups rallied behind their preferred candidates as they argued that a low turnout would favor the hard-liners. At the same

time, reformist participation in the elections contributed to the regime claims of popular legitimacy. As in the 2001 and 2004 elections,[35] the regime waged an energetic propaganda mission to make citizens vote. Khamenei declared that voting was a "religious duty."[36] In the end, participation was both low enough to allow the critics of the regime to question its legitimacy, and high enough to allow the regime to claim popular legitimacy.[37] The turnover was 63 percent in the first round and 61 percent in the second, in which Ahmadinejad defeated the front-runner, Rafsanjani. The defeat of Moin and Karroubi in the first round was a shock to the reformists. Karroubi, who narrowly finished third, accused the paramilitary forces and the Revolutionary Guard of interfering in the elections.[38] He argued that people had been paid to vote for Ahmadinejad, religious networks had urged their followers to support Ahmadinejad, and the paramilitary forces had intimidated people at voting stations. He issued a strongly worded letter charging that members of the Revolutionary Guard and the Council of Guardians had worked together to rig the elections. Newspapers that published his letter were temporarily banned. Moin joined Karroubi in questioning the fairness of the electoral results. However, they failed to stir public opinion. In the absence of any independent electoral monitoring system, which was crucial to democratic uprisings in Serbia in 2000 and in Ukraine in 2004, there was no way to know the magnitude of rigging involved in the Iranian elections. The reformist candidates were unable to provide substantial concrete evidence to support their allegations. Furthermore, they lacked the organizational capacity to challenge election results through mass demonstrations, as opposition movements had been able to do in Serbia and Ukraine.

In the runoffs, the reformists experienced a worst-case scenario. The choice was between their old foe Rafsanjani and hard-liner Ahmadinejad. The latter, a veteran of the Iran-Iraq War, an erstwhile provincial governor, and a professor of transportation engineering, was not considered a leading candidate before the elections. Many reformists thought that his election would result in a rollback of the accomplishments of the Khatami era. His rival, Rafsanjani, had been the most visible and established politician of the republic. Additionally, however, he had been a symbol of corruption and nepotism in the eyes of many citizens. During the 2000 elections, many reformists fiercely attacked Rafsanjani for authoritarian and corrupt practices during his presidency. Consequently, not many reformist-oriented citizens made a volte-face to support Rafsanjani. While Ahmadinejad increased his vote share from 19 to 62 percent, Rafsanjani's support climbed from 21 to only 36 percent. His last-minute attempts to join the populist bandwagon by promising cash flows and distribution of state assets to the public did not help.

A significant pattern of participation in the 2005 presidential elections was evidenced in regional variations. As Map 4.1 shows, turnout in the first round was generally low in the western regions inhabited by ethnic minorities, such as the Kurds, the Arabs, and the Azeri Turks.[39] For instance, fewer than 20 percent of all eligible voters supported any of the seven candidates in some districts of the Kurdistan province (Ostan). These figures may correspond to the relatively high level of political discontent and dissatisfaction with the regime among the Kurds, the Arabs, and the Azeri Turks. Their discontent with the regime occasionally erupted into violent clashes with the security forces.[40] Turnout in the runoffs further dropped in these minority regions, including from 33 to 23 percent in Kordestan, from 44 to 37 percent in West Azerbaijan, and from 55 to 51 percent in Khuzestan and Kermanshah. These figures were well below the national average of 61 percent. Calls for a boycott found the most receptive audience among these minority groups. Map 4.1 also shows the regional variation in support for Ahmadinejad. His support was concentrated in the central provinces, such as Esfahan, Tehran, Semnan, Qom, Markazi, Yazd, and in the eastern provinces, such as South Horasan. In contrast, he did poorly in the peripheral provinces, especially in Ardabil, where he was a governor during the 1990s, but also in Kordestan, Lorestan, Sistan and Baluchistan, and North Khorasan. Still, he significantly increased his vote share in almost every province in the runoffs. In fact, he received more votes than Rafsanjani in all provinces, except for Sistan and Baluchistan, and among absentee voters.

■ Conclusion

Elections in the Islamic Republic of Iran can be best conceptualized as the extension of factional conflict. While they are characterized by intense

Map 4.1 Turnout and Vote for Ahmadinejad in the First Round of the 2005 Presidential Election

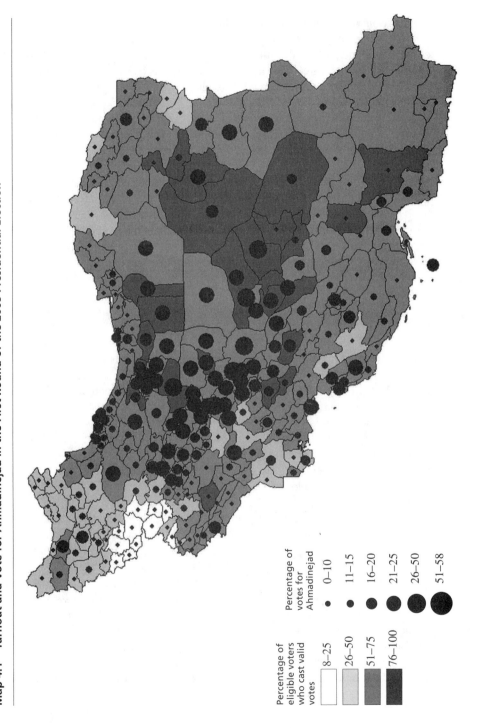

Percentage of
eligible voters
who cast valid
votes

8–25

26–50

51–75

76–100

Percentage of
votes for
Ahmadinejad

• 0–10

• 11–15

● 16–20

● 21–25

● 26–50

● 51–58

competition and dramatic political shifts, such as Khatami's landslide in 1997 or Ahmadinejad's victory in 2005, they do not ultimately produce outcomes that undermine the authoritarian structure of the regime. The guardians tightly control who participates in the elections, and elected officials are subordinate to nonelected officials. In most cases, only the "insiders" are qualified to run. Furthermore, the guardians do not hesitate to employ violent tactics to silence and demoralize opposition toward the regime. The judiciary bans newspapers and journals, imprisons journalists and intellectuals, and harasses reformist politicians. The rogue elements and paramilitary forces suppress student demonstrations, intimidate opposition figures, and occasionally murder dissidents. Moreover, different than in many other authoritarian postcommunist regimes, the Islamic Republic is built on strong nondemocratic ideological foundations (Tezcür and Azadarmaki 2008). The clerical rule is based on a distinctive understanding of Shi'i theology, and the guardians do not completely rely on popular mandate to justify their rule. Hence, in Iran, democracy does not seem to emerge as a by-product of short-term power needs and electoral calculations of the ruling elites, as elsewhere (Bunce 2000). An electoral strategy of regime change in Iran appears as a very remote possibility.

The reformist electoral victories created an aura of optimism that the regime would be democratized and the public would reject the regime's ideology.[41] In a similar fashion, the elimination of the reformists from the legislative and executive branches in 2004 and 2005 was interpreted as the consolidation of the authoritarian rule.[42] Both of these perspectives are misleading, as they portray electoral results as capable of diminishing or bolstering the authoritarian structure of the regime. While elections allow factions to develop platforms with public appeal and gain visibility, the structure of electoral competition does not lead to the formation of strong vertical links between factions and voters. The party system is in a very rudimentary state and democratic forces lack the organizational capacity to mobilize the grassroots. Political groups are not coherent and have little disciplinary control over their members. Huge fluctuations in participation between elections seem to reflect the underdevelopment of party identities and political orientations among the voters. As evidenced in the 2005 elections, the public does not generally categorize candidates as democratic and undemocratic. Hence public discontent within the regime does not necessarily translate into support for democratic candidates. The reformists who were in control of the presidency and the parliament received a lion's share of the public blame for economic problems. Hence public support for the legal opposition tends to be unstable. Elections create cycles of political change. However, these cycles are related to the changes in factional balance rather than the beginnings of democratic breakthroughs or other changes within the regime.[43] Thus elections are not agents of democratization or de-democratization (on this dual and continuous process, see Tilly 2007). Ultimately, elections in the Islamic Republic provide formal channels of sustainable political participation that regulate limited competition and pluralism within the boundaries set by the guardians. The formation of robust and strong political organizations that have extensive grassroots is likely to generate forms of political participation that are capable of transcending these boundaries.

▚ Notes

1. This section benefited from Azimi 1999.
2. Hard-liners include all political factions and individuals who have absolute commitment to the rule of the religious jurist *(velayat-e faqih)* and do not challenge the current distribution of power between elected and nonelected institutions. For a discussion of the differences between factions, see the Iranian daily *Aftab-e Yazd,* February 9, 2004.
3. See the Iranian daily *Kayhan,* February 25, 2000.
4. Some citizens seem to vote just because they want the stamp. See interviews in *The Independent,* February 21, 2004, and *Reuters,* June 15, 2005.
5. *Reuters,* February 2, 2000.
6. *Vision of the Islamic Republic of Iran, Network 1,* broadcast June 14, 2001.
7. *Vision of the Islamic Republic of Iran, Network 2,* broadcast May 28, 2001.
8. *BBC News,* April 7, 2004.
9. *New York Times,* February 2, 2004.
10. In an interview given to Hamid Algar in January 1980, Khomeini made it clear that, as a political system, Islam was immaculate and superior to all other political systems, including democracy. For Khomeini, Islam had nothing to borrow or learn from democracy (Khomeini 1981: 329–343).
11. Speech delivered during the Friday prayers, April 14, 2000.
12. Speech delivered during ceremonies marking the twelfth anniversary of Khomeini's death, June 4, 2000.
13. *Agence France-Presse,* March 11, 2000.
14. *Agence France-Presse,* July 1, 2000.
15. *Agence France-Presse,* April 18, 2000.
16. *Agence France-Presse,* February 6, 2004.
17. According to opinion polls, Nouri was the front-runner. See the Iranian daily *Abrar,* April 29, 1997.
18. See the Iranian daily *Kayhan,* February 25, 2000. For a description of the factions in the sixth parliament, see the Iranian daily *Hamshahri,* September 9, 2000.
19. See the Iranian daily *Bayan,* April 8, 2000.
20. *Reuters,* April 14, 2004.
21. *BBC News,* February 16, 2004.
22. *Vision of the Islamic Republic of Iran, Network 1,* broadcast on June 14, 2001.
23. For instance, immediately before the 2004 parliamentary elections, reformist parliamentarians issued a public letter that directly accused Khamenei of leading an oppressive regime (*Radio Free Europe/Radio Liberty,* February 18, 2004).
24. I conducted this survey, in collaboration with the University of Tehran. It

involved 412 respondents, employing multistage area probability sampling techniques. The response rate was 93 percent. For more information, see Tezcür, Azadarmaki, and Mehri, 2006.

25. For example, see the interview with Mohammed Reza Khatami, brother of President Khatami and general-secretary of the Islamic Iran Participation Front, in *Sharg,* April 24, 2004.

26. See the interviews with several reformists in *Aftab-e Yazd,* May 22, 2004.

27. According to Mohammed Reza Khatami, the hard-liners did not face any reformist candidates in 132 races out of 290 because of the disqualifications. *Reuters,* February 17, 2004.

28. On the one hand, the Islamic Iran Participation Front boycotted the elections and its secretary-general, Khatami, described them as illegitimate (*New York Times,* February 2, 2004). On the other hand, the Militant Clerics Association, led by parliament speaker Karroubi, decided to field candidates (*Agence France-Presse,* February 9, 2004).

29. *Aftab-e Yazd,* February 29, 2004.

30. On the growing influence of the Revolutionary Guard and second generation of hard-liners, see "Iran's Revolutionary Guards Making a Bid for Increased Power," *Eurasia Insight,* May 19, 2004.

31. For example, see the statements of Gholam-Ali Hadad-Adel, who became the speaker in the seventh parliament, *Reuters,* February 22, 2004.

32. The Guardian Council and the hard-liners may have been anxious that the hard-liner vote would be divided among so many candidates. See "Abundance of Candidates Worries Hard-Liners in Iran," *Radio Free Europe/Radio Liberty,* June 15, 2005.

33. Lack of transparency and corruption have beset the Iranian economy and have contributed to the political power of nonelected forces. Massive public funds are transferred and redistributed for political purposes, without public accountability and control (Esfahani and Taheripour 2002).

34. Personal communication with managers of Ahmadinejad's electoral campaign, Tehran, June 20, 2007.

35. Before the controversial 2004 parliamentary elections, Khamenei argued that voting in the elections would deliver a "slap in the face" to Iran's enemies (*BBC News,* February 13, 2004).

36. *Agence France-Presse,* June 13, 2005.

37. After the elections, Khamenei claimed that the people had full confidence in the "Islamic democracy" (*Islamic Republic News Agency,* June 19, 2005).

38. See the Iranian daily *Iran,* June 19, 2005.

39. The electoral data show voting results at counties, and second-level administrative units *(shahrestani).*

40. Mass demonstrations broke out in May 2006 in the Azeri Turkish regions following the publication of a cartoon derogatory of the Azeri Turks in the state-owned newspaper *Iran.* Riots, which resulted in dozens of fatalities, broke out in April 2005 in the Khuzestan province, populated by Arabs. In July 2005, mass demonstrations following the murder of a Kurdish oppositional activist resulted in a number of deaths in eastern Kurdistan.

41. For instance, see Bakhash 2000. See also McFaul 2005.

42. For example, see *Washington Post,* June 16, 2005.

43. For an article that conceptualizes recent developments in several post-Soviet states as swings in regular cyclical processes rather than transitions to democracy or authoritarianism, see Hale 2005.

5

Competitive Clientelism in Jordanian Elections

Ellen Lust-Okar

Why hold elections in authoritarian regimes? What purpose do they serve, and what is the nature of electoral politics? Some scholars conclude that elections in authoritarian regimes are inherently contested and destabilizing, while others have suggested that these elections are largely meaningless and highly orchestrated facades, intended primarily to legitimize the authoritarian regime. Adjudicating between these competing perspectives requires a careful analysis of electoral politics under authoritarianism.

This chapter is a step in that direction. Based primarily on an analysis of Jordanian parliamentary elections, it demonstrates how legislative elections under authoritarianism can provide an arena for significant competition over access to state resources, or "competitive clientelism." This competition is both systematic and shaped by institutions, although in ways that are fundamentally different from electoral politics in democratic regimes. The nature of this competition, combined with institutional rules, shapes both voter and candidate behavior and alters electoral outcomes. It also explains why elections can help stabilize authoritarian regimes, even in the absence of electoral fraud.

The disagreement in the relevant literature over the importance of elections lies, in part, in the fact that, while elections as an event have received attention, the politics of these elections remain largely unexplored. The conventional wisdom about the roles of these elections needs to be rethought, and the temptation to see authoritarian elections as simply early or incomplete forms of democratic elections needs to be abandoned. Rather, elections can be viewed as competitions over patronage in the absence of government alternance. This results in a very different form of electoral politics, with implications for both voter and candidate behavior.

■ The Conventional Wisdom:
Two Opposing Views of Elections

While some scholars have viewed elections in authoritarian regimes as extremely important, others see them as nearly meaningless. The view that elections are inherently contested underlies a great deal of scholarship, both on democratization inside and outside the Middle East and North Africa (MENA), as well as on public policies aimed at democratization. Political science has traditionally put elections front and center in understanding transitions to democracy. The expectation is that elections provide a mechanism for "chipping away at authoritarian regimes" (Posusney 2002). According to this theory, they do so both by creating space within which opposition can push for liberalization and democratization, and by socializing the public to participate in and look to democratic institutions for decisionmaking. It follows, then, that if elections are forced to be free and fair, and if political parties are strengthened, the road to democracy can be traveled more quickly. Democracy-promotion programs such as the Middle East Partnership Initiative, earlier efforts through the US Agency for International Development, and endeavors sponsored by a wide range of international foundations and organizations are based on these premises. They pour millions of dollars annually into strengthening political parties and civil society and in providing electoral observers.

In stark contrast is the view that elections are meaningless facades, simply intended as "window dressing" for purposes of gaining international or domestic legitimacy. This notion has been particularly widespread among scholars of the Middle East, who have increasingly dismissed elections now that the initial optimism accompanying openings in the early 1990s has worn thin (e.g., Chourou 2002; Sadiki 2002).[1] Such assumptions also underlie the work of scholars who study hybrid regimes (i.e., regimes that are neither "fully authoritarian" nor democratic; see Lindberg 2004, 2005; Mozaffar and Schedler 2002; Schedler 2002a, 2002b; Hartlyn, McCoy, and Mustillo 2003). For them, elections in "competitive authoritarian" regimes are interesting, but those in "full-blown" authoritarian regimes can be dismissed. Referring specifically to Egypt as an example of such a regime (and leaving one to wonder how they would view Syria, Tunisia, or other more repressive states), Steven Levitsky and Lucan Way state: "In full-blown authoritarian regimes, formal democratic institutions such as elections, parliaments, and courts either do not exist or exist merely as facades or legitimating mechanism. They do not yield meaningful contestation for power or generate uncertainty with regard to the allocation of political authority" (2003: 6). In general, then, these scholars easily eschew the *fallacy of electoralism,* which equates elections with democracy (Karl and Schmitter 1991), but they nevertheless accept a similar fallacy: namely, that "full-blown" authoritarian regimes cannot have elections that are meaningful in any significant way.

Problems with the Dominant Understanding of Elections

There are several problems with the dominant understanding of authoritarian elections in the MENA region. The first is theoretical. If we are to "unpack the gray zone" of hybrid regimes, it is critical to examine elections under the full range of authoritarian regimes (Carothers 2002). Gerardo Munck and Richard Snyder (2004) convincingly fault recent literature with conceptual imprecision and a failure to examine the "dark zone." Indeed, some scholars' very definition of competitive authoritarian regimes puts elections front and center, and yet, at the same time, pays very little attention to what makes these elections "competitive" or to understanding the nature of that competition (Levitsky and Way 2003; Diamond 2002). Until we understand the politics of authoritarian elections and the institutions that govern them across the full range of authoritarian regimes (and here, the MENA region provides an important arena of study), we cannot distinguish elections that create momentum toward democratization from those that reinforce the existing regime.

The second problem is practical. It is impossible to predict how successful current democratization programs will be, or to formulate more appropriate ones, without examining the relationship between elections and prospects for democracy. Democratization programs are based heavily upon assumptions that elections are inherently contested and destabilizing, but it is critical to determine when this is and is not the case. Indeed, to use a medical analogy, implementing such programs without understanding how authoritarianism "works" is akin to attempting to cure cancer without understanding how cancerous cells replicate.[2] We must examine the politics of elections in the MENA region if we are to distinguish who wins and who loses through electoral politics and to determine when promoting elections will foster democracy.

A third problem is empirical. It is difficult to reconcile the dominant views of elections with empirical evidence. If elections are inherently destabilizing, why is there strong evidence that electoral authoritarian regimes tend to "live longer" than nonelectoral authoritarian regimes? Jennifer Gandhi and Adam Przeworski (2001) have found, for instance, that the existence of (elected) parliamentary institutions corresponds to a longer duration of authoritarian regimes. Further, Gandhi and James Vreeland (2004) have found that parliamentary authoritarian regimes are less likely to experience civil conflict than their nonparliamentary counterparts. Examining slightly different factors, Barbara Geddes (1999) and Axel Hadenius and Jan Teorell (2005) similarly find that multiparty regimes are more durable than military regimes, indirectly supporting arguments that elections and parliaments may contribute to regime durability. Jason Brownlee (2004) is more skeptical that elections help to promote the survival of nondemocratic regimes. Nevertheless, the recent literature suggests that we should not quickly dismiss these elections as meaningless, but rather seek to understand how the politics and the impact of these elections vary according to regime types, across time, and under other social conditions.

It is similarly difficult to reconcile the view of elections as inherently destabilizing and meaningless with the fact that candidates, voters, and ruling elites invest enormous amounts of time, energy, and resources into the electoral process. Political elites take elections very seriously. Even where liberalization has been extremely limited or reversed, both incumbents and opponents vigorously debate rules governing participation. Candidates invest heavily in elections; even in the most seemingly repressive regimes, such as in Syria and in Iraq under Saddam Hussein, candidates spend large amounts of time and money on everything from lavish banquets and gifts to campaign materials and votes. It is hard to imagine that such debates would exist if institutions were completely meaningless, or that candidates would invest so heavily in elections if the outcomes were predetermined. In short, there exists a wide gap between our assumptions about elections under authoritarianism and the reality witnessed on the ground.

■ Rethinking the Politics of Authoritarian Elections

Making sense of these empirical regularities, and determining the prospects for democratization programs, requires rethinking the roles and politics of MENA elections. This begins with a reconsideration of the role of elections, more generally, and then a look at the behavior of voters, candidates, and incumbents.

The Role of Elections

Conventional wisdom holds that elections in authoritarian regimes, and the parliaments they produce, enhance the regimes' legitimacy, either with the domestic audience or with international actors. Yet this is not convincing. In authoritarian regimes such as those of Jordan and Egypt, many (and in some cases most) policy arenas are off-limits to parliamentarians, a fact that is not lost on either parliamentarians or voters.[3] A 2006 democracy poll by the Center for Strategic Studies found that only 7 percent of respondents believed that parliament played a major role in legislation in Jordan, while nearly 34 percent believed that the legislators had no effect whatsoever on Jordan's policies.[4] More important, the public has little confidence that the legislature makes laws regarding the most important problems facing Jordanians: unemployment, poverty, corruption, inflation, and public liberties. As Figure 5.1 demonstrates, both the general public and elites are skeptical that the parliament is able to influence the areas of pressing national importance. This skepticism holds across gender, age, and whether respondents are of Jordanian or Palestinian origin. There is broad agreement that parliament is not an effective policymaking institution, particularly regarding the policies that matter most.

Elections in authoritarian regimes are also not best understood as an arena for struggles over democratization. To some extent, these elections may be viewed as a two-level game, with one competition over the offices at stake and a second over the rules of participation (Schedler 2002b). However, this is only true in some cases and for some participants. In many countries, elections have continued for decades while democratization—and even expanded public participation—were not on the agenda. Syria, and Iraq under Saddam Hussein, are two clear examples of cases in which elections were held like clockwork and yet democratization was not on the table.

Even when elections were (re)instituted with the promise of liberalization, and sometimes murmurs about democracy—as they were in Jordan in 1989—contests over democratization do not drive electoral politics. Over

Figure 5.1   Is the Parliament Effective?

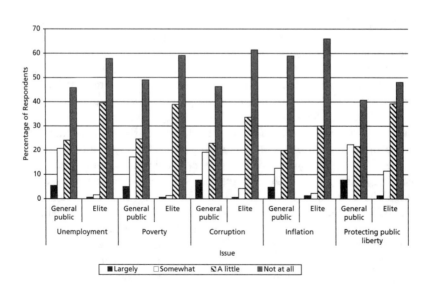

Sources: Center for Strategic Studies, *Jordanian Democracy Poll,* 2004; author's elite poll, 2005.

time, if democracy is not forthcoming, participants become increasingly skeptical that elections are vehicles for democratization. Most candidates and voters do not emphasize issues of democratization. For example, in the 1997 Jordanian elections, opposition to the 1993 electoral law was at its height and the retrenchment of democratization was being hotly debated, suggesting that rules of participation and democratization would be election issues. Yet, according to the 1997 Center for Strategic Studies democracy poll, less than a third of the candidates discussed "strengthening democratic life in Jordan," and fewer than 10 percent focused on such issues as the revision of the electoral law, strengthening of political parties, or further democratization.

Finally, some have argued that elections are important avenues for the identification and mobilization of new elites (Moench 1987; Landau, Ozbudun, and Tachau 1980). Highly entrepreneurial, upwardly mobile individuals can gain ruling elites' attention by doing well in elections. However, even if social mobilization is a primary goal of elections, it can only explain why candidates run in elections, not why voters cast their ballots. Why should voters be concerned with elite recruitment? Further, there is little evidence that the majority of elites gained parliamentary experience before attaining higher positions. If elections help to identify and recruit only a small number of new elites, why should regime elites invest in such a costly exercise?

Rather, authoritarian elections are best understood as an important arena for competition over access to a pool of state resources. Parliamentarians may not make laws, and certainly not in the most critical policy areas, but they can gain access to resources and distribute them to their supporters. They can call upon ministers and bureaucrats to allocate jobs to constituents, at times "threatening state institutions of scandalizing them in parliament if they did not react positively to their requests" (Kilani and Sakijha 2002: 58). That is, they can provide *wasta,* acting as an intermediary between the citizen and the state. They can also take advantage of the resources provided within parliament, hiring friends and relatives to serve in staff positions and distributing discretionary funds to fit constituents' (and their own) needs. Importantly, the acquisition of these funds is often at the government's discretion, which puts enormous pressure on the parliamentarians to "play by the regime's rules" in the parliament. As Sa'eda Kilani and Basem Sakijha conclude: "Parliament, whose main task is to monitor government's performance and legislate laws, is gradually becoming the haven for Wasta practices. Voluntarily or out of social pressure, parliamentarians' role in mediating, or, in other words, using Wasta between the citizen and the state is . . . becoming their main task" (2002: 58). This creates an inherent tendency for legislatures to adopt a pro-regime bias, even in the absence of ballot-box stuffing or other electoral manipulation. Voters will tend to elect parliamentarians who are close to the regime; candidates are drawn primarily from the ranks of those who are willing to accept, and play within, the status quo; and regime elites can thus use legal institutions to shape electoral outcomes.

Voter Behavior

Voters are likely to cast their ballots for those who can, and will, provide them access to state resources. That is, they vote for candidates who have (and will maintain) good relations with the incumbent elites, and with whom they also have personal ties. As long as the regime remains the major source of resources, competitive clientelism will promote a pro-regime legislature, even in the absence of regime manipulation.

Competitive clientelism promotes stability because weak rule of law characterizes most authoritarian regimes, and this makes *wasta* (that is, mediation) and informal institutions vital to maneuvering in the public sphere. Most people believe, and rightly so, that success in a wide variety of activities (e.g., obtaining licenses, landing jobs, entering university) requires *wasta*. Indeed, a survey conducted in 2000, reported by Sa'eda Kilani and Basem Sakijha (2002), found that the majority of Jordanians believed that they needed *wasta* to get business done at a government office, with 46 percent responding that they would seek *wasta* before beginning their task, and 19 percent indicating that they would seek *wasta* later. Given their parliamentarians' access to government offices, voters often turn to parliamentarians to play this role.

Consequently, voters seek parliamentarians who will have contacts with, or can remain in good graces with, the state, not those who will confront the government. A Jordanian voter voiced this well, stating:

> I came to seek a job from the deputy of our district. He told us that the government does not listen to them these days. . . . I wonder why the deputies oppose the government. They should comply with and obey the government's policies so that we can take our rights, because it is up to the government to pass anything. Frankly speaking, I will not elect anyone unless the government approves of him because we want to survive. (Kilani and Sakijha 2002: 59)

Of course, having a parliamentarian who can act as an effective mediator is only useful if that person will mediate on the voter's behalf; voters want parliamentarians who not only can deliver, but also will deliver to them personally. Thus, voters choose candidates not only on their ability to work with government, but also on their personal relations with the candidate. In Jordan, where kinship is extremely salient in determining loyalty and personal relations, voters tend to support candidates from their family and tribe. As shown in Figure 5.2, the 2007 Center for Strategic Studies survey found that more than half of voters cast ballots for candidates who were "able to work effectively with government," over 40 percent of voters cast ballots for a candidate because he or she was a member of their tribe or family, and more than 50 percent voted for a candidate with whom they had close personal ties. These relations were particularly important for Jordanians of Transjordanian (East Bank) origin, where tribal networks have remained stronger. Thus, as shown in Figure 5.3, while Jordanians of East Bank and Palestinian origin are similar in the extent to which religion factors into their choice of candidates, these populations differ in the extent to which tribal affiliations are important factors.

Understanding elections as competitive clientelism also helps explain voter turnout. Voters go to the polls when they believe that they can benefit from a candidate's success. In Jordan, where those of East Bank origin are more likely to have good relations with the state than those of Palestinian origin, there is an important relationship between the prevalence of Palestinians and voter turnout across districts. Districts with a large percentage of candidates of Palestinian origin have lower voter turnout than those in which candidates are of East Bank origin (Hourani et al., 1998: 207; Hourani et al., 2004: 196). Results of the 2007 Center for Strategic Studies survey corroborate this finding, with 61 percent of respondents of

Figure 5.2   Reasons for Voting for a Particular Candidate

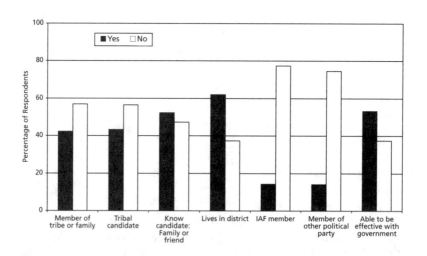

Source: Center for Strategic Studies, *Jordanian Democracy Poll,* 2007.

Figure 5.3   Reasons for Voting for a Particular Candidate (by national origin)

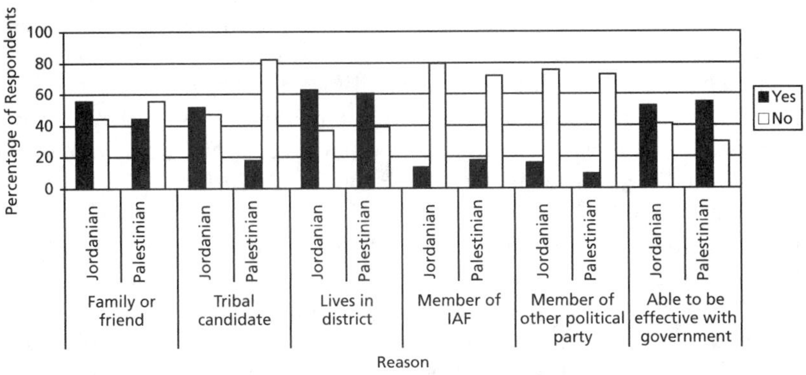

Source: Center for Strategic Studies, *Jordanian Democracy Poll,* 2007.

Transjordanian background reporting that they voted in the 2003 parliamentary elections, versus 44 percent of respondents of Palestinian origin. Jordanians of Palestinian origin, believing that their candidates can deliver neither *wasta* nor policies, prefer to stay home.[5]

Competitive clientelism also helps explain why voter turnout in rural districts tends to be higher than turnout in urban areas. Importantly, this stands in contrast to expectations of the early modernization literature, which in the 1950s and 1960s predicted that urbanization would spur political mobilization. Instead, voters in urban areas—where social networks are less developed and personal ties to candidates are weaker—tend to stay home, recognizing that they have little to gain regardless of which candidate wins the election.[6] In contrast, in rural areas, kinship networks tend to be stronger, and voters head to the polls hoping that if their friend, relative, or neighbor wins the election, he or she may be willing and able to help them in their dealings with the state.

That elections are primarily competitions over the distribution of patronage, and not policymaking, has important implications for public attitudes toward political parties. In general, political platforms around which parties are typically oriented are not significant when a parliament's policymaking role is limited, and consequently, the public pays little attention to political parties. The vast majority of voters do not consider party affiliation when casting their ballots. According to the 2007 Center for Strategic Studies survey, only 14 percent of Jordanians supported a candidate because he or she was a member of the Islamic Action Front (IAF) or another political party. Moreover, less than 1 percent of Jordanian respondents was, or planned to become, a member of a political party. Jordanians of both East Bank and Palestinian origin overwhelmingly view political parties as largely ineffective organizations that have been generally unsuccessful to date (see Figure 5.4).[7] Only 13 percent of Jordanians surveyed in 2007 believed that parties acted primarily in the people's interests, compared to more than 60 percent who believed that they acted in their leaders' interests. It is thus not surprising that when asked which, if any, political party would be able to form a government, more than 80 percent of Jordanians responded that no party was capable of forming a government, and only slightly more than 3 percent named the IAF (the party that received the highest level of support).

The exceptional support that the Islamic Action Front receives is easily understood within the context of competitive clientelism. Unlike other political parties, which were banned and heavily repressed between 1957 and 1989, the Muslim Brotherhood (which is closely connected to the IAF) was allowed to operate legally as a charitable association. This status allowed the brotherhood to develop an extensive social service network, including clinics and hospitals, schools, and other charitable organizations. As Hazem al-Amin (2006) notes, "While moving between their institutions and places in which they have a presence in Jordan, one feels that there is a shadow state set up by the Brotherhood. The feeling grows when one learns that the budgets for their various activities far exceed the money allocated

Figure 5.4   Are Political Parties Successful?

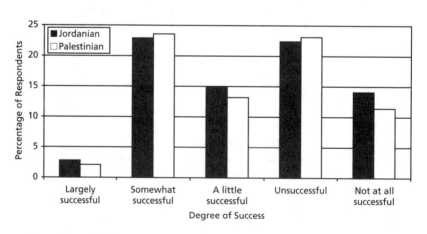

Source: Center for Strategic Studies, *Jordanian Democracy Poll, 2007.*

by the government for similar activities." These institutions not only provide an important point of recruitment for members into the Muslim Brotherhood, but they are an important source of revenue, reportedly yielding more than $1 billion per year (al-Amin 2006). Unlike other political parties, the IAF—through its relationship with the Muslim Brotherhood—has the ability to distribute its own resources. The exceptional support for the IAF is therefore not surprising, but it does not suggest that support for other Jordanian political parties will grow. Indeed, Center for Strategic Studies surveys have found that support for political parties had declined since the early 1990s.

The public also views parliament negatively. The vast majority of Jordanians do not believe that parliament can solve critical social problems, as discussed previously. Jordanians of both Palestinian and East Bank origin are also skeptical that parliament plays an important role, and remain largely dissatisfied with the institution (see Figures 5.5 and 5.6). According to the 2007 Center for Strategic Studies survey, only 17 percent of Jordanians believed that parliamentarians were primarily interested in the concerns of society and the nation, while 71 percent believed that parliamentarians were primarily concerned with their own personal and family interests.

Candidate Behavior

The opposition's perceptions of parliamentarians are perfectly consistent with candidate behavior. Elites know that the primary goal of elections is not to manage the alternance of power, nor is it to determine critical policy issues. The effect of elections on voter behavior influences candidates as well.

Figure 5.5   Does the Parliament Play an Important Role?

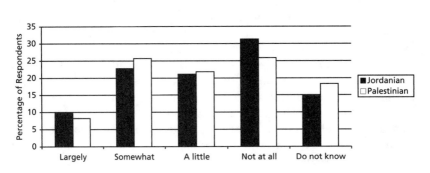

Source: Center for Strategic Studies, *Jordanian Democracy Poll,* 2007.

Figure 5.6   Satisfaction with the Parliament

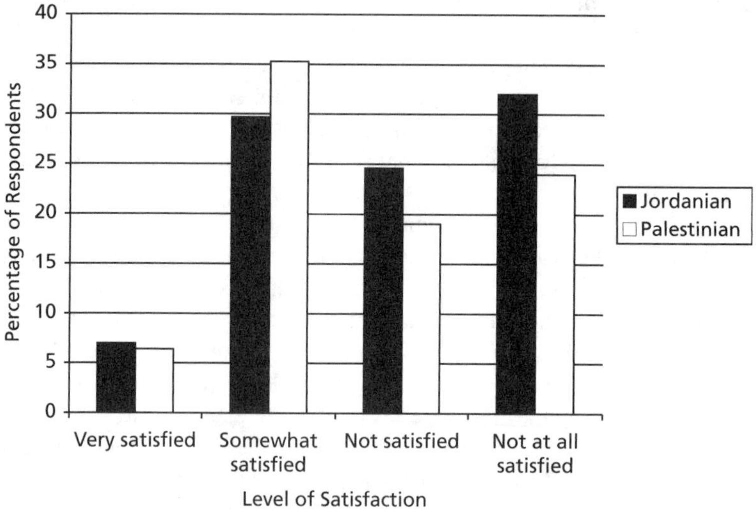

Source: Center for Strategic Studies, *Jordanian Democracy Poll,* 2007.

First, elites who are opposed to the regime are most likely to refrain from entering the electoral race. In interviews with opposition elites in Jordan and Syria, some individuals said that they refused to run in elections because they did not want to lend legitimacy to elections that they believed were nondemocratic. This stands in contrast to conventional perceptions that incumbent elites work actively to exclude opposition elites from elections. Rather, where elite alternance is highly proscribed and legislative powers of the parliamentarians are limited, opposition elites refuse to enter the race. The result: there is a self-selection of candidates who are only moderately opposed to or supportive of the regime.

Candidates are more likely to emphasize their family ties and personal relations than they are to concentrate on political platforms. This is not surprising. Candidates know that voters are primarily concerned with the deliverance of patronage. Thus, as Samer Shehata demonstrates in Chapter 6, campaign speeches and strategies are largely driven by the attempt to demonstrate the candidate's willingness and ability to deliver resources, not to discuss policy issues.

Moreover, as a 2005 survey of Jordanian candidates, conducted by this author in conjunction with the Center for Strategic Studies, demonstrates, it is the encouragement of family, friends, and the tribe that is the most important influence in determining whether Jordanian candidates will run. Political parties and government officials play little role (see Figure 5.7). Indeed, when individuals are not compelled to run on political party lists (due either to lack of electoral laws requiring party lists or to the logic of a dominant party regime), candidates are more likely to run as independents than as party candidates. Indeed, in Jordan, some candidates argue that they run as independents even when they are party members; they view party candidacy as a liability.

The result of elections over patronage is limited party allegiance and a tendency for the already weak parties to fragment into even weaker offshoots. High party volatility is not surprising: voters casting their ballots based on personal ties to the candidates and the candidates' relationship with the government are not likely to be loyal to political parties. Moreover, political party activists recognize that in the vast majority of cases, their party label is of limited relevance. In cases of internal party strife, it is often easier to walk away and form a new party than it is to remain inside the organization. Weak parties become even more impotent through a series of splits and splinters (see Lust-Okar 2001).

Weak political parties tend to make coordination among potential candidates difficult and lower the barriers to entry. In Jordan, an average of seven to eight candidates have contested each seat in the first four elections after 1989 (Hourani et al. 2002: 198). Importantly, the rate remained high (and the parties continued to be weak) despite changes in electoral laws, including the 1993 electoral law, which created a more majoritarian system and the 2003 law, which expanded the number of seats.

Figure 5.7   Who Encouraged You to Run in Elections?

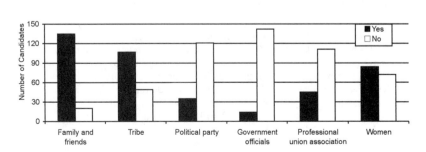

Source: Author's survey of elite candidates, 2005.

The cumulative result of weak parties, little coordination over entrance, and patronage-based voting is that there is high turnover in parliament. The logic of high turnover may not be immediately apparent. Yet if one realizes that it is much easier for candidates to promise (or voters to expect) the distribution of selective benefits to their supporters than it is for them to deliver these benefits, it becomes clear why incumbents are not advantaged. Moreover, the large numbers of entrants means that large numbers of votes are wasted; indeed, more than 60 percent of the ballots in the 2003 parliamentary elections were cast for candidates who failed to win seats (http://www.electionsjo.com). Not surprisingly, only 19 of the 110 members elected in 2003 were returning from the 1997 parliament, and only 20 of the deputies who won in the 1997 elections were returning from the 1993 parliament (Hourani et al. 1998: 204).

As long as state elites continue to control enough resources to distribute, elections in authoritarian regimes (where expectations for elite turnover and policymaking prerogatives of the legislature are limited) inherently promote pro-regime legislatures. Parliamentarians and their supporters become increasingly invested in using parliament as an arena of patronage distribution, not for promoting democracy or making policies. Indeed, for many parliamentarians, a move away from patronage functions and toward policymaking roles could only serve to weaken their influence. These conservative actors are more likely than opponents to participate in elections.

Elite Manipulation of Elections: The Importance of Electoral Institutions

To a large extent, ruling elites can be indifferent as to which candidates actually win parliamentary seats. Not surprisingly, Jordanians generally argue that direct manipulation of elections is relatively rare. Similarly, in Iran, the Guardian Council disqualified 569 candidates before the 2000 parliamentary elections, but this was not a large number compared to the total number of candidates or compared to previous elections. Moreover, as Haleh Esfandiari observed about that election:

> For the most part, the elections were fair, at least as far as reports indicate. Ballot boxes were not stuffed or altered. Voters were not bused to polling stations. In a few places where interference was suspected, skirmishes and fistfights broke out between the two sides. Some vote tampering may well have taken place at certain polling stations, but on the whole, the elections were clean. As one journalist told me, even if five percent of the votes in Tehran were tampered with, it made little difference, as the reformists won a clear victory. (2003: 129)

This example, along with many others, diverges from the standard belief that widespread corruption and overt ballot-box stuffing are always characteristic of elections in authoritarian regimes.

Rather, the history of elections in Jordan since 1989 demonstrates how incumbents can manage the competition through institutions. Through gerrymandering, malapportionment, and election laws, they can grant greater access to parliament—and the resources associated with it—to the traditional bases of regime support. These measures were particularly evident in Jordan through the 1993 and 2003 electoral laws.

Districting and Malapportionment

Electoral districts in Jordan are drawn to shift political access away from Jordanians of Palestinian origin and toward those of East Bank origin, as Table 5.1 demonstrates. Districts in which there were more Jordanians of Palestinian origin had fewer seats in proportion to the population size than did districts predominantly composed of Jordanians of East Bank origin. The most extreme case of malapportionment was found in Amman's second district, which had the highest proportion of candidates of Palestinian origin (and a high percentage of residents of Palestinian origin). This district had nearly seven fewer seats than it would have had were all Jordanians given equal representation.

This malapportionment has been a subject of debate in Jordan, but the new law enacted prior to the 2003 elections did not remedy the situation. Indeed, despite the strong complaints voiced by the opposition, the new parliament only exacerbated inequality. As Table 5.2 shows, both Amman and Zarqa, which had been heavily underrepresented, received some of the thirty newly added seats. Yet the increase did not outweigh the previous malapportionment; in fact, Amman went from nearly a twelve-seat deficit to a sixteen-seat deficit. Amman, Irbid, and Aqaba all became more underrepresented than they were prior to the 2003 redistricting, and districts with large populations of Palestinian origin remained largely underrepresented.

Electoral Rules

Election rules can also be used to shape outcomes. In Jordan, this was vividly demonstrated by the 1993 election law. In 1993 the palace faced challenges: the 1989 elections had resulted in a parliament within which the Islamic Action Front was the single largest election bloc, holding twenty-two of the eighty parliamentary seats. The IAF and palace historically had a conciliatory relationship, and thus Jordan did not abort liberalization in 1989 as Algeria would shortly thereafter. However, the IAF, as well as parties within the secularist opposition, were also notably opposed to peace with Israel. Thus, when the Madrid process and then the Oslo Agreement, between the Palestinians and Israelis, made a Jordanian-Israeli peace treaty a very real, immediate possibility, the palace sought a way to limit the IAF's presence in the upcoming elections.

The 1993 election law did just that. The fundamental change was a simple one: rather than allowing voters to cast multiple votes in multimember

Table 5.1   Seat Distribution vs. Proportional Representation, Jordan, 1997

Constituency	Population	Percentage of Candidates of Palestinian Origin	Seats Allocated	Seats Under Proportional Representation	Difference
Amman 2nd	517,269	73	3	9.9	−6.9
Amman 1st	318,821	63	3	6.1	−3.1
Zarqa	643,323	59	6	12.4	−6.4
Amman 4th	197,418	43	2	3.8	−1.8
Amman 3rd	160,445	32	5	3.1	+1.9
Aqaba	68,773	22	2	1.3	+0.7
Amman 5th	361,850	17	5	7.0	−2.0
Balqa	283,309	17	8	5.4	+2.6
Irbid	464,958	15	9	8.9	+0.1
Jerash	124,664	13	2	2.4	−0.4
Ramtha and Bani Kinana	143,002	12	3	2.7	+0.3
Karak	165,677	8	9	3.2	+5.8
Qurrah and North Ghor	146,831	7	2	2.8	−0.8
Tafileh	54,525	6	3	1.1	+1.9
Ajloun	95,698	3	3	1.8	+1.2
Madaba	104,062	0	3	2.0	+1.0
Central Badia	44,600	0	2	0.9	+1.1
South Badia	49,869	0	2	1.0	+1.0
North Badia	62,622	0	2	1.2	+0.8
Ma'an	58,635	0	3	1.1	+1.9
Mafraq	97,649	0	3	1.9	+1.1
Total	4,164,000	19	80	80	0.0

Sources: Abla Amawi, *Against All Odds: Jordanian Women, Elections, and Political Empowerment* (Amman: Konrad Adenauer, 2001), tab. 6, pp. 231–232; Hani Hourani et al., *Dirasat fi al-intikhabat al-niyyabiyah al-urdunniyah 1997* (Amman: Dar Sindbad Lil-Nashr, 2002), tab. 4., p. 24.

districts (with each allowed one vote per seat in the district), they were now allowed to cast one vote in multimember districts. The change, as expected, worked to the advantage of conservative forces. In elections that are primarily over patronage distribution, not policymaking, voters' most immediate concern is to elect parliamentarians who will deliver benefits to them personally. Thus, voters have incentives to cast votes for their friends, relatives, and neighbors, rather than for candidates with whom they are ideologically aligned. Before 1993, when given the opportunity to vote for both the candidate with whom they had personal ties and an IAF (or other) candidate whose platform appealed to them, voters cast ballots for both. After the 1993 election law, when faced with a choice between these candidates, voters most often cast their ballot for their friend, relative, or neighbor. The result was a much more fragmented parliament dominated by generally conservative independents. The IAF's representation dropped from twenty-two seats (of twenty-nine candidates) before the 1993 elections, to sixteen (of thirty-six candidates) elected in 1993.[8]

Table 5.2 Seat Gains Under Jordan's 2003 Electoral Law

Governorate	1997 Law Number of Districts	Number of Seats	Percentage of Total Seats Held by District	Difference from Proportionality, 1997 (number of seats)	2003 Law Number of Districts	Number of Seats	Percentage of Total Seats Held by District	Difference from Proportionality, 2003 (number of seats)	Increase in Number of Seats	Percentage of Seat Increase Granted to Governorate	Change in Proportionality (number of seats)[a]
Amman[b]	5	18	22.50	-11.9	7	23	22.1	-15.9	5	16.67	-4.0
Central Badia	1	2	2.50	+1.1	1	3	2.9	+1.8	1	3.33	+0.7
Zarqa[b]	1	6	7.50	-6.4	4	10	9.6	-6.1	4	13.33	+0.3
Balqa[c]	1	8	10.00	+2.6	4	10	9.6	+3.0	2	6.67	+0.4
Madaba	1	3	3.75	+1.0	2	4	3.9	+1.4	1	3.33	+0.4
Mafraq	1	3	3.75	+1.1	1	4	3.9	+1.5	1	3.33	+0.4
Northern Badia	1	2	2.50	+0.8	1	3	2.9	+1.4	1	3.33	+0.6
Irbid[c]	1	14	17.50	+0.1	9	16	15.4	-2.3	2	6.67	-2.4
Ajloun	1	3	3.75	+1.2	2	4	3.9	+1.7	1	3.33	+0.5
Jerash	1	2	2.50	-0.4	1	4	3.9	+0.9	2	6.67	+1.3
Karak	1	9	11.25	+5.8	6	10	9.6	+5.8	1	3.33	0.0
Tafila	1	3	3.75	+1.9	2	4	3.9	+2.6	1	3.33	+0.7
Ma'an	1	3	3.75	+1.9	3	4	3.9	+2.6	1	3.33	+0.7
Southern Badia	1	2	2.50	+1.0	1	3	2.9	+1.7	1	3.33	+0.7
Aqaba[c]	1	2	2.50	+0.7	1	2	1.9	+0.3	0	0	-0.4
Total	19	80			45	104			24	80.00	
Additional Seats for Women	0	0			0	6			6	20.00	
Total	19	80			45	110			30	100.00	

Source: Hani Hourani et al., *Who's Who in the Jordanian Parliament, 2003–2007* (Amman: Dar Sindbad lil-Nashr, 2004), p. 35.
Notes: a. Calculations for disproportionality of 2003 seat distribution are based on those of disproportionality in 1997 and are based only on the 104 seats (excluding seats reserved for women). The population figures for districts in 2003 were not available.

b. Denotes districts in which more than 25 percent of candidates were Palestinians in 1997.

c. Denotes districts in which 15–25 percent of candidates were Palestinians in 1997.

It should be noted that there is strong evidence that election laws have different effects in authoritarian elections, which primarily concern the distribution of patronage, than they do in democratic elections, which concern policymaking. For instance, we typically expect that more majoritarian election laws will reduce the number of political parties. Smaller parties are eliminated, and a few stronger parties remain. Yet, electoral rules appear to have the opposite effects when patronage, not policymaking, is at stake. When granted multiple votes, individuals often cast some votes for candidates who they believe will supply them with resources, and other votes for those who represent their ideologies. When restricted to one vote, however, voters cast their ballot for personal interests.

Consequently, across the Middle East and North Africa, we find that majoritarian electoral rules are more likely to produce greater political fragmentation and weaker parties (Lust-Okar and Jamal 2002). Despite this, however, the same lesson holds. Given the logic of competitive clientelism, and in the absence of a political or economic crisis, ruling elites can use institutions to shape election outcomes. Fraud and electoral manipulation exist, but are generally much more limited than would be necessary to keep the regime in power. Self-interested behavior and institutional structures shape election outcomes.

■ Conclusion

Viewing elections as a competition over access to state resources, or "competitive clientelism," helps to elucidate the behaviors of voters, candidates, and state elites. Voters, seeking to elect candidates who will act as intermediaries between themselves and the state, are likely to cast their ballots for candidates who are both able to act effectively in government and with whom they have personal connections. Elites, seeking a successful bid for election and aware of the constraints, are more likely to run if they have relatively good relations with the state, and will emphasize their kinship, ties to the region, and ability to perform services in their election campaigns. Regime elites, aware of the interests driving both candidates and voters, can largely rely on institutions—rather than fraud and manipulation—to shift opportunities and resources to their supporters and limit opposition success.

Of course, elections are not always the harbingers of stability for authoritarian regimes, and one can question the extent to which lessons learned in Jordan can be applied elsewhere. Where the regime appears to have an unchallenged monopoly over resources, elections are likely to remain competitions over patronage. Such appears to be the case in Egypt (see Chapter 6), as well as in Algeria, Syria, and Tunisia, and perhaps to a slightly lesser extent in Morocco. In other cases, elections may serve the purpose of creating more space for elite turnover. Güneş Murat Tezcür's analysis in this volume (see Chapter 4) suggests that this may be the case in Iran. The 2006 Palestinian Authority elections also demonstrated a much greater ability of elections to promote political change than the present analysis of Jordan suggests.

The reasons for such variation are likely to be found in the extent to which the state monopolizes resources. Where the state has an unquestionable monopoly on financial resources as well as a monopoly of force, the incentives for and behaviors of voters, candidates, and state elites should remain very much as described here. Given the strong state monopolies in the Middle East and North Africa (and willingness—at times—of external forces to step in and shore up these regimes; see Lust-Okar 2005a), the Jordanian experience is paralleled across the region.

However, where the state's monopoly is incomplete—either because of financial crises, the existence of militias, or the nature of the regime—elections are likely to have very different dynamics. In this case, if the regime faces a crisis, the election may serve as a focal point around which opponents can mobilize. Given these conditions, an "orange" or perhaps a "green" revolution is entirely possible within the Middle East and North Africa. The stability of nondemocratic regimes in the region, and seeming inability of elections to provide a catalyst for regime change, are not due to irrational behavior on the part of voters, candidates, and regime elites, nor to an inherent cultural resistance to either democratization or regime change, more generally. Rather, these are entirely rational response to incentives in regimes where the state elites' monopoly on resources remains unchallenged. This, to date, remains the case across much of the region.

▨ Notes

I wish to thank researchers at the Center for Strategic Studies at the University of Jordan for their valuable insights and feedback and for making data available. I extend particular gratitude to Fares Braizat, Mustafa Hamarneh, Ibrahim Saif, and Hekmat al-Khader for their exceptional support. Parts of this chapter draw from Lust-Okar 2006.

1. Anoushiravan Ehteshami argues, somewhat contrary to the arguments in this chapter, that elections serve an important role, helping "political forces in the Muslim world learn to play by the given rules of the game" (2004: 101).

2. I agree that this analogy reflects the normative judgments about democracy and authoritarianism embedded in democratization programs; for that, it seems particularly appropriate.

3. The dynamics of elections in the Palestinian Authority and Iran are somewhat different, in part because the strongest version of these assumptions does not hold. See Chapters 4 and 7 in this volume.

4. In the 2006 Center for Strategic Studies poll, respondents were asked, "To what extent do you believe that the party is able to influence the government on the

matters that pertain to its goals?" The results were as follows: 6 percent believed it played a large role, 25 percent that it had some effect, 22 percent that it played a small role, and 34 percent that it played no role; 13 percent did not know.

5. Results from the Center for Strategic Studies survey following the 2003 parliamentary elections found similar results, with 73 percent of respondents of Transjordanian origin reporting that they voted in these elections, versus 60 percent of respondents of Palestinian origin.

6. Jordanians of East Bank origin are more likely to live in rural areas than are those of Palestinian origin. An analysis including both national origin and percentage rural as determinants of voter turnout, national origin remained statistically significant, while percentage rural did not. However, the coefficient on percentage rural is consistent with the explanation given here. Higher turnout in rural areas holds in Egypt and Lebanon as well (see Harik 1980 as well as analysis of similar data by the author, in collaboration with Tarek Masoud, project in progress).

7. The 2007 Center for Strategic Studies poll found that only 1 percent of respondents believed that the political parties were capable of influencing government to respond in all situations, and 22 percent believed that they were capable in some situations. More than 50 percent believed that political parties were not capable at all.

8. The IAF's performance in the elections may also have been hindered by its performance in the Badran government in early 1991. The social policies it implemented met with a great deal of criticism.

6

Inside an Egyptian Parliamentary Campaign

Samer Shehata

Although a considerable literature about Egyptian parliamentary elections exists, mostly in Arabic, there are few works that deal with political campaigns in Egypt and even fewer that examine individual campaigns in detail.[1] This chapter addresses issues related to Egyptian parliamentary campaigns including how many Egyptians understand the role and function of a parliamentarian, voting behavior and the possible implications of this for governance and "democratization."

In Egypt, as elsewhere in the Arab world (see Chapter 5), people do not vote primarily on the basis of party affiliation, electoral program, or ideology, but rather on the provision of services, including individual services provided to district residents. This affects both voting behavior (e.g., *who* votes in Egyptian elections) and the character of campaigns. In contrast to many developed countries, in Egypt there is an inverse relationship between income and education, and political participation (e.g., voting): wealthier and better-educated Egyptians are less likely to vote. I explain the logic of this antinomy and speculate about what this and the related phenomenon of voting for services might imply for the functioning of parliament, good governance, and the relationship between voting and prospects for "democratization."

Political campaigns are also important, constituting one of the most basic components of electoral politics and a direct form of political participation for both candidates and voters. Campaigns often provide citizens with a chance to listen to candidates and hear contrasting views on political issues. They can also be opportunities for citizens to directly question sitting and future lawmakers and to make their own concerns heard. This is true of executive as well as legislative campaigns and elections.

But what are political campaigns in Egypt like?[2] What does campaigning entail and what are the most common features of Egyptian parliamen-

Mounir Fakhry Abdelnour campaigning.

tary campaigns? How do candidates "connect" with voters and how do citizens understand the role and function of a parliamentarian? And on what basis do people vote for candidates?

This chapter examines the political campaign of a single candidate who ran for reelection in 2005, Mounir Fakhry Abdelnour. Abdelnour, one of Egypt's leading liberal politicians, represented the El-Waily district in central Cairo, better known as Abbassaya, between 2000 and 2005 and served as the head of the Wafd Party's parliamentary delegation during that time. An analysis of his 2005 campaign demonstrates the strong emphasis on service provision over policymaking in Egyptian electoral politics, and yields broader insights into the character of Egyptian elections.

■ Mounir Fakhry Abdelnour

Until his defeat in the November 2005 elections, Mounir Abdelnour was one of the most visible opposition parliamentarians. He served on the parliament's Economic Affairs and Foreign Relations Committee and was a guest on both Egyptian state and Arab satellite television. As a prominent parliamentarian and a high-ranking Wafd Party official, his political statements were well covered in the national print media. He is a respected national personality and is also one of only a handful of independents on the government's National Council for Human Rights.

Abdelnour represents Egyptian secular politics with links to the nation's liberal era. He descends from a distinguished Coptic family with a tradition of political involvement long before the July 1952 "revolution." In an era of political Islam and the assault on secular politics, a Coptic parliamentarian is a rarity.[3] Before his defeat, Abdelnour was the most visible Coptic opposition deputy.

Abdelnour's opponents in the 2005, as well as in the 2000 and 1995 electoral races, represented more typical political trajectories. The first time he ran for office, in 1995, Abdelnour's opponent was Ahmed Fouad, a titan of Egyptian politics and a sitting parliamentarian. Ahmed Fouad embodied the Egyptian state in each of its various historical guises, from the 1952 revolution to the present: first during the socialist regime of Gamal Abdul Nasser in the 1960s, then as a parliamentarian under Anwar Sadat in the 1970s, and most recently as a leading member of Hosni Mubarak's National Democratic Party (NDP).

Fouad was a member of the Arab Socialist Union's Central Committee in the 1960s. He served in the Maglis al-Umma (National Assembly) from 1968 until 1979.[4] He joined the National Democratic Party when it was formed in 1978, already enjoying strong ties to powerful NDP officials. Fouad was then elected to the Maglis al-Shaab (People's Assembly) in 1990 as the representative of the El-Waily district, and quickly became the head of its Education Committee. In El-Waily, it was said that Fouad "owned" the district, which he represented until 2000.

In his first bid for parliament in 1995, Abdelnour lost to Fouad in a runoff election. In his second run for office in 2000, Abdelnour unseated Fouad after an intense and ugly campaign, followed by a runoff election. Realizing his seat was in jeopardy during the 2000 campaign, Fouad had begun politicizing religion and employed bigoted religious discourse against Abdelnour. Despite these techniques, Fouad lost and less than nine months after his humiliating defeat suffered a debilitating stroke. He died shortly thereafter.

Abdelnour's subsequent election experiences are even more intriguing, however. The 2005 electoral battle in El-Waily featured another member of the Fouad family. Ahmed Fouad's son, Shireen Ahmed Fouad, ran as the National Democratic Party candidate for the district in the November 2005 elections.[5] For the younger Fouad, however, the election went beyond politics: it was personal and familial. It was often said in the district that Shireen Ahmed Fouad blamed Abdelnour for his father's stroke and ultimate death. He considered the 2005 race a personal vendetta against Abdelnour; for him, the election was about avenging his father's defeat and ultimately his death.

If this was the end of the story, it would have the makings of a good television soap opera, but the drama continues. As often occurs in Egyptian elections, the circumstances in which Abdelnour "lost" gave rise to suspicion. After the votes had initially been counted and the preliminary results had been relayed to the candidates and announced on *Al Arabiya* television, the judge in charge of the district's elections left the school where the ballots were being counted and headed to the district's main police station across the street, paper tabulations in hand. There he locked himself in a room along with two assistants for more than three hours. When the judge finally reappeared, he announced entirely different results. Instead of 7,000 total votes cast with no single candidate securing more than 50 percent of the vote, thereby necessitating a runoff, the judge declared the NDP candidate, Shireen Ahmed Fouad, the winner. The total number of votes cast in the district had mysteriously risen by 2,000—all for Fouad—giving him the necessary margin (50 percent plus one vote) needed for victory without the necessity of a runoff (see Table 6.1).

Within days of the voting, an administrative court ruled that the district's elections were invalid, but for an entirely unrelated reason. The court declared that one of the candidates, Abdelhamid Sha'lan, competing for the "worker/farmer" seat, did not qualify to run as a "worker."[6] Sha'lan, an "independent NDP" candidate, the court ruled, should have been competing for the "group" parliamentary seat instead. Apparently, Sha'lan had previously run as a "group" candidate in local council elections, and his legal employment status, as an owner of a business and not an employee, disqualified him from running in the "worker/farmer" category.[7] Sha'lan, incidentally, received the most votes in the first round of the election for the "worker/ farmer" seat and ultimately defeated the sitting NDP incumbent, Fawzi Shaheen, in the runoff. Despite the court's ruling, which was never implemented, Sha'lan now sits in the People's Assembly representing the El-Waily district. After his election, like many other "independent NDP" candidates, he rejoined the party.

Table 6.1   Official El-Waily Results, Egyptian Parliamentary Elections, First Round, 2005

					Votes for Shireen Ahmed Fouad (NDP group candidate)	
Registered Voters	Votes Cast	Valid Votes	Spoiled Ballots	Turnout (percentage)	Number	Percentage
91,999	9,116	8,422	694	9.91	4,310	51.8

Source: Egypt State Information Service.
Note: For parliamentary elections, the Egyptian government only makes public the number of votes the winning candidate receives, not the complete vote breakdown.

In yet another interesting twist, less than two weeks after the election, the front page of the *Wafd* newspaper, the mouthpiece of Mounir Abdelnour's party, declared that he had been expelled from the party (Shehab 2005). The newspaper alleged that Abdelnour was a traitor and a spy, with questionable links to foreign powers, including the US government.

What had in fact happened was that Abdelnour had criticized his party's electoral performance and the party leadership several days earlier on television. This was not the first time Abdelnour had criticized the way the Wafd Party was being run. This time, however, the party's aging and autocratic leader, seventy-one-year-old No'man Gomaa, who two months earlier had stood in presidential elections against Mubarak and received less than 3 percent of the vote, unilaterally and unceremoniously kicked Abdelnour out of the party. Several weeks later the Wafd Party's Higher Council fully reinstated Abdelnour, and Gomaa eventually was removed as head of the party (Shehab 2006).[8]

■ Research Method

My primary research method was participant observation inside Mounir Abdelnour's reelection campaign, beginning shortly after the campaign's inception in early October 2005, and ending when the election results were announced on November 10, 2005. This entailed spending nearly every evening in Abbassaya at the campaign headquarters, following Abdelnour around the district, attending all campaign-related activities (e.g., *nadawat* [meetings], campaign walks, funerals, and weddings) with the candidate, speaking with campaign staff and supporters, and occasionally socializing with them in our free time. I spoke with Abdelnour throughout the campaign, either alone or in the context of wider conversations, and had a number of discussions with him about campaign strategy, which themes people reacted positively to, and which speakers were effective. On several occasions, he sought out my opinion about how a particular *nadwa* went or the audience's reaction to a speech.

I quickly became associated with Abdelnour's campaign in the district, and many within the campaign learned that I knew the candidate personally. During my second evening in Abbassaya, Abdelnour sat with a number of supporters and campaign workers, including myself, in front of his headquarters *(al-maqar)*. He ordered tea for everyone from the coffee shop across the street and, in the middle of general conversation, introduced me, telling those present, about twenty men of varying ages all associated with the campaign, that I was an Egyptian American professor at Georgetown University in the United States and that Georgetown was particularly well known for Middle Eastern studies. Abdelnour went further, exaggerating considerably, stating that I was a frequent commentator for the Cable News

Network and other English-language television channels on Middle Eastern politics, and added that whenever the Middle East was in the news, I would be invited to appear on television and give my opinion. Whatever the reason and regardless of the veracity of his statements, this seemed to impress those gathered more than my status as an Egyptian American professor. Abdelnour also mentioned that his daughter had taken several courses with me at the university and that this was how we had originally met.

After this evening, I became ingratiated with almost everyone involved in the reelection effort.[9] Whatever they thought of me or my research, they knew that I had a personal relationship with the candidate and that he was aware of and agreeable to my project. The candidate's words also reassured people about my loyalty. Campaigns are full of secrets and sensitive information, and I was warned more than once about certain individuals who sometimes appeared at campaign headquarters but who were less than completely trustworthy. I became part of the reelection effort, engaged in everything from giving my opinion about election-related matters to transporting campaign staff and supporters to election-related events.

In addition to participant observation, I gathered information on the election campaign from a number of additional sources. After the elections, I conducted multiple interviews with the candidate and a number of people involved in the campaign. Both the print and television media also regularly reported on Abdelnour's campaign.[10] Even after the elections, given Abdelnour's prominence in national politics and his leadership position in the Wafd Party, he appeared on a number of television programs, including *Malaf Khaas* (Special File) and the popular *Al-Bayt Baytak* (Your Home) on Egyptian state television. Finally, after the election, Abdelnour himself wrote several newspaper articles in *Al-Misry al-Yuwm* that concerned his own race and Egyptian politics more generally. These materials, and others, provided additional insights into the candidate, the district, and the reelection effort.

■ The Stakes

Getting inside an election campaign is not easy, since campaigns are electoral battles that produce winners and losers, with much at stake for political parties and especially for candidates. Anything that can potentially affect the outcome, even slightly, is taken into consideration. What hangs in the balance, of course, is power, and for candidates, membership in one of society's most prestigious institutions, with all of the privileges and opportunities this entails.

In Egypt, like elsewhere, elections are also serious business. For most candidates, campaigns constitute a major economic undertaking. The overwhelming majority of the more than 5,000 candidates (see Table 6.2) who ran in the 2005 parliamentary elections, did so as independents. Independent candidates, for the most part, receive virtually no support, financial or otherwise, from independent groups, organizations, or individuals. The legal opposition parties also have extremely limited funds to offer their candidates. Most candidates finance their own campaigns, and although the legal limit regarding campaign spending is about US$12,300 (70,000 pounds)—already a tremendous sum in a country where the average gross national product per capita is less than US$1,500 (9,000 pounds) per year—some spend millions trying to get elected.[11]

In the 2005 election, only the NDP and the Muslim Brotherhood provided substantial financial and organizational support to their candidates, although in neither case was it clear how much support was provided. And even in the case of candidates representing the ruling party, many spent significant sums, out of their own pockets, on their campaigns.

Why do people spend so much money trying to get into the People's Assembly?[12] What is so alluring about becoming a parliamentarian that many are willing to spend so much money, without any guarantee of success, in order to get elected? Of course, it is impossible to answer these questions definitively, because they concern the motivations of different candidates. Many undoubtedly are enticed by the glamour and social standing that membership in the People's Assembly confers. Others who have already achieved tremendous wealth through business and industry desire the political power that comes with being a parliamentarian. And still others, possibly the minority, seek to better their country through holding public office, serving the nation, proposing legislation, and keeping government accountable.

Many in Egypt, however, believe that the reason people are willing to spend so much money running for parliament is because membership in the

Table 6.2   Parliamentary Candidates in Egypt, 1984–2005

	Total Number of Elected Seats	Total Number of Candidates
1984	448	3,879
1987	448	3,592
1990	444	2,676
1995	444	3,980
2000	444	3,957
2005	444	5,177

Sources: 1984–2000, Ministry of Interior; 2005, Higher Commission for Parliamentary Elections.

Note: Election figures for 2005 do not include the number of candidates and voters in six constituencies in which elections had not yet been conducted (Essam el-Din 2005).

chamber provides legal immunity *(hasana),* which can be extremely rewarding financially.[13] The immunity that parliamentarians receive, in fact, can only be lifted by the People's Assembly itself. And it sometimes is.[14] Immunity from prosecution, it is said, allows some parliamentarians to engage in all sorts of extralegal and sometimes illegal practices and business ventures, making significant sums of money in the process. In addition, membership in the People's Assembly, it is believed, opens up all sorts of other opportunities for pecuniary gain (e.g., selling favors, including jobs, licenses, access to government land at below-market price). According to this logic, the money that candidates spend getting elected is recovered through the benefits of holding office; the money spent on political campaigns, at least in part, becomes a business expense. Regardless of these issues, given the amounts of money at stake, anything that could threaten the success of the enterprise, including my presence researching political campaigns, would be looked at unfavorably.

Campaigns also involve secrets and sensitive information about strategy, tactics, political alliances, campaign spending, and the timing of events. Similarly, candidates everywhere are sensitive about their image and how they are perceived. They do not want potentially damaging information about themselves or their campaign leaked. Because the stakes are so high, candidates and political parties are understandably reticent about letting people they do not know and trust into their campaigns.[15]

Still, I was able to secure the kind of access to Mounir Abdelnour's campaign that was necessary for ethnographic research. Other candidates and political parties allowed me to attend campaign events and conduct interviews with candidates and campaign staff. But for the most part, these other candidates were unwilling to give me complete freedom inside their campaigns. For example, I was invited to several campaign events of the NDP and Tagammu Party (National Progressive Unionist Party).[16] I was also able to interview high-ranking NDP officials about the parliamentary elections and other matters. I was even invited to the NDP's "operations room," and allowed to observe the high-tech command and control center in action, during the runoff election for the first phase of voting, on November 15, 2005. But most candidates and political parties were hesitant or even suspicious about my research.[17]

■ Choosing Cases

Although access was the most important factor in choosing to study Abdelnour's campaign, there were other important considerations. From the beginning I wanted to study more than one campaign ethnographically (through extensive, daily fieldwork), but I was limited by at least two factors in addition to the problem of entrée: the timing of the elections and the fact that ethnographic research is tremendously time-intensive, meaning that it would be impossible to study more than one campaign at the same time using this method.[18] Egypt's 2005 parliamentary elections, however, like those in 2000, were scheduled to take place over the span of an entire month, involving three separate phases of voting in three different sets of governorates (see Table 6.3). Therefore, I thought it would be possible to research only two campaigns thoroughly, if I studied one campaign in the first phase (November 9) and another during the third phase (December 1) of balloting. This would allow sufficient time to carry out the daily fieldwork I needed in each campaign.[19] Mounir Abdelnour's reelection bid was the campaign I chose to research in the first phase of the elections.

Importantly, Mounir Abdelnour represented the Wafd Party, which had more parliamentarians during the 2000–2005 period than any other opposition party. The Wafd publishes a widely circulated newspaper, giving it some influence, and has a long and distinguished history in Egyptian politics.[20] Abdelnour's incumbency meant not only would he mount a serious campaign, but also that he had a considerable chance of being elected.[21]

Mounir Abdelnour made for an especially interesting candidate. Like anyone who follows Egyptian politics, I knew of Abdelnour before meeting him or deciding to study his reelection bid. I had read about him in the press and seen him on television. He is an impressive and articulate politician who holds well-developed political and economic views, something that sets him apart from the majority of Egyptian parliamentarians. Abdelnour was also one of the few Coptic elected officials, and so I thought that following his campaign would also provide an opportunity to explore the dynamics of religion and politics in Egypt.

El-Waily (also known as Abbassaya) also presented a fascinating district to study. Neither an elite neighborhood nor a particularly depressed

Table 6.3 Egyptian Parliamentary Election Schedule, 2005

	Governorate	Election Day	Runoff Elections
Phase One	Cairo, Giza, Menoufiya, Beni Souif, El-Menya, Assiut, Matrouh, Al-Wadi al-Gadid	November 9	November 15
Phase Two	Alexandria, Al-Beheira, Al-Ismaila, Port Said, Suez, Al-Qalyubiya, Al-Gharbia, Al-Fayoum, Qena	November 20	November 26
Phase Three	Al-Daqahliyya, Al-Sharqiyya, Kafr al-Shayhk, Damietta, Sohaq, Aswan, Red Sea, North Sinai, South Sinai	December 1	December 7

Note: Mounir Abdelnour's campaign took place in the Cairo governorate.

area, Abbassaya is an older, middle-class section of Cairo, representative of much of urban Egypt. It is demographically diverse; home to one of Cairo's largest mosques (*Gama' al-Nur*) as well as the patriarchate of the Coptic Orthodox Church. The district includes commercial as well as residential areas, several government ministries (including the Ministry of Electricity), hospitals, schools, and public sector companies.

◼ Campaigning with Mounir Abdelnour

The *nadwa* (panel discussion or meeting) is the quintessential campaign event. It provides an opportunity for candidates to address the community and for members of the public to question the person running for office. Campaign *nadawat* are public events; anyone and everyone is encouraged to attend. After all, they are intended to get people to listen to the candidate (and his supporters), and ultimately vote for him on election day. In the weeks leading up to the election, Abdelnour usually held one *nadwa* each evening and sometimes two in one night. Each usually lasted no more than a couple of hours. The campaign tried to hold at least one *nadwa* in each of the district's dozen or so *shayakhas* (subdivisions of the district, or *dayra*). Usually, *nadawat* took place in the proximity of a neighborhood coffee shop and almost always occurred outdoors—on the street, in an alley, between buildings, or in any open space.

The Abdelnour campaign's *nadawat* varied in size from between several dozen to several hundred attendees. Chairs were provided by the nearby coffee shop, but if a particularly large audience was anticipated, or if the *nadwa* was being held far from a coffee shop, rented chairs were brought in. Audiences were almost always male, although women would occasionally stop and listen if they happened to be walking by.

Coffee shops did well during election season.[22] Politics is an evening sport in Egypt, and coffee shops see their fair share of campaign activity. The coffee shop in front of Mounir Abdelnour's headquarters, on Abbassaya Street, the district's main thoroughfare, for example, became the regular meeting place for many associated with Abdelnour's campaign. It also supplied (with the campaign picking up the tab) tea, coffee, and other drinks to the dozen or so people who were constantly gathered in front of campaign headquarters. One of the shop's workers could frequently be seen crossing Abbassaya Street (a four-lane road with a divider in the middle), delivering orders, and bringing back empty glasses. Sometimes he could even be seen lugging tables, chairs, and occasionally even a *shisha* (a water pipe used for smoking tobacco) from across the road.

In addition to the rows of chairs set up for the audience, a large table and a few chairs were placed in front for the candidate and any other speakers. Sometimes tablecloths, flowers, tissues, bottled water, and glasses for the speakers were also provided, depending on the sophistication of the event. And *nadawat* almost always included some sort of inexpensive audio system to amplify sound. One of the goals of these public meetings, after all, was to reach as many people as possible, not just those seated in the audience. Microphones and speakers ensured that if you lived—or just happened to be—in the neighborhood where a *nadwa* was taking place, there was a good chance you would hear it, even if you did not want to.

Hand-painted cloth campaign banners were usually placed behind the speaker's table. Large posters of the candidate displaying his name, symbol, and number were also frequently positioned nearby, further clarifying what was happening and who was running for office. Abdelnour's posters read "Together, for a new El-Waily," and included a palm tree (his symbol) and the number 7 (his ballot number), on either side of a large picture of his smiling face.[23]

More often than not, bright and colorful tent-making material—the kind also used in Egyptian funerals—was set up in the area where the *nadwa* was to occur. When raised as a backdrop or on the sides of where an event was being held, the material created the feeling of a semiprivate space, differentiating it from the surrounding public street. In the case of Egyptian funerals, the material is used to create what is essentially a large tent with three walls and a high ceiling.

Abdelnour's campaign never set up a proper tent, but at the very least a large piece of material was often raised behind the table where the candidate was seated and sometimes along one side of the area. Still, it was enough to create some sense of privacy. Of course, all of this cost money.

Candidates are rarely the first to speak at their own events. One, two, and sometimes three speakers would often first take the microphone to introduce Abdelnour in the most glowing manner possible. The individuals who introduced him sometimes varied from one event to another. People were chosen to introduce the candidate based on a number of factors. In addition to supporting Abdelnour, of course, being well known and somewhat respected in the immediate area where the *nadwa* was taking place was vital. Someone the audience knew and trusted, it was thought, would only further the candidate's standing in the community. It also helped if one could string a few sweet-sounding sentences together.

Hassan Heyba was not talented at introductions, but as one of the most visible members of the Abdelnour campaign, he was present at almost all of the *nadawat*. At most events, he managed to get hold of the microphone. Heyba was a real character: a foul-mouthed chain-smoker who appeared to be in his late sixties or early seventies who had been involved in the district's politics for nearly his entire life. Heyba always looked disheveled and often wore the same old maroon-colored cardigan. He also was most often unshaven. But because of his age and the color of his hair, his beard growth always took the form of white stubble. Short (around five feet six inches), slim, with a light complexion, thinning white hair, and a deep scratchy voice, Heyba was fond of telling me that he had "learned politics in Ahmed Fouad's kitchen."[24] It was partially because of his previous involvement in Abbassaya's politics as well as his age that he was known to many in the district. With a cigarette in one hand and the microphone in the other, Heyba was almost always one of the people who introduced Abdelnour.

Said Abdel Mon'em was another of the regulars at Abdelnour's campaign events. Only a few years younger than Heyba, Said was also a long-standing fixture in the district's politics. A tall, well-built man who often wore "third world suits," Said was a member of the National Democratic Party who had a history of involvement with the Egyptian state. From 1961 to 1967, under Gamal Abdul Nasser, Said was a member of the Youth Organization of the Arab Socialist Union. He reached the post of director of youth in the General Organization for Printing, in Imbaba, another neighborhood in Cairo.

Said fancied himself an orator and his introductions went on quite a bit longer than most. When making his remarks, he would usually mention that he was a member of the NDP but was supporting Mounir Abdelnour despite this. In fact, Said had backed Abdelnour's opponent, Ahmed Fouad, the NDP candidate, in both the 1995 and 2000 elections. Several months after the 2005 elections, Said told me that he had been officially summoned to NDP headquarters, where he was asked why he had supported Abdelnour instead of his own party's candidate.

Hassan Heyba and Said Abdel Mon'em often made many of the same basic points in their introductions. Both men emphasized that Abdelnour had roots in the district, was an honest politician and statesman, and was not running for personal benefit. For example, during one such introduction, on October 21, 2005, Heyba repeated the word "respectable" over and over again: "The respectable, the respectable, the respectable [one], the true son of El-Waily."[25] Heyba then shouted into the microphone, "He is really El-Waily's son, who was brought up in the lap of his grandfather, a colleague of Sa'ad Zaghloul's!" Heyba went on, asking the crowd rhetorically: "Why did he run? Not for immunity, not for personal interests, not for the accumulation of wealth, but for Egypt! He comes from a big, old, well-known family. His father and grandfather . . . were with Sa'ad Zaghloul."

The fact that Abdelnour's family villa once stood on Abbassaya Street, the district's main thoroughfare, on the current site of the Omar Effendi department store, was also often mentioned.[26] A street in the district had been named after his grandfather. At other times, Abdelnour's worldliness and diplomacy were emphasized, with speakers recounting that he had represented Egypt overseas, in the United States, France, and other countries.

Establishing a candidate's connection to his or her district is almost universal in electoral politics. This is particularly important in Egypt, however, because there are no legal restrictions or residence requirements in order to run for parliament and represent a particular district. Someone can be from Alexandria in the far north, for example, yet run for parliament in Aswan, in the far south. Parliamentarians are nonetheless supposed to represent the districts that elected them. This partially explains the emphasis, when introducing Abdelnour, on his relationship and connection to the district. In fact, although Abdelnour has a historical relationship to El-Waily, he does not live there. He resides in Zamalek, an island in the middle of the Nile and one of Cairo's most posh neighborhoods.[27]

◼ Mounir Abdelnour's Political Discourse

Abdelnour's speech was the main event of each evening's *nadwa*. He is a fairly skilled orator and, like candidates everywhere, he had a stock speech he delivered, changing the specifics depending on the circumstances. His first words were usually, "In the name of the one God that all of us believe in," followed by a few words thanking those in attendance and his supporters. The reference to God was a variation of the first line of the Quran ("In the name of God, the Merciful, the Compassionate"), which is how many Muslims begin speeches and other activities. This established to those present that Abdelnour was religious and that he too believed in God, the same God in which Muslims believe.[28]

Abdelnour's personality is frank and his speeches reflected this. After these brief opening remarks he would often proceed to say that the *nadwa* was being held so that he could present an accounting *(kashf hisab)* to the residents of El-Waily, and more specifically, to the residents of the particular *shayakha* where the *nadwa* was taking place. The *kashf hisab* was about what he had accomplished as the district's representative over the preceding five years. Abdelnour would then say that he also wanted to hear from district residents in attendance, and that after his remarks people would have a chance to ask questions and state whatever was on their minds.

It was about this time each evening that the campaign staff would distribute a short pamphlet *(kutayib)* bearing on its cover a color picture of Abdelnour delivering a speech in the People's Assembly, and detailing within what he had accomplished in parliament over the preceding five years. This short document of no more than ten small pages served as both Abdelnour's *kashf hisab* and his political program.

To provide an example of Abdelnour's discourse, the language he employed, and the arguments he made, in addition to allowing his own voice to emerge, I have quoted extensively here from one of his typical speeches. I heard variations of this stock speech at each *nadwa* I attended:

I need to correct something that has been said. The introductory speaker said that you are here to support me. That's not what we're here for but for you to listen to me, to find out what I've done, to keep me accountable and then to support me or not, it's your decision . . . to see what I have done in the last five years.

. . . It has been said, especially in this area, that I got into parliament and did not do much, forgot about the area, did not deliver as much as I should have.[29]

Next, Abdelnour proceeded to explain to the audience (as he usually does) the proper role and function of a parliamentarian, who has three basic obligations—the first is to legislate or to make laws *(al-tashre')*, the second is to keep the government accountable *(al-rikaba)*—especially concerning the budget and government expenditures, and the third *(al-khadamat)* is to serve the district and its residents: "I know that according to the people in the community, the priorities are reversed. People are concerned with services . . . for a number of reasons. Although according to the law the priorities are not supposed to be this way. We suffer from a lack of jobs, inflation, and poor education."

At this point a lower-middle-class, veiled woman standing behind the last row of chairs interrupted him and said that a teacher had hit her son in school. Abdelnour asked her to reveal the teacher's name, and promised to look into the matter and do something about it. He continued:

We all suffer from the poor quality of health care and public health services. And the private hospitals are incredibly expensive.

. . . No one can solve any of these problems—not a minister, not the prime minister, not the president. The only thing that can solve these issues is *good policy;* reasoning, analysis, and sound policy. And therefore the first duty of the parliamentarian is what will solve our problems [meaning, formulating good policies] and not the providing of services.

Abdelnour had brought with him all the statements he had made in parliament over the preceding five years, published in book form. He next accused the government of misspending government resources instead of solving problems such as unemployment, stating: "I have not let any of you down with regard to this—legislating and keeping the government accountable." He gave the example of his objection to the increase of commercial rents on stores by 10 percent a year "in these especially difficult economic times." His view had won out and rents had been raised by only 2 percent a year. He also spoke about some of the policies that he wanted and the things that he has called for. For example, he has called for the transfer of the mental hospital out of Abbassaya, because when it was built, Abbassaya was a desert, outside Cairo, empty space. Now Abbassaya is crowded and the space could be used for much better purposes. He has also called for the transfer of the police academy, to be replaced by space for youth centers and other projects that could benefit the area and its residents, including housing. Abdelnour continued:

> The solving of our problems will come through good policies—encouraging private capital to invest so that they can create jobs—I called for this—and the lowering of taxes . . . and this law went through. I also called for the lowering of customs . . . and I succeeded . . . and all of this was in my 2000 platform. I encourage you to look at my pamphlet.
>
> I put all of this aside—unfortunately—because I know what is important to you. It is services. My little pamphlet describes what I have done for the district in terms of job creation.
>
> In the last five years, 9,022 people have come to my district office. We have responded to 6,400 of them; 5,780 people have been from El-Waily and 693 were from outside El-Waily but had some connection to the district.
>
> . . . I have found employment for 431 people . . . 253 of them are people with low degrees and they were employed in security companies and other companies; 127 were employed in Ministries and state organizations including the Ministries of Petroleum, Agriculture, Electricity, the Central Agency for Public Mobilization and Statistics, Military Factories.

He went on to state the number of people he had employed in the private sector, and said that this figure had risen in the preceding two weeks.

At this point, a man in his late sixties or early seventies who was standing off to the side and whom I had never seen before, interrupted Abdelnour—"Don't forget my son. You got my son a job!"—and then added one person to the figure that Abdelnour had just cited.[30] Abdelnour continued:

> This number is a small number, a drop in an ocean. I think—my estimation is that the number of unemployed in the district is 25,000 to 30,000. The answer is good policies, reviewing laws, suggesting laws. . . . Not in a parliament that only knows how to raise their hands in agreement and clap.[31] This will not solve our problems.
>
> . . . I have served you honestly [at which point someone stood up and recited a line of poetry, in rhyme, about Abdelnour: *lafayna El-Waily lafayna, zay Mounir ma laqayna*].[32] I have served and it has been at a cost, personally, and on my family. . . . I ask you to hold me accountable.

Abdelnour's understanding of the role of parliamentarians and legislative bodies—to legislate, to keep the government accountable, primarily by reviewing government budgets and expenditures, and to provide services and look after constituent interests—is fairly standard in Egypt, and the Egyptian constitution states as much almost explicitly.[33] Articles 109–126 discuss the functions, responsibilities, and powers of parliament. Article 109 states that "the President of the Republic and every member of the

People's Assembly shall have the right to propose laws." Article 114 states that "the People's Assembly shall approve the general plan for economic and social development." Article 115 states that "the draft general budget shall be submitted to the People's Assembly." Article 118 outlines the oversight powers of the People's Assembly over other state organizations regarding the budget (the Central Agency for Accounting). And Articles 124–126 provide the People's Assembly with the power to question government ministers, including the prime minister, and even to withdraw confidence from "any of the Prime Minister's deputies or from many of the Ministers or their deputies."

Not only would Abdelnour devote a good part of each evening's speech to recounting the "services" he had provided to the district, but his campaign pamphlet provided a comprehensive accounting—in greater detail and with statistics—of the services he had provided to the community and its residents. For example, Abdelnour arranged for a pedestrian bridge to be built over Ramsis Street, a busy thoroughfare with speeding traffic, at a crossing where pedestrians were often involved in traffic accidents. He also lobbied the government to build a "Heart Institute" in the district (which is currently under construction). This took tremendous coordination on Abdelnour's part between the Ministries of Health and Higher Education and other government bureaucracies. In addition, he also undertook a major restoration of Maktabat al-Barudi (Barudi Library), transforming it into a neighborhood cultural and educational center in the district; established educational services for the district's school-age children; and, in response to the educational crisis in Egypt and the phenomenal expense of private lessons *(durus khussussaya,* which many parents cannot afford), purchased educational videos intended to strengthen the academic skills of students.[34]

The questions that district residents asked after Abdelnour's speeches frequently reflected the overwhelming concern with personal "services." For example, the first person to speak on the evening of the above-quoted speech proceeded to describe his own problems dealing with the Ministry of Housing. In fact, his remarks were not stated in the form of a question but rather as an appeal to the district's representative.[35] The man had apparently received legal authorization from the ministry, based on his socioeconomic condition, for a subsidized apartment more than a year earlier, but had still not received an apartment. His remarks concerned his own personal situation, and not the general state of housing policy or community services. Abdelnour took a stack of documents from the man, promised to look into the matter, and said:

> Personal services *(al-khadamat al-khassa)* will not solve all of our problems. Personal favors and services will not solve the problem. We need to attract foreign capital, Arab capital and Egyptians to invest in big and small industry. [Abdelnour went on to briefly explain how this would help

the economy and unemployment.] And democracy is the only way to deal with corruption. It will provide accountability . . . and a parliament that has the right to withdraw its trust *(thiqqa)* and support from the government. . . . The Egyptian constitution must be changed, it must be amended.[36]

The constant requests for services from parliamentarians were literally never-ending. It was quite common, for example, for streams of people to approach Abdelnour during the *nadwa* itself, often when someone was introducing him or during someone else's speech, and begin explaining their problems to him there and then, and ask for his help. Sometimes people even interrupted Abdelnour while he was delivering his speech, recounting their dilemmas loudly in front of everyone gathered, and then appeal for his assistance.

The appeals to Abdelnour often became even more pronounced once the *nadwa* had concluded. Dozens of men would surround Abdelnour as he tried to walk back to his district offices, pushing, nudging, and sometimes shoving each other to get close to the parliamentarian and say something or make a request. Usually, Abdelnour was remarkably pleasant and calm considering the circumstances, and he could frequently be heard during such moments saying *"hader, hader"* (yes, yes) and suggesting to these people that they come to his office to speak about their concerns in detail. Abdelnour was also quite plainspoken about what he could and could not do for constituents. After one such *nadwa,* for example, Abdelnour turned to someone who had apparently asked for something he could not possibly deliver, looked him directly in the face, and simply said, "I do not have magical powers."

Later during the evening of the above-quoted *nadwa,* I spoke with Mohamed Serrafi in the coffee shop across from Abdelnour's headquarters. Serrafi was one of the lower-level workers in the campaign, someone I would eventually become very close to. He was almost always present at campaign headquarters and attended all of the public meetings, unless he had work to do elsewhere for the campaign. For the most part, he did the simplest of tasks: carrying pamphlets to the evening meetings, helping with event preparations, preparing posters of the candidate and political banners, and the like. Serrafi was a short, thin, man in his early fifties, always unshaven, a smoker, divorced, with two kids; he was very smart but somewhat unstable. He wore the same clothes most evenings and had a down-and-out quality to him. It was clear that life hadn't gone his way and he was paying the price. His ex-wife and children lived in Maadi while he rented a single room in a boarding house in a poorer section of Abbassaya. But Serrafi loved politics and had a history of political activity in a nearby area, Bab Al Shaa'raya, Ayman Nour's district. Serrafi was also fiercely opposed to the government. Our conversation that evening focused on the campaign, parliamentary elections, and more specifically, how people view parliamentarians in Egypt. Speaking about the poorer sections of El-Waily, Serrafi said: "Those people consider the parliamentarian a God—able to deliver all of the personal services and favors they want . . . with a magic wand."

◼ Voting for Services

What I have described in this chapter is neither specific to the El-Waily district or to Mounir Abdelnour. It is also not specific to sitting parliamentarians: providing services for the community and, more importantly, providing personal services for constituents, is the name of the game in Egyptian parliamentary elections. I witnessed the same phenomenon in other districts and with other candidates. No one better symbolized this than Hisham Mustapha Khalil, an "independent" NDP candidate in the Qasr el-Nil district of central Cairo.

Khalil is the son of Mustafa Khalil, a former prime minister and head of the NDP, and his electoral contest received intense national attention. In addition to his father's status, Khalil was one of the hundreds of NDP members who, when they were not nominated by the party to run for office, subsequently resigned from the party so they could run as "independents," competing against the party's official candidates. Making the electoral contest more interesting, the official NDP candidate and incumbent whom Khalil ran against—Hosam Badrawi—is a prominent reformer known to be close to Gamal Mubarak, and a member of the influential NDP policies secretariat.[37]

I interviewed both Hisham Mustapha Khalil and Hosam Badrawi and I also attended campaign functions organized by both candidates. The race was thought to be one of the costliest in the entire country, with each candidate spending exorbitant sums of money on their campaigns. In addition to posters and other forms of political advertising, Hisham Mustapha Khalil spent significant sums of his own money on infrastructure and beautification projects in his district. In fact, late one evening after one of his campaign events, Khalil took me on a personal tour of some of the projects he had financed, including trash removal, painting of buildings, and restoration of once badly deteriorated steps and alleyways in poorer areas.[38] Khalil paid for these improvements out of his own pocket and promised the district's residents that he would continue to do so, even if his election bid was unsuccessful. Khalil's political posters, in fact, were particularly distinctive, because they featured "before" and "after" photographs of the neighborhoods and streets where he had financed improvements, visually referencing the services he provided to the community, even before being elected to parliament.[39] Of course, his own picture was positioned in the middle of the photos, as a reminder of who had paid for the improvements and local services.

Hisham Mustapha Khalil clearly understood the logic of voting behavior in Egypt, and if he ever forgot, local residents were always present to remind him. Khalil had been invited to speak to residents of Maʿaruf, one of the *shayakhas* in the Qasr el-Nil district, known for its car-repair shops and mechanics, on one of the evenings, October 22, 2005, that I accompanied him. Not much of an orator, he usually spoke no more than a few minutes. The following question was the first he received that evening, from a mechanic who worked in the area: "I know that a legislator is not primarily supposed to provide services. And the members of the local councils are supposed to do this—but—unfortunately with respect to the members of the local councils—they are powerless, they have no power. So, what will you do for us?"

The importance of providing services to constituents came through time and time again during my research. For example, Ahmed Ezz (the director of membership of the NDP, a parliamentarian, a member of the policies secretariat, and arguably one of the most powerful people in the party), during an interview on October 18, 2005, declared that Egyptian parliamentary elections were about two things: "What voters care about is: (1) how are you negotiating with government to get us the services before others—other areas—get them, and (2) personal relationships: Do they see you enough? Do you attend weddings, funerals? Are you in the district and visible, shaking people's hands? If you are rich, are you philanthropic?"

◼ Conclusion

The cases presented in this chapter are not simply "anecdotal," based on casual interactions, but representative of hundreds of other cases, based on months of daily fieldwork with candidates and voters. Based on their speech and actions, Mounir Abdelnour, Hisham Mustapha Khalil, and Ahmed Ezz, two of whom were sitting parliamentarians in the 2005 Egyptian parliamentary elections, seem to believe that Egyptian voting behavior is primarily based on the provision of services and not on ideology, party affiliation, or campaign programs. Moreover, they seem to operate largely based on this assumption. Local residents, based on their questions and actions, also seem to confirm that voting behavior is governed by this logic.

For those who follow Egyptian politics, in fact, the terms *naʿib khidma* (service representative) and *naʿib umma* (national representative) have become part of the local political language.[40] Sometimes used disparagingly to criticize parliamentarians who are said to be only capable of delivering services (e.g., as opposed to the "more important" functions of legislating and keeping the government accountable), and at other times used to explain electoral outcomes (e.g., "service representatives" are thought to be more likely to win elections), the discourse of "service representatives" and "national representatives" further indicates the extent to which this type of voting behavior is thought to occur in Egypt.

Most Egyptians do not vote on the basis of party platforms or political programs, policy issues, or ideology. Many if not most vote for candidates who they believe will provide them with *khadamat* (services). Services, however, are understood to be not just public goods for the entire community or the electoral district (e.g., better roads, improved schools, sewage systems, public improvements). They are also frequently understood to be individual services for district residents and include things like helping residents and their children find employment, secure housing, and gain access to healthcare, in addition to facilitating all sorts of dealings between individuals, the government, and its bureaucracy.

Why is this so? Why do many if not most Egyptians understand the role of a parliamentarian as one of providing individual services (let alone collective services for the district) and not one of legislating, holding the government accountable, considering policy options, and debating foreign affairs?

Several factors most likely explain this phenomenon. Most Egyptians realize that parliamentarians simply do not have the power to make major policy decisions or undertake significant political change.[41] They understand, quite accurately, that parliamentarians have only limited powers, much less than those outlined in the constitution, and that the overwhelming concentration of government power resides in the executive branch and, more specifically, in the person of the president. Like political scientists, Egyptians are very aware of the fact that they live in an authoritarian or semiauthoritarian political system, a system in which the legislature or parliament (in this case, the People's Assembly) functions neither ideally nor according to the principles of democratic theory.

Moreover, the socioeconomic context is such that many if not most Egyptians are in desperate economic need and find themselves in a social, political, and economic system based largely on connections. Without connections themselves, their district's representatives in parliament represent one such connection (and as such, an opportunity) for socially and economically disenfranchised citizens who otherwise lack many connections with other powerful and networked individuals. Furthermore, candidates and district representatives need something from district residents (i.e., their support and, more specifically, their votes) and at the same time are supposed to represent their interests.

The logic of voting behavior in Egypt might also shed light on the question of *who* votes in Egyptian elections. Participation in Egyptian elections is extremely low. In the country's first-ever presidential election, in September 2005, for example, voter participation was less than 24 percent. Similarly, overall participation rates in the November–December 2005 parliamentary elections were below 28 percent. Unlike in the United States and other developed countries, I postulate that in Egypt there is an inverse relationship between participation and voting, and education and income. In other words, while the better educated and wealthy are more likely to vote in the United States and other developed countries, there are indications that the situation is exactly the opposite in Egypt: the better educated and wealthy are less likely to turn up at the polling station.

We can begin to explain why this might be the case based on what we have established about the logic of voting behavior in Egypt. Middle- and upper-middle-class Egyptians are less likely to need a candidate or parliamentarian as a *wasta* (a connection) to find them jobs, provide low-cost healthcare, and navigate the government bureaucracy, because they already have connections themselves or can gain access through their families and friends. Poorer people, however, are less likely to have such connections and therefore are more likely to participate and vote in parliamentary elections, in hope of establishing a connection with a candidate or parliamentarian and securing services in return. Poorer people are also more likely to participate in elections in order to "sell" their votes, a phenomenon that is fairly widespread in Egypt. Of course, this question is in need of much further investigation.

We can also only speculate here about the larger macropolitical consequences of this type of voting behavior on Egyptian politics and more specifically on issues of good governance and the possibilities of democratization. It would seem that voting for candidates primarily based on the provision of services (and particularly individual services) would have negative consequences on governance. Simply put, in such a system, parliamentarians must spend much if not all their time providing services for individual members of their constituencies rather than attending to national interests, keeping government accountable, and proposing sound legislation.

If Egyptian parliamentarians concentrate primarily on providing constituent services, as many parliamentarians frequently claim, one might reasonably ask whether the Egyptian parliament actually functions as a check on the power of the other branches of government, the way a parliament is supposed to function according to democratic theory. It could very well be the case that the Egyptian parliament (and legislative bodies in semiauthoritarian states more generally) functions in a thoroughly different manner than legislative bodies in democratic states, and also in vastly different ways than prescribed by the Egyptian constitution itself. These are surely fruitful questions for further research.

▧ Notes

1. See the series of books published by the Al-Ahram Center for Political and Strategic Studies on Egyptian parliamentary elections, including Moustafa 1995, 2001. See also al-Minoufi 1995; al-Sawi 2004; Bin Nafisa and al-Din Arafat 2005; and Mineesy and Lutfi (2001). See also Hamdy 2004. For an account of Amina

Shafiq's campaign efforts in 2000, see Shafiq 2001; Shafiq also writes for *Al-Ahram* and is a longtime member of the Tagammu Party. She ran unsuccessfully in the 2005 elections in Boulaq.

2. Stated differently, are political campaigns in Egypt different from campaigns elsewhere, or are they similar to campaigns in other countries, including democracies? Or alternatively, do political campaigns in semiauthoritarian states have unique characteristics?

3. There were no more than seven Coptic parliamentarians in the People's Assembly during the 2000–2005 session. In the current parliament there are only six, five of whom were appointed by the president. According to Article 87 of the Egyptian constitution, the president has the power to appoint up to ten individuals to parliament. President Mubarak has traditionally used this power to appoint under-represented groups such as women and Copts to the People's Assembly. The only Coptic candidate who was elected to parliament in the 2005 elections was Yousef Boutrus Ghali, the current minister of finance. Many speculate that his election was rigged, however, as he is a long-serving cabinet minister who previously held the position of minister of foreign trade. The National Democratic Party only nominated two Copts out of 444 candidates in the 2005 elections, while the United National Front for Change, a broad coalition of antigovernment parties and political forces, nominated thirteen Coptic candidates.

4. The Egyptian parliament, now known as the Maglis al-Shaab (People's Assembly), was officially termed the Maglis al-Umma (National Assembly) until the late 1970s.

5. As in other countries, political families or dynasties are a phenomenon in Egypt. Although I do not have precise data about this, my impression is that this occurs in Egypt more often than in most democratic states (see "Zahrat tawrith" 2006).

6. Article 87 of the Egyptian constitution prescribes that half the members of the People's Assembly "must be workers and farmers." Candidates are registered before an election as either "worker/farmer" or "group/professional," and compete under this classification system. In accordance, each electoral district is represented by two parliamentarians, most often one "worker/farmer" and one "group/professional." As such, voters in each district choose two candidates to represent them, one of whom must be a "worker/farmer."

7. Things are even more complicated, apparently. I was told by a candidate who filed a legal appeal against Sha'lan that, according to the court ruling, Sha'lan could not be both an employee and the owner of a company simultaneously. Another complicating factor that speaks to the exceedingly convoluted character of Egyptian parliamentary elections is that Sha'lan's victory has put the entire district's elections (and its parliamentary representation) into question. Because Sha'lan has been categorized as a "group," the El-Waily district presently has two "group" representatives in the chamber. This, in itself, is unconstitutional, and many speculated that further legal action regarding the district's elections would take place.

8. Gomaa was removed as party head on January 18, 2006. On April 1, 2006, in an attempt to restore his control, Gomaa stormed the Wafd Party's headquarters with a group of armed supporters and thugs. The resulting violence lasted ten hours and left twenty-eight people, mostly journalists in the party's daily newspaper, injured. The incident, which involved gunshots and a fire, also caused significant damage to the party's headquarters, not to mention its reputation.

9. I experienced a few tense moments with people over the course of the campaign, but this was the normal result of working closely and intensely together in difficult circumstances.

10. A number of articles were written about Abdelnour in *Al-Ahram* and in *Al-Misry al-Yuwm* in November and December 2005.

11. It is virtually impossible to obtain accurate information about campaign spending in Egypt. Most who spend over the legal limit, of course, are unwilling to admit this. And as far as I know, no government agency systematically collects data about campaign spending. Nonetheless, it is perfectly clear that some candidates spent vast sums of money on their campaigns. In the few districts that I followed—for example, Abdelhamid Sha'lan (El-Waily), Hisham Mustapha Khalil and Hosam Badrawi (Qasr el-Nil), and Momahmed al-Massoud (Boulaq), each spent at least US\$180,000 (1 million pounds) on their campaigns. Khalil and Massoud, it is speculated, each spent over \$550,000 (3 million pounds) on their election efforts.

12. Another important and related question is why so many people in Egypt run for parliament. The number of candidates competing for the same number of seats has approximately doubled since 1995. This also has an impact on campaign spending and the intensity of electoral competition. By comparison, India, the world's largest democracy, with a population over 1 billion, only saw 5,398 candidates in the 2004 elections, with 675 million registered voters electing 545 parliamentarians (two parliamentarians were appointed). See http://www.indian-elections.com/facts-figures.html.

13. Article 99 of the Egyptian constitution states, "No member of the People's Assembly shall be subject to a criminal prosecution without the permission of the Assembly except in cases of flagrant delicto." In theory, of course, this article is included in the constitution in order to provide greater guarantees for the independence and freedom of parliamentarians to question government, criticize policies, and otherwise perform their jobs uninhibited by the possibility of politically motivated prosecution. In actual practice, however, the immunity provided to parliamentarians is a tremendous perk of office, commonly thought to be used unethically by parliamentarians for personal gain.

14. The infamous case of "the loan parliamentarians" is only one example. During the two previous parliamentary sessions, a number of parliamentarians were stripped of their immunity and prosecuted for taking advantage of their parliamentary status to obtain millions of pounds in unsecured loans. Much of the money was never paid back. In an *Al-Ahram Weekly* article, Gamal Essam el-Din noted, "Politically, it is expected that the harsh verdicts will thrust under sharp public scrutiny the increasing use of parliamentary immunity and political clout to make illegal profits" (Essam el-Din 2000a). In another article, Essam el-Din wrote, "Because the defendants included five former members of parliament (MPs) from the ruling National Democratic Party (NDP), the rulings reignited the debate on MPs' abuse of parliamentary immunity to secure ill-gotten gains" (Essam el-Din 2002). See also Essam el-Din 2000b.

15. Academics and researchers are also interested in "objective" research and neutrality. Although these might be considered noble objectives when conducting research, they are potentially damning traits from the perspective of a candidate.

16. See Chapter 9 in this volume for more information on Egyptian political parties.

17. Yet another example of this concerns an acquaintance whose father happens to be an NDP parliamentarian from the Boulaq district in central Cairo. Although I was invited to attend several campaign events with his father, he was noticeably reticent about my research and seemed to be conscious that it could potentially portray his father in a negative light.

18. In fact, I hired four young researchers from the Al-Ahram Center for Political and Strategic Studies to help conduct election-related research. I assigned

three of the researchers to different districts—Qasr el-Nil, Boulaq, and Imbaba—to follow the first phase of the elections. Although I had initially hoped they would be able to carry out ethnographic fieldwork in these districts, this soon proved unrealistic.

19. Most of the research for the campaign in the first phase of voting started in early October and continued through November 9, or November 15 if there was a runoff election. After the conclusion of the first phase of voting, I immediately began researching the campaign I had chosen for the third phase of the elections, scheduled for December 1.

20. The Wafd was for many years the only opposition party with a daily newspaper. This has changed somewhat with the appearance of Ayman Nour's Hizb Al-Ghad (Tomorrow Party), although that party's daily publication has a much smaller circulation.

21. Over 5,000 candidates ran for 444 seats in parliament, according to the Higher Commission for Parliamentary Elections. Many candidates, however, were people no one had heard of, and were not even residents of the districts where they were running for office. The majority of these candidates were not serious contenders, and their "campaigns" often reflected this. Although I met with a number of such candidates, I thought it would be more interesting and worthwhile to study candidates and campaigns that had some chance of success.

22. Elections were thought and said to be a *muwsim* (season) by many. People spoke of *muwsim al-intikhabat* (election season). This made sense in that certain types of activities (e.g., campaigning, *nadawat*) and opportunities (e.g., employment in campaigns and other opportunities to benefit from candidates) only took place when elections were held, or during election season.

23. Election ballots in Egypt display candidates' names along with corresponding symbols and numbers, or ballot positions. In a country with high illiteracy, the use of pictures and numbers for candidates makes some sense. Ostensibly, numbers and symbols are assigned based on when individuals register their candidacy (e.g., the earlier one registers, the more likely one is to receive a low number). In practice, however, ruling-party candidates always receive the first and second positions on the ballot and their corresponding symbols. The NDP "group/professional" candidate is always first on the ballot and is represented by the crescent moon, whereas the NDP "worker/farmer" candidate is always second and represented by the camel. A few days before the election, two candidates withdrew from the race and the numbers for all the candidates below them on the ballot changed accordingly. So although Abdelnour's number was 7 during the entire campaign—and much of his campaign material displayed the number 7 (e.g., posters, banners, printed material)—a few days before the election his number became 5. Those days saw campaign workers furiously making changes to banners, cutting off the number 7 on printed material and otherwise attempting to cope with what can only be described as incompetence in electoral administration. The only candidates whose ballot positions did not change were those who originally had lower numbers than the two candidates who withdrew. As number 1 and number 2 on the ballot, the NDP "group/professional" and "worker/farmer" candidates remained the same in terms of ballot position.

24. What Heyba meant, of course, was that he first learned about politics and campaigns by working for Ahmed Fouad. This, in itself, is interesting, as it means that one of the most important people in Abdelnour's campaign (a leading member of the largest opposition party) had previously worked for and led the election and reelection efforts of a member of the ruling party. Heyba once told me that during one such election for Ahmed Fouad many years ago, he stuffed so many ballot boxes

that his fingers began to bleed. He recounted this with a contorted look on his face as if to demonstrate both the pain involved and the disgusting sight of blood literally dripping from his fingernails. Heyba said that he stopped supporting Fouad when Abdelnour first ran for office in the district in 1995.

25. This was clearly intended to differentiate Abdelnour from many if not all of the other candidates running for parliament in the district. Moreover, *al-na'ib al-muhtaram* (the respected representative) is how parliamentarians are referred to in parliament. This is roughly the equivalent to "honorable congressman" in the US political system.

26. The irony of the fact that the Abdelnour family villa was located where the Omar Effendi department store in Abbassaya now stands cannot go without comment. Although Omar Effendi has its origins in the early twentieth century, since the store's nationalization in the 1960s it has come to be associated with some of the negative aspects of the country's socialist era in the Egyptian imagination: state control of the economy, low-quality goods, and limited selection. The Abbassaya store in particular is also an example of uninspiring socialist-era design and poor-quality construction. Abdelnour—and his family's once-grand villa—by contrast, represent the politics and economics of an earlier liberal capitalist period. The irony continues, as the Egyptian government recently privatized Omar Effendi.

27. Zamalek is located in the Qasr el-Nil electoral district.

28. Abdelnour could also often be seen with a *sibha* (worry beads) in hand. As a Copt, his religion was an issue; it was used against him by some of his opponents in his two previous campaigns, and I heard his religion discussed among supporters and campaign staff on several occasions.

29. These excerpts come directly from my field notes of October 17, 2005.

30. This scene was actually quite endearing. I believe this man was sincere. Interestingly, I never saw him again, possibly further indication that he was not a paid supporter.

31. Here he was referring to parliamentarians from the ruling party, who can regularly be seen sleeping in the chamber and are known to approve everything the government puts in front of them, by either clapping or raising their hands in approval.

32. Abdelnour, like some other candidates, had a campaign worker/supporter who functioned as a "poet," attending events and occasionally standing up to recite a line of *zagal* (colloquial poetry) about the candidate. This line roughly translates as: "we went around El-Waily [searching], we went around; the likes of Mounir we have not found."

33. The Egyptian constitution is available at: http://constitution.sis.gov.eg/en/enconst1.htm.

34. The videotapes as well as many other "services" not recounted here were financed by Abdelnour's own money.

35. The resident's timing was important. Election season is the time during the course of a five-year parliamentary session that a parliamentarian is most vulnerable and in greatest need of support from constituents.

36. What Abdelnour meant by this is that under the current constitution, even if the parliament withdrew its confidence in the government, the matter would then go to the president, who would likely dismiss the vote of no confidence in his ministers, resulting in absolutely no change.

37. Many in Egypt considered this electoral contest to be a battle between two wings of the same party, the "old guard" of the NDP versus the new, modern, and younger-oriented generation of NDP reformers, led by Gamal Mubarak.

38. On October 22, 2005, Khalil drove me around the district himself, in his new BMW sport utility vehicle (bearing "customs" license plates, indicating that import taxes had not been paid on the car), so that I could see for myself what he had accomplished.

39. Some of his posters featured pictures of medical equipment he had purchased (again out of his own pocket) for local hospitals. These posters featured photographs of the hospital rooms before equipment and after the equipment had been installed.

40. What is meant here, of course, is a differentiation of two types of parliamentarians—those who primarily provide services to their constituents (*na'ib khidma* or "service representatives") and are either incapable or uninterested in the other functions of a parliamentarian, and those parliamentarians (*na'ib umma* or "national representatives") who concentrate on the larger issues of national political importance. Also see "Representatives Win with Services" 2006.

41. See Ellen Lust-Okar's quotation (2005b) of one Syrian parliamentarian who reportedly exclaimed, "We're members of parliament. We don't make laws!"

7

Local Elections in Gaza

Dag Tuastad

Based on anthropological fieldwork conducted in the Bureij refugee camp during the 2005 Palestinian elections, this chapter examines how Palestinians engage in conflict over authority. The Palestinian Authority is based on, and shaped by, tensions between two sources of power.[1] The first is the power of massive grassroots-based political participation. This is the popular power, which could be observed during the first intifada and during elections held in Palestine. The second basis of power is the Palestinian Authority itself, which has ruled through a chain of alliances combining informal structures of primary solidarity groups, family, and factions, with the formal and legal structures of the semi-state (Parker 1999: 57). This is what Rex Brynen calls the "neopatrimonial" dimension of Palestinian politics (1995: 24).

Politics in the aftermath of the local elections held in Gaza in 2005 reflected the tension between these bases of power. In Bureij the local elections generated intrafactional democratization processes, massive popular mobilization, and participation during the election campaign.[2] However, the accomplishments of the elections were undermined by elites who were intent on preserving their own positions. To do so, power-holders allied with and co-opted strong solidarity groups, cultivating tribalism and factionalism in an effort to preclude power-sharing.

▮ The Palestinian Authority and Neopatrimonial Rule

When the Palestine Liberation Organization (PLO) leadership returned from exile after 1993, they were met by a deeply antielitist local leadership. New leaders had emerged during the intifada, taking positions against the old landed elites. Indeed, many alleged that mukhtars and family leaders had collaborated with the occupation forces and put them on death lists.[3]

Returning Palestinian leaders needed to marginalize this local, antielitist leadership in order to build their own power base. Building on the traditional power structures of Palestine, they sought to revitalize the personalized power system in two ways. First, they reinforced the Fatah cadre system, penetrating the bureaucracy of the authorities with various police and security forces at their disposal. Second, in spite of the "collaborator" accusations of the large landowning families in Gaza, they aligned with such families. In this way, proximity to key individuals defined the distribution of power. Whom one knew became more important than the process of decisionmaking (Robinson 1997: 186). The electoral system governing the first national Palestinian elections, in 1996, also reflected this re-personification of politics. The system was based on a "multi-member majority vote" (Vollan and Butenschøn 1996: 29). Votes were thus cast for persons rather than for parties, and the candidates given the most marks by their names were elected. In this first-past-the-post, multivote system, there were significant discrepancies between the various constituencies regarding how many votes were needed to become elected. In Salfit, three of the five candidates received fewer than a thousand votes each. This meant that for some large families, a collective voting pattern was sufficient to elect their candidates. The election system thus favored familism, which helps explain why 507 of the 672 candidates competing for the eighty-eight seats ran as independent candidates. Of those eighty-eight elected, forty-nine were from Fatah, only three were from other parties, and the rest were independent candidates (Vollan and Butenschøn 1996: 114–120).

After the 1996 elections, the Palestinian Authority started a campaign to restore the mukhtar institution. Every resident was to have a representative in civil matters, and for court cases and civil affairs like marriages and births, the mukhtar was to be the witness. Small families were thus to affiliate themselves with mukhtars of larger families. As Muhammed al-Farra, from the Ministry of Local Government in Gaza, explained, "Every person should have a mukhtar, unless the family is of less than 200 persons, then they can not have a mukhtar."[4] The ministry was thus responsible for approving the official mukhtars of the families, first checking their background, including their security file. The ministry also negotiated between various segments of a family when they could not agree upon who their mukhtar should be. Thus, part of the work of the mukhtar was regulated by semiofficial tradition, not by law. However, it was still necessary to have a signature from the mukhtar for certain tasks. For instance, in order to receive an identification card from the ministry, one needed verification from a mukhtar. Certain conflicts were also regarded as open for "traditional" reconciliation rather than court procedure, and it was the mukhtars who

were to be responsible for mediating conflicts and for facilitating reconcili-
ations. The mukhtars were to take initiative in such cases, leading either
committees of *lajnat al-wi'a* (cool off) or of *lajna al-sulha* (reconciliation).

The refugee camps in Gaza, where close to half of the 800,000 refugees
in Gaza live, are not administered by the Palestinian Authority. Rather, the
United Nations Relief and Works Agency (UNRWA), in conjunction with
various refugee committees formed exclusively of members from the
camps, administers them. The autonomy of the camps is a crucial question
for the refugees, as less autonomy would signal resettlement of the refugees
without addressing a solution based on refugee demands. In Bureij, some
considered the institutionalization of the mukhtar as a control measure, and
others saw it as a form of interference in the refugees' affairs. For example,
a family from Mughar, where a considerable number of families were sympathetic with the Popular Front for the Liberation of Palestine (PFLP), did
not want to have their own mukhtar. They regarded it as a reactionary institution: "In our family, we have a council, but we do not have a mukhtar. In
the council, the branches are represented. Our branch, the Darwish branch,
has four, Abel Ghour has two, Mustafa has two and Muhammed has one.
We do not want a mukhtar in Jaber—but there are three or four from
Mughar. We do not like it. Arafat appointed them. What can he do? A
mukhtar before [1948] had land, he had much. Now he cannot afford to
serve his own guests."[5] The reestablishment of mukhtars, then, seemed to
some to misrepresent the current political reality within Palestine and within smaller, local communities.

Thus it was not uncommon to reject the mukhtars whom the officials
assigned. "We refused it," Yusef Nabaheen, from one of the large families of
Bedouin origin in Bureij, told me. He continued: "It was a big campaign in
1996–97, but we did not want them to approve our mukhtar. They wanted the
mukhtar to be elected; we had a meeting; we rejected. We inherit the position. They wanted it to be with the wealthy ones, with those with many sons.
We have our mukhtar, but he is not registered. He does not have the stamp of
the authorities. When we need a signature, we go to another family."[6]

These examples reflect a genuine skepticism toward the authorities' way
of reinforcing familism, especially because of the widespread perception that
the returning PLO cadres used familism to build a power-base in Gaza
through the old, large landowning families. Many regarded the Dughmush
family as having become rich through collaborating with the Israeli occupiers: "When the Egyptians left, Dughmush took all the sand-land in Gaza
city. It was private land and *waqf* land [land for the mosque to be used for
common good and charity] but they took it," an anonymous refugee from a
Bedouin family in Bureij told me. "Then they sold the land that was not
theirs, and the Israelis did not care. As long as they permitted it, they would
not get resistance from them. And that was how Dughmush got rich."

The solidarity of families like the Dughmush was of the *'asabiyya* kind, the special group feeling of corporative, endogamous, patrilineal groups (Lindholm 2002: 52). It was a particularistic solidarity that was based on family rather than political ideology. However, this solidarity was consistent with factional political association, and factions would in most circumstances be complementary rather than competing. The factions would in theory be composed of members from different families, in the same way that different families would have members belonging to different factions. However, if a family, like the Dughmush, was in conflict, the faction members would be allied despite potentially different political leanings. It was unlikely that different family members would fight against each other if there was a clash between Hamas and Fatah. This was especially the case for the large families in Gaza, where the primary loyalty appeared to be to the family. Families with strong internal solidarity and cohesion were assets that factions could use in their political conflicts. This made the Palestinian Authority shun confrontations with leading families and instead cultivate their support.

However, this familial focus generated a further fragmentation during the militarized second intifada. The high level of violence in the confrontation with the occupation undermined the rule of law. Some of the leading families of Gaza started to seek their own interests, even if these were detrimental to the community at large. They knew that they could do so without too much interference from the Palestinian Authority.

This autonomy contributed to the fact that some of the large families originating in Gaza, such as the Dughmush and the al-Shawiye, became uncontrolled, armed groups. These family bands have engaged in such activities as kidnapping foreigners in order to have a (criminal) relative released from prison. Rather than being prosecuted for such an act, they would frequently achieve their demands through negotiations. Negotiating with criminals in this way encouraged such violations and undermined the people's trust in the Palestinian Authority, which was responsible for maintaining the rule of law. Consequently, the rule of law gradually fell apart during the second intifada.

The ultimate effect of reestablishing the mukhtar system was the creation of an alliance between the landowning, nonrefugee families of Gaza, and the authorities. Concomitantly, the underprivileged, including those living in refugee camps, became further marginalized. Moreover, fragmentation of the center also generated similar patterns in the peripheries. If violence gives birth to itself, so does factionalism (Scheper-Hughes and Bourgois 2005: 1). In the camps of Gaza, armed groups formed around new patrons who had been born in the "gray zone" between armed resistance and crime. These groups also made alliances within the Palestinian Authority. This potentially benefited both, but it also undermined the rule of law.

However, there are some resistant traits against this "decommuniza-tion" that are inherent, so to speak, in the spirits of local communities. Ted Swedenburg (1995) has shown how a rural community-based ethos of col-lective action and responsibilities underscored and propelled the great Palestinian uprising from 1936 to 1939. Similarly, the first Palestinian intifada was largely organized along similar lines, even using the same names of the resistance committees, and based on mass mobilization and self-reliance (Abu-Amr 1996). This dimension of Palestinian politics reflects a grassroots, democratic ethos that "builds community," in the sense that it builds upon the trust among people.

Under these conditions, elections strengthen Palestinian politics and culture. Yet such opportunities have been intermittent. The national election of 1996 was to be followed by local elections in 1997. But the Palestinian Authority postponed the local elections again and again. Only when Yasser Arafat died and Mahmoud Abbas was elected his successor did the antici-pated elections take place, in spring 2005. The spring 2005 local elections appeared to be the means necessary to counteract the spinning fragmenta-tion and deinstitutionalization resulting from the second intifada.

◼ The 2005 Local Elections in Bureij

The local elections held in the Bureij refugee camp in April 2005 illuminate general phenomena concerning aspects of political participation, on the one hand, and neopatrimonial authoritarianism of Palestinian politics, on the other. Bureij is located in the middle area of Gaza, 13 kilometers southeast of Gaza City. The camp measures 0.48 square kilometers, and according to UN sources is home to 29,700 registered refugees (McCann 2002). Population density is around 60,000 per square kilometer, one of the highest in the world. Today the inhabitants of Bureij live in 4,627 different house-holds, in twelve adjacent "blocks" *(wihdat)* or neighborhoods. For the local elections in 2005, 15,482 voters were registered in Bureij. Elections took place at thirty-one polling stations in eight election centers.

Officially, according to the Ministry of Local Affairs and the Higher Election Committee, the local elections were to be "unpolitical elections"—regarding "services," not "real" politics. The parties would thus run under local names rather than as parties. However, everyone knew that in deeply politicized and contested Palestine, the idea of having "unpolitical" elec-tions was a farce. In Palestine, where every local election to any branch of any union represented a competition between the factions, local elections would be hyperpolitical, not unpolitical. In 1996, the Islamic Resistance Movement, Hamas, had already stated its intent to participate in local elec-tions, which it considered to be outside the Oslo framework. This was also consistent with the political strategy of the movement, building power from the ground up, moving from mosques to local councils, and from local councils to national institutions. This was a strategy that had led Islamists to win in Algeria (where the results became annulled, leading to a civil war) as well as in Turkey (where a moderate branch of the Islamic movement was then in power).

When the election campaign started in Bureij on April 21, 2005, two weeks before the elections, the main parties, Hamas and Fatah, had already been campaigning "informally" for some time. The parties conducted home visits, community work, and public opinion "research" (i.e., asking people in the various quarters of the camp about their priorities and concerns). In addition, Hamas had a list of candidates prepared years prior, in anticipation of the elections, which had been postponed time and again. Fatah, on the other hand, had been preoccupied with internal struggles and was thus much less prepared when the campaign started.

When the Hamas list was revealed in Bureij, it shocked the local Fatah members. All thirteen Hamas candidates were university graduates, and some had earned postgraduate (including doctoral) degrees; they included imams, engineers, social workers, and university lecturers. Some of the candidates were well known from their leading roles in the resistance. Muhammed Taha, who was number one on the list, had lost a son and been arrested by the Israelis during the second intifada. He was also one of the founders of Hamas in Gaza.

When Fatah members in Bureij saw the candidates that their own party had nominated to compete with Hamas, they revolted against the central Fatah leadership. The elections revealed the undemocratic culture within Fatah. Upon its founding, Fatah was spiritually and organizationally inspired by the Muslim Brotherhood in Egypt, but later organized according to Leninist principles of "centralized democratization" (Pappe 2004: 192). Hence, whether at the national, regional, or local level, the executive committee maintained control over the selection of members in subordinate committees (Pappe 2004). The system may have been efficient in terms of military organization, but it was not compatible with genuinely democratic elections. The residents in Bureij sent in their suggestions of candidates based on interviews in each "block" of the camp, but they found that Fatah's central committee in Gaza refused most of the candidates. Instead, the committee placed other names on the list.

Khaled Safi, number three on the Fatah list, provided a useful perspective on this subject:

> It smelled of the *mukhabarat* [the intelligence service] appointing the names; no one wanted to work for the list. The blocks of the camp are the grassroots. Everywhere there was frustration. People said, "If you impose these candidates, we will not work in the election." The *iklim* [regional

leaders] said, "We do not want to lose again," referring to the results of the first round of the elections. Hamas won in Deir al-Balah [the neighbor camp and town of Bureij in the middle area of Gaza]. We did not want this to happen again. Then various names from the leaders of the middle areas were discussed; the names were sent out like balloons. We discussed them in the camp, but people said, "We refuse!" Then the Fatah leaders of Bureij said, "We are with the *iklim* [the regional leaders]." Still, people in the blocks, in the grassroots, refused. Face to face, it was then said to our leaders, "We refuse that you are our leaders!"

Then a new nomination process started. Each block again chose three to six names in the first half of March. Each of the names from the blocks was then seen together. I was nominated by ten blocks, and was then asked to become a candidate. . . . So that way we got thirteen names chosen by the Fatah members of the camp.

If we do not win, the "old guard" would say that we lack the experience, the long history, the prison, etcetera. Now we have technocrats!

I accepted the nomination after a few days of thinking. We were then taught by NDI in Gaza during a week of training for all the Fatah candidates for the second round of the voting in Gaza.[7]

We made a name for our list, *Al-'Ata wa al-Bina,* "Building and Supporting," but Fatah in Gaza refused this. They sent us another name: *Al-Wafa li Al-Aqsa,* "The Effort or Sacrifice for Al-Aqsa." We refused! We did not want Al-Aqsa now; we wanted our own name, reflecting who the candidates of the list were. This was our list. We demanded that we could keep it; this was our name, so then we kept it.

If we had been chosen from above as usual, and not directly from our members, I think we would have accepted it—the name sent us from above. But now, we were chosen from below. They respected us; our loyalty was with them, not with Gaza.[8]

The members of Fatah's central committee in Gaza then ostensibly felt that they had no choice but to follow the "order" from below, recognizing that otherwise they would be humiliated through the ballot box. Elections, and the quality of the Hamas campaign, thus forced Fatah to restructure, and to democratize its nomination procedures. Fatah was reactive; it saw what Hamas did and thought that it would have to do the same.

The Fatah candidates in Bureij hoped that their independence from Fatah's central committee in Gaza City, which the camp largely despised, would be recognized. Additionally, they hoped that they were now, in fact, represented by talented experts and technocrats, rather than party cadres, as in the past. Like the Hamas candidates, most of the Fatah candidates, eleven out of thirteen, were university graduates, and some had earned postgraduate degrees (including one doctorate); most were engaged in engineering, business administration, and project management.

However, people recognized that Fatah had tried to copy Hamas, rather than stressing their differences. On the posters for Hamas in Bureij, the female candidates were not pictured (although female candidates were pictured for Hamas in the Rafah camp in southern Gaza). Consequently, Fatah did the same: no pictures of the female candidates appeared on the posters for Fatah in Bureij.

Through such imitation, the local Fatah leaders thought they had avoided catastrophe. Simultaneously, they accepted that the main issues of interest regarded moral questions defined by Hamas: corruption, sacrifices, religion, and safety. The mosques represented control and purity rather than violence and anarchy. It was striking, however, how representatives of the largest and most significant families, as well as the militants in the Al-Aqsa and Jenin Brigades, were not nominated when the selection process derived from below in the camp. Although the Fatah list appeared to be an improvement in terms of voter appeal, it was too late for Fatah to change people's perspectives about the party and its candidates.

■ Interfactional Cooperation on Election Day

Before the elections, the factions of Bureij had gathered and agreed to establish a joint cooperation committee *(lajnat al-ta'awun)* to keep the peace on election day. The committee had one member of each faction present in all eight election centers in the camp, designated by a cloth tied around their arms. This joint effort emerged from the camp's spirit of joint resistance against the occupation, not as something prescribed by the rules and regulations of the Higher Election Committee. Their function was to intervene if any trouble erupted, with each member of the committee responsible for his faction. The committee apparently worked as it was supposed to: calming and controlling *tanzim* members, and ensuring that their faction did not do any campaigning inside the polling centers.[9]

Amid an excited atmosphere, people of all factions participated with commitment and pride. On election day, the green banners, stripes, caps, and head scarves of Hamas dominated the camp landscape, outnumbering Fatah supporters in terms of visibility.[10] In the evening, the ballot counting at Bureij Sports Club (Center 885, Station 5) took place without interference or complaints; every ballot was checked by election staff and also by the numerous local election observers. When the counting had finished, none of the observers inside had any objections to the process. The results were then published outside; they were hung on the doorstep of the center, while the other copies were sent to the local election center in Bureij and to the Higher Election Committee in Gaza.

Leaving the election center, one learned that the results there were rather similar to the results in other centers of the camp: Hamas had won. Some Fatah supporters who were watching Hamas celebrate claimed that the results were not clear and that the outcome could change, but in fact there was no doubt about the results. The Fatah supporters, with their yellow banners, were left to watch as Hamas took to the streets, singing and shouting. As midnight neared, hundreds of Hamas supporters entered the square of Block Four in the camp, marching in the street while shouting, "Qassam! Qassam! Qassam!"[11]

◼ Annulling the Results

The victory was a tremendous blow to Fatah. In fact, it was the greatest defeat ever for Fatah in local or national elections, and it had occurred in all three main urban centers in Gaza where elections were held: Beit Lahya, Rafah, and Bureij. The Fatah defeat was staggering. Of the councils elected during this round of the local elections, Fatah won thirty-eight, which covered a population of approximately 230,000. Hamas won in thirty local authorities, but here the population exceeded 600,000 people (Regular 2005a).

Fatah hard-liners would not accept the results. On the evening of election day, Mahmoud Nashabat took control of the municipality building. Nashabat had been an intifada leader in both uprisings, and had formed a group of armed men through his work for the preventive security forces of the Palestinian Authority, the Kataib al-Jenin, or Jenin Brigades. He was associated with the Palestinian Authority and Fatah, but was a de facto warlord who had the reputation of killing anyone who stood in his way. After occupying the municipality building on the evening of the election day, he threatened to blow it up if the results were not overturned. He issued a leaflet stating that he had filled the whole building with explosives, and if anyone from Hamas entered, he would detonate the building. The next day he left the municipality building after entering into negotiations led by Hassan Jibrin, the regional Fatah leader. Fatah in Bureij subsequently issued a leaflet in which it stated that serious cheating had taken place during the elections, and that it would send a complaint to the central Higher Election Committee. It seemed as if an agreement had been reached within Fatah; they would not accept the defeat. "It is the first time that the party in power organizing the election accuses the opposition of winning through cheating," Hamas succinctly responded at a May 10, 2005, press conference convened in Gaza City.

As Fatah decided not to accept the Hamas victory, the calm of the election period dissipated. During the summer of 2005, outbursts of interfactional violence escalated. Khaled Safi, the Fatah candidate quoted previously, was worried that Fatah, not Hamas, would resort to violence, noting that the latter had better control over its military branches. He continued:

> If the "emir" says do this, they do this. Fatah, they discuss or refuse. Arafat established committees. Extra sugar, like to have better coffee. So it became extra sugar, and extra sugar committees. . . . In Fatah the military branch does not listen to the political branch; they listen to nobody. In

> Bureij, Nashabat, Kataib al-Jenin, they follow no one. They are sometimes
> with Fatah, and under the Fatah umbrella, but they do exactly what they
> want to do themselves.[12]

But Khaled and several other candidates from the Fatah list were exceptions. The majority of Fatah activists could not admit the loss, and thus
started searching for ways to explain how mistakes had been made during
the election process.

They did so in spite of the fact that they acknowledged Hamas's better
preparation and organization for the elections. In the crucial moments,
Hamas had mobilized all known sympathizers during the registration
process. No comprehensive civil registry existed in the Palestinian entity
that could be used in the elections, and thus out-of-date registration lists and
special voter registration lists were used. The voter registration lists were
thus based on two sources: an incomplete civil registry, received on com-
pact discs from Israel, and a list of those who had registered during autumn
2004. At that time, Fatah was in turmoil, with younger intifada leaders
demanding reforms against the old guard and returnees. Few inside Fatah
had bothered to undertake a registration campaign for Fatah supporters.
Hamas, on the other hand, had mobilized its members. "Hamas won
because they mobilized in order to register," Abu Ghanem, a young local
Fatah member admitted, and added that the problem was also with the
Higher Election Committee, which some believed had failed to fulfill its
duties.[13]

Those who rejected the election results argued that the Higher Election
Committee "was not good enough." Paradoxically, international advisers
had also been critical of the committee, because they regarded it as too
politicized.[14] The concern was that the committee was composed of people
controlled by the ruling party, Fatah, a criticism echoing the one against the
election committee that oversaw the parliamentary elections of 1996. The
election committee that oversaw the presidential elections of January 2005,
following the death of Yasser Arafat, had been less politicized in that
regard. It seemed awkward that Fatah would criticize the election committee that they themselves had appointed for the local elections through the
Ministry of Interior.

It was specified in the law on local government by the Palestinian
Legislative Council of 1996 that the election committee for local government should be different than the one for national elections. According to
the law, the central election committee should be responsible for subelec-
tion committees, and also had the power to monitor the performance of
these committees and their subcommittees at the local level. This implies
that these election committees are independent from the Ministry of Interior
itself. As such, in 2005, the election committees were not directly under the
control of the Fatah regime. However, the authorities appointed the Higher

Election Committee, and many regarded it as loyal to the Palestinian Authority, which was under Fatah control. Thus it seemed contradictory that Fatah should take the Higher Election Committee to court for misconduct in the elections. But eventually Fatah did just that. "Fatah is suing Fatah," people said in Gaza.

The controversy continued. Ali Diab al-Din, a lawyer who had been on the candidate list for Fatah, formulated Fatah's complaint regarding the election results in Bureij. The election law stated that complaints could be issued within one week of the declaration of the results. There were two kinds of complaints, he explained in an interview: one concerning "names and stories," and the other concerning electoral rules. They had gone through the list of the election staff and found that some of them belonged to Hamas.[15] This was denied by Anis Abd al-Rahman Abu Shamala, number seven on the Hamas list. He argued that some may have sympathized with Hamas, but none were members, and furthermore that the claim made by Fatah would be impossible to verify, as the membership lists of Hamas were not public (the members of the movement were targets of Israeli assassinations).[16]

Questioned as to why the complaint against the members of the Higher Election Committee was not raised before publication of the election results, al-Din of Fatah answered by extending the complaint: "Many dead people voted." In other words, people who were on the civil registration list, which had not been updated, were marked as having voted, though they were actually deceased. He claimed that almost twenty such cases existed. Furthermore, he said that the families of the mentally handicapped could vote in their stead (ten to twenty such cases), as could the families of prisoners (eight to nine cases), although according to the election law there was no room for absentee voting. He also claimed that Hamas had more than one observer at every voting station, though the law specified the presence of only one observer. Finally, he stated that when the counting started, the candidates had been unable to observe it. Because of this, Fatah demanded a new election.

"Why did Fatah claim there was foul play only after the results came out, which favored Hamas?" Issa Nashaar from Hamas aptly asked (Hamad 2005). The complaints, like "dead" people having voted, could hardly be verified, and in any case it could not be established who it was that allegedly had cheated. Some of the complaints were not legally valid. In terms of the complaint that the candidates had not been able to observe the counting, it was established that, in fact, this was not a right at all according to the election law. Finally, even if the numbers of individuals who had allegedly cheated were added up, it would still not change the balance of power; each of the Hamas candidates had on average won about 400 more votes than each of the Fatah candidates.

Claims of significant irregularities were not something for which members of the local election committee were prepared. In Bureij, the local election committee had eight members: two from Hamas, two from Fatah (including the chairman), one from the Popular Front for the Liberation of Palestine (the vice chairman), one from the Democratic Front for the Liberation of Palestine (who did not participate), and two "independent" lawyers (who were considered pro-Fatah). The committee had been established three months before the elections, and its initial work had concerned voter registration. The Popular Front member of the committee, Yusef Awad, stated, "It was Fatah's fatal mistake not to work harder on the registration. On the election day, crowds came to the election committee because they had not been registered."

Awad had been educated as an agricultural engineer and worked for the Ministry of Agriculture. He did not support Hamas and took pride in the elections being conducted according to the rules and regulations of the law. "The results were fair," he said. "It was what the people wanted. The problem with Fatah is that they do not want to work with the reasons behind their failure."[17]

■ Canceling the Agreement with Hamas

Two weeks after Hamas won the main urban centers in the elections, Palestinian courts ruled to nullify the results in Beit Lahya, Bureij, and Rafah. Hamas leaders were furious. They claimed that Fatah leaders and the Palestinian Authority had pressured the court to void the results (*Reuters* 2005). "These rulings are a plot that was born in the dark whose aim is to forge the will of the Palestinian people and rob Hamas of its achievements in local councils under the guise of a court ruling," Mahmod Zahar, then–political leader of Hamas in Gaza, said at a press conference (Regular 2005c). The court had ordered that the results in 12 out of 31 polling stations in Bureij, 5 out of 42 in Beit Lahya, and 51 out of 141 in Rafah be canceled, and called for new elections for voters registered at these stations within ten days. However, this new ruling was soon annulled by the Ministry of Interior.[18] In an interview, I later asked the chairman of the Higher Election Committee in Gaza, Usama Abu Safiyah, whether anything unusual had occurred in the places where Hamas had won that Fatah had complained about compared to other places. "No," he said, "nothing was special there."[19]

Hamas did not recognize the court ruling and made clear that it would refuse to participate in an eventual new round of elections. "Hamas has the right to use all means to defend its [May 5] victories. The crisis we have reached is Fatah's responsibility alone," Hamas spokesman Abu Zuhri said at a news conference in Gaza (Baker 2005). Episodes of confrontation between Hamas and Fatah now became more and more frequent. All over Gaza, Hamas organized protests against the attempts "to steal their victory," Abu Zuhri said.

On May 24, 2005, in Bureij, several Hamas supporters were injured in one of these demonstrations. According to one bystander, the driver had apparently panicked as he mistook fireworks for being gunshots, and then lost control over the vehicle, which burst into the crowd. Hamas militants, thinking they were under attack, fired back and accidentally injured two children.

While international observers stated that the Higher Election Committee had carried out its duties and that the local elections had been fair, Fatah elements moved not only to cancel the results of their main losses in the urban centers, but also to postpone the national parliamentary elections scheduled for two months later, on July 17, 2005. Thus, on June 5, 2005, when Palestinian president Mahmoud Abbas announced the postponement of the national elections, Hamas promptly took this as evidence that Fatah was not taking seriously the agreement reached in Cairo with Hamas. The Hamas spokesman warned that it would lead to "more chaos and confusion in the street" (Baker 2005).

Essentially it appeared as if Fatah was replacing its attempt to include Hamas in the political process with an attempt to exclude it. In March 2005, there had been a breakthrough in the negotiations between Palestinian factions and the Palestinian Authority (PA) in Cairo. In the Cairo Agreement, Hamas, along with eleven other Palestinian organizations, agreed to suspend all military activities against Israel throughout the year, to participate in the parliamentary elections scheduled for July, and to commence discussions about joining a new PLO. "This is a turning point for the region," said the Palestinian Authority negotiator, Nabil Abu Rideina (Usher 2005).

A postponement of the election meant annulling the Cairo Agreement and putting the interests of Fatah before national unity. Nevertheless, few were surprised when the Palestinian president decided to postpone the elections; even members of the international community expressed relief: "We advocate postponing the elections until December 2005. This will allow the PA to benefit from the achievement of the disengagement, manage an orderly disposal of the settlement assets in Gaza, and put an end to the existing chaos. The public will then support the Authority against Hamas," an Egyptian official said (Usher 2005: 4).

A warlike situation evolved between Fatah and Hamas in the aftermath of the postponement of the national elections and the annulling of the Hamas victories in the municipal elections in Gaza. Several members of the factions were killed during the summer, many in mutual attacks on the offices of the political branches in Gaza (Regular 2005b). The Hamas leader, Mahmoud Zahar, declared that the party had now lost all faith in the

Palestinian president (Usher 2005: 4). The trust generated by popular participation in the election withered.

However, some Fatah leaders regarded the postponement as inevitable. It was essentially the same as annulling the victory of Hamas in the urban centers in the local elections. Fatah could not let go of its power.

■ Fatah First

Hassan Jibrin was the regional leader of Fatah in the middle areas of Gaza, and the leader of the Refugee Committee of Bureij. Hassan was one of those who had worked to have the Cairo Agreement with Hamas annulled. "Hamas threatens, if elections are postponed, they will break the Cairo Agreement," he said, referring to the March 2005 breakthrough whereby Hamas had agreed to participate in parliamentary elections. "But if Abu Mazen insists on having the Parliamentary elections in July, we will break the agreement."[20] Hassan spoke deliberately, and simultaneously the Al-Aqsa Brigades carried out a "campaign" in Gaza, forcefully closing voter registration offices (Regular 2005d).

Jibrin believed that the national elections had to be postponed in order to restructure Fatah, and he was also skeptical about Hamas's victory in the local elections. "Someone came and voted in the name of a martyr. We went to Muhammed al-Taha [number one on the Hamas list] and said this. 'It is a miracle,' he said. He did not question whether someone had actually cheated. How can we deal with people like this?"[21] When I later asked Anis Abd al-Rahman Abu Shamala, a candidate on the Hamas list, about what Jibrin had told me, he denied that Muhammed al-Taha had called the victory "a miracle." He rather saw it as an example of Fatah's fabrications about Hamas.[22] From Hassan's perspective, it was impossible to accept Hamas taking over Bureij, as he was convinced that people did not know what they had voted for. "They want to have separate schools, one for boys and one for girls," he said, alleging that Hamas would change everything and that this was in their program. When asked if the people should not get what they voted for, he replied, "We are not in Oslo. The people who voted Hamas, the majority did not read the program. The results are due to other factors."[23]

Nasser Jabber, also from the Refugee Committee in Bureij, added, "The results do not mean that people voted for the Hamas program; you cannot say that people support this." The members of the Refugee Committee in Bureij are not formally elected through ballots, which leads some to claim that the election results were a response to the belief that it is the PLO and Fatah who control the camps, rather than an expression of who people want to be led by. This claim is supported by Hamas's establishment of institutions to parallel those of the PLO. "We are not elected, but I think that we represent the people," Hassan Jibrin said. When I asked if the Refugee Committee should include representatives of the majority of the camp who voted for the Islamists in order to be more legitimate, he replied, "We want them to be a part, but before they get in, we need to change their culture. We do not want them as a snake; we need to pull out their teeth."[24]

Hassan Jibrin had become a local leader before the first intifada, and had served fourteen years in an Israeli prison. He was a typical, smart camp politician. He gained his leadership position through competence, and he had both rhetorical and organizational skills. He did not gain power through an alliance with a powerful Fatah faction in Gaza City or close relations to a family there. He admitted that these kinds of alliances infected Fatah, but that it was something he despised: "We do not deny ten years of corruption, through Fatah and the Palestinian Authority. But when it comes to Hamas, they have a hidden agenda. They are a black box. They are mosque and religion."[25]

For Jibrin, what mattered was restructuring Fatah. He wanted to have the central point of power relocated back to the camps, away from the axis of PLO returnees, and large Gazan families. This was to be done by having the long-awaited internal elections in Fatah. Yet to relocate this central point of power, he had to ally with darker forces of Fatah.

One of these darker forces was Mahmoud Nashabat, the notorious warlord. "You cannot touch him, and not protest. He has 200 men and he pays them $2,300 every month. If you say anything against him, he will have you killed, then write a memo that you were a collaborator," an anonymous man in Bureij relayed to me. "He even took Jabali into Bureij, and then released him," the man continued, referring to an incident during the summer of 2004 when gunmen, Mahmoud Nashabat and his Jenin Martyrs Brigades, abducted Ghazi Jabali, the Palestinian police chief in Gaza, and took him to Bureij. Following negotiations with the Fatah secretary-general in Gaza, the chief of Gaza's Preventive Security, and the governor of central Gaza, the police chief was later released. The abductors demanded jobs for unemployed gunmen and a halt to the corruption in the Palestinian territories, a spokesman for the kidnappers said on *Al-Jazeera* television ("Gunmen Release Gaza Police Chief" 2004). Hassan Jibrin was perhaps the only man that Nashabat would listen to, and it was Hassan who convinced Nashabat to give up his occupation of the municipal building in Bureij. "We asked them not to take any stupid actions, to wait. They respected that," Jibrin said of the incident.[26] I declined to ask him what it was that Nashabat should wait for. I met Mahmoud Nashabat half a year later at his new offices in January 2006, at the time of the parliamentary elections. He and his men had now become integrated into the police forces of the Palestinian Authority. The whole gang of the Jenin fighters were on the payroll of the same Gaza police force whose leader they had kidnapped a year and a half earlier.

Conclusion

Ziyad Abu-Amr argues that Palestinian politics are characterized by sociopolitical pluralism; the social powers have been balanced, in terms of familial and tribal interests as well as the interests of the various Palestinian political factions, and no single group has been strong enough to crush or dominate the others (1996). This point underscores the idea that the neopatrimonialism of the Palestinian Authority is not a uniform system that coordinates the flow of power from the centers to the peripheries, but rather a system of fragile alliances that embeds latent intrafactional conflicts waiting to implode. In the case of Bureij, warlord Mahmoud Nashabat and his Jenin fighters have become co-opted into the police forces of the Palestinian Authority. It should be noted that, according to Hassan Jibrin, in the Bureij camp alone there are five other similar military factions operating under the umbrella of Fatah: Al-Aqsa, Al-Awda, the National Resistance Committees, the Ahmed Abu Risik Brigades, and Al-Haq.[27] These groups evolved during the two intifadas and were products of the resistance. They were influenced by the brutalization of the increasingly militarized resistance, rather than by the strong civil society that had flourished in Palestine until the establishment of the Palestinian Authority in 1994. The military factions form an utterly fragile basis for any political structure. Apparently the Palestinian Authority not only lacks control over the means of violent force, but also inadvertently strengthens forces that undermine its own authority.

It is important to note that neopatrimonialism, as analyzed by Rex Brynen (1995), is a form of rule employed by power-holders that generates uncontrollable processes of fragmentation. This does not mean that fragmentation is *the* defining characteristic of Palestinian political culture. Rather, it means that fragmentation is an intrinsic dimension of the neopatrimonial form of rule in Palestine. There is a counterdimension as well: an antielitist and egalitarian ethos of collective political participation. A lesson throughout Palestinian history and occupation is that politics conducted over the heads of the masses will sooner or later lead to a backlash (Kimmerling and Migdal 2003: 356).[28] The experiences of external occupiers are not different from the experiences of internal power-holders who concern themselves with power alone, in spite of having lost the popular basis upon which that power ought to be secured. These leaders sit on political volcanoes. The tension between the two forms of power—the grassroots popular power and the Palestinian Authority power—guarantees the unsustainability of neopatrimonialism in Palestinian politics.

Postscript

During the 2006 parliamentary elections in Palestine, I witnessed an incident concerning a handicapped man who had difficulty walking and speaking. "He is retarded, he shall not vote," the Fatah observers said. The president of the election center had arrived at the polling station, where people were starting to gather outside. She left to phone the Central Election Commission, and returned shortly afterward. "What is your name?" she asked the man. He replied, stating his name. "How old are you?" "Where do you live?" Slowly the handicapped voter managed to answer the questions. "Do you know who to vote for?" "Yes—Hamas!" the man answered. Some people smiled at his response, but the Fatah observers still protested—the man was being influenced by his brother, who was following him, they claimed. "Go and vote, and God bless you," the president of the polling center told the voter.

I mention this incident because the picture that emerged from the 2005 local elections was similar to that for the 2006 parliamentary elections, which were also "free and fair," with genuinely opposing parties competing for the authority and with high levels of mobilization and voter participation—and in which many of the underprivileged people voted for Hamas, which eventually won. Another similar feature between the 2005 and 2006 elections was that, in their aftermath, the Palestinian Authority resorted to nondemocratic measures to avoid handing over power as prescribed by law,[29] a policy endorsed by the international community following the fundamental antagonism by the United States and Israel toward Hamas. This is important because it reminds us of how the Palestinian situation is different from the situations in other Middle Eastern countries, where elections are micromanaged in order to keep the ruling leaders in power. In the Palestinian context, elections could have been genuinely democratic, leading to de facto regime change, had it not been for the intervention of external forces.

An aspect of Palestinian authoritarianism is thus that it involves international patronage, extending the neopatrimonialism described in this chapter. However, following the June 2007 seizing of power by Hamas in all of Gaza, the lesson should be that in the deeply politicized Palestinian context, patrimonialism backfires.

▓ Notes

I am grateful to Ellen Lust-Okar, Gudrun Bertinussen, and Svein Tuastad for constructive comments on a draft of this chapter, to Jacob Høigilt for "correcting" transcriptions, and to Jamal Safi for very helpful assistance during fieldwork.

    1. This chapter views the Palestinian Authority as an authoritarian regime. Neopatrimonial authoritarianism is regarded as a form of rule that generates uncontrolled processes of fragmentation. Such fragmentation need not be the intention of the rulers, but it is an inevitable consequence of their policy. In Gaza, fragmentation has spread from the center to the peripheries.

    2. Elections in the fragile situation of Palestine differ in this regard from elections held in the more stable regimes of the Middle East, where they may contribute

to preserving forms of semiauthoritarianism (see Chapter 5 in this volume). In Gaza, elections can have a genuine catalytic effect on the political system.

3. Mukhtars are "headmen" of extended families. During the Ottoman period, they were the "leaders" or administrative contacts between villages and the authorities.

4. Personal interview with Muhammed al-Farra, undersecretary, Ministry of Local Government, Gaza City, July 12, 2005.

5. Personal interview with Nasser Jaber, member of the Refugee Committee in Bureij, June 13, 2005.

6. Personal interview with Yusef Nabaheen, candidate for Fatah in local elections in Bureij, July 10, 2005.

7. The US Democratic Party is affiliated with the National Democratic Institute, "a nonprofit organization working to strengthen and expand democracy worldwide" ("About NDI" 2006).

8. Personal interview with Khaled Safi, candidate for Fatah in local elections in Bureij, July 11, 2006.

9. At one station (PS 5100) I observed a man from Fatah while I visited the Bureij secondary school. The man became furious when he was ordered by election staff to take off his Fatah headscarf, which he refused to do. The member of the committee from Fatah was quick to calm him, accompanied by other Fatah sympathizers inside the center.

10. Some Fatah people said, as others had claimed during the campaign meetings of Hamas, that most of their supporters had been bussed in from outside. I asked a couple of camp people where they were from and if they had been bussed in from other camps. None of them were from outside Bureij. Some claimed that this was a typical accusation from Fatah people, whose *shabab* (youth) dressed in yellow but could not match the number of people dressed in green.

11. The name of the rocket that Hamas's military wing frequently fired into Israel.

12. Personal interview with Khaled Safi, May 4, 2005.

13. Personal interview with Abu Ghanem, Bureij, May 9, 2005.

14. Personal interview with an international adviser for the presidential elections in Jerusalem, January 6, 2005.

15. Personal interview with Ali Diab al-Din, candidate for Fatah in local elections in Bureij, May 9, 2005.

16. Personal interview with Anis Abd al-Rahman Abu Shamala, candidate for Hamas in local elections in Bureij, June 12, 2005.

17. Personal interview with Yusef Awad, member of the local election committee in Bureij, May 9, 2005.

18. By November 2006, new elections still had not been held, and Fatah thus remained in control over these local councils.

19. Personal interview with Usama Abu Safiyah, chairman of the Higher Election Committee, Gaza City, June 13, 2005.

20. *The Economist,* June 9, 2005. The national elections were postponed, but Jirin would still be disappointed: Fatah's party congress, the reason why the local activists of Fatah wanted to have the national elections postponed, got postponed. Now the congress was to be held after the new election date for the national elections. By November 7, 2006, a date for the Fatah congress still had not been set.

21. Interview with Hassan Jibrin, political leader of Fatah in Gaza's "middle areas," Bureij, June 11, 2005.

22. Interview with Abu Shamala, June 12, 2005.

23. Interview with Jibrin, June 11, 2005.

24. Ibid.

25. Ibid.

26. Ibid.

27. Ibid.

28. The interests of the Palestinian aristocracy of the 1930s, of profiting from selling land to Jewish colonialists, led to the biggest national revolt ever experienced in the Middle East. The might of Great Britain, which was then the world's greatest imperial power, was efficiently challenged from 1936 to 1939 (Swedenburg 1995: xxi). Fifty years later, the world's fourth strongest military, Israel, would be forced to start rethinking its occupation of Palestine following the outburst of the first intifada, and in 2005 would be forced to retreat from Gaza following the armed resistance of the second intifada.

29. See the illuminating commentary "What Can Abu Mazin Do?" by Nathan Brown of George Washington University, at http://www.carnegieendowment.org/files/brownabumazincommentary.pdf.

PART 3

Beyond Electoral Politics

8

Opposition Groups in Bahrain

Katja Niethammer

During the first legislative period (2002–2006) of Bahrain's reform era, political progress was severely impeded by the conflict between "participants" (those political forces that opted for work within the parliamentary framework) and "boycotters" (political groups that chose not to join the elections of 2002 and not to recognize the parliament's legitimacy).[1] Trying to avoid public dialogue, both contending camps engaged in coalition building behind the scenes. Hence, political actors often resorted to surprising tactics that made them the source of gossip. For example, the deputy heads of the appointed Shura Council and members of the elected chamber of representatives secretively discussed possible future changes to the mode of Shura appointment with the interior minister during their trip to the funeral of Rafiq Hariri in Beirut on February 16, 2005.[2] A possible compromise, so they hoped, could persuade the boycotters to join the upcoming elections of 2006. Then, another deputy chairman of the elected chamber did something rather unusual for a functionary supposedly devoted to institutions and laws.[3] Instead of first trying to convince the boycotters to participate, he went directly to the *majlis* of Bahrain's most prominent oppositional Shiite cleric, Isa Qassim, to gain approval for a line of compromise, thereby circumventing formal political arenas. The reasoning behind this act was that the cleric functions as the "gray eminence" behind the main boycotting Shiite group. Resorting to their formal representatives would have been futile without first securing the consent of the cleric, who has no formal connection to any political society.[4]

This example shows how, as Laila Alhamad notes in Chapter 3, the spheres of formal and informal institutions (a formal parliament and a rather informal *majlis*) ought not be regarded as separate political arenas. Rather, they often overlap in sometimes surprising, sometimes more predictable ways. To gain a more comprehensive understanding of the forms of political participation in Bahrain, this chapter analyzes the formal and informal arenas and the interactions between these spheres, based primarily on interviews and participant observations in Bahrain.[5]

I begin by presenting the background and structural setting of Bahraini politics, including descriptions of some of the legal and structural limitations to formal political participation, and identifying the institutions (in their varying degrees of formality) in which political actors pursue their aims. I next focus on three groups of actors that (during the first legislative period, 2002–2006, the focus of analysis here) maintained different positions toward state institutions, ranging from adoption to rejection, and developed divergent strategies to promote their positions. These groups illustrate the wide range of participatory tools, some quite unconventional, that political activists in Bahrain developed during the first four years of the new parliament's existence. However, the focus here is extraparliamentary opposition groups, a decision not intended to devalue the parliamentarians' efforts, but rather to highlight the opposition groups' more complex strategies aimed at establishing (oppositional) discourses and at influencing political decisionmaking.[6]

Through this analysis, the chapter reveals the dynamics of Bahraini political participation and obstacles to reform. During the 2002–2006 period,[7] Bahraini political actors' strategic options were defined, to a great extent, by their respective positions toward parliament. While actors within parliament could participate to a certain degree in legislation and government supervision, those outside could not influence the details of legislation. They could, however, participate in agenda-setting. The more they incorporated less formal arenas of discussion into their strategies, the more influential they became in their agenda-setting efforts. After all, the regime has proven to be receptive toward street agitation, a phenomenon that may be manipulated through informal connections. However, strategies that appeared to be directed toward exerting pressure on the government to achieve certain policy outcomes might in fact have been aimed toward quite a different goal. Often, oppositional groups were caught in competition with each other, thereby losing sight of influencing the government altogether. The fragmentation of Bahrain's society and the resulting high level of distrust between participants and boycotters, and more fundamentally, between the various ethnoreligious groups, put severe constraints on most political actors.

■ The Bahraini Political Setting

The Kingdom of Bahrain does not constitute a democracy,[8] but it has entered a process of political liberalization that has significantly expanded the margins for formal and informal political participation.[9] Shaikh Hamad bin Isa Al-Khalifa came to power after the death of his father in March 1999, and since then Bahrain has pursued a top-down liberalization process. This process is partly motivated by economic objectives: the country's oil supplies are almost depleted. Other than oil, Bahrain's national income stems mainly from financial services (offshore banking and insurance), weekend tourism from neighboring Gulf states, and industrial production (Bahrain Monetary Agency 2004).

Political unrest, which was a prominent feature of Bahraini politics in the 1990s, negatively impacts these sources of finance. Thus the opposition's fight for limiting the ruling family's autocratic rule and resuming parliamentary life, which Bahrainis had experienced for less than a short two years (1973–1975), culminated in wide mass mobilization during the 1990s, locally referred to as the "Bahraini intifada."[10] The unrest was also motivated by the perceived and real discrimination of the Shiite majority (roughly 70 percent) by the dominant Sunni ruling family and its clientele. While not all Shiites are economically and politically deprived, poverty and unemployment are concentrated within the Shiite population, and Shiites have been barred from holding senior positions in the security forces.[11] The unrest in the 1990s met with government suppression and the extensive violation of human rights.[12]

Although the Sunni-Shia conflict dominates much of the public discourse, Bahraini society is fragmented in much more complex ways. Bahrainis are identified by their fellows not only as adherents to sects, and law schools in the Sunni case or *marja'iyya* in the Shiite case, but also as originating from different locations. Some Sunnis, as well as some Shiites, have roots on the Iranian Gulf side; the Sunnis claim to be Arab, while the Shiites have retained their Persian native tongue and close, often marital ties to Iran. In addition, there are also those identified as peninsular Arabs. Especially for the Sunni population, having tribal affiliations or not remains a very important identity marker.[13] Social distinctions determined by living circumstances (village, city, new neighborhoods), profession, education, and wealth are more fluid than ethnic and religious ascriptions and might play an increasingly significant role for political affiliations in the future.

Nonetheless, to reduce political opposition to sectarian conflict would be an oversimplification. In fact, the liberal elite come from both Sunni and Shiite backgrounds. As elsewhere though, liberals (who have mainly demanded the resumption of parliamentary life)[14] have steadily lost ground. The religious trend has been growing since the 1980s, partly spurred by the Islamic revolution in Iran and partly mirroring the general shift toward Islamism. In the Bahraini setting, however, Islamism inevitably carries a sectarian dimension. Hence the intifada has been increasingly understood in sectarian terms.[15]

To overcome the entangled problems of economic crisis, social strife, and political conflict, the ruling elite opted for a top-down liberalization process. The first steps of the reform process were received enthusiastically. Shortly after coming to power, Shaikh Hamad issued a general amnesty for political prisoners and invited exiled activists to return.[16] A committee was appointed to draft a "National Action Charter." This, however, was a first point of contention. Of the six prominent liberal opposition figures in the drafting committee, four withdrew; one of them, lawyer Hassan Radhi, expressed the lack of any sense of ownership of the process:

> We had assumed that a drafting committee would be constituted from among the members of the National Action Charter committee, but instead a ready-made draft had been presented. I don't know where it came from, but it was very bad. I had been present for three meetings, but then I resigned, actually four of us resigned. Obviously this made them think again, because later a better draft emerged. I believe an Egyptian did the bulk of the work, but there were also Jordanians and Tunisians involved. It's not known officially, though.[17]

Nevertheless, the National Action Charter was published and subjected to a referendum. In general terms, the document promised the resumption of constitutional rule and parliamentary life. It proposed two amendments to the original constitution of 1973: the transformation of the "State of Bahrain" into the "Kingdom of Bahrain," and the introduction of a bicameral parliament.[18] The definition of the second chamber's role remained deliberately vague. Chapter 5 of the document began by evoking the example of "deep-rooted democracies" *(ad-dimuqratiyyat al-'ariqa)* and went on to explain: "It is in the interest of the state of Bahrain to adopt a bicameral system whereby the legislature will consist of two chambers, namely one that is constituted through free and direct elections whose mandate will be to enact laws, besides a second one with people of experience and expertise who would give advice as necessary." Since this left the question open as to whether the Shura Council would advise the elected chamber or share in decisionmaking on equal footing, the document generated a good deal of controversy prior to the referendum. The government tried to dispel any fears by having the crown prince and the minister of justice and Islamic affairs (then-chairman of the National Action Charter Committee) declare in interviews that the elected chamber would be superior to the appointed one *(Al-Ayyam* February 5, 2001, February 9, 2001).[19] Perhaps reassured by these deliberations, the public overwhelmingly endorsed the National Action Charter (98.4 percent yes votes) in February 2001.[20]

When the king issued the amended constitution one year later, reactions were not as enthusiastic as they had been for the National Action Charter. The amendments provided the Shura Council with the same legislative powers as the elected chamber, which gave the king (who appoints Shura members) huge leverage over the legislative process.[21] Moreover, the amendments were drafted behind closed doors, and the promulgation of the constitution came as a surprise even to circles close to the government.[22] Not only were the different political factions not involved in debating the document (giving rise later to a debate on the "contractual constitution"), but the government then claimed that the constitution was legitimized by the referendum on the (opaque wording of the) National Action Charter.[23]

Under the new constitution, the king allowed political societies to register under the law governing civil societies,[24] although this law explicitly forbade political activity. Hence, political societies were allowed to function as de facto political parties, but they were not given legal security. Nevertheless, all political societies participated in the municipal elections of March 2002. However, the situation was different for the parliamentary elections held in October 2002. An alliance of four societies, including the large Islamist Shiite society Al-Wifaq, decided to boycott because they objected to the "amended" (in official parlance) or "new" (in theirs) constitution.[25] In summer 2005 a law was passed to govern political societies explicitly,[26] and a large number of political societies registered.[27]

Another point of contention has been the electoral law. Through gerrymandering of constituencies, Sunni and Shiite votes have been made roughly equal.[28] Resulting from the partial Shia boycott, Sunni Islamist societies played a disproportionate role in the chamber,[29] as the two Sunni Islamist societies, Al-Minbar al-Islami (Islamic Platform) and Al-'Asala ("Purity"), together secured 31 percent of the seats.

While the legitimacy of the constitution was hotly debated, other areas of the reform process were less contentious: few denied that the margins for free expression of thought, in public events and in the media, were considerably expanded. Political debates were, as a rule, conducted freely and reported in the press, especially in the Shiite daily *Al-Wasat*. This newspaper is owned and edited by one of the most prominent former exiles, Mansur al-Jamri. Previously an activist of the London-based Bahrain Freedom Movement,[30] al-Jamri was offered the position of running the country's first oppositional newspaper as part of his return package.[31]

Probably more influential than the press have been the numerous blogs and Internet forums. Many of the Shiite villages ran their own, as did most clerics. Websites like Bahrain Online, Duraz.net, and Al-Montadayat had a significant readership; they sent their reporters to political events, announced demonstrations, and often streamed seminars live.[32] The Internet magazines also illustrate a characteristic feature of the reform process: a decisive lack of legal certainty. On February 27, 2005, three moderators of Bahrain Online were arrested and accused of being responsible for other users' defamation of the government on the website pages.[33]

Demonstrations also occurred on a regular basis. Generally neither government nor security forces interfered unless they felt threatened.[34] As is the case with other civil liberties, political practice or participation was generally tolerated, but the necessary legal foundation for political activity was not provided. The lack of legal certainty was deliberate. "You have to see what we practice, not what is written in laws. Our practice is very liberal," said Shaikh Muhammed bin Atiyatallah Al Khalifa, then-head of the Central Informatics Organization and now minister of the Royal Court.[35]

Generally, civil society flourished, at least numerically. In 2005 a total of 386 civil societies, including charitable societies, excluding sports clubs, were registered with the Ministry of Social Affairs.[36] Bahrain's nongovernmental organizations (NGOs) were fragmented, however. Many NGOs were spin-offs of political organizations and drew only a narrow ethnic-sectarian sector to their activities.[37]

The liberal atmosphere, the mostly tolerant handling of civil liberties, the sheer existence of political societies,[38] and the existence of a parliament and a constitutional court all suggest a favorable environment for political participation; however, a closer look at the legal basis of the reforms and at political practice calls for a more cautious assessment. The executive remained completely outside political competition: members of the ruling family held the most important ministries, the king had an indirect final say on legislation through his control over the Shura Council, and a large number of restrictive laws were in force. Political and civil freedoms guaranteed by the constitution were limited by law and could be restricted by ill-defined references to national cohesion. Finally, the electoral law was biased against the Shiites.

◼ Venues of Participation: Clubs, *Majalis,* and *Ma'atim*

Bahrain's society offers a complex matrix of interlinking social institutions, mobilized to varying degrees for political ends. Perhaps due to Bahrain's small size and its population density,[39] institutions mediating individual interests have existed for a long time. The most important of these are clubs, *majalis* (literally "sitting rounds"), and *ma'atim* (literally "funeral houses").

Catering to the urban elites of both sects, clubs were opened in Manama earlier than in the rest of the Gulf region. Most notably, the 'Uruba Club, home to most prominent liberals, was founded in the early 1930s and still serves as an important meeting place. In addition to clubs that share only a broad orientation but no clear set agenda, a plethora of professional associations can be found, from lawyers' to engineers' societies. Some of these professional societies, especially the Bar Society, are politicized. Of those, most are leftist-liberal rather than Islamist, as is the case elsewhere in the Arab world.[40]

Often less elitist than clubs are *majalis*.[41] These are regular gatherings in private houses, usually held in reception rooms with separate entrances. In general, there are regular attendees at nearly every *majlis,* but there is a degree of openness as well. *Majalis* can be quite different in form: some are just social gatherings, while others have more fixed agendas, with set topics and guest speakers. Members of the royal family, heads of families, religious figures, intellectuals, and political activists all host *majalis.* While on a certain level the state's reform project is also about channeling political discussions into formal institutions, namely parliament ("appropriate channels"), these semiformal meetings have also been encouraged: the state has financed the addition of *majalis* to the houses of municipal councilors and deputies.[42] Most deputies entertain a fixed weekly *majlis* to which friends and members of their constituencies come and address their grievances. Most *majalis* are exclusively male, but there are also exclusively female ones, like the rather formal meetings to which the king's first wife occasionally invites women. Mixed *majalis* are rare and tend to focus on cultural and academic topics. Whenever female voters wish to discuss a problem with a deputy, they are expected either to talk to him on the phone or to speak with his wife.[43] Sectarian fragmentation is often mirrored in *majlis* attendance. There are Sunni and Shiite *majalis;* mixed meetings tend to be academic, as is the case with gender-mixed *majalis.*

Bahrain also has a dense web of Shiite *ma'atim.* Endowed by individuals, many Shiite families can pride themselves on having established one or more *ma'atim,* which vary greatly in size, exist for both sexes, and perform a variety of functions. They are places where religious festivals like the birthdays of imams are held and 'Ashura festivities are prepared.[44] Moreover, clerics lecture in both male and female *ma'atim,* on a variety of topics ranging from pious readings to political questions. *Ma'atim* are also places for social gatherings, where marital engagement parties are held or visits take place. There is a class and gender dimension to the visiting pattern: generally speaking, lower-class women seem to visit these places most frequently, probably due to a lack of acceptable alternatives.

Both Sunnis and Shiites have religious, missionary, and charitable societies that often also offer offices and conference rooms for specific lectures. Other venues for political and social interactions are the headquarters of political societies. Several of these have regular weekly or monthly lectures. Many headquarters of NGOs and trade unions are located very close to each other,[45] since the king donated a block of apartments for that purpose in 2001.[46]

▓ Multiple Governments?

To assess the ability (or lack thereof) of political groups to participate in political decisionmaking, we need to identify the loci of decisionmaking.

This is not as easy as it may seem. Bahraini conventional wisdom held that there were two governments: the more reformist king and crown prince on one side, and the anti-reformist prime minister on the other. This was a simplification of a complex reality, but there was some truth to this assessment. The ambiguity in the decisionmaking process caused by this structure created tangible obstacles to reform.

When Shaikh Hamad became the ruler of Bahrain in 1999, his uncle Shaikh Khalifa bin Salman had been prime minister for almost thirty years.[47] Since Emir Isa was not actively involved in daily politics, the prime minister was the de facto ruler. Shaikh Hamad, however, intended to reign and rule. The prime minister, accustomed to autocratic rule, was unenthusiastic about reforms. Or perhaps, as a former adviser to the prime minister's court rather cautiously explained, "It [was] not that the prime minister [was] completely against reforms as such. He just want[ed] them his way. . . . He felt so marginalized at the beginning of the project. You have to understand how people like our prime minister were raised and have lived. He [was] not used to encountering opposition."[48] Rather than risking severe strife within his family,[49] the king ordered two limited cabinet reshuffles,[50] and replaced other ministers when the opportunity arose. The appointment of a new minister of interior in May 2004 serves as an illustrative example. What began as a peaceful demonstration by a few thousand Shiites in support of the Najaf-based cleric Ali as-Sistani turned violent, provoked by riot police who fired rubber bullets and injured a number of demonstrators. Following this incident, the king dismissed the long-serving minister of interior, a fellow shaikh. The dismissal of a royal family member was unprecedented. Further complicating the situation, as the minister had been sick for some time, a son of the prime minister had been deputized for him. Thus the son was rather elegantly removed as well, causing some scandal.[51]

More profound perhaps was the king's decision to withdraw responsibilities from the prime minister and his old guard by creating new administrative bodies. The Economic Development Board—created in 2000, composed of ministers and heads of private companies and chaired by the crown prince—increasingly appropriated decisionmaking functions formerly endowed to the cabinet. The board was responsible for an ambitious program to restructure the country's economy, involving drafting legislation.[52] The crown prince also commissioned the McKinsey consultants to design the reforms, thus further reducing the old guard's influence.[53] Similarly, the crown prince chaired a housing committee,[54] the king disbanded the oil ministry (headed by the prime minister's son), and replaced it with an energy commission in September 2005 (*Gulf News* September 28, 2005).[55] This outsourcing of governmental functions—a process experienced in Morocco as well (see Chapter 11 in this volume)—weakened the little accountability the decisionmaking processes possessed.

The lack of clarity regarding the functions and prerogatives of "royal executives" added to this opacity: king, crown prince, and prime minister all maintained their own courts, each staffed with its own consultants in diverse policy fields. As a disgruntled consultant at the Royal Court put it, coordination was absent. He complained, "It is chaotic, all these parallel advisors. . . . The crown prince has bypassed us Bahraini experts, he has only commissioned foreigners who do not understand a thing."[56]

Not surprising for an authoritarian regime, it was unclear to most political actors (apart from the innermost circles) who had the right and power to decide. As a deputy put it:

> Me, for example, I have a very good contact with the crown prince. He does have an open door, really. You can talk to him like to a normal person, like we are talking. He even takes notes. You cannot talk to the prime minister or to the king. There, you only listen. The prime minister, when he meets us deputies—he has to, sometimes—you can feel he despises us, doesn't even want to shake hands. Let alone listen. But who will decide? I want to believe it is the crown prince but what do I know?[57]

■ Parliamentarians, Boycotters, and Protesters

Bahraini actors used three notable strategies to influence political decision-making. The three examples are not comprehensive, but they illustrate a range of tools used by Bahraini political participants, defined in distinction to decisionmakers (see Chapter 2). The first example shows how parliamentarians and boycotters were caught at an impasse, which they managed to escape only by external intervention. I argue that this conflict strengthened the executive. The use of mass mobilization and informal *majlis* politics by the opposition outside parliament is demonstrated in the second example, and the ambivalent outcome of this tactic is depicted. The more radical opposition, described in the third example, used sectarian agitation in order to win supporters from their competitors. This oppositional infighting also strengthened the government.

Parliamentarians and Extra-Parliamentary Opposition in Deadlock

Political societies had operated under the law governing other NGOs until August 2005—a situation that all political actors agreed required correction. This lack of political legal certainty affected the work of societies within parliament (the two Sunni Islamist societies, Islamic Platform and "Purity"; and the third society in parliament, the leftist Al-Minbar at-Taqaddumi (the progressive platform), as well as those outside (the four boycotters). However, Bahraini political societies found it difficult to establish common ground even amid such common interest. As the boycotters did not recognize parliament's legitimacy, they thus believed that even to lobby deputies would be inconsistent with their boycott. The political left was particularly fragmented for such reasons. The lack of cooperation and dialogue also pertained to the members of the Shura Council, even though most of its appointees were liberal secularists,[58] which could have made them strategic allies regarding "liberal" legislation.

Given these divisions, bargaining between boycotters and participants was hard to achieve, and consensus-making across the institutional barrier of parliament was blocked. The only exit from this impasse was the intervention of a mediator. Contrary to the practice of other Middle Eastern monarchs to act as arbitrators between conflicting political groups (see Chapter 11), this is not an option for King Hamad, as the Bahraini ruling family is not seen as a party above conflicts but as ally to the "Sunni side." Hence an external mediator was needed. The US National Democratic Institute (NDI) routinely brought conflicting parties to a joint table.[59] In the case of the law governing political societies, the NDI's representative, Fawzi Juleid, initiated meetings to discuss the new bill immediately after the government's bill was leaked in autumn 2003. But until late 2004 the societies were still caught up in their mutual refusal to dialogue.[60] Only when it became clear that the new law could outlaw the boycotters (since it forces political societies to acknowledge the constitution) were their representatives willing to join deputies in an NDI-organized workshop.[61] Another contentious point in the government's bill was a ban on financial or organizational foreign assistance, combined with the lack of state financing for political societies, a demand raised mainly by leftist societies (whose membership is smaller than the Islamists').[62]

It was particularly problematic for Islamist groups that a US institute played the role of external mediator. Shiite Islamists had to maneuver quite a bit to make their views on US involvement consistent: they welcomed the forced removal of Saddam Hussein, but rejected the US presence in Iraq. They wanted reforms from within Bahrain to be consistent with Islamic values, while at the same time believing in the necessity of US pressure on their government.[63] Political activists therefore did not always volunteer information on the "outside" involvement. The president of Al-Wifaq, (religious) Shaikh Ali Salman, recounted: "We came all together united in that problem, us four boycotters and five other societies. We agreed on a common proposal. We've sent the proposal to the king, the others to parliament [because, of course, the boycotters cannot recognize this parliament]. Some compromise will be achieved, I think."[64]

The parties agreed on some points: external funding for training should be allowed, a minimum age of eighteen should be set for membership, and state funding for all societies should be guaranteed. These features were actually similar to a proposal that the leftist deputies of the "Democratic

Bloc" had initiated in late December 2003.[65] An interview with Abdunnabi Salman of the bloc uncovered the following: "We are few liberals in parliament and we have to deal with all the [Sunni] Islamists. . . . The problem is that Al-Minbar at-Taqaddumi [Salman's political society] is the only real party in parliament. The others are new and their existence is big on paper only. Those have less interest in a law on political parties than us."[66] There is some truth to this assessment. Only 39 percent of deputies were actually members of a political society.[67]

Islamist societies in general—including Sunni ones—developed out of wider movements organized in charitable funds and societies.[68] Thus they did not have as much difficulty obtaining financing as do the leftist and liberal societies. Moreover, Sunni Islamists feared Iranian financing of their Shiite counterparts, leading Sunni Islamists to remain loyal to the government on all general questions. This overrode their common interest with other political societies. (Religious) Shaikh Adil al-Mu'awda, a religious man and then-head of the Salafi society Al-'Asala, illustrated this: "Quite honestly, I have not even read the law on political societies yet. I am convinced that whoever works honestly and in the open has nothing to fear. Moreover, we have to go very gradually towards more participation, which we'll get eventually. Besides, our people are interested in housing and in the money they find in their pockets."[69]

Other members of the legislature also did not support the proposal. No one had tried to convince the 61 percent of deputies who were not organized in any political society to support their initiative. Nor had the Shura members been addressed. It is therefore not surprising that the government's bill passed without any amendments shortly before the summer break in 2005.[70]

Events surrounding the development of the law on political societies reveal a basic dilemma in which Bahraini politics were caught: the avenues for meaningful participation in the legislative process were unavailable to a substantial portion of political actors. The situation constituted a vicious cycle. The opposition outside parliament did not recognize this institution. Hence, as a matter of principle, boycotters did not talk to its representatives except in the final hour, and even then, they did not talk to all parliamentarians. Parliamentarians, on the other hand, saw no reason for cooperation with groups that otherwise ignored them. This feeling was exacerbated by the basic distrust between the Sunni Islamists in parliament and the Shiite groups outside it. If forced to decide, the Sunnis have proven to have more common interests with the government than with their Shiite counterparts.[71] No group—neither the liberal and leftist deputies, nor the opposition outside parliament—tried to win over the Shura Council, which, after all, could veto any legislation. This dynamic gave the government an upper hand, which in turn reinforced the opposition's conviction that parliament was useless.

The Extra-Parliamentary Opposition's Campaign for Constitutional Changes

Bahraini actors also attempted to influence fundamental political decision-making through social institutions like *majalis* and mass mobilization. This strategy was particularly prevalent among the coalition of election boycotters, which was formed during the years 2002–2006 by four partners: Al-Wifaq, Al-'Amal al-Islami, Al-'Amal al-Watani ad-Dimuqrati (al-Wa'ad), and Al-Tagammu' al-Qawmi. The first two societies, the Shiite Islamist Al-Wifaq and the Islamist Al-'Amal al-Islami, differed more in their constituency than in their programs. The former had thousands of members, while the latter was a smaller organization of *shiraziyun,* followers of the *marja'* Muhammad ash-Shirazi, a Shiite jurisconsult considered by his followers to be a model of religious emulation.[72] The other two societies were leftists. Al-'Amal had popular exiles and intellectuals among its ranks,[73] and managed to influence public discourse significantly, while Al-Tagammu' was a much less influential, formerly Baathi organization.

The point around which these four societies coalesced was their rejection of the constitutional amendments of 2002.[74] They rejected the content of the amendments (above all the legislative powers of the Shura Council) as well as their mechanism (royal promulgation without consultation). In their opinion, no meaningful progress could be achieved without first correcting the constitution of 2002. The boycotters demanded a "contractual constitution" *(dustur 'aqdi),* agreed upon by the ruler and the ruled.[75] In 2004, activist Aziz Obol, one of the intellectual heads of the opposition, explained: "It is a question of credibility for us—we cannot legitimize this constitution. . . . The Americans always try to convince us to go slowly and gradually. Going gradually is fine with us but the path has to be the right one. There has to be a real constitutional monarchy at the end of the way."[76]

This "fundamental" approach also implied that the boycotters could not distinguish between the different power circles within the government. Jalila as-Sayyid, an activist lawyer, explained: "To me talk of the anti-reform prime minister and the pro-reform camp around king and crown prince is meaningless. They are much two sides of the same coin."[77]

While the ideological side to the boycott was clear, there was a pragmatic side to it as well: considering Bahrain's majority voting system,[78] it was highly unlikely that the three small societies could win more than one or two seats, although this was certainly not the case for Al-Wifaq.[79] The boycott also stabilized the societies' internal hierarchies; it made it harder for new politicians to achieve a profile and allowed societies to postpone a lot of tactical decisions. Both Islamist and secularist societies were comfortable with this. The leftists still struggled with their communist exile and underground identity, and Al-Wifaq hardly managed to integrate its returned exiles with the former intifada activists.

The coalition's strategic options were limited. They could not directly influence legislation, since discussions with members of parliament were easily interpreted as betrayal of the boycott's ideals. However, Al-Wifaq, in particular, had other means to exert pressure on the executive. A mass integration party,[80] the society has developed from a wider social movement demanding equality and justice for Bahrain's Shiite population.[81] It has a massive support base and is composed of former intifada activists, returned exiles, and a number of clerics. Typical for this type of party, Al-Wifaq features a plethora of auxiliary organizations (women, youth, human rights, etc.) and local branches. Through its cleric-activists, it has an "automatic" connection to the *ma'atim* and mosques.

The boycotters' campaign had three distinct (if overlapping) phases. At first the boycotters tried to influence public discourse from conference tables. Dominated by the intellectuals of Al-'Amal al-Watani,[82] the campaign started in February 2004 with a conference titled "Toward a Contractual Constitution."[83] The government reacted sharply against the meeting, discouraging the hotel where conference rooms had been booked from hosting the event and barring foreign guests from entering Bahrain. Nevertheless, the conference fostered the coalition's cohesion, but it clearly did not achieve dialogue with the government on the constitutional question. Later the strategy built on Al-Wifaq's assets as it moved toward a combination of show of force on the streets and behind-the-doors dialogue with the government. The third phase was dominated by mass mobilization and the use of *majalis*.

The boycotters' standard assertion was, "Pressure is needed from within and from outside."[84] Relying on a "traditional" way of addressing Gulf rulers,[85] they wrote a petition to the king asking for constitutional changes and hoped thus to express their discontent to both the government and the outside world. The petitioners confidently expected a minimum of 50,000 signatures, because gaining support with religious backing and infrastructure had proven to be easy in the past.[86] The petition was launched on 'Ashura, "since that day, the whole world is on its feet. . . . The leftist parties will get Sunni signatures, but generally the Shiite population is more active."[87] In April and May 2004, events escalated as Al-Wifaq managed to efficiently collect the signatures. Young activists had been deployed in every village, while others were touring the *ma'atim*.

The king would have had a difficult time responding to the petition, since following the rationale of the reform process, he could only change the constitution through the new institutional channels—that is, through a two-thirds majority in both parliamentary chambers. Reacting to a petition would thus only invalidate his reforms. Instead, a legal squabble between the government and the campaigners ensued: the government declared that petitions would only be accepted if submitted by a legal body, not a coalition of legal bodies that was itself not registered.[88] Al-Wifaq then proposed to couple a signature to the petition with membership to the political society, which allowed its membership to grow to 70,000.[89] The government was becoming increasingly nervous, and on April 30, 2004, arrested seventeen signature collectors[90] in order to prevent the potential embarrassment of the petitioners collecting more signatures than there were voters in the elections (Amnesty International 2005; *Gulf Daily News* May 1, 2004, May 3, 2004; *Bahrain Tribune* May 1, 2004).[91]

An impasse resulted, and once again an outside mediator needed to intervene. The editor of *Al-Wasat,* Mansur al-Jamri, invited nine contending political societies to his private home to discuss the constitution.[92] The "publicly private" nature of the gathering facilitated its attendance. As a discussant from the boycotters' side recalled: "We met on four Thursday evenings at Mansur's house. After discussing the problem we moved to solutions and agreed to write a letter to the king asking for the release of the activists and the initiation of a national dialogue on the constitutional question. But the king was quicker than us and had ordered their release before our letter reached him."[93]

Later the king met with the heads of those nine political societies in a formal audience, not to discuss the constitution, but as a symbol of openness to dialogue. To offer a face-saving excuse for the boycotters to stop their petition drive, a "dialogue on constitutional questions" was initiated between the minister of labor,[94] as government representative, and the boycotters.[95] Clearly, constitutional questions do not fall in this minister's portfolio. Indeed, it would be surprising for the king to have been interested in including these groups, which were responsible for delegitimizing his reform project, in decisionmaking. Rather, he was interested in de-escalation. Abdunnabi al-'Ikri, a participant of the meeting, said, "Obviously, our aims were very divergent. They want us to participate; we want to change the constitution."[96] The dialogue's inherent futility influenced a shift in the internal balance of the opposition coalition. Up to that point the boycotters had relied on constitutional experts, which secured the leftist societies' influence. However, as the coalition had to modify its strategy, opting for mass demonstrations for constitutional changes, quite naturally Al-Wifaq took control of the operation.

It is impossible to establish any causal relationships, but clearly the mass demonstrations in Ukraine and Lebanon in February and March 2005 had a strong impact on Bahraini activists. Following the Lebanese example, banners and stickers in national colors were created. Before, Shiites often carried Iranian or Hezbollah flags, which infuriated the government and also alienated many Sunnis.[97] But the demonstrations for constitutional reform received a branding: every participant was given stickers in Bahraini red and white that read: "Constitutional reform first." This statement sparked a reaction among Sunnis, who marked every other lamppost with "Bahrain first" stickers.

Two massive rallies were held, one on Sitra Island, a traditional stronghold of Al-Wifaq, and another in front of a main shopping mall, Dana Mall.[98] Estimates of the number of participants varied greatly. For the Sitra rally, organizers estimated 120,000, while the pro-governmental newspaper *Al-Ayyam* estimated between 5,000 and 7,000 (clearly an underestimate).[99] The coalition of boycotters had abandoned dialogue with the government. The dangers of this strategy were quite obvious to those who adopted it. The mobilization of youth in rallies was hard to sustain without risking an escalation to violence. Another constant concern was the sectarian nature of protest. Shiite youth dominated the street rallies, while only few Sunni intellectuals and activists participated. In fact, mass demonstrations rallied the economic elite and the Sunni population around the government. To counter that, the head of Al-Wifaq, Shaikh Ali Salman, and others made use of the *majlis* structure of Bahraini society and embarked on a tour through the "Sunni *majalis* of Muharraq."[100] Salman expounded: "The basic sectarian division of our society is there and we have to take it into account although none of us likes sectarianism. But we always have to put Bahrain first, then other loyalties. We have to get our Sunni brothers to participate. In the end, we are citizens, not Shiites."[101] While this *majlis* tour was well received, it did not add more Sunni supporters to the campaign. Pressure on the government did not increase.

At the same time, Al-Wifaq, as the potential winner of elections, started to bring other issues back into its discourse, slowly. As Shaikh Ali Salman explained in his opening speech at Al-Wifaq's 2005 General Assembly:

> There's no movement in the constitutional question. . . . We have many different opinions with our brothers in the constitutional alliance in many other topics, but we stand firmly together in the constitutional question . . . which is the key to all other questions. . . . But we need a strategy for all the other problems: one, illegal nationalizations; two, unemployment; three, discrimination; four, corruption; five, housing; six, bills in parliament like the law on political societies and the antiterror law.[102]

With Al-Wifaq indicating potential readiness to join the next elections, deliberations for some possible compromise on the Shura Council started to develop behind the scenes. As described previously, parliamentarians addressed Shaikh Isa Qassim informally with suggestions for a possible compromise. It was leaked through some *majalis* that the Royal Court had elaborated different potential forms of compromise on the Shura Council, proving some receptiveness to the massive popular protest without giving the impression of being coerced "by the street."[103] Discussions involved a change of the procedure of appointment to the Shura Council.[104] Al-Wifaq itself was not compromised by such talk with "illegal" parliamentarians, since it involved only Isa Qassim, who was not a member.

In early summer 2006, Al-Wifaq announced its intention to participate in the next elections. The three smaller societies subsequently followed suit: they could not sustain the boycott without their biggest partner, but the lengthy discussions in their boards and general assemblies attested to the uneasiness of reconsidering their position.

Trying to wield influence outside state institutions produced ambivalent results. For the coalition of the boycotters' biggest partner, Al-Wifaq, it was quite successful; by showing its massive following in the petition and in the demonstrations, it became a major player with which the government had to seek compromise. Moreover, Al-Wifaq could retain its grassroots activism even with deputies in the chamber. While during its boycott Al-Wifaq missed opportunities to influence legislation (like the law on political societies), these losses were offset by the potential gains it made through the boycott. Al-Wifaq proved to be a real opposition, impossible for the government to ignore. It renewed its organizational capabilities in the villages (e.g., through petition activists) and developed an intellectual profile through its alliance with leftist intellectuals and the debate on a contractual constitution. The organization's president, Shaikh Ali Salman, managed to gain more trust from Sunni circles through his *majlis* tour and his constitutional, rather than Islamist, discourse.

The results for the three other parties of the coalition were rather different, and indeed they were not to enjoy success in the elections in 2006. Even then, it was clear that winning any seats without an electoral alliance from Al-Wifaq would be extremely hard, making them very dependent on their larger partner's self-restraint. Even in August 2006, it seemed unlikely that Al-Wifaq would support more than one or two leftist candidates.[105] Other than Al-Wifaq, which had demands apart from the constitutional question, the smaller societies had not built up a profile of their own. Considering their small numbers, they will not be able to pursue agenda-setting regarding constitutional reform outside the parliament, either.

Redressing the Past Through Public Seminars? An NGO as Radical Opposition

Other groups had fewer strategies that they could employ to demand reform. The most radical, although not militant, Bahraini opposition group, the Bahrain Center for Human Rights (BCHR), put questions of social justice at the forefront of its agenda: discrimination, poverty, and the redress of past state violations against parts of the Shiite majority population. Consistent with this rationale, it organized as an NGO with political goals, led by Abdulhadi al-Khawaja.[106] Al-Khawaja is a follower of the *marja'* Muhammad ash-Shirazi, and hence belongs to a small minority of Bahraini

Shiites. Since sectarian identity plays a prominent role in Bahrain, this poses an obstacle to gaining political support.[107]

The BCHR thus aimed to attract the more radical (or less patient) fringes of the Shiite movement, which was an obvious choice. It was not possible, though, to draw a clear-cut line between Al-Wifaq supporters and those of the BCHR: both have the same roots.[108] The BCHR's more confrontational approach was more attractive to the youth than to elders. The BCHR and its allies[109] addressed two main audiences and hence employed two different rhetoric strategies: a pro-democracy vocabulary directed mainly to US and UK audiences,[110] and a language of sectarianism addressed to the Bahraini audience.

The BCHR's radicalization strategy crystallized when Abdulhadi al-Khawaja gave a speech at a seminar on poverty designed to launch a report highlighting the concentration of poverty within the Shiite community. In this speech, he called for the resignation of the prime minister.[111] More importantly, the authorities construed his remark as inciting hatred. The activist had overstepped the boundaries of permissible critique, apparently attempting to provoke a strong government reaction.[112] The next day he was arrested and the BCHR was legally dissolved.[113]

The preceding day the crown prince had launched a similar report, also highlighting poverty and unemployment. This implicitly voiced an extremely harsh critique against the government of his great-uncle,[114] and marked a spectacular departure from the previous dominant practice of family solidarity. Al-Khawaja's direct attack on the prime minister the following day, however, played immediately into the prime minister's hands. On the evening of al-Khawaja's arrest, the king and the crown prince had to rush to see the prime minister at his court. During subsequent weeks the prime minister used all opportunities to show the strength of his supporters. Companies, Sunni city quarters, and tribes published huge declarations of solidarity in newspapers. Banners praising the prime minister were displayed all over the country, except in the Shiite villages. Delegations visited his *majlis* daily and received publicity in all newspapers but *Al-Wasat.* As one observer summarized: "His solidarity machine works like in the old days. His office calls you and says, 'We want a sign from you and your brothers, from you and your tribe, you and your company.' And the crown prince is marginalized for the next months."[115]

During the two months that al-Khawaja remained in custody, his supporters held regular protests and managed to elicit several press releases from Human Rights Watch and Amnesty International.[116] The court sentenced al-Khawaja to one year in prison on October 21, 2004. Later the same day, the king pardoned him. The BCHR has remained unlicensed but active nonetheless.

Although the BCHR's strategy actually strengthened that part of government most resistant to reform, it did not modify its position. Rather, al-Khawaja founded a subsidiary to the BCHR, the Unemployment Committee, which started on a similar confrontational trajectory. The committee mobilized a series of demonstrations (with probably a hundred participants) down Manama's main street at rush hour. Angry Bahrainis were quick to label them "bread and mobile demonstrations," after the utensils the unemployed carried, but the demonstrations did not produce any police reaction.

The group escalated its tactics. It changed venues and started to demonstrate in front of the Royal Court on June 19, 2005, and later threw rotten eggs at parliament on July 17, 2005. In both incidents, riot police severely beat protesters. However unjustified the excessive police violence, clearly the protesters were seeking confrontation, since both the Royal Court and parliament are implicitly off-limits for demonstrations.

The BCHR, meanwhile, remained active. To counter Al-Wifaq's constitutional rallies, it concentrated on the question of past human rights violations and the government's unwillingness to tackle them. The BCHR invited the public to a seminar *(nadwa jamahiriyya)* in a Shiite village.[117] The topic of discussion was a meeting that had been held in Geneva between the Bahraini government and the UN commission concerned with the Covenant Against Torture.[118] The seminar drew an audience of 2,000–3,000 Bahrainis.[119]

In stark contrast to Al-Wifaq's constant effort to appear nonsectarian, the BCHR pursued the opposite strategy. Their rhetoric directed at international NGOs was consistent with the vocabulary of "Western" democracy promotion, but the symbolism the BCHR used inside Bahrain was overtly Shiite. Even the water dispensers at the seminar's venue were decorated with swords from which Hussayn's blood dripped.[120] Moreover, while the seminar discussed redress of past state torture, its focus was political. This was amply demonstrated by a live phone call to Sa'id Shihabi, the only person still in London with the Bahrain Freedom Movement, who read an anti–ruling family pamphlet.[121]

The strategy of the BCHR and its subsidiaries did not focus on influencing the government's decisionmaking process. The BCHR did not enter into discussions with either government or parliamentarians on concrete demands (e.g., possible compensation to torture victims or official acknowledgment of past state violations). Rather, it voiced demands that attracted the more radical supporters of Al-Wifaq. One such demand was to have seventy intifada victims proclaimed "national martyrs," which the government found unacceptable. When addressing the unemployment issue, the activists' influence was detrimental to the cause, as they strengthened the anti-reform camp within government, probably because the primary aim was to seek Al-Wifaq supporters rather than influence political decisionmaking.[122] The BCHR's main aim seemed to be an attempt to carve out a share of votes from the Al-Wifaq–dominated Shiite population with Islamist leaning.

■ Conclusion

Bahrain, a reforming but still authoritarian state, has created structures that allow for limited formal participation. The deputies in the elected chamber can participate in legislation and supervise government actions, but the appointed Shura Council can veto any legislation. During the 2002–2006 legislative period, elected deputies' powers were hampered by two other factors as well: an unwillingness by the deputies to bargain with the members of the Shura Council, which, after all, did not act as a monolithic actor; and the unbalanced set-up of the chamber itself, which was partly due to the election boycott in 2002 by four political societies. Given this boycott, Shiite communities were not represented adequately in the chamber. Moreover, the majority of deputies of Shiite background were not organized in political societies, while their Sunni counterparts—who had more common interests with the government than they had with the Shiite political activists—were.

The Shiites largely opted to stay outside the institutions and therefore could not influence any concrete legislation. However, they could participate in agenda-setting. The coalition of election boycotters, consisting of two Shiite Islamist and two leftist societies, did this efficiently with regard to the "constitutional question." The more the coalition incorporated mass demonstrations and *majlis* dialogue into their strategy, the more influential their agenda-setting efforts became. The regime has shown some receptiveness toward street agitation. Still, if the strategy of exerting pressure on the government by means of massive demonstrations has proven to be beneficial for the biggest party of the coalition, it was less so for its small leftist partners, who found themselves marginalized after the elections of 2006.

Finally, the strategies of the most radical opposition appear to have been directed toward the government, but might in fact have aimed at quite a different end. These groups tried to attract supporters from their political competitors. By seeking confrontation with the government, they succeeded, particularly with disenfranchised youth. This oppositional infighting strengthened the anti-reform camp within the government but otherwise failed to influence decisionmaking. Moreover, escalation strategies aggravated the very sectarian conflicts that obstructed meaningful political participation in Bahrain in the first place.

To genuinely broaden the scope of political participation, political actors of all kinds involved in Bahraini politics would have to change their behavior. Not only should the government provide a better framework for political progress, particularly by strengthening the rule of law but also, in order to achieve concrete policy outcomes, political activists should seriously strive to overcome their fragmentation and try to put less stress on principled and legalistic viewpoints that inhibit dialogue. However, the government has reverted to previously used autocratic policies rather than pursuing the reforms any further. Therefore, such desirable changes seem less than likely.

▨ Notes

An extended version of this chapter was originally presented at the workshop "Political Participation Under Authoritarianism in the MENA" at the Seventh Mediterranean Meeting, March 22–24, 2006, and was published as a Robert Schuman Centre for Advanced Studies working paper (Florence). I thank the participants for their valuable comments, most of all the workshop directors, Ellen Lust-Okar and Saloua Zerhouni, and my discussant Samer Shehata. I also thank my colleagues Guido Steinberg and Isabelle Werenfels at the Stiftung Wissenschaft und Politik, Berlin, and Nadja-Christina Schneider at the Center for Modern Oriental Studies, Berlin, for comments on an earlier draft. The research that this chapter builds on has been financed mostly by the Thyssen Foundation.

1. The election boycotters' coalition consisted of: Al-Wifaq (Shiite Islamist), Al-'Amal al-Islami (Shiite Islamist), Al-'Amal al-Watani ad-Dimuqrati / Al-Wa'ad (liberal-leftist), and At-Tagammu' al-Qawmi (former Baathi).

2. Personal interviews with Fawzi Juleid, National Democratic Institute representative, May 15, 2005; Shaikh Adel al-Mu'awda, vice president of the Council of Deputies, May 17, 2005; Abdurrahman Jamsheer, vice president of the Shura Council, May 17, 2005; and Aziz Obol, opposition activist, April 27, 2005.

3. The deputy was Abdulhadi Marhoon, a liberal Shiite.

4. Political groups are called "political societies" in Bahrain. They function like "parties" in every respect.

5. I interviewed seventy-six political actors (some repeatedly), from all sides involved (parliamentarians of both chambers, representatives of political societies, government functionaries, royal family members, representatives of nongovernmental organizations, clerics, journalists, and intellectuals), attended innumerable political discussions (ranging from formal conferences at hotels to more informal *majlis* meetings and private parties), and participated in demonstrations. Written materials collected range from pamphlets to draft legislation. The fieldwork was conducted in February–March 2004, September–October 2004, and April–June 2005.

6. For a discussion of this rather wide definition of political participation, see Chapter 3 in this volume.

7. This chapter was written in January 2006 and August 2006. Its does not include changes that occurred in the elections in November 2006. Note that the four societies that boycotted the elections in 2002 have since participated. However, only Al-Wifaq has been successful, securing nineteen (of forty) parliamentary seats.

8. At least one integral qualification is missing: the Bahraini executive is not elected. Thus, Bahrain does not constitute a democracy, regardless of how one defines "democracies with adjectives." On the vast body of literature that has been produced on this subject, see especially Collier and Levitsky 1997; O'Donnell 1993; Carothers 2004; Brumberg 2002; Ottaway 2003. For the German debate particularly, see Mackow 2000; Merkel and Croissant 2000.

9. Political participation should not be measured against an ideal democracy; this would only result in a "minus list" but fail to explain the citizens' agency within the system; see Chapter 1.

10. The only comprehensive academic "Western" study on that subject is, to the best of my knowledge, the PhD dissertation Meinel 2002. Different exile groups have published various booklets.

11. See, for example, as-Sayyid 2003; al-Khawaja 2003. These publications are written by activists, but nonetheless seem trustworthy regarding the basic facts.

12. The extent and gravity of governmental human rights violations are disputable. The undersecretary of justice, Shaikh Khalid bin Ali Al-Khalifa, acknowledged in a personal interview (May 22, 2005) that grave human rights violations took place in the 1990s. However, in his opinion, out of the seventy martyrs claimed by the opposition, only ten could be substantiated as legal court cases. For the opposition's view, see Human Rights Watch 1997; Parliamentary Human Rights Group–London 1996.

13. The matrix of ethnic and sectarian affiliations is most comprehensively described in Khuri 1980: 141.

14. As expressed in the "Petition of the Elite" of 1992. Personal interview with Munira Fakhru, coauthor of the petition, May 10, 2005.

15. Personal interviews with Munira Fakhru, May 10, 2005; Shaikh Ali Salman, of Al-Wifaq, May 9, 2005; and Baqir an-Najjar, sociologist, May 6, 2005.

16. Legislative Decree no. 10 (2001), concerning general amnesty for crimes affecting national security, and Legislative Decree no. 56 (2002), concerning interpreting of certain provisions of Legislative Decree no. 10. Copies of both can be found on numerous websites (e.g., http://www.mahmood.tv). These decrees are criticized by opposition groups for effectively granting impunity to state officials involved in human rights violations.

17. Personal interview with Hassan Radhi, lawyer, September 27, 2004.

18. The 1973 parliament was unicameral: thirty deputies were elected, the ministers were ex-officio members. Hence, ministers made up roughly one-third of the assembly's members. In 1992, then-emir Shaikh Isa introduced the appointed consultative Shura Council to counter public discontent.

19. The interviews were published in all local media.

20. See http://www.pogar.org.

21. According to the constitution, proposals may be written by members of both chambers. The government can initiate bills. For a bill to become law, both chambers have to adopt it. If both chambers fail twice to reach the same decision, they hold a joint meeting chaired by the chairperson of the Shura Council, who casts the deciding vote in case of stalemate. See Article 85 of the constitution.

22. Personal interviews with Shura Council members Jamal Fakhru, April 22, 2005; Faisal Fulad, April 26, 2005; and Aburrahman Jamsheer, also secretary-general of the National Action Charter Committee, May 17, 2005.

23. Among many other sources, see al-Khalifa 2005. A rather absurd exegesis (absurd to the outside observer) started where all sides legitimized their respective views in the wording of the National Action Charter.

24. Law no. 21 (1979), concerning social and cultural societies, clubs, special committees working on youth and sports issues, and private foundations.

25. The other three boycotting societies are Al-'Amal al-Islami, Al-'Amal al-Watani ad-Dimuqrati (al-Wa'ad), and Al-Tagammu' al-Qawmi at-Taqaddumi. The boycotting alliance therefore consists of two Islamist societies and two leftist societies. The Wifaq outnumbers the other three by far. See Figure 4.2. Voter turnout was 53 percent. See also http://www.pogar.org.

164   Beyond Electoral Politics

26. See Figure 4.1. The law governing political societies was published in the official gazette on August 3, 2005.

27. There was a total of twenty-four political societies (Summer 2005), not all of them active. The ones actually functioning were Al-Wifaq al-Islami (the major Shiite Islamist society), Al-'Amal al-Islami (Shiite Islamist, *shirazi*), Al-Amal al-Watani ad-Dimuqrati (changed its name to Al-Wa'ad in 2005, leftist-liberal), At Tagammu' al-Qawmi at-Taqaddumi (Baathist), Al-Minbar at-Taqaddumi (leftist-liberal), the Mithaq al-'Amal al-Watani (liberal, pro-government), Al-'Asala (Sunni-Salafi), and Al-Minbar al-Islami (Sunni Muslim). Two more societies are somewhat undecided as to whether to be social or political: Al-Muntada (liberal) and Al-Ikhwa (Persian Shiites).

28. Bahrain is divided into forty constituencies, each of which sends one representative to the Majlis an-Nuwwab. Candidates must win a majority in the first round or a relative majority in the runoff. For details on the voting process, a critique, and statistics, see Bahrain Transparency Society 2002.

29. The elected chamber of 2002–2006 was constituted as follows: the Islamic Bloc (Shiite), 20 percent; the Independents (Sunni conservative), 19 percent; Al-Minbar al-Islami / Islamic Platform (Sunni), 18 percent; Al-'Asala / (Islamic) Purity Society (Sunni Salafi), 13 percent; the Democrats (liberal-left), 8 percent; individuals, 22 percent.

30. Two other heads behind the Bahrain Freedom Movement have come back: (religious) Shaikh Ali Salman is now the head of Al-Wifaq; Majid al-Allawi has become minister of labor. Only Sa'id Shihabi stayed in London; he still runs the website of the movement (www.vob.org), more or less on his own.

31. Television and radio is state-owned and very much pro-government.

32. The most frequented ones are http://www.bahrainonline.org and http://www.montadayat.org/index.php.

33. This is congruent with the Bahraini press law, which does not specifically deal with the Internet. After a series of demonstrations, the three were released. For a detailed account see http://chanad.tk ("Free Ali").

34. Clashes between demonstrators and the police have increased since 2005, following the quiet of the period between 1999 and 2003.

35. Personal interview with Shaikh Muhammed bin Atiyatallah Al Khalifa, then-head of the Central Informatics Organization, February 25, 2004.

36. Personal interview with Fatima al-Balushi, minister of social affairs, May 7, 2005.

37. Generally, the more elitist the NGO, the less narrowly defined its constituency in sectarian terms.

38. In the Gulf Cooperation Council, protoparties can only be found in Kuwait, which has the region's longest parliamentary tradition.

39. Size: 665 square kilometers; population: 688,345. Note that this population includes 235,108 nonnationals (estimated in July 2005). See Central Intelligence Agency 2006.

40. Personal interviews with Baqir an-Najjar, May 6, 2005; Isa Ibrahim, lawyer, February 26, 2004; and Muhammad Ahmad, lawyer, May 21, 2005.

41. The word *majlis,* meaning "sitting round," can refer to the room, to the assembly, and to the institution as such.

42. Personal interviews with councilors and parliamentarians, such as Jawwad Fairouz, September 17, 2004; and Abdulaziz al-Musa, May 10, 2005.

43. Personal interviews with then–elected members of parliament Abdunnabi Salman, also member of the Islamic Platform, September 28, 2004; Jassim Abdul'al, October 2, 2004; and Farid Ghazi, February 17, 2004, among others.

44. 'Ashura is the Shiite holiday commemorating the martyrdom of the Prophet's grandson Hussain.

45. Among the Gulf states, Bahrain has the longest tradition of leftist mobilization, due to its being the first state to discover oil, in 1932. Trade unions worked underground until legalized in the framework of the reform project. Personal interview with Abdallah Hussein, General Federation of Bahrain Trade Unions, September 16, 2004.

46. Personal interviews with several NGO representatives, including Abdulla ad-Durazi, Bahrain Human Rights Society, February 25, 2004, September 16, 2004; Jassim al-Ajmi, Bahrain Transparency, May 1, 2005; and Abdulhadi al-Khawaja, Bahrain Center for Human Rights, February 21, 2004.

47. In fact, he has been Bahrain's only prime minister, taking his post immediately after independence in 1971.

48. Personal interview, anonymous, February 23, 2004.

49. The family is not homogeneous in its political outlook. As Shaikh Khalid bin Khalifa Al-Khalifa, put it, "We, the Royal Family, are no bloc: We have Salafis, one is in Guantanamo, do you know; we have liberals, I guess I'm counted among those; we have conservatives and people not interested in politics. We have old guard, new guard, all." Personal interview with Al-Khalifa, May 23, 2005.

50. The last comprehensive reshuffle was announced in January 2005. It added a second female minister, Fatima al-Balushi (social affairs) to the Ministry of Health. For the first time, a Persian-speaking Shiite, Abdulhussain Mirza, was made a minister, of the prime minister's court.

51. Among others, see lively online discussions of the event at http://bahrainiblog.blogspot.com and http://chanad.tk (English); and http://www.montadayat.org/index.php and http://www.bahrainonline.org (Arabic).

52. Key areas are labor-market reform, educational reform, and land reform. Personal interviews with Zakariya Hijris, deputy chief executive of the Economic Development Board, and desk officers Khalid Janahi and Maysoon Sabkar, June 1, 2005. See also http://www.bahrainedb.com.

53. The land reform aims at controlling the widespread corruption by designating legally binding development plans for industrial and housing areas.

54. The provision of housing is an important policy field for a Gulf welfare state; lack of housing is immediately connected to lack of legitimacy.

55. Moreover, the head of the energy commission will be part of the Economic Development Board, hence working under the crown prince.

56. Personal interview, anonymous consultant at the Royal Court, May 18, 2005. Adviser and consultant positions are often offered as rewards for past services and do not entail real functions.

57. Personal conversation, anonymous Shiite deputy, September 28, 2005.

58. One motivation for creating the Shura Council is to fend off Islamist legislation—particularly with regard to economic legislation. Personal interviews with Shaikh Muhammed bin Atiyatallah Al-Khalifa, February 25, 2004; and Abdurrahman Jamsheer, general secretary of the National Action Charter Committee, February 24, 2004.

59. The NDI was invited by the ruler in 2002 and worked with all political societies, both within and outside parliament. Personal interview with Fawzi Juleid, September 27, 2005. However, in the run-up to the 2006 elections, Juleid's residence permit was revoked (on May 13, 2006), terminating the NDI's work in Bahrain.

60. Interview with Fawzi Juleid, September 27, 2005.

61. Held in Manama at the Diplomat Hotel on October 7, 2004.

62. Moreover, the government draft stated a minimum age of twenty-one for

membership; the societies wanted a minimum age of eighteen. The extent of the executive's power to withdraw licenses from political societies was also a contentious issue. Foreign funding is a problematic issue in other countries as well; see, for example, Chapter 9 in this volume.

63. Personal interview with Shaikh Ali Salman, May 9, 2005. See also Al-Wifaq 2005.

64. Personal interview with Shaikh Ali Salman, May 9, 2005.

65. Proposed law on political parties in Bahrain. Presented by Abdulhadi Marhoon, Yousif Zainal, Abdunnabi Salman, Sameer ash-Shuwaikh, and Fareed Ghazi on December 22, 2003. See http://www.nuwab.gov.bh. Another draft, "Proposed Law on Regulating Political Societies," was presented by Ahmed Bahzad, Ali al-Samaheji, Hammad Khalil, Al-Mohandi, Jassim Abdul'al, and Abdulaziz al-Mousa on December 22, 2003.

66. Personal interview with Abdunnabi Salman, September 28, 2004.

67. Others who ran as independents later pooled into parliamentary blocks. They might become protosocieties down the road, but at that time their political outlook was not coherent. Interviews with Abdulaziz al-Musa, of the Sunni bloc Al-Mustaqilun, May 10, 2005; and Ali al-Samahiji, of the Shiite bloc Al-Islamiyun, May 2, 2005. Another 22 percent of the deputies were independent.

68. Al-Minbar al-Islami is the political organization of the Muslim Brotherhood and Al-'Asala (Salafi) is affiliated with Jami'at at-Tarbiya (Development Society). Both have been active for decades. Personal interviews with Saadi Abdulla, of Al-Minbar, February 16, 2004, September 23, 2004; (religious) Shaikh Adil al-Mu'awda, head of Al-'Asala, September 28, 2004, May 17, 2005; and Baqir Najjar, May 6, 2005.

69. Personal interview with Adil al-Mu'awda, September 28, 2004.

70. The new law forced the societies to reapply with the Ministry of Justice. This triggered a lot of protest by the boycotting societies, including a strike of Friday sermons. But by the end of the three-month period provided (beginning with the law's publication on August 3, 2005), all societies had reregistered.

71. Sunni Islamists have concentrated their parliamentary activism on questions of decency of women, alcohol, and other moral issues, but also on topics of social security and pensions.

72. For a self-description of the school of *marja'* Muhammad ash-Shirazi, who is actually the only deceased "Model of Emulation" (died 2001), see, for example, http://www.imam-shirazi.org and http://www.alshirazi.com. The majority of Bahraini Shiites seem to follow Khamenei, then as-Sistani. No exact data exist.

73. The welcome that exiles like Abdunnabi al-'Ikri or Abdurrahman an-Nu'aimi received on their return to Bahrain demonstrates their status as popular heroes.

74. For a comprehensive account of their viewpoint, see "Legal Opinion Concerning the Constitutional Matter of the Kingdom of Bahrain," written by a group of lawyers close to the boycotters, at http://mahmood.tv/index.php/docs/500.

75. The boycotters' discourse has become unitary on that point. Personal interviews with Hassan Radhi, lawyer, September 27, 2004; Aziz Obol, opposition activist, April 27, 2005; Shaikh Ali Salman, May 9, 2005; Abdullah ad-Durazi, of the Bahrain Human Rights Society, February 25, 2004, September 16, 2004; and Jalila as-Sayyid, of the Constitutional Conference Organizing Committee, February 26, 2004.

76. Personal interview with Aziz Obol, October 11, 2004.

77. Personal interview with Jalila as-Sayyid, February 26, 2004.

78. For details on the voting process, a critique, and statistics, see Bahrain Transparency Society 2002.

79. This is exactly what happened in the 2006 elections. Nineteen members of al-Wifaq won parliamentary seats, as did independent leftist Aziz Obol. The two leftist societies, as well as the *shirazi* society, failed to win any seats, although some government meddling against Al-'Amal al-Watani's candidates seems likely to have occurred.

80. This type of party emerges out of a social movement and aims at integrating its members, in most aspects of their lives, into the party, with the help of subsidiary organizations. Typically, mass-integration parties demand some degree of ideological commitment from their members. See Jonasson 2004: 35–44.

81. In Chapter 2, Holger Albrecht differentiates between Islamist social movements and elitist political parties. In Bahrain, however, Al-Wifaq actually has both qualities: it is a social movement *and* a legal political party at the same time.

82. The debate on the "contractual constitution" shows this clearly: the vocabulary is pure leftist lawyers' parlance without Islamic links.

83. Papers and programs of the constitutional conferences in 2004 and 2005 had been posted at http://www.al-deera.net/motamar2005/html/2004/daleel.htm. However, by late 2006, the website had been disabled.

84. Personal interviews with Aziz Obol, April 27, 2005; Shaikh Ali Salman, May 5, 2005; Abdullah ad-Durazi, September 18, 2004; and Jalila as-Sayyid, February 26, 2004.

85. Bahrainis have petitioned their rulers periodically since the beginning of the twentieth century (e.g., the previous emir, in 1992 and 1994). Petitions have become popular recently in Saudi Arabia as well.

86. "Isa Qassim had managed to collect 32,000 signatures against the reform of the family law in one week only," said Mansur al-Jamri in a personal interview on February 27, 2004. Personal interview with Jalila as-Sayyid, February 26, 2004.

87. Personal interview with Abdulhadi al-Khawaja, February 21, 2004.

88. Article 29 of the constitution reads: "Any individual may address the public authorities in writing over his signature. Group approaches to the authorities may only be made by statutory bodies and corporate persons."

89. Personal interview with Shaikh Ali Salman, May 9, 2005. In 2006, the number of official members had to be corrected: only roughly 1,500 were paying members.

90. Besides collecting signatures, the youths had allegedly distributed leaflets, produced by the Bahrain Freedom Movement, calling for regime change (an offense according to Bahraini penal law).

91. Government officials saw the voter turnout of 53 percent as indirect proof of the constitution's acceptance. Personal interview with Shaikh Muhammed bin Atiyatallah Al-Khalifa, February 25, 2004.

92. Personal interview with Abdunnabi al-'Ikri, of the Bahrain Human Rights Society and the Committee for Returned Political Exiles, September 16, 2004.

93. Ibid.

94. The minister, Majid al-Allawi, is a returned exile himself (formerly with the Bahrain Freedom Movement).

95. Four meetings were held during summer 2004. At the last meeting, on September 11, the societies were told to present a draft constitution as a basis for discussion. Personal interview with Abdunnabi al-'Ikri, September 16, 2004.

96. Personal interview with Abdunnabi al-'Ikri, September 16, 2004.

97. Shaikh Ahmad remarked: "What are we supposed to think when they raise

their Khamenei flags and their Hezbollah banners . . . oh, of course, now we have demonstrations Lebanese-style." Personal interview with Shaikh Ahmad bin Atiyatallah Al-Khalifa, May 25, 2005.

98. Sitra Island on March 25, 2005; Dana Mall on May 6, 2005.

99. On March 26, 2005, the United Arab Emirates–based newspaper *Gulf News* estimated 20,000, and the pro-opposition paper *Al-Wasat* estimated "thousands." Aerial photos point to a number lower than the organizers' claim, but surely higher than *Al-Ayyam*'s estimate. Similarly, the Dana Mall protest was estimated to have drawn around 15,000 by the convenors, and considerably less by others. My own estimation would amount to probably 5,000–7,000. A final demonstration was carried out in the town of Hamad on June 17, 2005, attracting fewer participants, but still numbering in the thousands.

100. Muharraq is one of Bahrain's islands. Its old quarters host some traditional Sunni areas.

101. Personal interview with Shaikh Ali Salman, May 9, 2005.

102. Opening speech of Shaikh Ali Salman, April 28, 2005.

103. Interviewees preferred to remain anonymous on this issue.

104. For example, by conducting indirect elections to the Shura Council. This could be done by changing parliamentary bylaws and would not violate the National Action Charter or the constitution. However, a reduction to half the Shura Council's seats to twenty (instead of forty) or a limitation of the Shura Council's veto power (the model then favored by Al-Wifaq) seem less likely.

105. Among them most likely Aziz Obol, who is close to the leftist Al-'Amal al-Watani, but is not a member. Obol is indeed the only former boycotting leftist who secured a seat in the new parliament.

106. The BCHR was cofounded by leftists who were marginalized by al-Khawaja and his circle and later left it. Personal interviews with Aziz Obol, April 27, 2005; and Faisal Fulad, May 10, 2005. Al-Khawaja had been in exile for twenty-four years. In Copenhagen he was a member of the Bahrain Human Rights Organization, which was a subsidiary of the *shirazi* Islamic Front for the Liberation of Bahrain. See Meinel 2002: 157.

107. To insinuate the presence of "hidden agendas" of the respective other sectarian/ethnic group is omnipresent, even with seculars. It is not a religious question, but one of national loyalty. Phrases like "as a *shirazi* he's with Iran" are heard from non-*shirazi* Shiites and Sunnis alike. For earlier relations between the *shiraziyun* and the Iranian revolutionaries, see Meinel 2002: 152–159.

108. Both developed from the social movement for equality that emerged through the intifada.

109. Mainly the Committee for Martyrs and Victims of Torture, led by Abdurra'uf Shayib.

110. Both governmental bodies and NGOs.

111. At the 'Uruba Club, Manama, September 24, 2004.

112. This is how virtually everyone judged his speech, including those sympathetic to him.

113. This occurred on the grounds that it was not licensed for political work, but for human rights business only. The venue, the 'Uruba Club, was closed for forty-five days.

114. See the September 24, 2004, issues of *Al-Ayyam, Al-Wasat,* and *Akhbar al-Khaleej.* For the crown prince's initiative, see http://www.bahrainedb.com.

115. Personal interview, anonymous.

116. See http://www.hrw.org and http://www.amnesty.org (public statement MDE 11/003/2005, *[Public] News Service* no. 196, July 19, 2005).

117. In collaboration with the Committee for Martyrs and Victims of Torture, led by Abdurra'uf Shayib in Bilad al-Qadeem, on May 25, 2005.

118. Other Bahraini human rights NGOs had also participated, but only the Bahrain Human Rights Society participated officially. The others had missed the deadline to hand in their reports. The following NGOs were present: the Bahraini Human Rights Society, the (dissolved) Bahraini Human Rights Center, the Bahraini Human Rights Watch Society, the Committee for Martyrs and Victims of Torture (Shiite), and the Committee for the Victims of Terror (ad hoc Sunni organization depicting the Shiite intifada activists, among them activists from the Committee for Martyrs and Victims of Torture, as terrorists). The Bahraini Human Rights Watch Society and the Committee for the Victims of Terror seemed to be government-sponsored, a practice aimed at weakening existing "bottom-up" NGOs. See Chapters 3 and 10 in this volume for co-optive practices in Morocco.

119. My own estimate.

120. Equating of current suppression of Shiites with the oppression and murder of Hussayn, and of the Al Khalifa with the Umayyads, is widespread and surfaces in decorations for religious festivals, foremost 'Ashura.

121. Like those found on the Bahrain Freedom Movement's website, in English and Arabic, at http://www.vob.org.

122. This interpretation can be seen as analogous to Ellen Lust-Okar's findings (see Chapter 5) on the motivations that drive people to run for elections in authoritarian settings: often, these candidates do not seek a role in decisionmaking either.

9

Mapping Participation in Egypt

Nihad Gohar

This chapter examines political participation under authoritarian or semiauthoritarian regimes, and prospects for democracy, through an in-depth study of the Egyptian political system. Political participation is defined here as any activity intended to induce political change. Egyptians voice demands for change and offer programs and ideas that might present alternatives to the existing ones through both formal and informal institutions. Formal channels of participation, such as political parties and electoral processes, trade unions and professional associations, and similar institutions whose roles are defined by laws and regulations, offer a means of expressing demands as well as guaranteeing upward mobility and personal gains. Importantly, however, they may also be used in ways that clearly deviate from their counterparts in Western democracies. Informal institutions that entail co-optation and clientelism also offer a channel for making demands, particularly to politically conscious individuals who perceive formal channels to be blocked or ineffective.

This chapter begins by mapping the venues for participation in Egypt. It demonstrates the varied sites of activity, from political parties and membership in unions and syndicates, to activism within the framework of both secular civil society associations and religious ones. It then identifies the obstacles and limitations to political participation in Egypt.

■ Main Actors and Legal Framework

The most obvious locus of political participation is found in political parties, but these are not the only, nor the most important, venues. The judiciary, civic associations, religious organizations, trade unions, and secular nongovernmental organizations (NGOs) all play important roles, both providing their own channels for participation and affecting the participation within political parties.

Political Parties

The activities of political parties in Egypt are regulated by Law no. 40 (1977), which a score of democracy advocates have criticized due to the difficulties it creates for applicants hoping to form opposition parties. According to this law, a precondition for the formation of any political party is that its principles and objectives conform with those prescribed by the state. These include the principles of Islamic *sharia,* which is the main source of Egyptian legislation, and the principles behind the July 1952 revolution and the corrective revolution of May 1971, which sought to preserve social cohesion, national unity, and socialist democratic principles. Under Law no. 40, no political party can be formed on the basis of a social class, sect, geographic region, race, or religion—an important provision that excludes groups such as the Muslim Brotherhood from formal political life.

Within Law no. 40, Article 8 grants the ruling party significant control over the formation of political parties. This article provides for the formation of a Committee on Political Parties, composed of the head of the Egyptian senate (the Shura Council), the minister of justice, the minister of interior, the minister of parliamentary affairs, and three nonparty members chosen from among former judiciary bodies, to be selected by the president of the republic.[1] This committee has been responsible for rejecting the applications of a great number of parties, many of which have turned to the judicial system to contest the committee's decision. Because the president of the republic, who is also head of the ruling party, forms the committee, composed of ministers of the ruling party, the committee gives de facto control over party registration to the ruling party.

Despite these limitations, there are more than twenty political parties in Egypt. Some, however, have been frozen by the Committee on Political Parties, while others fail to make a visible impact on political life at all. Thus this section maps only a selected number of the most active Egyptian parties in an attempt to sketch a picture of the present party system. This section is ordered more or less in terms of party vitality and impact on political life, beginning with the most powerful actor, the ruling party, and moving on to less powerful opposition parties. The Muslim Brotherhood, one of the most viable opposition movements, is discussed in the section on civil society, due to the fact that the government has not legalized it as a political party.

The National Democratic Party. The most powerful political party in Egypt is the National Democratic Party (NDP), headed by the Egyptian president himself. The dual role of the president demonstrates a serious entanglement of executive and legislative powers, which has a long history. Indeed, the National Democratic Party is the oldest of Egypt's contemporary parties, derived from the ruling Misr (Egypt) Party, which represented the center of President Anwar Sadat's first attempt to create a pseudo-democratic, multiparty system in 1976.

At that time, Sadat formed three wings within the new ruling party, the Arab Socialist Union, representing the right, the center, and the left (Khalafallah 2001). Those wings were to practice mutual criticism within the existing political organization, adhering simultaneously to the principles of the July 1952 revolution and Sadat's "corrective" movement in 1971. The regime's objective in controlling political life was also translated into the appointment of opposition leaders. For example, Ibrahim Shukri, then–minister of land reclamation, was appointed head of the Socialist Labor Party, described by Sadat as the "honest opposition" (Khalafallah 2001: 90). Within the framework of this artificial multiparty system, the National Democratic Party became the ruling party and has remained so to the current day. After Sadat's assassination at the National Day parade in October 1981, President Hosni Mubarak became both president of the republic and head of the ruling party.

Linked to both the government and the state since its establishment, the National Democratic Party has at its disposal all available political, economic, financial, and publicity resources. This has deprived other parties of resources and helped the NDP to cement its status within the political system. At the same time, however, the NDP's monopoly on power and resources has deprived it of any lessons that can be learned through real friction with an effective opposition. Only in the 2000 parliamentary elections was the NDP's artificial protection, which shields it from the reality of authentic political life, somewhat threatened.

Gamal Mubarak, son of the Egyptian president and policy secretary of the National Democratic Party, has described the 2000 parliamentary elections as a wake-up call for the party.[2] Official NDP candidates failed to receive more than 48 percent of the seats, far below the Egyptian norm. This minor crisis was quickly remedied, however, when successful independent candidates rejoined the NDP immediately after the elections. Some of these successful candidates had been NDP members who had left the party when it nominated other candidates to run under the NDP banner. Through reincorporating these candidates, the NDP increased its representation to its usual, safe majority.

According to Gamal Mubarak, the party has undergone extensive changes since this watershed event, including changes to its organizational structure to enhance the level of engagement between the party leadership and its grassroots.[3] These massive changes include the creation of the political secretariat headed by the president's son, Gamal, and composed of a number of young reform-minded intellectuals. The party has since been divided between the old and the new guard, a division set against rumors that the president was grooming his son to take over the presidency. Nevertheless, party membership has become one of the most important channels of upward mobility. Leading businessmen, academics, and prominent personalities from all walks of life have come to look upon membership in the NDP as a sure way to accumulate power and in some cases amass personal wealth.

In its new form, the party prepared a program to tackle Egypt's economic problems, including issues such as tax reform, monetary policies, investment policies, and the development of small enterprises.[4] However, the persistent problems of poverty and unemployment tarnished the party's image. During the presidential elections of May 2005, opposition parties and the public at large voiced one recurrent accusation: Why had the NDP failed to implement a reform program to tackle chronic economic problems earlier in its twenty-four-year rule?

The Wafd Party. One of the main opposition parties, Al-Wafd, is also one of Egypt's oldest political parties. It derives from a 1919 movement that represented national resistance to the British occupation of Egypt. The party dissolved after the 1952 revolution along with all other parties.[5] Given its early history, Al-Wafd has had experience with a real multiparty system, during the prerevolutionary era known now by many scholars and practitioners as the liberal era, that other modern parties lack.

Despite the many restrictions imposed on postrevolutionary political life and those imposed by Sadat after his launching of the three democratic platforms, Al-Wafd resurrected itself in 1978. The regime felt threatened by the historical foundation of this party and its political significance, however. The regime's insecurity led it to issue Law no. 33 (1978), aimed at preserving social cohesion. The law prevented the leader of the New Wafd Party, Fouad Serageddin, from practicing his political rights, thereby forcing it to dissolve itself three months later (el-Shubki 1997: 89).

The New Wafd Party was reestablished yet again in 1983, presenting itself this time as a rightist liberal party. During the 1984 legislative elections, it entered into an alliance with the Muslim Brotherhood, representing the so-called conservative right. The Muslim Brotherhood, which will be discussed later, attempted to strike such alliances in its quest to become an active player on Egypt's political scene. Yet, like other parties' alliances with the brotherhood, the 1984 alliance with the New Wafd Party dissolved.

The Nasserist Democratic Arab Party. The Nasserist Democratic Arab Party was formed in 1992 under the leadership of Diauddin Daoud. The party's discourse is based on the adaptation and application of the ideology of Gamal Abdul Nasser to contemporary conditions, including emphasis on economic self-reliance and control over natural resources. The party calls for pan-Arab unity along the lines of Nasser's Arab nationalism, and stresses the importance of resistance to US hegemony. Party members adamantly reject the Camp David Accords and the normalization of Arab-Israeli relations. Like other contemporary parties, the Nasserist Party suffered from internal divisions and a power struggle between the old guard and the younger generation, providing yet another example of the lack of internal harmony within Egypt's political parties.[6]

Contradictory party statements reflect an internal controversy between democracy and Nasserism. In an interview with Diauddin Daoud, published in *Al-Araby,* the party's official newspaper, the party leader defended the authoritarianism of Nasser's regime on the grounds that a revolution, by definition, is a forceful change of the status quo. Daoud pointed to land reforms, the nationalization of capital, and other radical policies that would never have succeeded in a democracy. At the same time, Daoud stressed the importance of social democracy, the primacy of social justice, and the redistribution of wealth over political freedoms. Radical changes, he stressed, have never been the result of democracy.[7] Such a lack of confidence in the power of democracy reveals a discrepancy between the current discourse of the Nasserist Party and its condoning of the antidemocratic practices of the Nasser regime.

The National Progressive Unionist Party. The National Progressive Unionist Party, also known as the Tagammu Party, emerged from a coalition of Nasserists, Communists, and Nationalists. It was established in 1975 as the left wing of the Arab Socialist Union. After the disbanding of the latter, Tagammu became its own independent party in 1976. The party was led by Khaled Mohyiddin, a former member of the Free Officers Movement and one of the leading members of the Revolutionary Command Council, which led the 1952 revolution.[8] Not surprisingly, given the leader's background, the party is based on the principles of the 1952 revolution: defending national identity and independence from imperialism, stressing Egypt's Arab identity, and promoting ideas such as independent development, social democracy, and equality. Mohyiddin, an unwavering supporter of the Nasser regime, was also an adamant opponent to the Sadat regime. He considered Sadat's initiation of a semi-multiparty system and his adoption of the open-door policy to be a sacrifice of social democracy under the guise of increased political democracy.[9]

The party has generally had tense relations with Egyptian regimes. It constantly opposed President Sadat, criticizing government repression in the aftermath of the 1977 food riots, which included closing Tagammu's official newspaper, *Al-Ahali,* opposing the Camp David Accords, and more broadly opposing US interference in Egypt's domestic affairs. Under the Mubarak regime, the party adopted a more moderate policy toward the government. It boycotted, along with other parties, the 1990 elections, and contested the results of the 1995 elections.[10] However, it took part in the 2000 and 2005 parliamentary elections.

The Ghad Party. The Ghad (Tomorrow) Party has been the subject of controversy since the Committee on Political Parties approved its inception in November 2004. The approval came after three previous rejections on the grounds that the party's political program did not differ significantly from that of existing parties. Its founder, Ayman Nour, an attorney and a former leading figure in the Wafd Party, had left the latter in 2001 following a dispute with Al-Wafd leader, Noaman Jom'a, who accused him of trying to split the party. According to Nour, 25 percent of Al-Wafd's members have joined Al-Ghad. Nour argues, however, that his sole objective was not to stage a political war against Al-Wafd, although he symbolically chose the historic residence of 1919 revolutionary leader Sa'ad Zaghloul (a leading Wafdist) as the site for the press conference announcing the inauguration of his party.

Al-Ghad projects itself as a party for youth. In 2004, 64 percent of its members, according to its leader, were under age forty-five. Al-Ghad also advocates women's rights, as demonstrated by its selection of Mona Makram Obeid, a prominent academic and granddaughter of one of the pre-revolutionary political figures, as party secretary-general (el-Nahhas 2004). However, Obeid's tenure did not last. She resigned in the aftermath of the criminal charges directed at Ayman Nour.

The charges against Nour tested the resilience of Al-Ghad. Nour was arrested after being stripped of his parliamentary immunity and accused of falsifying two thousand applications of membership presented to the Committee on Political Parties. His detention was extended for forty-five days, attracting international attention (Hamzawy 2005). After his release, Nour remained in the spotlight by running in Egypt's first presidential elections, in September 2005. He won 8 percent of the votes, placing ahead of the Wafd candidate. In the parliamentary elections, Al-Ghad nominated 200 candidates in 70 percent of the districts, including twelve Copts and three women. According to *Al-Ahram Weekly,* Al-Ghad managed to attract a number of NDP members who were not officially nominated by their party (el-Nahhas 2005a). Despite having served two terms in the People's Assembly, the now-imprisoned Nour failed to win reelection to that body in 2005.

The Judiciary

The judiciary has played an important role in regulating political parties and elections, and has also served as an independent arena of participation in

Egypt. In general, the independence of the judiciary is a prerequisite for the separation of powers—the conceptual backbone of any democracy. In Egypt, however, Rule no. 66 (1943), amended by Law no. 35 (1984), constrains the independence of this important power. Article 9 of Law no. 35 gives the minister of justice the final word in assigning or renewing judgeships on the appellate courts, which supervise the work of primary courts. The same law, in Article 78, establishes a department for judicial inspection within the Ministry of Justice. This department is responsible for inspecting the performance of judges, holding them accountable, and deciding upon their promotion, demotion, transfer, among other things, under the total control of the minister, who is accorded, by a number of other articles, the authority to discipline those judges. The existence of such authority is a sheer violation of the concept of the independence of the judiciary power (al-Rifa'i 2005).

Judicial independence has been the subject of constant debate in Egypt, surfacing notably before the 2005 presidential and parliamentary elections. The Association of Judges, known as the "Club of Egyptian Judges," unanimously called for full judicial supervision of both the presidential and parliamentary elections, and the General Assembly that was convened prior to the presidential elections asked the Egyptian government to amend the law on political rights to include sufficient guarantees for the independence of judges in carrying out their mandate to supervise the elections. The judges opposed a law drafted by the government, insisting on their own draft law, which had been discussed for over two years by the parliament. The judges' proposed law called for restricting the role of the minister of justice to administrative supervision and restraining the minister's power to select heads of court. It also stipulated the Supreme Judicial Council's approval of presidential appointments of the public attorney, public prosecutor, and members of his office. Judicial opposition to the law proposed by the government centered on the government's proposal to form a Supreme Supervisory Committee, which would be responsible for supervising the presidential elections in conjunction with five other public figures, selected from outside the judiciary. The judicial movement fully rejected these conditions, developing its objections into a campaign demanding complete judicial independence.

The Egyptian Center for the Independence of the Judiciary organized a conference in April 2005 to reiterate the call for independence. There was some internal strife between those who called upon the judges to join the popular and political forces requesting reforms and those who insisted that the judicial power should keep its traditional neutrality and stay away from the increasingly vocal opposition.

Nevertheless, during the General Assembly meeting of the Alexandria Judges Club on April 15, 2004, 1,200 judges decided to boycott both the presidential and the parliamentary elections, scheduled for September and December 2005, respectively. They made their acceptance of the mandate to supervise any upcoming elections conditional on establishing an independent judicial authority in charge of supervising all stages of the electoral process, from monitoring voter registration to declaration of the results. They also reiterated their demands for a law on judicial authority that would liberate the judges from government control. Judicial supervision of the election process started during the parliamentary elections of 2000, but was flawed nonetheless: the Ministry of Interior was in charge of registering the voters, supervising the vote count, and declaring the results.[11]

Civil Society Organizations

Egypt, according to Mustapha Kamel al-Sayyid (2000), has had the prerequisites for a vibrant civil society, in terms of social differentiation and the emergence of a middle working class, ever since the reign of Mohamed Ali. However, civil society in contemporary Egypt faces two problems. First, it lacks experience and suffers isolation from other more experienced global partners. In addition, the government fosters this isolation, attempting to prevent organizations from maturing and gaining enough experience and connections to become truly effective.

Like other states of the developing world, Egypt has gradually lost power to international bodies, such as the International Monetary Fund and the World Trade Organization. In order to carry out economic reforms and structural adjustment policies, the Egyptian government has largely withdrawn from the social domain, giving up its responsibilities to the private sector in the fields of health, education, and other welfare activities. Thus the state has encouraged the private sector and civil society to step in and provide services in the voluntary sector, preaching such notions as participatory development and the role of civil society in promoting the development process.

However, a wide gap divides rhetoric from practice. The Egyptian government has not voluntarily relinquished its monopoly over domains affecting the political sphere. Thus it encourages civil society to act within certain boundaries. NGOs are encouraged only if their activities remain within the service provision sector, and only if those activities do not reflect any political stance or attempt at social transformation. A similar trend is seen among civil society actors in Morocco (see Chapter 10).

There are a host of examples to substantiate this claim. NGOs that work in the fields of human rights, participatory development, and similar areas that require advocacy are usually banned by the government. Several Egyptian NGOs that have pursued advocacy as a primary objective have been denied the right to register according to Law no. 84 (2002), such as the New Women Research Center, which advocates gender issues, as have networks of other women's organizations that have called for more democratization and a vibrant civil society. Another example is the Land Center for Human Rights, which works in the arena of child labor, among other things, and also focuses on advocacy.

Law no. 84 was designed to guarantee that all working NGOs are controlled by the government; only those approved by the Ministry of Social Affairs are allowed to register. This law is a regression from the law of 1999—the former gives the Ministry of Social Affairs the right to dissolve an NGO without court appeal, simply by administrative decree.[12]

Religious organizations. Some question the idea of linking civil society only to secular institutions. Egypt has a range of religious organizations that provide social services, but the most important, in terms of political participation, are the Muslim Brotherhood and the Wasat Party.

The Muslim Brotherhood. The Muslim Brotherhood is one of the oldest political organizations in Egypt. It was established in 1928 by Hassan al-Banna, a schoolteacher who called for a regeneration of society on the basis of Islamic principles and for political and social reforms. The organization started essentially as a philanthropic society, but it became one of the most important political actors, championing the cause of the poor and taking an active part in the Egyptian nationalist movement against British occupation.

The brotherhood has had a troubled relationship with Egyptian regimes. In spite of its commitment to nonviolence, the brotherhood established a secret military wing in 1939, engaging in a number of violent incidents. The regime then assassinated al-Banna in 1949, and Hassan al-Hudaybi, his successor, tried to abolish the secret wing of the brotherhood. After the July 23 revolution of 1952, however, relations between the ruling elites and the brotherhood, which had initially supported the Free Officers Movement, deteriorated. In 1954 the regime accused the brotherhood of attempting to assassinate Nasser. Consequently, it abolished the brotherhood and imprisoned thousands of its members. In the wake of this ordeal, several former members, notably Sayyed Qutb, who was executed in 1966, pursued a violent ideology. The Muslim Brotherhood has since distanced itself from militant groups, however, adhering instead to its nonviolent reformist stance.

Under Sadat, imprisoned members were gradually released, but the brotherhood remained illegal. In the 1990s the government attempted to curb the brotherhood's increasing influence. Nonetheless, it remained an active political force, as reflected in brotherhood members' performance as independent candidates in several parliamentary elections, most notably the 2005 legislative elections. During the latter, the brotherhood's candidates won eighty-eight seats (20 percent of the total), making them the largest opposition bloc in parliament. Their success came despite many violations of the electoral process by the government, including the arrest of hundreds of brotherhood members. In comparison, legal opposition parties performed poorly in the 2005 legislative elections, winning only fourteen seats. This has led some Egyptian elites to argue for legalization of the Muslim Brotherhood, as well as its participation in the Kefaya political-reform movement.

The Wasat Party. One of the most interesting manifestations of the government's rejection of political parties with an Islamic reference, in addition to its refusal to legalize the Muslim Brotherhood, has been the establishment of the Wasat (Middle) Party. The idea of forming the party was the brainchild of a number of religiously oriented youth who had been active within the student movement of the 1970s, and later within the professional syndicates during the 1980s and 1990s. By the end of 1995, their idea had translated into a project they called "Al-Wasat." The founders, who included former members of the Muslim Brotherhood, as well as a number of Copts and women, applied to register a party under that name in January 1996. The party's objectives, combined with its relationship to the banned Muslim Brotherhood, sparked media uproar.

In April 1996, the party-to-be had its first confrontation with authorities when its main founder, Abul Ela Madi, and two other founders were detained alongside thirteen leaders of the Muslim Brotherhood. The detention was based upon their alleged attempt to form a party that would become a facade for the banned brotherhood. On May 8, 1996, the detainees were to be tried before a military court; five days later, the Committee on Political Parties officially rejected the formation of Wasat. A Wasat attorney, well-known, moderate Islamic thinker and writer Selim al-Awwa, appealed this ruling. Three months later, the three detainees of the Wasat Party were declared innocent of the charges against them, which had been modified from attempting to form a facade party for the Muslim Brotherhood to membership in a banned group. The party made three further attempts to win the approval of the Committee on Political Parties, to no avail. The last attempt, in May 2004, was made in spite of the inclusion of a number of prominent moderate Islamic-oriented thinkers, such as Selim al-Awwa and Abdel Wahab al-Messiri.[13]

The party's relations with the Muslim Brotherhood have also been tense. Founding members of the Wasat Party claim that the brotherhood exerted pressure on a number of prospective members to withdraw from Wasat. In response, Wasat's founding members attempted to portray the party in a positive light, pointing to its independence from the Muslim Brotherhood and its image as a civil party with an Islamic background. It presented itself as better able to represent the aims and ideas of a larger section of the Egyptian citizenry than could a religious advocacy group.

The attempts by Wasat to form a civil but religiously oriented party and its confrontation with both the ruling regime and the Muslim Brotherhood elicit an analysis of the secular nature of the regime, its rejection of any religious party, and its fear of the possible popularity of this trend among its citizens. The deep-rooted fear of such Islamic parties can be traced to the long history of the Muslim Brotherhood and its active participation in Egypt's political life.

Professional syndicates. Professional associations and trade unions also have a long history of conflictual relations with the regime. Syndicates, which emerged in the twentieth century as the backbone of Egyptian civil society, have played an active role in a host of issues. They have raised funds for various causes, such as disaster relief, the Palestinian intifada, and fellow Muslims in Bosnia. In this way, they are similar to Islamic organizations, which have also played important roles in social relief.

Indeed, religious organizations and professional associations in Egypt have been closely related at times, which has exacerbated their difficult relations with the government. Al-Sayyid (2000) notes an attempt of prohibited religious organizations to infiltrate and work through professional associations. Consequently, the government sequestered some of those associations, which then appealed to the judiciary to put an end to those infiltration attempts. The success of Islamic groups in infiltrating professional syndicates, groups that the Committee on Political Parties prohibited from forming political parties based on religious grounds, prompted the government to pass new laws aimed at containing Islamic influence. The result was the so-called Unified Law of Professional Syndicates no. 100 (1993), described by the government as "the democratic guarantees law on professional syndicates." The actual objective of the law was to constrain syndicates that were controlled by Islamists.

The first article of this controversial law stipulates that 50 percent of the members of a syndicate's General Assembly (i.e., half of all registered members) must participate in elections in order for them to be valid. If elections fail to meet this threshold, they have to be repeated, in which case 30 percent of the members must vote in order for the elections to be valid (again, a very high percentage that is unlikely to materialize). If this threshold is not reached, the government assigns a committee to administer the syndicate under judicial supervision. This law has single-handedly brought the election process to a complete stop in ten professional syndicates, including those for doctors, engineers, dentists, pharmacists, agriculturalists, teachers, and lawyers.

This law stands in stark violation to the rules of democracy. For instance, the Egyptian law on political rights stipulates that a candidate for the People's Assembly must receive at least 51 percent of the votes cast (not of possible registered votes) in the first round of elections in order to win. If no candidate reaches this threshold, a runoff is held between who those received the highest number of votes. The winner is then the candidate who receives the majority of the votes cast in that runoff. This has led, in some cases, to candidates winning seats in the People's Assembly by receiving only 2,000 votes in districts comprising more than 100,000 registered voters.[14]

Ironically, compared to the weak and paralyzed parties, syndicates have been a stronghold of democracy, despite the regime's attempts to force them out of yet another legitimate channel of participation. In 2003, elections within the press syndicate resulted in the defeat of the government-backed candidate, the head of the newspaper *Al-Ahram,* in favor of Galal Aref, a Nasserist. The Nasserists won four seats of the twelve-member board and the banned Muslim Brotherhood won another four seats, together giving them control over two-thirds of the board. According to some, these results did not reflect the political orientation of the journalists, although they did reflect real voting behavior (Hilal 2003). It is unlikely that a third of Egypt's journalists belong to the Nasserist camp and another third have Islamist orientations. It is more plausible that the results indicate the organizational skills of those two groups.

There are two interpretations of the motivations behind the elections within the press syndicate. Some interpret the outcome as resistance to government control over the syndicates and political life more generally, and as a protest against the deteriorating conditions that journalists must endure. Others see the results as a direct consequence of increased Islamic and nationalist feelings among Egyptian journalists in the aftermath of the 2003 US invasion of Iraq, which proved detrimental to the government-backed candidate.

This possible development of increased Islamic and nationalist sentiments reflects a general fear among the secular intellectuals of both the Nasserist and the Islamic parties, both regarded as having a history demonstrating clear hostility toward democracy and intolerance of opposition. These intellectuals also fear that this development could spread throughout Egypt. The unexpectedly successful performance of the Muslim Brotherhood during the 2005 legislative elections only exacerbated that fear.

Labor Unions

Another important actor in Egypt's political life is the labor movement. Literature covering the labor movement has usually focused on its role in democratization, rather than the channels it used under authoritarianism. Some analysts have referred to the role played by labor movements not in solely triggering a democratization process, but in entering with other social actors into pacts that might help speed the democratization process. Reference is also made to the role of labor movements during transition periods, which is manifested in strikes and demonstrations (Valenzuela

1989). Under authoritarian regimes, labor unions might be eliminated altogether, but given the role of international pressure, different types of organizations are allowed under restrictive arrangements. Because labor organizations can be used to coordinate labor actions, disrupt production, or serve as a platform for political opposition to the regime, labor policy is a critical issue for governments under authoritarian regimes (Valenzuela 1989: 447).

The labor movement in Egypt is organized by Law no. 12 (1995), which introduces some amendments to Law no. 35 (1976). One of the most restrictive aspects of this law is Article 13, which refers to the right of workers or apprentices within an industry to form one single union at the national level. Contributory or complementary industries are considered part of the specified industry. The General Union has the mandate to defend workers' rights, improve their working conditions, raise their cultural and social levels, take part in designing and implementing vocational training programs, supervise the activities of labor committees, conduct collective bargaining processes, and conclude collective labor contracts. The General Union is also mandated to comment on legislation that influenced the vocation or the industry and, most importantly, to approve of the organization of worker strikes in accordance with legal restrictions and the establishment of funds to absorb the financial burdens resulting from strikes. The Egyptian Trade Union Federation (ETUF) is by mandate the leader of the Egyptian labor movement, and formulates its general policies. It has the mandate of defending the rights of Egyptian workers.[15] Workers in Egypt—particularly in the private sector—suffer from low wages and long hours; improvement of these working conditions, rather than political participation per se, is their main concern.

A number of workers' movements have attempted to formulate a political position, though, such as the Committee for Coordination of Union Rights and Liberties, which held its second conference on May 27, 2005, at which it issued a common statement on the political position of workers toward reform, emphasizing worker demands. With few exceptions, though, most labor demands have revolved around wages and working conditions. Some industrial regions, though, have witnessed pockets of labor resistance. The asbestos workers, for instance, organized a sit-in to demand a clean environment and healthy working conditions as well as compensation for workers whose health had been ill affected by such a hazardous environment (Abbour 2005). The company that witnessed the labor unrest had been closed by a decree of the prime minister, who requested that the ETUF, under the leadership of its longtime leader Al-Sayyid Rashed—a national party member and a also longtime parliamentarian who had lost both his parliament seat and his position as head of the ETUF—ensure the protection of workers' rights. The ETUF had justified its failure to extend its protection to those workers on the grounds that they were not members of trade unions.

In 2006 and 2007, a series of labor strikes took place in a number of sectors, revolving largely around demands such as benefits and wages amid fear of how privatization might affect the rights that workers enjoyed within public companies. Those strikes, however, did not reflect a political ideology, but rather more interest in better working conditions, irrespective of the type of ownership. Work in the public sector had been preferable to a great number of workers, not because of the type of ownership, but rather because of the benefits (Abbour 2005).

Egypt's single union system has been an attempt by the government to control the labor movement, and has been criticized by international organizations as hampering the rights of workers to collective bargaining and freedom of association. Members of the single union are mostly public sector workers, which leaves private sector workers completely unprotected. The ETUF has been accused of being co-opted by the government, in a striking resemblance to the co-optation of civil society organizations in Morocco (see Chapter 10), a fact reflected in the ETUF's leadership as well as in its connection to the ruling National Democratic Party and the government in general. Changes in the leadership of workers' movements have not translated into more independence for the labor unions. Parallel structures such as the Labor Union Services Association, an NGO that was recently closed by the Ministry of Social Solidarity, have been unable to break the siege imposed on the labor movement in Egypt.

■ Obstacles and Limitations to Political Participation

Formal Restrictions on Political Participation

Perhaps the most important impediment to expanding political participation in Egypt was the notorious Emergency Law no. 162 (1958), revived after Sadat's assassination, which vested the president of the republic with immense powers. The law has been shelved following constitutional amendments introduced in the aftermath of a "national referendum" held on March 26, 2007, and has been boycotted by large sections of the population. It has been replaced by Article 179, on terrorism, which vests the security organs with the powers to arrest citizens, search their houses, and monitor their correspondence and phone calls without court order, in violation of other articles of the constitution, namely Articles 41, 44, and 45, which protect personal freedoms.[16]

The laws governing political parties, syndicates, and associations in Egypt are designed to restrict participation. These laws have been the subject of long debates between various actors demanding a wider realm of political activity and the regime attempting to hold all the strings and allow only calculated doses of freedom. This debate recently turned into an open confrontation, as the regime was forced to partly remove the lid on bottled-up frustrations of the numerous but constrained political actors.

To some extent, this has been the result of international pressure. The US government, among others, has criticized the Egyptian government through its Greater Middle East Initiative. Global civil society organizations, intergovernmental organizations, and donors have also stressed such issues as good governance and democracy promotion. However, not only external but also internal pressures have played a part in forcing the government to (somewhat) succumb to vocal opposition in the media.

The Kefaya (Enough) Movement has mobilized to oppose Mubarak's rule and the anticipated hereditary succession to his son, Gamal. Its membership, claimed to be approximately 15,000, includes a number of middle-class intellectuals, academics, parliamentarians, and students. The movement has gained visibility through the organization of a number of campaigns, conferences, and demonstrations in the venues of syndicates and even in downtown Cairo. Some of those demonstrations have been peaceful, while others have ended in clashes with security forces.

The issue is not whether the movement can be considered a real and visible opposition to the ruling regime, but rather whether it reflects a relatively new era in which more open opposition to the system is condoned, provided it does not cross too many lines. In this same vein, the Muslim Brotherhood has organized a number of demonstrations, usually following Friday prayers. It has voiced a number of demands, including the freedom to establish a political party. During the 2005 parliamentary elections, the brotherhood organized demonstrations to contest results that many described as scandalous. Thus, one could argue that the regime has tolerated, at least to a greater extent than previously, political participation and opposition in the form of collective, peaceful action. These changes have not been formalized, however, in a legal framework, indicating that the regime is more concerned that it appears to be making strides toward democracy, and less concerned with actually taking major steps.

A look at the NDP's discourse also suggests a change in attitude, but one that has not yet resulted in significant institutional reforms. The NDP initiated a national dialogue with a wide range of stakeholders, including opposition parties but not the Muslim Brotherhood, in January 2005. In a statement following the first round of dialogue, President Mubarak stressed that the NDP does not seek to monopolize policymaking. The party, according to this discourse, believes firmly in the principle of dialogue with the other parties, to discuss realistic political and economic reforms that serve Egyptians' interests. Regarding political reforms, the party stresses the importance of implementing free and fair elections under judicial supervision, guaranteeing freedom of expression and the rule of law, dismantling the state's supreme security courts, ending the exceptional powers enjoyed by the public prosecution, canceling most of the military decrees, establishing a national council for human rights, and empowering civil society. The party has also suggested constitutional reforms (an obvious reference to a constitutional amendment suggested by the president in March 2005), as well as amendments to laws that regulate political and syndicate life. The latter include the law on political life, which discusses the establishment of an independent electoral committee; the law on political parties, which reviews the conditions and procedures required; the law on democracy in professional syndicates, which guarantees their independence; and an ethical charter to regulate the relationship between parties and candidates during elections.

The NDP has remained true to some of its promises, but because it has not made significant changes—most notably, abolishing emergency laws—the ruling party has not significantly expanded the arena for political participation. The National Council on Human Rights was indeed established, in January 2004, but human rights organizations are skeptical about the council's value, given the emergency laws. The Cairo Center for Human Rights Studies even accused the president of the council of making biased statements in favor of the candidate of the ruling party during the 2005 presidential elections.[17] Similarly, the People's Assembly canceled Law no. 105 (1980), on the state security courts, in June 2003, and hence abolished those courts. This is a small step forward, except that it does not abolish the ad hoc courts established under the emergency laws.[18] The Committee on Parliamentary Elections is charged with oversight of the elections process, but is headed by the minister of justice, which again puts the process under the executive's control. In short, reforms have fallen short of significant expansion of the Egyptian political sphere.

Societal Obstacles

The tendency of Egyptian society to passively rely on the government for aid, refusing to engage in any open confrontation with the ruler, is also an obstacle to expanding political participation. There is a general perception among both intellectuals and the public that Egyptians generally resort to pretense while nevertheless mistrusting the ruling regime and harboring feelings of hostility.

This reluctance has persisted even since the establishment of a restricted multiparty system in 1976. Membership in political parties remains negligible, at best 10 percent of the adult population or 20 percent of the male adult population. Newspaper readership is also low, as is participation in syndicates and general elections. During the 2005 parliamentary elections, an estimated mere 28 percent of registered voters (and a much lower number of eligible voters) participated. Despite the high levels of inflation, the relative increase in the cost of living, and the poor performance of the national economy—all circumstances that should have instigated collective protest—there are few demonstrations, sit-ins, and strikes.

According to Negad Bora'i, the emergency laws have shaped Egypt's political culture. Media campaigns portray activists working in the human rights field in a negative light. According to him, the Group for Democratic Development, headed by Bora'i himself, attempted in 1999 to organize a workshop in upper Egypt to instruct teachers on the use of democratic tools inside the classroom. Security forces limited the number of participants, and the Ministry of Education disciplined those who ventured to participate in this workshop (Stacher 2001). These and other experiences not only affected the development of secular civil society, but also shaped perceptions of those who attempted to participate within it.

Egyptians are much more likely to appeal to members of parliament or government ministers. Members of the elite, particularly prominent business elites, do not hesitate to use the channels of direct contact with decisionmakers, whether individually or collectively through their respective organizations, to serve their interests (al-Sayyid 2000). Indeed, the functions that Egyptian parliamentarians perform reflect an unwritten social agreement. Many describe the Egyptian parliament as the "service parliament." This indicates that parliamentarians restrict themselves to providing constituent services in order to secure their reelection, rather than acting as policymakers and as a collective check and balance on the executive. Consequently, Egyptian elections are characterized by a display of money politics, family solidarity, services, occasional violence, and rigging, with rural areas displaying higher levels of participation due to family ties and tribal solidarity.

Funding Limitations

Limited funding also thwarts the growth of legitimate channels of participation, such as civil society organizations. Religious charity organizations are particularly active in providing services and in gaining the confidence of the masses. A 2003 study by the United Nations Development Programme on subjective poverty and social capital in Egypt found that religious organizations enjoyed a particularly high degree of trust. The religious NGO Al-Gameya al-Sharia stood out in its ability to gain the confidence of members of the community and succeeded in promoting principles of volunteer and community work based on religious teachings. Not surprisingly, Al-Gameya receives massive funding from local donors.[19]

Egyptians tend to place less trust in secular, and particularly foreign-funded, NGOs. For example, a secular NGO that was active in Manshiet Nasser, a low-income squatter settlement, was founded to meet the needs of female-headed households. It relied on foreign funding and conducted credit programs predicated on the principle of collective loans (a traditional way of saving used by many Egyptian households). It also provided legal-council and awareness programs focused on the law on personal status, and trained adolescent girls to prepare them for motherhood. This NGO was strongly criticized by the Islamic Gemeya for charging interest on their loans. The legal-council program was also harshly criticized by men, who considered it an attempt to encourage their wives to rebel.[20]

Restrictions on funding can hinder development of NGOs. Law no. 84 (2002) prohibits the raising of funds and the collection of donations without the prior authorization of the Ministry of Social Affairs. The ministry is obliged to respond within a period of two months, during which time civil society organizations are placed under the total control of the government. The law also restricts foreign funding, even of organizations that operate in Egypt according to bilateral agreements with the government (e.g., the United Nations Children's Fund, the World Health Organization, the United Nations Educational, Scientific, and Cultural Organization).

The source of foreign funding also poses a problem. Egyptian advocacy NGOs in fields such as democratization, women's issues, and human rights have proliferated during the past two decades, many funded primarily by external sources. However, their reliance on foreign funding has become a curse due to accusations by both the government and the (controlled) press that those NGOs serve foreign interests. They have even been branded as "human rights boutiques" in an attempt to discredit them (el-Gawhary 2000).

In short, both religious and secular NGOs are constrained by funding restrictions. Religious NGOs are popular and very effective in mobilizing the public and in sustaining themselves through voluntary donations. However, the Egyptian government, as well as foreign donors and Western governments (many of the latter question anything Islamic as a potential terrorist incubator), distrust religious NGOs. Secular NGOs are sometimes distrusted by the public, particularly if they receive foreign funding. They are also monitored closely by the government, lest they become involved in sensitive political activity, and are restrained by donor priorities. Indeed, secular NGOs lose their appeal when they take what one might call a "foreign approach." For example, a host of gender programs that failed to take the Egyptian cultural context into consideration led to the perception that they were a form of foreign intervention and an attack on Egyptian morals and cultural values (el-Gawhary 2000: 39).

Internal Party Practices
Egyptian political parties, in particular, also find it hard to demonstrate their commitment to democratic practices, either internally or within the regime more broadly. Even the 2005 parliamentary elections demonstrated the weakness of Egyptian political parties. The National Democratic Party won

311 seats, which amounted to 68.5 percent of the vote; the New Wafd Party won 6 seats, or 1.3 percent; the Progressive National Unionist Party won 2 seats, or 0.4 percent; the Ghad Party won 1 vote, or 0.2 percent; the Nasserist Party failed to win any seats; and the independents won 24 seats, or 4.6 percent. The Muslim Brotherhood won 88 seats, or 19.4 percent of the vote.[21] Irregularities affected the results, but at least part of the outcome must be understood as the result of party actions.

All of the parties, including the NDP, suffer from weak party commitment. The NDP saw a large number of independent candidates entering the race when they failed to win the party nomination. Similarly, the Wafd Party performed poorly in both the presidential and the parliamentary elections, due to an internal battle, between the Wafd leader and other central figures within the party, that threatened its very existence. The same was true for the Ghad Party, which also witnessed internal strife during the 2005 parliamentary elections. A dissident faction headed by the party's former deputy chairman nominated sixty-five candidates who in some districts competed against fellow members of the Ghad Party. The 2005 elections demonstrated the difficulties that Egyptian parties face in grappling with their own problems of internal democracy, not to mention the indifference of a large segment of the population toward them.

Another indication of the weak internal democratic structure of Egyptian opposition parties was seen in Khaled Mohyiddin's decision to voluntarily relinquish his position as a leader of the National Progressive Unionist Party to his successor, Rif'at al-Said. This was an unprecedented move, hailed as demonstrating the uniquely democratic nature of this party. Elections for the new leader took place in late 2003.[22]

Not only is the internal democracy of opposition parties in question, but so too is their outlook toward democracy at large. A case in point is the Nasserist Party. Although the party leader defended the authoritarianism of Nasser's regime, he also stressed the importance of social democracy, the primacy of social justice, and the redistribution of wealth over political freedoms.[23]

This leaves only the Muslim Brotherhood, whose outstanding performance in the 2005 elections leaves no doubt about it being the only viable opposition on Egypt's political scene. During those elections, the regime departed from earlier policies by condoning the participation of the Muslim Brotherhood in an open manner under their traditional motto "Islam is the solution," in spite of that fact that the brotherhood was a banned association. Before, the brotherhood had to ally itself with another party and enter the elections under the latter's banner, as it did with the Wafd Party and the Labor Party. However, in the 2000 elections, the Muslim Brotherhood was able to display its viability as an oppositional force. In the 2005 parliamentary elections, the ruling regime took a calculated risk by allowing the brotherhood the partial freedom to attain a certain number of seats. There were cases of forgery and rigging to limit its success, and the brotherhood entered the elections with only 150 candidates, below the threshold required to approve the nomination of a presidential candidate. The regime had not acquiesced to the brotherhood's demand to form a political party, in spite of its obvious viability compared to the other secular opposition parties, whose performance had been feeble despite the formation of a united opposition front.

Skeptics and opponents who fear that the Muslim Brotherhood will end prospects for democratic change watch its performance closely. These critics accuse the brotherhood of undemocratic practices and even claim that its outstanding performance in 2005 was the result of good organization, money politics, and the lack of a viable alternative, rather than its popularity. It remains to be seen how the strong presence of the Muslim Brotherhood will affect the parliament, given the war that the government has waged lately on brotherhood leaders and financial supporters.

Conclusion

This mapping of the most important political actors in Egypt and the legislative framework that regulates their performance sheds light on the nature of participation under the authoritarian regime. Formal and informal channels of participation include elections, political parties, syndicates, and civil society organizations. However, even elections, which are one of the landmarks of democracy in any society, have come to acquire a different meaning under the current political conditions. Money politics, family ties, and services performed by actual and potential parliamentarians give a different meaning to the concept of elections. Political participation has been shaped by a host of factors, with legal limitations providing only one facet of the issue. Funding and even societal limitations have come to play a role in shaping the way political actors approach the issue of participation. All these factors have defined the concept of political participation in Egypt in a manner that clearly deviates from the general understanding of the term in more democratically developed societies.

Notes

1. See http://www.aljazeera.net/nr/exeres/41686drf-59d6-4c42.b&ed-9495ff2ac06.2003.
2. Interview with Gamal Mubarak, October 10, 2001, at http://www.ndp.org.eg.
3. Ibid.
4. See http://www.ndp.org.eg/en/platform/parliamentary.aspx.
5. See http://www.arabdecision.org/show_func_3_14_8_1_3_326.htm.

6. See http://www.arabdecision.org/show_func_3_14_8_1_3_4057.htm.

7. See http://www.al-araby.com/articles/897/040222-11-897-dlg01.htm.

8. See http://www.arabdecision.org/show_func_3_14_8_1_3_330.htm.

9. Interview with Mohyiddin on the website of Kefaya movement, May 28, 2005, at http://www.kefaya.org/05reports/050531mossadhegazy.htm.

10. See http://www.arabdecision.org/show_func_3_14_8_1_3_330.htm.

11. See http://www.egypt.com/top4/egyptian_judge.asp.

12. See http://www.eohr.org/ar/report/2002/ngo-law.htm.

13. See http://www.alwasatparty.com/modules.php?name=content&pa=showpage&pid=6.

14. See http://www.aljazeera.net/nr/exeres/989d3bcd-9360-4c7e-86C0-9a3f109218e.htm?wbc_purpose=basic.

15. See http://www.aljazeera.net/knowledgegate.

16. See http://www.islamway.com/?iw_s=article&iw_a=view&article_id=2236.

17. See http://hrinfo.net/egypt/cihrs/2005/pr0829.shtml.

18. See "Subjective Poverty and Social Capital: Towards a Comprehensive Strategy to Reduce Poverty" at http://www.ndp.org.eg/2nd_conference.

19. Ibid.

20. Ibid.

21. See http://en.wikipedia.org/wiki/egyptian_parliamentary_election,_2005#overall_results.

22. See http://www.arabrenewal.com/index, 2006.

23. See http://www.al-araby.com/articles/897/040222-11-897-dlg01.htm.

10

The Dynamics of
Civil Society in Morocco

Driss Maghraoui

With the move toward more economic liberalization in the 1990s, the Moroccan regime started to open up to different political and economic reforms. While keeping the stability of the regime and its legitimacy as an important imperative, the monarchy gave signs of opening up the political and economic fields, allowing for more political participation of civil society organizations in key national issues and debates. This chapter examines the strengths and limits of civil society participation in Moroccan politics. In the past decade it has become clear that the political vacuum that was left as a result of discredited political parties is gradually being filled with a more active civil society. I argue that as part of its strategies of self-renewal, adaptation, and co-optation, the Moroccan regime has sought to bring more nongovernmental organizations (NGOs) into its political orbit. In addition, the attempt to contain the rising popularity of the Islamists by formal inclusion has been more recently supplanted with a parallel strategy of involving more civil society actors that are outside the spectrum of religious ideology. This chapter focuses on the changes in those groups that have identified themselves with a more secular project of Moroccan society rather than on Islamist associations.

This chapter treats "political participation" in a dynamic way that better reflects the multidimensional strategies for participation of both the monarchy and the Moroccan civil society. Without such an understanding of participation, the various ways in which the Moroccan regime and civil society actors act and participate—such as negotiation, resistance, co-optation, or coercion—would not be well captured and grasped. Succinctly stated, different civil society actors have participated in different ways, and these differences ought to be acknowledged. This chapter focuses on two key examples in which Moroccan civil society actively participated: the Instance

193

Equité et Réconciliation (IER; Equity and Reconciliation Commission), and the Institut Royal pour la Culture Amazighe (IRCAM; Royal Institute for Amazigh Culture). These examples represent some of the more recent attempts by the Moroccan monarchy to deal with major social, economic, and political problems that civil society actors were instrumental in raising as part of the national debate. All of the royal committees that were created to examine these issues included members from the Moroccan civil society. Thus, while this chapter focuses on the IER and IRCAM, one could undertake similar analysis of a whole array of institutions that have mushroomed under King Mohammed VI, including but not limited to the Royal Commission for the Reform of the Moudawana, the National Initiative for Human Development, the Royal Consultative Council for Saharan Affairs, and the High Authority for Audiovisual Communication.

It would be a mistake to assume that the role of civil society under nondemocratic rule is only artificial and manipulated by the state. Instead, this chapter suggests that the participation of civil society in the royal committees has been relatively effective in giving them more legitimacy. The regime takes up causes raised initially by civil society and appropriates them within committees and institutions that then aspire to serve as monopolies for the same causes. Co-opting members of civil society into these committees is part of the strategy. It is important to note, however, that the continuous existence of a contested space illustrates resistance to the regime's attempt to monopolize the debate in the public sphere, making the nature of civil society participation more heterogeneous. I do not intend to make blanket statements about civil society actors or about the ways in which the Moroccan regime deals with them. While civil society in Morocco can still be part of an independent political activity to challenge state hegemonic rule in the Gramscian sense, it can simultaneously and may inadvertently be serving the monarchical regime.

If we were to accept the arguments of scholarship on authoritarianism, we would quickly underestimate the role of this dynamic civil society, stripping it of its impact even within well-established authoritarian structures. On the other hand, if we were to accept the premise of the democratization paradigm that assumes that civil society is a major source of empowerment for democratization, we should normally expect a full-blown democracy in Morocco within the next decade, about which many observers are already skeptical. Instead, this chapter suggests a middle-ground position whereby our conception of authoritarianism becomes more elastic and allows for the possibility of different forms of political participation. This chapter asks the question of how civil society can exist within an adaptable and more flexible form of authoritarian state, and yet not yield any significant democratic change.

While I agree with Laila Alhamad's argument (see Chapter 3) that it is hard to draw a causal relationship between the role of civil society and top-down reforms in the Arab world, and that we should also be more attentive to informal modes of political participation, it would be rather restrictive in the Moroccan context to underestimate the role of formal civil society organizations and to relate these reforms mainly to pressure exercised by Western governments. Political participation of civil society has gradually emerged as part of a growing space of contention in an attempt to press for reforms within the existing political system and not against it. On the one hand, I want to show that the Moroccan regime has allowed this space of contention as long as it does not challenge the monarchy's legitimacy or go beyond the "red lines." It is therefore part of a regime-regulated form of liberalization that does not entail a retreat of the monarchy from its absolute control over the decisionmaking process. Instead, it simply means a shift in the strategies and mechanisms of political control. On the other hand, my analysis here does not seek to imply that civil society actors will in the long run become irrelevant in the face of the state's growing hegemonic powers. Rather this analysis is intended to shed some light on how the monarchy can use civil society actors and appropriate their causes and discourses in order to increase its control and monopoly over the decisionmaking process.

The presence of such an active civil society can be effectively instrumentalized by appropriating it into the political machine of the monarchy as part of liberalization under coercion. Involving civil society will in some ways strengthen state capacity, instead of weakening its authoritarian power. Contrary to the bleak image that Nihad Gohar presents of civil society in Egypt (see Chapter 9), active and diverse NGOs in the Moroccan context have played an important role in advancing the potential for liberalization. However, this is not to suggest that these NGOs will ultimately ensure collective empowerment, the solidification of liberal values, or the institutionalization of democracy. The Moroccan context of political participation, then, allows for some understanding of the process by which an authoritarian regime adapts itself to a new conception of "political modernity" in order to rejuvenate and recast itself into the twenty-first century. After independence, King Hassan II could occasionally afford extremely violent measures in the face of political and social pressures. Army and police repression of different social movements between 1956 and 1991 were very common. But for the past decade, the use of coercive measures against social movements has become less acceptable, especially under different international pressures.

To understand political participation as a dynamic force, we can apply Jules Pretty's concept of participation (1995: 4–5) to the present case. Pretty distinguished between different levels of participation in the decisionmaking process, ranging from "manipulative" to "self-mobilization," presenting participation in a complex, nuanced way. Participation can be simply a matter of pretense in which all the power and decisionmaking reside with influential people. Alternatively, participation can be part of what Pretty calls "passive participation," which involves unilateral decisions. In this case, social actors participate in what has already been decided upon. Another dimension of participation is the consultative one. Participation by consultation does not necessarily imply that the views of social actors are really taken into consideration or that they are actively involved in decisionmaking.

While I join Holger Albrecht in his argument (see Chapter 2) that political participation is critical for further understanding of the authoritarian nature of the state in the Middle East, I believe civil society organizations in Morocco cannot simply embrace a high degree of illusion. This chapter suggests instead that the areas of political participation within which civil society in Morocco acts are more often within the parameters of manipulative, passive, and consultative participation than within the areas of interactive or self-mobilization participation. One could argue that civil society participation has moved from being more passive under Hassan II to being more interactive and consultative under Mohammed VI. Yet the manipulative and passive participation has not been entirely eclipsed.

▣ Historical Background

In 1998, King Hassan II allowed the election of a transitional government under opposition leader Abderrahman Youssoufi, while simultaneously allowing the establishment of the Consultative Council on Human Rights. Because of international pressure and growing internal social and economic problems, the late king was in a way also preparing the ground for a smooth and successful transition of power to his son in 1999. The arrival of King Mohammed VI created a better context for political opening. Young and reform-minded, the new king undertook some positive changes, including the sidelining of the longtime minister of the interior, Driss Basri, the return of political activists to Morocco after many years of exile in Europe, the release of political prisoners who were victims of the so-called *années de plomb* (years of repression and extrajudicial incarceration known as the "years of lead"), and the reform of the *moudawana* (civil code), which granted more rights to women. Partly a genuine policy of reform, but also a strategy on the part of the regime to promote its image abroad, the political opening nevertheless facilitated the rise of a more active civil society. From an economic perspective, the programs of "structural adjustment" imposed by the International Monetary Fund and the World Bank beginning in the late 1980s gradually weakened the traditional role of the state to generate jobs, provide services for the people, and satisfy their different demands (Desrues and Moyano 2001). This situation has led to increased poverty in major cities and in the countryside. Neighborhoods such as Darb al-Sultan, Hay al-Mohamadi, Sidi Ma'arouf, Sidi Othman in Casablanca and

Taqadoum, Douar al-Doum in Rabat, and others have some of the highest levels of poverty and unemployment. According to the World Bank (2001: 10), one Moroccan in five currently lives below the poverty level. Morocco is now known for what are commonly called *les barques de la mort* (the boats of death), which illegally transport hopeless young people across the Mediterranean Sea, though this search for a "better life" usually ends in death. Therefore, the social role of the state started to be filled by Moroccan civil society, supported most often by international NGOs. In addition, confronted by the problem of terrorism after the May 16, 2003, attack in Casablanca, the Moroccan civil society is increasingly perceived to be an integral part of the strategy to challenge the threat of religious radicalism. Representatives from Moroccan human rights associations, women's solidarity groups, and many local civil society groups are trying to capture the attention of a growing number of marginalized youth who are easily attracted by radical religious ideologies.

The process of economic liberalization, as it was associated with the phenomenon of structural adjustment and free-market economics, manifested itself along three different processes. First, like other trade unions in various parts of the world, the most important union organizations in Morocco (the Union Marocaine du Travail [UMT] or the Moroccan Labor Union, the Confédération Démocratique du Travail [CDT] or the Democratic Confederation of Labor, the Union Générale des Travailleurs Marocains [UGTM] or the General Union of Moroccan Workers, and the Fédération Démocratique du Travail [FDT] or the Democratic Labor Federation) became riddled with internal divisions, leaving them incapable of facing the challenges of neoliberalism (Jibril 2005). Economic hardship has contributed to the atomization of Moroccan society, which in itself has led to a gradual weakening of trade unionism. Consequently, trade unions have lost their political stamina to mobilize the people. Second, although there was a significant economic opening, the process of economic liberalization was not accompanied by a serious process of political liberalization and more significant moves toward institutionalized democracy. Morocco continued to cling to its "Hassanian democracy" as a good example of what has been termed "liberalized autocracy" without meaningfully engaging in democratic reforms. In the face of this political disillusionment, and with the lack of a viable and democratic system of representation, the main political parties in Morocco gradually lost their credibility with the population. Third, the process of economic liberalization inadvertently made it possible to further "internationalize" the "local" discourse about change and "modernity," broadly defined. This political and social context favored the growing role of a vibrant civil society, perceived to be outside the control and orbit of both the authoritarian state and the quiescent and corrupt political parties.

The logical consequences and inherent contradictions of economic liberalization in Morocco have subsequently resulted in a crisis of the authoritarian and hegemonic structures of political rule; hence a more dynamic civil society became possible, which has been able to benefit in varying degrees from a growing transnational discourse about democracy, human rights, and the environment. This discourse could not be structurally detached from the liberalizing economic project the Moroccan state had to embark upon. In a way, liberalization had to come as part of a whole "package," and civil society filled the political gap that was missing.

■ Civil Society and Political Participation: A Sample

Since the 1980s the Moroccan state has become much more open to the creation and political participation of numerous associations, as long as they do not confront the system. As part of its strategy of appropriation, the Moroccan regime has even contributed to the establishment of a number of regional associations. By the end of the 1990s, Morocco could count more than 30,000 local associations, while Tunisia had about 5,000. In Algeria the civil society potential has been muffled in a context dominated by a repressive political and military regime. Due to more openness on the part of the monarchical regime, Morocco has been a fertile ground for the emergence of a more vibrant civil society. About 37 percent of the Moroccan associations are concentrated between Rabat and Casablanca. According to the Johns Hopkins Comparative Nonprofit Sector project, in 1999 the civil society work force in Morocco represented 1.5 percent of the economically active population. Even though this is a small percentage, it represents a major development compared to two decades ago, when civil society sectors were very limited. Volunteer work, according to the same source, represented 52.8 percent of the civil society work force (Salamon 2004).

The Association Marocaine des Droits Humains (AMDH; Moroccan Human Rights Association), created in 1979, is one of the oldest and most respected human rights associations in the country (Mouaquit 2004). The AMDH presents itself as a progressive association based on both national and international standards. Over the years the AMDH has played an important role in defending human rights. The association strives to work independently from political parties, even though it was initially established by activists from the Union Socialiste des Forces Populaires (USFP; Socialist Union of Popular Forces). The association has encouraged mass action, and has regularly supported the principles and implementation of political, social, and cultural democracy as the basis of Moroccan society. In 2007 the AMDH had at least forty-five active sections throughout Morocco.

The AMDH has been at the forefront of the human rights debate since it started condemning the repressive system of King Hassan II. Since its inception it has played an important role in making public pronouncements, exposing human rights violations, and pressing for justice for victims. The AMDH was instrumental in organizing awareness campaigns about human rights violations and training various human rights associations. As part of its attempt to press for change in the judicial system and establish more democratic institutions, the AMDH has published general annual reports as well as specific reports concerning human rights violations in Morocco. In addition to organizing conferences and workshops, the association publishes books and brochures as well as a monthly human rights newspaper *(Al-Tadamoun)* in Arabic and French.

The second major civil society actor is the Organisation Marocaines des Droits Humains (OMDH; Moroccan Human Rights Organization), created in 1988; it too has a well-established reputation in the country. Since its inception, it has stressed the necessity to be politically independent and nonpartisan (Waltz 1991: 487). The OMDH is involved in many activities, often in conjunction with the AMDH. In fact, the two groups are also both part of various regional and international civil society networks. The OMDH has been instrumental in organizing awareness campaigns concerning human rights through its individual, collective, socioeconomic, cultural, civil, and political activities. The organization focuses part of its attention on education in the field of human rights, and protection and defense of victims. The OMDH has regularly called on the Moroccan government to adhere to international human rights conventions. It also presses for legal reinforcement of civil, political, socioeconomic, and cultural rights, and supports the independence and impartiality of the Moroccan judicial system as part of the consolidation of democracy and the rule of law. The OMDH's human rights agenda is similar to that of the AMDH. It has organized several workshops and conferences, and oversees many reports and publications.

The Forum de la Citoyenneté (Citizenship Forum) is a nonprofit cultural association that has concentrated on disseminating information regarding the principles of citizenship within Moroccan society. Three aspects of this forum make it important as far as political participation is concerned. First, it advocates dialogue among various national actors, including the government. The forum was conceived as a space for political actors to communicate their divergent perspectives. The Citizenship Forum works as a framework for the interaction of various social initiatives and points of view concerning major issues such as development, freedom, justice, and democracy in Morocco. Second, the Citizenship Forum attempts not only to imprint a culture of democracy and citizenship in Morocco, but also to involve various actors in political participation. Third, the forum insists on the creation of permanent institutions to guarantee the existence of the notion of Moroccan citizenship. Finally, the Citizenship Forum targets youth in order to engage them in current issues and problems in Moroccan society. The forum is also active in promoting and developing values of tolerance and a spirit of dialogue in the social and cultural spheres.[1]

The Citizenship Forum has developed some innovative programs for educating the public about citizenship, democratic transition, and citizen participation. These educational programs have focused particularly on strengthening the principles of citizenship among youth in high schools, through training sessions as well as cultural, artistic, and environmental workshops implemented in collaboration with the Ministry of Education and local, national, and international civil society actors. The Citizenship Forum has also created the Obsérvatoire de la Transition Démocratique au Maroc (Oversight of the Democratic Transition in Morocco), in collaboration with scholars and cultural actors. This is a scientific institution that specializes in issues concerning democratic transition in Morocco. Its members work to identify and define the concept of "democratic transition" by examining its intellectual origin and historical background. For the Citizenship Forum, identifying the mechanisms by which transition may occur, as well as the various signs indicating such transition, is an important aspect of measuring the prospects of democracy in Morocco. Finally, a citizen participation program, in the form of a study group comprising various actors such as civil society leaders, academics, human rights groups, business groups, social workers, and professionals, has been undertaken in Casablanca. This group forms a kind of civil "tissue," acting as advisers and observers concerning human rights abuse; it works to strengthen and upgrade local social groups, which in turn serve to buttress the core of development and democracy in Morocco. On a number of occasions, this group has worked closely with local government representatives, potential candidates for local elections, and mayors, informing them about the role that civil society can play in their neighborhoods and towns.

The Citizenship Forum has been instrumental in organizing conferences, workshops, and projects to consolidate the conditions of citizenship. It wants to create what it calls "bridges of communication"—networks of dialogue and cooperation to reinforce a "relationship of solidarity" between local and international actors as well as cooperation and coordination between public and private institutions in the promotion of the "values of citizenship and . . . its success." The Citizenship Forum has published some useful books with such revealing titles as *L'éducation à la citoyenneté* (2002), *Transformations démocratiques au Maroc: enjeux, handicapes et limites* (2003), and *L'Amazigh et les problématiques de l'identité composée* (2004).[2]

The Forum des Alternatives Maroc (FAM; Moroccan Alternatives Forum), a more recent association, was created in June 2003. It seeks to contribute to the establishment of an autonomous democratic, social, citizen movement. The FAM identifies itself as a civil society forum that defends and promotes economic, civil, political, social, and cultural rights without racial, ethnic, linguistic, religious, or gender segregation. It works with various social actors, including the government. The FAM has played an important role in encouraging political participation, emphasizing the role that civil society can play in promoting democracy in Morocco. In addition, its vision for solving local problems is to relate them to the international context.

One of the main objectives of the FAM is to "renew the terms of the debate about the role of the associative movement in the democratization of Moroccan society" (http://www.forumalternatives.org/article9.html). It encourages political participation by contributing to research and looking for appropriate and egalitarian avenues for partnership among various social actors and government officials. The vision of the FAM is to "inscribe the social movement in Morocco in an international dynamic of globalization and involve Moroccan social actors in the international dimension of the movement for peace" (http://www.forumalternatives.org/article9.html). The forum seeks to encourage all social alternatives that aspire to democracy and participative citizenship by creating a new context for debates regarding and among youth and students, associations, trade unions, and political parties. The activities of the FAM revolve around organizing regional workshops on civil rights and reform of the judicial system regarding civil rights. One important goal of the FAM is to create a consortium of networks in the form of a permanent research and training center for various civil society actors. The forum has organized six regional conferences intended to educate youth about the socioeconomic problems associated with globalization.

As previously mentioned, civil society actors in Morocco have regularly worked in collaboration with international NGOs or institutions. The Actions Positives pour le Droit des Femmes au Maghreb (APDFM; or Positive Action for Women's Rights in the Maghreb) is a good example of such collaboration. The APDFM was part of the Euro-Mediterranean Partnership initiative, especially in the framework of the European Union Euro-Mediterranean Democracy programs. In 1994, prior to launching the APDFM, Italy's Mediterranean Institute, with the support of the European Commission, started a research action program. The first stage of this program was undertaken in Morocco and Tunisia from 1994 to 1997. The second stage was undertaken in Algeria from 1997 to 1999. A network of Moroccan civil society actors, known as the Réseau Espace de Citoyenneté (REC; Citizenship Network) was involved and included the Association pour la Défense des Femmes Victimes des Violences (ADFVV; the Association for the Defense of Female Victims of Violence), the Réseau Associatif de Dévelopement Social et Démocratique (RADSD; the Network for Social and Democratic Development), the Forum des Jeunes Filles du Maroc (FJFM; Forum for Young Women in Morocco), the Union de l'Action Feminine (UAF; the Union for Feminine Action), and the UMT and the UGTM.

The APDFM is a good example of how an outside institution can create the context and dynamics necessary for coordination and political participation at the regional North African level. Involved in the project were women's associations, civil society organizations from the Maghreb (Algeria, Morocco, and Tunisia), and trade unions. The goal of this project was to promote women's rights and the democratic development of North African society through strengthening the work, action, and communication of civil society organizations. The APDFM was involved in various fields, including awareness days for women's rights, judicial and psychological assistance, training, and activities related to awareness campaigns and women's rights, all utilizing video, theater, and radio. The project also organized transnational training sessions specifically tailored for women's associations, trade unions, and various civil society groups in the Maghreb and the Euro-Mediterranean.

The Réseau Amazigh pour la Citoyenneté (RAC; Amazigh Network for Citizenship) was established in February 2004. This network concentrates on issues concerning cultural identity, human rights, women's rights, and the environment in Morocco. One of its main objectives is to promote and safeguard the Amazigh culture, identity, and language in Morocco and in North Africa in general.

Moroccans, Algerians, Tunisians, and Arabs residing overseas are among the most important actors in consolidating civil society in Morocco, the Maghreb, and the Middle East in general. This has become an important factor in encouraging more political participation in the Arab world. In the case of the Maghreb, citizens abroad are important for a number of reasons. First, historically, North Africans in Europe and in France, more specifically, were instrumental in the emergence of nationalism in North Africa. Young students from Algeria, Morocco, and Tunisia were the backbone of the nationalist movement against French colonialism. In the 1990s the Amazigh (Berber) cause, which has been the subject of debate in Algeria and Morocco, has gradually gained significant success in both countries, though it originated in Europe. Second, North Africans in France have much in common, since they face similar discriminatory problems in Europe and are critical of government in their home countries. Third, Moroccans in Europe are the most important source of foreign currency: 85 percent of Moroccans who reside overseas live in Europe and bring in more foreign currency than phosphate (Morocco exports the largest amount of phosphate in the world). Finally, North Africans in Europe can be effective in mobilizing local European associations for the same causes.

A good example is the so-called Congress, an international NGO conceived by the constituent assembly of the Tangier congress in November 2001. This event was the historical result of a long process, undertaken by an established committee, to give a voice to the Moroccan citizens (or those of Moroccan origin) living in the European Union countries and other regions of the world. The Congress aspires to function as a representative and consultative body and to create synergy between Moroccan groups who are dispersed internationally. Its main objectives are to defend the rights, freedoms, and interests of Moroccans or people of Moroccan background who live in Europe, especially in relation to immigration issues, and to encourage political participation.

Though such examples indicate that civil society and political participation are alive and well in Morocco, does this mean that the coercive and repressive measures associated with authoritarianism will cease to exist? This chapter does not propose such an outcome. While civil society is active in the public sphere, and while some NGOs are involved in royal commissions, Moroccan citizens can still be jailed simply because of political opinions that go against the "sacred foundations" of the nation. In 2000, when the AMDH published a list of names of Moroccan officials it considered responsible for human rights abuse, and then organized a demonstration in front of parliament, thirty-six of its members were eventually tried and condemned to imprisonment for three months. Since the advent of the new monarch, various civil society activists throughout Morocco have been harassed, intimidated, tried, imprisoned, and tortured because of their political views. Other targeted civil activist organizations have included the Western Sahara branch of the Forum for Truth and Justice, the UMT, and the Association Nationale des Diplomés Chomeurs du Maroc (ANDCM; National Association of Unemployed Moroccan Graduates).

◼ The Monarchy Reacts to Civil Society Pressure

It was under the late king Hassan II in the early 1990s that the initial reaction to pressure from civil society actors was witnessed. The first sign of this reaction was the fact that human rights issues started to become part of debates in the public sphere. In newspapers and booklets, public authorities were criticized for their involvement in human rights abuses. A number of prisoners—among the more famous of whom were Abraham Serfati, the Bourekat brothers, and the Oufkir family—were released from prison. The town of Tazmamart, which Hassan II once referred to as the "capital of flowers" in a television interview with a French journalist, became publicly associated with the most horrible atrocities, torture, and arbitrary detentions of the *années de plomb* (years of lead). Other "sites of memory," such as Derb Moulay Cherif in Casablanca, Dar al-Mokri in Rabat, and Qalat Mgouna in Agdez, became representative of the harsh and repressive political system in Morocco.

Longtime opposition leader Abderrahman Youssoufi returned from exile in 1980 and was charged in 1998 with the constitution of a *gouverne-*

ment d'alternance, which lasted until 2002. Under the leadership of Youssoufi, the new government stressed the necessity of democratic change, the rule of law, and transparency. A number of important political reforms took place, even though they did not reduce the power of the monarchy. These reforms were mainly concerned with constitutional changes regarding the two chambers of parliament, which started to approve actions taken by the government and vote on various bills. The constitutional reforms also made possible the establishment of commissions of inquiries to investigate measures taken by the government.

One of the most important reactions came when the king decided to create the Conseil Consultatif des Droits de l'Homme (CCDH; Advisory Council for Human Rights) in 1990. Morocco set the example for other Middle Eastern authoritarian states to create a panoply of national human rights institutions in a less overt and heavy-handed way to counter private civil society actors (see Cardenas and Flibbert 2005). In an important speech in 1990, Hassan II stated: "We have decided to fulfill our goal for the establishment of the rule of law, which will first and foremost put an end to a plethora of viewpoints about human rights, in order to close this chapter. It is otherwise supposed to provide the citizens with diligent, serious and efficient judicial means to defend their rights vis-à-vis the administration, the police and even the state." In the same speech, however, the king warned that "he, who in banners, speeches or newspapers, calls for another regime other than constitutional monarchy, has undertaken not a political action but a subversive act against the will of the people and the constitution."[3] It was clear that Hassan II was speaking about human rights and the means to attain them, while at the same time asserting the means by which to repress them. The CCDH addressed a case regarding 112 people who had "disappeared," 56 of whom had died, whose families were eligible for financial compensation. In November 1993, Hassan II created the Ministry of Human Rights and appointed one of the founding members of the OMDH, Omar Aziman, as its head. In hindsight, the appointment of a civil society human rights figure appears to have been one of the first steps in a strategy that Mohammed VI would refine and master.

It seemed clear that Hassan II wanted to close this chapter on human rights issues as quickly as possible, because it was affecting the image of the monarchy. On October 9, 1998, he addressed parliament, stressing the importance of human rights and insisting that this issue "should definitely be closed" to release Morocco from "the burden of a reputation that does not reflect its real face." The CCDH was responding to the will of Hassan II when it published a report in April 1999 that was clearly intended to "close this chapter" as the king intended, three months before his death. The CCDH's role was mainly technical, as it focused on financial considerations and disassociated itself from the major political ramifications of human rights abuse in Morocco. It was also very vague and obscure about the context and conditions in which human rights abuses were taking place. Furthermore, the 112 cases that it presented did not reflect the real numbers and realities of disappearances.

Many civil society actors, including the OMDH, the AMDH, and other international NGOs, reacted positively but skeptically to the CCDH. They were critical of its findings and stressed that the number of unresolved disappearance cases was much higher than that presented by the royal council. An important criticism was the fact the state was not being held responsible for human rights abuses. Some NGOs criticized the CCDH for working in an obscure manner without much presence in the public sphere via media coverage. For many, its report lacked the methodological rigor associated with investigations into past human rights abuses. Some viewed the CCDH as mere window dressing for Morocco's image on the international scene. Others viewed it as part of a strategy to appropriate human rights causes and to contain civil society activism. Finally, the financial dependence of the CCDH on the regime deprived it of autonomy and legitimacy (Bouandel 1999).

Whatever the CCDH's worth, it seemed clear that the pressure exerted by Moroccan and international NGOs resulted in some recognition of human rights abuses. Though the regime retained its authoritarian nature, it nevertheless realized that it had to react to this pressure and adapt itself to a new local and international context. Guilain Denœux and Abdeslam Maghraoui observed: "The powerful Interior Minister, Driss Basri, found himself on the defensive during the council's deliberations. Basri also seems to have understood that he could not confront the council head-on, or try to intimidate its members by flexing his muscles" (1998: 72). In addition to revising its penal code in 1992, the government in 1993 started to ratify a series of conventions, including the Convention Against Torture and Other Cruel, Inhuman, or Degrading Treatment or Punishment; the Convention on the Elimination of All Forms of Discrimination Against Women; and the Convention on the Rights of Children. A more lasting effect has been the presence of human rights issues on the public agenda. Local and international human rights organizations can work relatively freely and Moroccan NGOs are regularly consulted by the state on various issues. A certain degree of openness made it possible for courageous newspapers, such as *Le Journal, Tel Quel,* and *Assahifa,* to criticize the government and write about human rights abuses. However, some subjects remain taboo, such as Islam, the monarchy, and the Western Sahara; journalists who write critically about them have either been imprisoned or fined large amounts of money for transgressing the "red lines." Political participation has been allowed, but only within the limits accorded by the regime.

■ The Monarchic Umbrella of Civil Society

After Hassan II died in July 1999, the new king brought with him a fresh style to the monarchical institution and presented himself as a liberal leader with new conceptions of political, social, and economic matters. In a famous speech in August 1999, Mohammed VI reiterated his attachment to the ideals of constitutional monarchy, respect for human rights, and individual liberties by announcing the creation of an independent arbitration panel within the Advisory Council for Human Rights. He called for a new conception of authority based on accountability, and proclaimed that defining a new status for women and fighting against corruption and poverty were his top priorities. Mohammed VI confirmed the *gouvernement d'alternance* and has not interfered in the internal affairs of political parties. He has urged reform of the electoral law to ensure representation. He has also called upon Moroccans to take elections seriously. The first legislative elections held under Mohammed VI, in September 2002, orchestrated by Interior Minister Driss Jettou, occurred under relatively transparent conditions. Many observers perceived the elections to be an important moment for the prospect of democratization in Morocco.[4] The most significant sign of the king's more liberal policies came in 2004, when parliament adopted reforms of the *moudawana* (family code), a major step toward granting more rights to women, especially in matters concerning divorce and child custody.

The aftermath of the 2002 elections, however, revealed the limited potential for meaningful democratic change. Sidestepping the wishes of the majority in parliament, the king selected Driss Jettou as prime minister, even though he was not a member of the parliamentary majority, which included the USFP and the center-right Istiqlal. Additionally, Mohammed VI appointed, as had been the tradition, the ministers of interior, foreign affairs, and Islamic affairs. Politically, these appointments represented a step backward in the process of democratic transition for which the king had called. Jettou had no party affiliation, and his appointment—a surprise—created tension among the political elite. The appointment reconfirmed the traditional supremacy of the monarchy and its position as the only significant force in the decisionmaking process.

The new king's declared democratic intentions were simultaneously accompanied by measures that reinforced his powers through the creation of royal committees on strategic issues. Hassan II had started a trend in the monarchy of asserting monopoly control over key matters, and under Mohammed VI this trend has increased markedly. While power was established through the personification of authority under Hassan II, with the succession there has developed an "institutionalization" of royal powers. Whether the rationale behind this tendency is modernization of the monarchical institution, more efficiency, or tighter control over the decisionmaking process, clearly it is leading toward a hybrid system—that is, a combination of royal committees and state institutions with the same functions. Mohammed VI has both continued with the same policy of allowing more political participation by civil society actors, and injected the policy with a new strategy of appropriating actors' causes, mainly through the establishment of various committees and institutions such as the Equity and Reconciliation Commission and the Royal Institute for Amazigh Culture, discussed below.

To include more civil society actors in political participation can be seen as an extension of the push toward privatization in Morocco. The emergence of more technocrats at the expense of more politically oriented elite explains the new king's propensity to see liberalization and modernization via the lenses of economic development. The process of co-optation of civil society from this angle has at least three goals. First, civil society actors are genuinely becoming a new vector for mitigating the failures of the development process. In this case, civil society plays an alternative role to facilitating development, and the regime seems to be myopically focused on its economic agenda and unwilling to balance its vision with a more systematic and consistent project of political liberalization. The creation of the National Initiative for Human Development can be seen as part of this strategy.

Second, the inclusion of civil society can be seen as an apolitical tool that fits well within the development scheme and goals of the monarch. In this case, civil society works with the regime within the logic of a political continuity, not without it. While some segments of civil society irritate the regime, they do not appear to challenge or antagonize it. Therefore, the idea of development through local civil society actors becomes consistent not only with the privatization process of solving social and economic problems, but also with the "depoliticization" of the Moroccan political scene (Maghraoui 2002). When the monarchy stresses the discourse of privatization and good governance, it is simultaneously evoking a technical language that sees efficiency and procedural questions, not structural political issues, as the main problems that face Moroccan society.

Third, it seems that the new king is responding to a classical liberal concern that Jean-Jacques Rousseau evoked when he stated: "In a well ordered city every man flies to the assemblies. Under a bad government no one cares to stir a step to get to them, because no one is interested in what happens there, because it is foreseen that the general will will not prevail. . . . As soon as any man says of the affairs of the state, what does it matter to me? The state may be given up for lost" (Scaff 1975: 455). The new king might be responding to such an interpretation of the importance of participation, and this might be one of the reasons why he is sometimes portrayed as a more liberal monarch. However, it seems that the king's, or his advisers', interpretation of the philosophies of Rousseau, and perhaps Adam Smith, are overwhelmingly informed and influenced by those of Thomas Hobbes, thus resulting in a version of liberalism that is seriously restricted by an entrenched authoritarian political culture that has dominated Moroccan politics for a long period of the nation's history. The same syncretistic process that had produced "Hassanian democracy" is producing another kind of authoritarianism that is sprinkled with an updated lexicon of words and concepts drawn from neoliberalism, human rights discourse, and the language of human development. Mohammed VI's liberalism is often constrained by the authoritarian practices to which he is still structurally attached. This may be part of a new form of "authoritarian liberalism" or what has been termed the "liberalized autocracy" (Brumberg 2002).

In the current context of a fragmented opposition, Mohammed VI retains full control over the political and decisionmaking processes. The creation of royal councils and committees that include civil society actors, to deal with human rights abuse, poverty, women, the civil code, cultural diversity, the education system, and the Western Sahara question, are all part of the new "technologies of control." Here we are also reminded of a still useful distinction between political participation as part of an "interaction" and political participation as part of "instrumental action." While interactive participation is based on an individual's choice to identify with the common good of a social group's shared goals, purposes, and political "virtues," participation as instrumental action is associated with power relations and influence within a competitive political context. As Lawrence A. Scaff succinctly put it, instrumental action participation "functions to provide a cloak of 'legitimacy' for elite decisions and hence for the system in which decisions are made" (1975: 455).

■ The Equity and Reconciliation Commission

At the end of 1999, following Hassan II's death, a group of victims of human rights abuse and various civil society members created the so-called Moroccan Forum for Truth and Justice (MFTJ) to criticize the work of the CCDH (Slymovics 2001). The president of the MFTJ was the late Driss Benzekri, a political prisoner between 1974 and 1991. After receiving a PhD in international law in 1993 from the University of Essex in the United Kingdom, Benzekri went back to Morocco to become more active in the defense of human rights and later founded the MFTJ. The MFTJ engaged in a large campaign to create an independent truth commission with more extensive goals and long-term visions. The most important and symbolic acts of the MFTJ, along with the AMDH and the OMDH, came through organizing commemoration activities and the so-called *caravanes de la vérité* (truth caravans), which visited former detention centers as "sites of memory." In April 2001, Mohammed VI reacted by reorganizing the CCDH, reducing the number of seats assigned to political parties and unions, and involving more civil society actors. In November 2001 the MFTJ, the AMDH, and the OMDH proposed to the king the creation of a truth commission to further investigate past human rights violations and to make the issue more public. In a speech on January 7, 2001, Mohammed VI officially approved the establishment of the seventeen-member Equity and Reconciliation Commission (IER; Instance Equité et Réconciliation) to pursue out-of-court settlement of human rights abuses that had occurred between 1956 and 1999.

The king appointed Benzekri as president of the IER. From a linguistic and symbolic point of view, Benzekri has moved from being the president of "truth and justice" to being the president of "equity and reconciliation." In fact, he resigned his position at the MFTJ soon after his nomination to the IER. Other than its president, the membership of the IER reveals a clear preponderance of civil society figures. Eight of its members were from the CCDH: Driss Benzekri, secretary general of the CCDH; Ahmed Chaouki Benyoub, lawyer and vice president of the OMDH; Abdelaziz Benzakour, former president of the Moroccan Bar Association; Mbarek Bouderka, human rights activist in various associations in France; Mahjoub el-Haiba, university professor of human rights; Mustapha Iznasni, journalist and founding member of the OMDH; Latifa Jbabdi, president of the Women's Action Union; and Mohamed Mustapha Raissouni, also a former president of the Moroccan Bar Association. The remaining members were human rights activists: Abdelaziz Bennani, former president of the OMDH involved in the Euro-Mediterranean human rights network; Brahim Boutaleb, university professor of history; Mae el-Ainaine, first chairman of the Western Sahara's appellate court; Salah el-Ouadie, writer; Abdellatif Mennouni, lawyer and professor of constitutional law; Abdelhay Mouedden, university professor of political science; Mohamed Nechnach, physician and member of the International Committee of the Red Cross and Red Crescent; and Driss el-Yazami, vice president of the International Human Rights Federation.

With a mandate to provide monetary reparations to more than 20,000 cases, propose measures for assistance, aid the return of victims' bodies to their families, and create public "memory" sites, the commission was an important achievement in the political history of Morocco. The IER organized public hearings on television, prepared historical records about acts of repression that were perpetrated between 1956 and 1999, and made information available to the public through the creation of a website. It was clearly the most important step ever taken by Moroccan authorities to recognize human rights abuses committed under their regime.

The focus of criticism was the level of independence the commission actually possessed. The fact that some members of the IER were still de facto members of the CCDH meant that they operated within a limited space. In the eyes of some civil society leaders, the ambiguous relationship between the IER and the CCDH conferred less legitimacy to the final report drafted by the IER on human rights abuse. Furthermore, the IER had no legal basis, could not name perpetrators, and had to maintain "full secrecy." These constrictions can be attributed to inconsistent clauses that relate to the royal decree established for the commission. While Article 9 of that decree clearly stipulates that the IER will "examine the responsibility of the state or other institutions in the violations," Article 6 states that the commission does not have any judicial powers and will not determine individual responsibility for violations.[5] The limited definition of "human rights violation" was also a matter of concern. Article 5 states that the IER will deal with "grave violations of human rights," which were interpreted mainly as "enforced disappearance and arbitrary detention." The commission did not consider the various forms of human rights abuse defined by international standards and recognized by international NGOs such as Human Rights Watch.

The IER also worked in total detachment from parliament and the government, depriving it of potentially major political dimensions. The nature of the regime, which was at the heart of the human rights abuses, was not questioned. The political dinosaur upon which responsibility should have been based was somewhat eclipsed by more focus on the technicalities of the IER. While the IER was conducting its work regarding the 1956–1999 period, the Moroccan regime was still violating human rights. Moreover, military officials who were allegedly involved in the perpetuation of human rights abuses were not interviewed by the IER, and these state agents still operate with impunity.

In general, the Moroccan human rights organizations reacted positively to the work of the IER, but there was nevertheless some criticism. Some local civil society actors felt that they were being sidelined in terms of participation and consultation, while others believed that the mandate of the commission was limited and did not take into consideration the issue of accountability. This set in motion a conflictual relationship between the IER and the major associations, such as the AMDH, the OMDH, and the MFTJ, that were monitoring the work of the commission to counter its proposals for structural change and sweeping political and legal reform. It is unknown whether the Moroccan regime intended to create these divisions within civil society, but it is tempting to apply what Daniel Brumberg called "dissonant politics," in which the "rulers of liberalized autocracies strive to pit one group against another in ways that maximize the rulers' room for maneuver and restrict the opposition's capacity to work together" (2002: 61).

■ The Royal Institute for Amazigh Culture

The first glimmering of identity politics around Amazigh emerged in Morocco within the context and intellectual mood of the student movement in Rabat. In November 1967, young Amazigh activists established what became known as the Association Marocaine de la Recherche et de l'Echange Culturel (AMREC; Moroccan Research and Cultural Exchange Association), which sought to promote Berber culture and history. In the 1970s and 1980s, AMREC was concerned with cultural activities and scientific research; it later began to call for the recognition of cultural rights. Its more moderate stand was one of the reasons for the emergence of another important association, known as Tamaynut, in October 1978. Since its inception, Tamaynut was much more politically oriented. Its objective was to pressure the regime by giving an international dimension to the Amazigh cause (Kratochwil and Lakhbassi 2004). As opposed to Algeria, where the issue of Amazigh cultural identity has taken a confrontational and sometimes violent turn since the 1980 "Berber Spring," in Morocco it has remained more peaceful but no less assertive. Today AMREC has sections in at least eleven cities in Morocco, including Rabat, Casablanca, Marrakech, and Agadir.

One of the key moments of the Moroccan Amazigh movement came in 1991 in the southern city of Agadir, when six cultural associations joined their efforts to denounce the institutional and cultural marginalization of the Amazigh people and to press for the recognition of the Amazigh language in the Moroccan constitution, and its inclusion in the school system.

Mohammed Chafik was one of the first founding members of AMREC and the author of what became known as the "Agadir Chart" (La Charte d'Agadir). The manifesto was the first direct challenge to the homogeneous conception of Moroccan nationalism based predominantly on the notion of Arabhood. By returning to the past, Chafik and all those who signed the document wanted to rejuvenate Amazigh linguistic and cultural components that had been eclipsed from the prevalent Arab nationalist paradigm.

Since the Berber Manifesto, Amazigh civil society activists had been seriously harassed by Moroccan authorities. In 1982, poet Ali Sedki was sentenced to one year in prison for publishing an article about the history of the Berbers. In May 1994, a number of Amazigh activists were arrested because they had carried banners written in an Amazigh dialect known as Tifanagh. In defiance of the arrest, Berber activists organized a conference in May 1994 around the theme of "national information and Amazigh." Under instruction from the late king Hassan II, Moroccan authorities asked the Amazigh activists to draft a list of precise appeals. It did not take long for Hassan II to react. In August 1994, he announced publicly that the Amazigh language should be included in the primary school system. Though perceived as a lukewarm reaction by some, this was nevertheless a major step forward for the Amazigh activists, who kept pressing for the cause until it was recognized in September 2003. Also in 1994, Moroccan television began broadcasting short segments of the news in three different Amazigh dialects.

Amazigh cultural awareness in Morocco became a much more important component of the politics of identity in the late 1990s. In 1995, a number of cultural associations had established the Congrés Mondial Amazigh for the defense of Amazigh culture and identity. A key moment in the awakening of this awareness happened in 1997, when the World Amazigh Congress met for the first time in the Canary Islands in order to call once again for the preservation of Amazigh cultural identity and language. Propelling that event was the gradual emergence of a vibrant transnational civil society activism, especially among young students within both Europe and Morocco.

One of King Mohammed VI's most important reactions came in his famous Ajdir speech on October 17, 2001:

> The plural nature of our history and identity is indissociable from the unity of our nation, revolving around its sacred values and inviolable basis, which are a tolerant and generous Islam, the defense of a unified and integral homeland, allegiance to the crown and the king, and attachment to a social, democratic, and constitutional monarchy. We would like also to state that the Amazighty that looks deep into the history of the Moroccan people should belong to all Moroccans without being used for political ends.[6]

IRCAM was clearly created under the umbrella of the executive power. The royal *dahir* (decree) that was promulgated for its establishment referenced the "Kingdom's holy and intangible values: faith in God, love to the Fatherland, allegiance to the King—Amir al-Mouminine, Commander of the Faithful—and attachment to the constitutional monarchy." The royal decree began: "Our Sharifian Majesty, pursuant to Article 19 of the Constitution, has decided that in Article 1: An institution called 'Royal Institute of Amazigh Culture' . . . shall be created by Our Sharifian Majesty and be set under Our tutelage."

Reference to Article 19 invoked the king's title as Commander of the Faithful and the guarantor of the liberties of individuals. Article 2 went on to state that "the Institute, created to this end by Our Majesty, shall provide us with opinions on the measures to take in order to ensure and promote the Amazigh culture in all its expressions." Articles 6 and 7 of the royal decree were unambiguous: "The Institute's director shall be appointed by Our Majesty" while the other forty members of the institute's administrative board "shall be appointed, and reappointed if necessary, by Our Majesty, on the basis of a proposal made by the Institute's director." In addition "the

Institute's director shall submit all decisions made by the board to the High approval of Our Majesty." Upon the establishment of IRCAM's administrative council in June 2002, the king further reminded the new members of their specifically advisory role: "We are convinced that based on your intellectual probity, your consciousness of the plural nature of Moroccan culture, your sincere patriotism, and your distinguished qualities, you are well qualified to provide me with your sage advice."[7]

The idea behind the creation of an Amazigh institute was not new. Upon request from Hassan II in 1979, the idea was presented in a report prepared by Mohammed Chafik, but no action was taken. The idea of creating an Amazigh institute was again formulated in the 1991 Berber Manifesto, as the second major objective of Amazigh associations. A five-member royal committee was later established to ponder the Amazigh question and advise King Mohammed VI; it included four close advisers and Mohammed Chafik, the founding member of AMREC and the architect of the Berber Manifesto (Antara 2007). Chafik would become the first president of IRCAM. In November 2005, the king appointed Ahmed Boukouss as the second director of IRCAM. Boukouss was known for his moderate position in the Amazigh movement. In 1967 he was one of the founding members of AMREC, and he was also one of the first people who signed the Berber Manifesto. Upon his appointment, Boukouss was already on the defensive when he declared to the newspaper *As-Sahra al-Maghribia* (December 5, 2005, p. 2) that IRCAM "was not meant to contain Amazigh culture but to fulfill the aspirations of the Amazigh cultural movement."

IRCAM has been criticized by various Amazigh associations both inside and outside Morocco. The better-known and more public criticism has come from Tamaynut, the Amazigh Network for Citizenship, in Morocco; the International Amazigh Congress, in Paris; and the Amazigh Committee for Development and Human Rights, in Lausanne. Most of these associations stress the fact that Amazigh identity, culture, and language should be officially recognized in the Moroccan constitution, especially because Morocco is still referred to as an "Arab and Muslim state with Arabic as the official language." A number of local NGOs have condemned the discriminatory laws that do not allow people of Amazigh background to give their children Amazigh names. The judicial system still ignores some Amazigh customary laws (*'urf*) in its official codes.

In August 2006, the Amazigh Network for Citizenship invited forty different associations to a national workshop in order to propose a draft law that would create an alternative body to IRCAM. Perhaps an unrealistic goal, it was nevertheless symbolic and revealing. Ahmed Arhmouch, president of the network, told the newspaper *Al-Maghribia* that the purpose behind the creation of an alternative body for Amazigh language, culture, and civilization was to achieve real independence and more extensive power in decisionmaking. Arhmouch stressed the fact that IRCAM is mainly "a consultative body for the king and not a decisionmaking body; its budget is dependent on the royal palace, which hampers its independence" (*As-Sahra al-Maghribia,* December 5, 2005, p. 2). The president of Tamaynut also drafted a long list of recommendations that were indirectly meant to challenge the legitimacy of IRCAM.

Conclusion

Political participation by civil society actors is possible under a flexible and adaptable form of authoritarianism. As part of its strategies for self-renewal, adaptation, and co-optation, the Moroccan regime has been able to bring more NGOs into its political orbit. Because of its recent history, the most important event being the advent of a more liberal monarch, Morocco has become an ideal ground for testing how an entrenched authoritarian regime is capable of metamorphosis. In an ambiguous but sustainable way, a nondemocratic regime can use the tools and social forces that should theoretically threaten its continuity, but that in reality are appropriated and integrated into a political force that further ensures its legitimacy and existence.

Political participation of civil society, however limited or usurped by the monarchy for its own purposes, is evident in Morocco in various ways. The authoritarian nature of the Moroccan political regime has not prevented it from calling on the importance of "partnership" with local NGOs. In 2003 the office of the prime minister called upon the ministers and secretaries of state to work closely with civil society associations. Even though the nature of this partnership remains ambiguous, it has become part of the language and official discourse of the highest level of state officials, including King Mohammed VI. No matter what strategies the monarchy undertakes to engage civil society actors, and no matter how the regime reacts to political pressure, these actors can in the long run play an important role in facilitating the transition to a more liberal political system. This relationship between the Moroccan state and civil society has the potential to contribute to the nation's political and economic development only if civil society actors strive to retain their independence from the government, and only if this relationship becomes institutionalized outside the stronghold of the monarchical regime. If supported and strengthened, civil society organizations in Morocco could accumulate enough legitimacy and credibility to become an effective venue for political participation, and could eventually contribute to the creation of a structural basis for democracy.

Notes

1. See http://www.enda.org.ma/article.php.
2. See http://www.alternatives.ca.

3. Royal speech delivered on May 8, 1990, "Discours de Sa Majesté le Roi Hassan II lors de l'installation du Conseil Consultatif des Droits de l'Homme, le 8 mai 1990" (Speech of His Majesty King Hassan II at the time of the dedication of the advisory council of human rights, May 8, 1990.) Accessed at http://www.ccdh.org.ma/_fr_rubrique.php?id_rubrique=113 on February 5, 2007.

4. On the results of the 2002 elections, see http://www.afrol.com/news2002/mor029_poll_results.htm and http://www.elections2002.ma.

5. Royal Decree no. 1.04.42 of April 10, 2004, on the Commission on Equity and Reconciliation, at http://www.ier.ma/article.php3?id_article=221.

6. Speech given by King Mohammed VI on October 17, 2001, in Ajdir.

7. Ibid.

11

The Moroccan Parliament

Saloua Zerhouni

Many analysts have underestimated the role of parliament in authoritarian regimes and focused their studies instead on the strategies of these regimes to maintain and exercise their power. They have often paid little attention to the role of legislatures and the internal dynamics within these institutions. Most scholars have emphasized the weakness of legislative bodies under authoritarianism in order to show their limited power and influence on political outcomes (Claisse 1985). While this chapter recognizes that political openings in the Middle East and North Africa (MENA) have given rise to new hopes and expectations regarding the role that parliament can play in a transition from authoritarian to democratic rule, it departs slightly from the more optimistic view presented by the "democratization paradigm." In *Legislative Politics in the Arab World,* the authors stated in a rather confident manner that parliamentarians "have begun to exercise their constitutional functions of oversight of the executive branch. They also are becoming more effective in assisting their constituents to obtain services from the executive branch. . . . [parliamentarians] and their staffs are typically genuinely interested in building their institution into a major force for democracy" (Baaklini, Denœux, and Springborg 1999: 4).

I present in this chapter a more nuanced, albeit less rosy picture of the Moroccan parliament. The parliament is a "formal structuring framework" set up by the regime in order to ensure its stability and continuity. It serves as a channel through which the monarchy and political parties reach compromise and resolve conflicts. I suggest that the parliament's role in the field of legislation and government oversight is very limited, and that it is more a space for "doing politics" than for "producing policies." Despite the monarchy's discourse about the necessity of political participation, strengthening this institution is not a priority for the monarchy nor the political parties.

To better understand the role of the parliament within the Moroccan political system, and the politics of participation within this institution, this chapter analyzes political participation in Morocco and how the parliament's functions and powers have evolved through different legislatures. Indeed, over the years, the parliament has become a necessary institution for the overall functioning of the political system, despite its limited constitutional powers and "bad image." Based primarily on interviews, this chapter examines parliamentarians' motives for participation, as well as the internal dynamics of parliament and the obstacles to effective participation within it.[1]

▣ Political Participation in Morocco: Strong Discourse but Weak Reality

Morocco is one of the first countries in the Middle East to have encouraged political participation. In its first constitution, in 1962, the monarchy created a parliament and established a multiparty system, after which national and local elections were held on a regular basis. Over the years, the regime strove to project an image of Morocco as a democratic state with modern political institutions. Indeed, the 1990s carried the discourse of democratization, respect for human rights,[2] and more consensual relations between the monarchical institution and the opposition parties to new levels.[3] Morocco held relatively transparent national and local elections in 1993, 1997, and 2002. It also enhanced the powers of the parliament after the 1996 constitutional revision. Opposition newspapers and a number of nongovernmental organizations (NGOs) and political parties flourished, bringing to the forefront of the public debate many issues that were previously considered taboo.[4]

When King Mohammed VI came to power in 1999, he undertook measures to improve citizen representation and participation in the political life. The first elections under his reign remain the most transparent ever held in Morocco. In 2002 he urged reform of the electoral law to ensure more representation. In 2003, discussions about reforming a fragmented partisan scene were launched and resulted, after two years of negotiation between the Ministry of Interior and the main political parties, in the adoption of a law on organizing political parties. This brought with it a number of measures that called upon political parties to adopt more democratic and transparent mechanisms and procedures in their internal organization and financial management. Finally, in various speeches, the king urged the parliament to take full responsibility and to rationalize its activity.[5] Together, these actions reveal much about the importance that the monarch accords to the institution of the parliament.

However, the monarchy still concentrates most political power within its orbit and controls the venues of formal and informal participation. It is clear that the various modes and institutions of political participation do not tell us much about the "politics of participation" in Morocco. The monarchy has the ability to undermine formal modern political institutions through recourse to informal processes. For instance, the reform of the family code was dealt with mainly through a royal committee, and in the end the parliament served only as an institutional instrument to formally pass the reform.

In Morocco, there is a dilemma between an artificial and official discourse about the necessity for political participation and its reality as orchestrated by both the monarch and the political parties in order to achieve their own specific goals. The monarchy's discourse on political participation is motivated by at least three interrelated considerations. First, since independence, the Moroccan regime has always aspired to present itself as a modern state whose functioning is based on formal institutions, no matter how void of substance they are from within. The monarchy needs to have those institutions to shield it against criticism and inefficiency.[6]

Second, the idea of having a parliament goes beyond its classical role in developed democracies, notably that of legislation and government oversight. As discussed by Holger Albrecht in this volume (see Chapter 2), the objectives and functions of formal and modern institutions in authoritarian regimes differ from those of their counterparts in democracies. Rather than a legislative body, the parliament in Morocco is a "legitimizing tool" for decisions taken by the monarchical institution, which bases its strength on the relative weakness of the parliament. In general, the monarchy gains more power if other formal institutions are perceived to be weak. The monarchy needs weak institutions, but not "dead" institutions, in order to guarantee its survival. This holds true for other institutions such as civil society actors, which are instrumentalized by the regime to ensure its self-renewal (see Chapter 10).

Third, the parliament has been instrumentalized during a long period of King Hassan's reign for elite compensation, manipulation, integration, or co-optation. It provides the regime with an ideal space to manage or prevent conflicts between different stakeholders, allowing Hassan to present himself as the sole arbitrator for resolving differences and conflicts within society. It allows the regime to enlarge the space of negotiation and to bring political actors into play according to the rules of the game.

Political parties are motivated to participate by considerations that serve their interests and ambitions. First, the parliament is an avenue for aspiring individuals to become part of the elite, in order to approach the inner circles of power, most notably the government and the monarchy. Second, the parliament is an ideal space for parliamentarians to defend their interests, whether personal or professional. The parliament is also a channel through which conflicts are resolved. For the monarchy and the political parties, this institution is the sphere par excellence for conducting politics.

▦   The Moroccan Parliament:
"Backbone" for the Monarchy

Morocco experienced seven legislatures between 1963 and 2002. Despite the short period during which the parliament was dissolved by the monarchy,[7] it has generally continued to exist on a permanent basis. From one legislature to the other, the powers of the parliament were reinforced in a "homeopathic" manner. Aware of the crucial role of the parliament in the stability of the regime, the monarchy maintained the institution, but without giving it the necessary tools to exercise a real impact on the decisionmaking process. Instead, the parliament was instrumentalized to serve the interest of both the monarchy and the elite.

With the first legislatures, the parliament was considered a "rubber-stamp chamber"; its role was that of consultation and legitimization of decisions taken outside it. With the sixth and the seventh legislatures, the parliament played an increasingly effective role in the field of lawmaking and government oversight. Its prerogatives have been strengthened through the 1996 constitutional reform. Following the 2002 elections, the increasing number of representatives of the Islamist Party of Justice and Development (PJD) contributed to the revitalization of the parliamentary life.

Despite the image crisis of the Moroccan parliament, many programs and efforts have been implemented in coordination with international donors to strengthen the institution. Whether the reason behind this strengthening is to push further for democracy or to ensure the predominance of the monarchy, these efforts help to avoid a regime crisis. Various protagonists are aware of the importance of having a parliament with limited powers instead of having no parliament at all. A quick look at the history of different legislatures since 1963 reveals how the parliament has served as a stabilizing and structuring framework of the political scene.

Experiencing the Two Extremes:
The 1963 and 1970 Legislatures

When Hassan II came to power in 1961, he declared his intention to continue the reforms that his father, Mohammed V, initiated in the field of administrative decentralization and democratization. King Hassan promulgated the first constitution, which stipulated in Article 1 that Morocco is a "democratic, social, and constitutional monarchy." The powers of the government and the parliament were defined, but preeminence was given to the monarchical institution. In addition to the prerogatives recognized in Article 19, the king appoints the prime minister and the other cabinet members, and can dissolve the parliament and declare a state of emergency.[8]

According to this constitution, the parliament is bicameral and has considerable legislative and oversight powers. In terms of lawmaking, the parliament votes on laws as well as on the budget, and initiates laws concurrently with the prime minister. The legislature has the right to initiate the revision of the constitution, which can become definitive after its submission to referendum. In terms of the executive oversight, the parliament may question the government's responsibilities by adopting a no-confidence vote (Article 81).

Defining the parliament's constitutional framework was not sufficient to make it function. The political class needed to become familiar with the new mechanisms and techniques associated with legislation. After twenty months of existence, the chamber of representatives was faced with a number of crises that inhibited the normal functioning of the institution. There was a scission within the majority,[9] and the nationalist party Istiqlal started to question the fact that the monarchy had the exclusive prerogative of appointing the government.

The opposition parties, mainly Istiqlal and the Union Nationaliste des Forces Populaires (UNFP; National Union of Popular Forces), called for an agrarian reform and more state control of the economy. In June 1964, in a vote of no-confidence, the opposition pushed the government to resign.[10] This dynamic opposition permitted the emergence of an independent spirit that aspired to make the parliament an autonomous center of decisionmaking. It is in this context of parliamentary activism, coupled with the failure of political parties to reach an agreement concerning their participation in a government of national union, that King Hassan declared a state of emergency in June 1965 and decided to revise the constitution. The king suspended the parliament and concentrated all powers in his hands during the five-year state of emergency.

The resumption of parliamentary life took place in 1970 through a new constitution. This constitution brought about a number of measures aimed at reinforcing the powers of the monarchy and limiting those of the government and the parliament. A unicameral system was established to maintain only the chamber of representatives. This chamber was composed of 240 members, among whom 90 were elected directly and 150 indirectly. Though the parliament's lawmaking powers had not changed, its prerogatives for government oversight had been significantly reduced. Use of the no-confidence vote as a censure motion became more difficult, now requiring signature of one-fourth of parliamentarians instead of one-tenth in the previous legislature (Article 74). It became more difficult to invoke extraordinary sessions as well, and the right to initiate a constitutional revision was burdened by procedural measures and a signature requirement of two-thirds of parliamentarians.

In this atmosphere of constrained political participation, the opposition parties decided to boycott the chamber, 214 members of which supported the government. The absence of an opposition and the marginalization of political parties had a negative impact on the functioning of the parliament, which became a rubber-stamp chamber for the government. The lack of conditions for autonomous parliamentary action, as well as the turbulent political context of the early 1970s, contributed to the failure of this experience.[11]

In the first legislature, the monarchy experienced a parliament with strong prerogatives and a strong opposition. In the second legislature, the regime experienced a legislature with very limited powers and no opposition. In both scenarios there was political chaos and crisis. In the end, the monarchical regime became more aware of the importance of having a parliament that was neither strong nor weak.

Restoration of Parliamentary Activity: Prerequisite for Regime Stability (1977–1992)

The 1972 constitution reintroduced a degree of equilibrium between the various institutions and subsequently defined the prerogatives of the 1977 and 1984 legislatures. The monarchy maintained its centrality in the political system, while the powers of the parliament and the government were relatively reinforced. The unicameral system was maintained, but with a change in the proportion of directly elected parliamentarians (two-thirds of parliamentarians were elected directly and only one-third indirectly, according to Article 43). The legislative powers of parliament were extended to cover new areas such as the election of local assemblies and councils. Moreover, the chamber of representatives was given the power to vote on the so-called *lois-cadres,* which define the economic, social, and cultural action of the state. The parliament maintained the ability to revise the constitution, a right shared with the king and not with the government as in 1962.

The parliament resumed its work in 1977 after a five-year hiatus during which the monarchical institution had tried to restore unity around the throne.[12] The third legislature was one of "rehabilitation" of parliamentary politics and the integration of parties into the political system. Indeed, both the monarchy and opposition parties became aware of the importance of creating a more stable framework "within which social and political violence could be contained" (Khaldouni 1984: 22). Various actors perceived the parliament as an instrument to achieve specific objectives. For the monarchy, the most important thing was to have "a regime of representation, a democratic life with modern institutions." For the opposition parties, the most important thing was to have "a privileged framework for political protest within which they [could] oppose, protest and propose change" (Khaldouni 1984: 637).

The third legislature was charged with negative connotations that showed the marginalization of this institution and its subordination to the executive branch. For some researchers, the parliament played a necessary but symbolic role. Others emphasized the fact that the parliament was a marginalized institution (see, e.g., Claisse 1985: 113, 147–157). Scholars paid little attention to the fact that this institutional framework was necessary for political participation and to prevent the creation of a political vacuum. Between having a weak parliament and no parliament, the monarchy preferred the former. Negotiating between what was possible and what was wishful thinking, the opposition parties opted for the first scenario and integrated themselves into the political scene.

Following the 1984 legislative elections,[13] a centrist coalition dominated the parliament. There was a relative increase in the number of seats won by opposition parties (85 seats out of 306), and Istiqlal and Union Socialiste des Forces Populaires (USFP; Socialist Union of Popular Forces) parties became an important force.[14] This change in the composition of the parliament contributed to "reenergizing" the institution. The debates became less ideological, and more criticism was directed toward the liberal policies of the government. Lively debates took place when the budget, fiscal reform, structural adjustment, and privatization were discussed.

The confrontation between the government and the opposition culminated in a no-confidence vote in May 1990.[15] Despite the fact that the majority had rejected the censure motion, it was an important moment in the life of the legislature. It created an atmosphere of debate and resulted in more pronounced participation by the opposition parties. It also gave opposition parties the opportunity to use their constitutional prerogatives and to portray themselves as politically active. By the end of the legislature, the monarchy and the opposition had reached an implicit agreement about the importance of normalizing political life. In the late 1980s, however, liberalization was interrupted, with the king placing restrictions on the opposition and occasionally banning their newspapers when they criticized the government. The beginning of 1990 was characterized by labor unrest and strikes in Fez and other cities. Once again, King Hassan had to react by submitting a new constitution to referendum.

From Resurgence to Assertion:
A New Parliamentary Era (1993–2007)

Despite the fact that the monarchy has maintained its hegemony over the political system, the 1990s marked the beginning of a new era in legislative development in Morocco. The parliament was playing a more active role in a new context characterized by consensual interactions between the monarchy and opposition leaders from Istiqlal and left-wing parties. Part of a united front known as the Koutla al-Democratiya (Democratic Bloc),[16] opposition parties drafted a memorandum to the king in which they requested direct universal suffrage in parliamentary elections. Hassan II reacted in March 1992 by stating his intention to revise the constitution and to hold free elections. For the first time, the opposition parties were consulted and involved in revising the constitution.

A series of reforms were introduced after the constitutional revision of 1992. For instance, parliament was given the power to establish committees of inquiry following a majority vote. The government was ordered to present its program before the parliament for a vote of confidence. The Constitutional Council and the Social and Economic Council were established. Minor restrictions on the powers of the monarchy were also introduced, including removal of the king's power to dissolve the parliament during states of emergency (Article 35).

Besides constitutional reforms, the composition of the fifth legislature witnessed some positive changes.[17] For example, 75 percent of elected members were new, which helped revive the parliament. Women made a timid entrance when Badia Skalli from the USFP and Latifa Smires-Bennani from Istiqlal became the first female parliamentarians in Morocco. The opposition parties increased their seats in parliament (to 122 seats out of 333, among which 52 were for the USFP and 50 were for Istiqlal) and formed a front that the government had to consider more seriously. As a result, the debates were livelier and the parliament started to play a more visible role.

The activism of the parliamentarians did not spare the parliament from criticism. Parliamentarians were often criticized for their lack of rigor in plenary debates. The confrontational attitude of opposition parliamentarians toward the government reflected their lack of professional skills and, more importantly, their inadequate understanding of legislative rules and functioning. Repeated scenes of shouting between ministers and parliamentarians during televised plenary sessions were denounced by King Hassan, who in a speech referred to the parliament as a "circus" (Idrissi 1995: 6).

The parliament was suspended, and the king announced new constitutional reforms. Following the legislative elections in 1993, Hassan held negotiations with Koutla leaders in an attempt to form a new government. The royal offer was rejected, mainly because Hassan wanted to keep the most important ministries, commonly referred to as *ministères de souveraineté* (sovereign ministries), under his control.[18] Opposition parties repeatedly contested the presence of an indirectly elected tier in the chamber of representatives. The first round of negotiations failed, but they led to a dialogue between the two protagonists.

It is out of this context that the 1996 constitutional revision developed. All the opposition parties voted for the amendments introduced, because these amendments satisfied some of the demands presented in the memorandum. Among the most important reforms introduced was the abolition of indirect suffrage of members of the chamber of representatives and the reestablishment of a bicameral system. The sixth legislature was composed of a chamber of representatives elected entirely by direct universal suffrage and a chamber of councilors elected indirectly.[19]

In 1997, legislative elections were held, and one year later the king convinced Abderrahman Youssoufi, leader of the largest opposition party, the USFP, to head a *gouvernement d'alternance*.[20] Formed in 1998, the government was primarily drawn from opposition parties that had largely been excluded from power in the past.[21] The new government announced an ambitious program of reforms in the social, political, and economic fields, symbolizing a new era in relations between the monarchy and the opposition parties.

The new bicameral system was different from the one that Morocco had in 1962. The two chambers currently have almost the same prerogatives in the field of legislation and government oversight. They can both form fact-finding committees. The chamber of councilors was given also the power to present warning motions to the government (Article 77) and to draw its attention toward more specific issues. The initiative to revise the constitution is also a common prerogative among the two chambers.

The similarities in the prerogatives of the two chambers had a negative impact on the functioning of the legislature. Most of the criticism addressed to the sixth legislature related to the reestablishment of this system. The bicameral system had resulted in protracted legislative procedure and incoherent, redundant parliamentary work, given the lack of coordination between the two chambers. When comparing the internal rules of the chamber of representatives to those of the chamber of councilors, it seemed as if Morocco was confronted with two parliaments and not one parliament with two chambers.

Despite this criticism, this legislature was one of the most productive. Bills of great importance, concerning issues such as reform of the educational system, a five-year plan for economic and social development, reform of the media code to allow more freedom of expression, and the organization of the 2002 legislative elections, were voted on. The parliament, under its constitutional prerogative, established fact-finding committees. Indeed, the lower house formed a fact-finding committee to investigate the Crédit Immobilier et Hôtelier (Credit for Real Estate and Hostelry), while the upper house investigated the Caisse Nationale de Sécurité Sociale (National Fund for Social Security). In this way the parliament was able to assert its role in the legislative process and gain some relative control over the government. The political opening of the 1990s, as well as the more consensual relations that characterized the relationship between the monarchy and the opposition, were all encouraging factors that paved the way for a more active parliament.

However, the constitutional powers of the parliament and its new composition were not sufficient to make it more efficient. The internal dynamics of parliamentary participation were still characterized more by "politics" than policy. The parliament served as a space for negotiation and building consensus and compromise, and as a result, most bills were unanimously approved. The role of the opposition was very limited, if nonexistent. After more than thirty years in the opposition, it was more difficult for the USFP to take up the role of the majority. The same criticism applied to the new opposition, which did not have the necessary experience. Finally, most of the important bills were initiated and discussed outside the auspices of the parliament, whose main role was to vote on them.[22]

The adoption of a bicameral system provided the monarchy with new mechanisms for maintaining its predominance over the political scene. The creation of an upper house that has the same prerogatives as the lower house but whose composition consists of rival political alliances helped the king maintain his position as the sole arbiter. The bicameral system was part of the king's strategy to satisfy the demands of the opposition parties concerning the election of a chamber of representatives entirely through direct suffrage, while the upper house would play the role of a counterpower in case of a political crisis. This was again part of the monarchy's strategy to guarantee its stability and to keep the parliament in a weak and subordinate position.

With the 2002 legislature, the internal dynamics of the parliament have changed. Following the 2002 legislative elections, the PJD increased its number of representatives in the parliament from nine in the previous legislature to forty-three. In addition, these elections brought thirty-five female members to the parliament, thus increasing Morocco's ranking in the MENA region in terms of women's representation in political institutions.

The involvement of the Islamists in Moroccan politics is a very recent phenomenon, because of the history of confrontation that has characterized their relationship with the monarchy. In 1996, a group of Islamists moved from a strategy of criticism and opposition to one of participation in the established institutions of the regime. After that, they integrated an existing political party from the center right, Mouvement Populaire Constitutionnelle et Démocratique (MPCD; Constitutional and Democratic Popular Movement), and participated in the 1997 legislative elections. In 1998 they changed the name of their party from the MPCD to the Parti de Justice et de Développement (PJD, Party of Justice and Development), and managed to enlarge their electorate basis and representation in parliament. Currently, the representatives of the PJD constitute the third largest power in parliament after the USFP and Istiqlal.[23]

The PJD's participation in parliamentary politics brought a new dynamic. The party's parliamentary caucus is one of the most organized and active groups in parliament. It sits in the opposition bloc, thus reinforcing the parliament's control over the executive. It takes its work very seriously and has participated actively in committee and plenary session debates. During the 1997–2002 legislature, PJD participation in the parliamentary sphere was shaped by both religious concern and the desire to normalize their presence in parliament. In the 2002 legislature, ideological considerations were not applied with the same rigor for all draft bills. As the PJD became more integrated into the system, its emphasis on religious issues tended to dwindle in favor of more pragmatic goals, which require compromise.

The May 16, 2003, terrorist attacks in Casablanca constrained the PJD's participation. Under pressure to compromise concerning certain proposed legislation, most notably the reform of the family code and the anti-terror law, the Islamists demonstrated a great ability to adapt to new circumstances. For instance, the ideological disagreements that had characterized the discussion of the family code were bypassed when the monarchy took over this matter. The Islamists were also forced to cooperate on the anti-terror law, despite its irregularities and contradictions with respect to human rights. The mere fact that the Islamists have changed their position under pressure from the regime reveals the kind of limitations that the opposition encounters in exercising its powers in parliament.

The current legislature is also characterized by the increasing number of important laws that have been voted upon favorably. The reform of the family code and the nationality law, which allow Moroccan women to transmit their nationality to children born of non-Moroccan fathers, are two examples. These bills can have a significant influence on gender equality and human rights. Other bills include measures to enlarge and better organize political participation, reform the electoral law, and establish better conditions for electoral participation. In 2007 the legislature voted on a law to allow Moroccan residents outside Morocco to participate in the 2007 legislative elections.

Other bills have aimed at reinforcing the rule of law and enhancing public morality. The internal rules guiding the function of judges are currently under revision, and a draft bill to establish financial tribunals is under discussion. To ensure more transparency in the management of public funds, a bill imposing a declaration of estate for some local elected and high officials was voted on, despite the heated discussions and resistance that it had created in parliament. The minister of justice announced that other bills would be presented in order to generalize the spirit of this text to all elected members and to members of the government.

The Moroccan parliament is still subject to the same types of constraints. Despite Mohammed VI's liberal discourse on the necessity to energize this institution and his many invitations to parliamentarians to take full responsibility, in reality there has been no change in the monarchy's strategy toward the power of the legislature. The most important bills that were voted on during the 2002 legislature, such as reform of the family code and the party bill, were initiated by the monarchy, and consensus was built outside the parliament. The new king is still exercising his monarchical role as an arbiter. This role seems to have been accepted by the various political actors, including the opposition. Moreover, most of the draft bills have been undertaken at the initiative of the government, and bicameralism still inhibits the functioning of the legislature. In addition, working conditions have not improved. Since 1997, the two chambers have coexisted in the same building, and the number of staffers has not increased to provide better assistance for parliamentarians.

This synopsis of the various Moroccan legislatures clearly reveals the centrality of the parliament in building consensus and initiating conflict resolution. What becomes clear, as well, is that the parliament provides the monarchy and political parties with a formal context through which they can bargain, negotiate over resources and privileges, and reach compromise. More important, the parliament serves as a channel through which the relationship between the monarchy and the parties is normalized and trust is built.

■ Incentives for Parliamentary Participation: Self-Interest vs. Democratization

Political elites' attitudes toward political power have tended to be characterized primarily by concern for their own interests. Identifying the incentives for parliamentary participation will help us understand why the parliament in Morocco is more a space for engaging in "politics" than producing policies. Parliamentarians' motives can be explained by a multitude of factors that differ from one parliamentarian to another. Despite this diversity, two main incentives can be identified based on an analysis of the interviews I conducted.[24] The first shows the priority given to local and professional interests. Parliamentarians seek to defend the interests of their districts or the professional sectors to which they belong. These interests are not conceived in the context of a national strategy, but as part of an individualist achievement. The second incentive for Moroccan parliamentarians is their ideal and genuine interest in changing the political system.

Promoting Democracy and Introducing Change

For many observers, the Moroccan political scene is in a phase of "recomposition," as evidenced by the political openings of the 1990s and the advent to power of a new king. The motive for political engagement for one tier of interviewed parliamentarians was their desire to bring about a measure of "change," defined differently by different parliamentarians, but with a common denominator of democratizing the regime, as well as achieving further equality and social justice. This view was expressed by parliamentarians belonging to many political parties, including Istiqlal, the USFP, the Parti du Progrès et du Socialisme (PPS; Party for Progress and Socialism), the Front des Forces Démocratiques (FFD; Democratic Forces Front), the PJD, and the Confédération Démocratique des Travailleurs (The Workers Democratic Confederation), and crossed generational lines.

The perception of "change" differed according to the parliamentarian's ideological background. For instance, one parliamentarian from the PJD noted: "Establishing democracy should be intertwined with the teaching of the principles and values of Islam." For all left-wing parliamentarians, change meant democratization of the regime through elections. The key to change for most depended on the ability of the regime to do away with the "old practices" and to ensure conditions for transparent and fair elections. Indeed, local and legislative Moroccan elections in the 1970s and the 1980s were largely manipulated by the Ministry of Interior.

While all parliamentarians of this tier believed that parliament could play a role in advancing democracy in Morocco, their strategies for introducing change varied. The first strategy suggested participation within the structures of the regime, despite the lack of transparency and manipulative practices that characterized the 1970s and the 1980s. The second strategy recommended avoiding involvement in politics until electoral conditions could be improved. Thus the political opening of the 1990s largely determined participation in elections.

Aware of the limits of the political context within which parliamentarians participate, one interviewee from a left-wing political party explained his strategy in the following way: "Since the mid-1970s, we opted for the strategy of democratic participation in order to achieve change. For us, despite the fact that elections were highly falsified, organizing an electoral campaign was one way to contribute to citizens' awareness, and to present our choices and programs to the citizens so that they adhere to them." Despite their will to run for elections and their belief in the ideals of democracy, parliamentarians did not participate until the 1990s. That was the case not only for representatives from the PJD, who ran for the first time in the 1997 legislative elections, but also for parliamentarians from left-wing political parties, who explained their attitude as a result of the climate of mistrust that had characterized their relationship with the regime.

Promoting Local and Professional Interests

The parliament has often served as a space to preserve the parliamentarians' interests. Indeed, two-thirds of the interviewees declared that their participation in parliament was motivated by their will to defend the interests of the districts they represented and the professional sectors to which they belonged. These views were expressed by parliamentarians of diverse political affiliations, from different generations and professional backgrounds. Greater emphasis on defending local interests was expressed by parliamentarians who were active with NGOs and who had held or were holding local mandates,[25] while desire for political change was expressed mainly by parliamentarians working in the business or private sectors and by farmers.

There is an increasing awareness among parliamentarians about the merit of participation at the local level. Their national mandate is the only way through which they can achieve their goals at the local level. There is therefore a complementary relationship between working at the local level and working at the national level.[26] For some parliamentarians from political parties such as the Mouvement Populaire (MP; Popular Movement), the Mouvement National Populaire (MNP; National Popular Movement), and the Parti National Démocrate (PND; National Democratic Party), work at the local level means defending the interests of the city, district, or region to which they belong. Regional identity was very often related to the ethnic background of the parliamentarian. One parliamentarian expressed this view as follows:

> I belong to the rural area, which has been largely marginalized after independence, perhaps not intentionally. The people who were in power after independence were [mostly] from the urban areas and concentrated much of their efforts in developing [those] areas. When the children of peasants earn degrees from universities, they [decide] to get organized in order to defend the rural world. There is also the ethnic and the cultural dimension that has pushed us to run for a seat in parliament.

The group of parliamentarians who are keen to preserve their professional interests is composed mainly of councilors and deputies working in professional sectors ranging from commerce and industry to agriculture.[27] For these parliamentarians, the parliament functions as a space that allows awareness of decisions to be taken and, moreover, allows them to communicate their messages to the government and influence the orientation of the decisionmaking process. According to a parliamentarian from the Rassemblement National des Indépendants (National Assembly for Independents): "To defend a professional sector, one should be in parliament, this way we can know what are the policies that are undertaken and we can take the necessary action in order to influence them. We can have a well-organized professional federation, but if we are not represented in parliament, we cannot do much. Why do we have to create a lobby group if we can "invade" the political field from within?"

Participation in Parliamentary Meetings
Parliamentary caucuses and committees constitute important structures within which parliamentary work is done.[28] Parliamentarians' participation

within these "structures" varies according to their hierarchical status in parliament. While the heads of parliamentary groups and the committee chairs control and influence decisionmaking processes, the space for maneuver for parliamentarians who are just members is very limited. Most members do not try to challenge the decisions taken by the president of the group or by the committee chair; rather, their participation in these two structures is mainly an opportunity to speak about the issues that they want to stand up for either in their district or in their professional sector.

Because of their status, presidents of parliamentary caucuses[29] and committee chairs[30] play an important role in organizing parliamentary activity. They participate in the meetings of the so-called *conference des presidents,* in which the most important decisions related to the work of committees and the plenary session are discussed and voted on. Presidents and committee chairs participate actively in the parliament, and can be considered an "elite within the elite." They are closer to the centers of power within the institution and in their own political parties; their positions allow them to have a relative influence on decisionmaking processes.

Parliamentary Caucuses and the Predominance of Party Politics

Besides coordinating the meetings and activities of parliamentary caucuses, all presidents of these caucuses seek coordination between their own political parties and the caucuses. All caucus presidents consider themselves spokesmen of the political parties that they represent. A president's principal role consists of communicating the party's politics and views and convincing the members of the caucus that the party's position should be respected.[31] For one president: "The bureau of the political party gives its vision and orientations concerning a specific question, I communicate those ideas and I explain them to the members of the group. Parliamentarians should accept and follow what the party has decided. Sometimes, there is some resistance and [there are] differences between the parliamentarians' views and those expressed by the party, but we end up . . . making the position of the party prevail." The predominance of party politics over political outcomes in parliament is evident.[32]

Parliamentary caucus members' participation in and influence on decisionmaking processes are very limited. When caucus members attend the meetings, their main objective is to communicate the problems of the districts and professional sectors that they represent. As a result, the plenary sessions have lost their importance and have become redundant meetings about local and professional issues. When it comes to making decisions within the group, members rarely express their disagreement vis-à-vis the decisions and recommendations of their party. For well-educated and experienced parliamentarians, adopting decisions taken within the party is a question of "partisan discipline," while for less educated and new parliamentarians, the party is thought to know better about the decisions to be taken. A minority of parliamentarians express their disagreement, but because of their limited number, their ability to maneuver is restricted and they cannot influence the decisionmaking process.[33] Oppositional reaction is limited to either resignation from the parliamentary caucus or boycotting the caucus meetings. One parliamentarian explained the reason behind his resignation from the caucus in the following way: "We asked the leader of our political party to recruit financial advisers to assist us with our work in committees, especially the budget bill. Every parliamentarian gives 2,500 DH per month to the party . . . the equivalent of 150,000 DH [approximately US$15,000] per month if we count parliamentarians from both chambers. The leader of the party did not accept and did not even dare to explain his position."

Parliamentary Committees:
"Useless Spaces for Complaints"

The committee chairs play an important coordinating role that provides them with more power and influence on decisionmaking processes. Committee chairs coordinate with the government and establish the agenda for the committee meetings over which they preside. They direct the discussions and contribute effectively to building consensus among parliamentarians when it comes to voting on bills. One committee chair from the majority provided his perspective: "I try to bring closer the views expressed by parliamentarians in order to build consensus, we are the ones [committee chairs] who make votes; in certain cases, we present the amendments together as a majority."

All committee chairs were very critical of parliamentarians' participation in the meetings. One suggested: "Very often, parliamentarians' contribution to the discussion has a local, broad, and superficial character." Another's opinion was that "parliamentarians do not respect the agenda, and committee meetings [become] a 'space for useless complains.' The parliamentarians discuss [regional problems], they don't discuss the proposed bills. . . . I think there is a minority that is competent and a majority that has not yet the necessary qualifications to sit in parliament."

Committee chairs also emphasized the high rate of absenteeism in committee meetings. Bills are sometimes discussed and voted on among five or six parliamentarians, though each committee is composed of fifty-four members. One chair suggested: "The parliament's survival is dependent on the participation of a minority of parliamentarians—that is, 10 percent or 15 percent from both chambers—and without them and their participation the parliament would not continue to exist."

If the committee chairs are more influential when it comes to decisionmaking processes, the members of the committee play a more limited role. First, their lack of expertise and material resources make the discussion of bills, especially when they relate to the budget, more difficult. This has a negative influence on legislative production and government oversight. Second, most of the parliamentarians whose education is limited to primary or secondary schooling do not participate much in the discussion of bills, they just raise their hands during voting and vote according to party lines. However, committee meetings represent an opportunity for a minority of parliamentarians to discuss proposed bills, present amendments, and formulate oral and written questions to the government. The national dimension of parliamentary participation was put forward by representatives from the PJD and from left-wing parties such as the USFP and the PPS.

It is clear that the decisionmaking process in the Moroccan parliament is highly centralized within a small group of parliamentarians, and that political parties dominate political outcomes. When a parliamentarian does not hold a position in the hierarchy, his or her ability to maneuver remains very limited. If the parliament is instrumentalized by the regime to ensure its stability and continuity, it is also used by the parliamentarians themselves to achieve their own specific objectives. The participation of most parliamentarians is determined by their interests. The parliament is more a space for negotiation over resources and access to the "circles of power" than a space for producing general policies. In addition, the lack of human resources to assist parliamentarians in their work makes their task more difficult. Participation in the Moroccan parliament reveals a great deal about the weakness of this institution and the image crisis it suffers.

▪ Conclusion

The Moroccan parliament is perceived as a weak institution in terms of its powers, its internal functioning, and the image it portrays. The rules of the game have been set up in a way to make it function as an "empty shell." However, one should not underestimate the importance of this institution for the continuity and the stability of the regime. In Morocco, the primary role of the parliament is not that of legislation and government oversight; rather, the parliament is a space for "managing the field of politics." Despite its weaknesses, the mere existence of the parliament is important for giving a permanent "pulse" to the political scene. There, elections are organized and seats are negotiated among the political parties. It acts like a game card, where roles are redistributed, rules are redefined, the majority rules, and coalitions and oppositions are created. The parliament is an ideal space for creating debates.

Moreover, the parliament is the ideal arena for resolving differences and conflicts within the society. The monarchy has always pronounced, as a major political strategy, its ability to serve as the motor of change and the "prime mover" that mobilizes everything for its own benefit. According to elite and public views, the monarchy is perceived as an efficient institution, a perennial political structure, and an indispensable political system. There is no consensus about the role and function of the parliament; instead, there are debates about abolishing the upper house.

If the parliament is to resolve its image crisis, it will need to assume new roles and to become a vibrant and dynamic institution within which key policies are initiated and voted on. The Moroccan parliament needs to transform itself from a body that has served as a vacuum and a channel of conflicts and politics, to that of a policymaker. A change in the legal, constitutional, and institutional frameworks may create an environment conducive to legislative development.

The parliament will continue to play a role in forging compromise between various stakeholders. It is an ideal channel for consensus building and conflict resolution among the political parties. The opposition parties have learned that radical rhetoric is not the best way to achieve their objectives. Strengthening the Moroccan parliament could be beneficial for all political actors, but this will not result simply from the short-term financial and technical support of international donors. Rather, the power of the parliament should be enhanced through constitutional change, separation of the branches of government, elite renewal, and establishment of solid democratic institutions.

■ Notes

1. The sample of interviewees comprised forty-three parliamentarians from the chamber of representatives and thirty-nine from the chamber of councilors. It included presidents of parliamentary groups and committee chairs. The majority of the interviewees (fifty-one) had a university degree; twenty-one had attained secondary-level education, and ten had attained only primary-level schooling. Fifty-five of the interviewees were working in the private sector, fourteen were professors, eleven were farmers, and two were working in the public sector. Ten of the interviewees were under forty-five years old, the majority was between ages forty-five and sixty, and eighteen were older than sixty. The interviews were conducted in 2000. From 2004 to 2006, in collaboration with the Center for International Development at the State University of New York, I contributed to the implementation of a program on strengthening the Moroccan parliament. Insights gained during that experience were used in developing this chapter.

2. Due to domestic and international pressures, the king released political prisoners, created a human rights ministry (1993), and announced the destruction of the Tazmamart death camp (1994). Moreover, administrative tribunals, a council responsible for the control of the constitutionality of laws, and a consultative council for social dialogue were set up in 1994. In general, important steps were being taken to "moralize" public life, including the launch of antidrug campaigns.

3. For instance, following the 1997 legislative elections, King Hassan II suc-

ceeded in convincing Abderrahman Youssoufi, leader of the largest opposition party, the USFP, to head government of *gouvernement d'alternance*.

4. For instance, King Mohammed VI established the Equity and Reconciliation Commission in order to reimburse the persons who had been subjected to torture or injustice.

5. The king's speech in the opening session of the legislative year, October 2004.

6. When it comes to unpopular social and economic policies, the use of formal institutions can relieve the monarchy from the burden of accountability. To put it bluntly, in Morocco, we have never heard that the monarchy is responsible for unemployment or raising the prices of oil—rather it is "the government." The king imparts justice but is not responsible for social injustice.

7. Between 1965 and 1970, Morocco was under a state of emergency, as declared by King Hassan II.

8. According to Article 19, the king is "Commander of the Faithful, [and] shall be the Supreme Representative of the Nation and the Symbol of the unity thereof. He shall be the guarantor of the perpetuation and the continuity of the State. As Defender of the Faith, He shall ensure the respect for the Constitution. He shall be the Protector of the rights and liberties of the citizens, social groups and organizations. The King shall be the guarantor of the independence of the Nation and the territorial integrity of the Kingdom within all its rightful boundaries."

9. There was tension between the Front for the Defense of Constitutional Institutions and the Popular Movement. The latter complained about its representation in the government and wanted more ministerial portfolios.

10. The government escaped this first attempt because of an insufficient number of votes (a small number of votes were missing). For more details on the content and positions of the political parties, see al-Missioui 2000: 7–77.

11. Morocco witnessed two attempted coups d'état, in 1971 and 1972.

12. After the interruption of the political opening in 1965, King Hassan's attempts to restore the relationship between the monarchy and the opposition parties were unsuccessful. This relationship was put back on track in the mid-1970s with the emergence of a "national consensus" concerning the monarchy's claim to the Western Sahara. Since 1975, Morocco has asserted territorial claim over the Western Sahara, the former Spanish colony (1884–1975) that was ceded by Spain to Morocco and Mauritania without the consent of Western Saharans. For more on the Western Sahara dispute, see Zoubir and Volman 1993.

13. The parliament's four-year term was extended to six years through a constitutional amendment adopted in May 1980. The legislative elections that were initially planned for 1981 were postponed because of serious economic and social crises.

14. The USFP was created in 1972 as a breakaway from the UNFP.

15. The legislature's term was extended for two years by the 1989 referendum. King Hassan grounded his decision in the idea that there should be no interference between the elections and the referendum in the Western Sahara.

16. Koutla was composed of four political parties: Istiqlal, the Socialist Union of Popular Forces, the Party for Progress and Socialism, and the Organization for Democratic and Popular Action.

17. For more on the strengths and weaknesses of the fifth legislature, see the chapter on Morocco in Baaklini, Denœux, and Springborg 1999: 111–132.

18. These ministries are Interior, Justice, Islamic Affairs, and Foreign Affairs. See Tozy 2000.

19. Three-fifths of the members of the chamber of councilors were elected by regional electoral colleges. Chamber members were elected for nine-year terms. The terms of one-third of house members were renewed every three years.

20. In liberal democracies, *alternance* means the assumption to power of opposition parties as a result of their success in free and transparent elections. Many interpretations were given to the king's initiative of *alternance*. For some observers, it pointed to the possible evolution of a more pluralistic political system, but also to Hassan preparing conditions for a smooth succession. For others, such as Michael Willis, it was "a cynical attempt to tempt critics of the system or in the system itself so they compromise themselves" (1999: 118).

21. The *gouvernement d'alternance* was a coalition drawn from a parliamentary majority formed by seven parties: the Democratic Forces Front, Istiqlal, the National Popular Movement, the Social Democratic Party, the Party for Progress and Socialism, National Assembly for Independents, and the Socialist Union of Popular Forces.

22. For instance, in regard to reform of the educational system, the king appointed a royal committee to oversee this dossier, and the parliament later intervened to vote on the reform law after committee discussions.

23. Despite the criticism that had been addressed to the Socialists during their control of *gouvernement d'alternance,* they gained fifty-seven seats in parliament. The Socialists continue to constitute the majority in parliament, together with ideologically different political parties such as the Popular Movement. In addition, the USFP remains in government and holds some important portfolios, such as the Ministry of Finance.

24. Data were gathered during the sixth legislature.

25. A third (36 percent) of the interviewees held a local mandate in parallel to their national mandate.

26. The fact that the national level serves the local level is very revealing about the limits of decentralization in Morocco, despite all the efforts that were devoted to this matter.

27. Private sector workers (34 percent) dominated the parliament during the sixth legislature, followed by businessmen (25 percent).

28. The core of the parliamentary activity is undertaken within the committees. Proposed bills are discussed, amended, and voted on in committee before being presented to the plenary session.

29. Eighteen out of twenty-one presidents of parliamentary groups were interviewed. Two-thirds of the interviewees had a university degree; one-third had a high school degree. Presidents came primarily from the private sector; a minority were school or university teachers. The majority were between forty-five and sixty years of age, and were serving their second or third national terms apart from PJD presidency. This shows that only experienced parliamentarians are appointed to preside over the parliamentary groups. Finally, it is worthwhile to note that all presidential parliamentarians are men; no women occupy these positions.

30. Eleven out of the twelve committee chairs were interviewed. All of the interviewees had a university degree, and the majority were older than forty-five and serving their second or third term. Most of them worked in the private sector. No women occupied these positions.

31. Apart from the PJD parliamentary group, in which the president is elected, the presidents of other groups are appointed directly by the bureaus of the political parties, and the members of the group are then consulted to approve the appointments. In many cases, the parliamentary president is a member of the political bureau of the party.

32. The predominance of party politics in parliamentary groups was challenged by two presidents from the opposition who were trying to ensure more autonomy in the parliamentary decisionmaking process.

33. Most of them belong to left-wing political parties, have a university degree, and are serving their second or third term. The majority hold positions in parliament, as members of chamber bureaus, vice presidents of committees, and the like.

12

Trade Unions in Tunisia

Delphine Cavallo

Compared with its Maghreban neighbors, Tunisia projects an authoritarian image in which a single party, the Democratic Constitutional Rally (DCR), exercises effective control over the political process. Following the example of other countries in the region, the past fifteen years in Tunisia—that is, since 1993—have brought mitigation of controls in favor of more open-minded, "liberal" policies. These include the creation of election laws reserving a number of seats in the national parliament for the legal opposition,[1] a more flexible procedure to register one's candidacy for the office of president,[2] well-defined rules for engineering of electoral campaigns, the opening of media ownership to the private sector,[3] and the withdrawal of copyright registration for the newspaper industry.[4] Together, these measures, and many more, intended to show signs of liberalization as part of a democratic "toolkit."

However, such liberalization barely opened the way for political participation. Electoral reforms have allowed for opposition-party candidates, but the ruling party itself selects these, leaving little doubt as to the election outcomes.[5] Financial regulations and restrictions on media access outside election periods, pervasive police pressure to limit protest, and government regulations of political parties all limit public interest in general elections and party membership outside the DCR.[6] Furthermore, as the presidential party's quasi-monopoly on the distribution of material and political patronage attracts large numbers of diverse members, political debates become limited by strong social controls and one major taboo: the public incontestability of the president. Moreover, such debates are only rarely opened to the public. The process inevitably leads to overpoliticization through depoliticization; in other words, as more and more issues become of interest to the central regime, the authorities assert more and more control, leaving only secondary or technical issues to be debated openly.[7]

Nevertheless, the machinery of control, repression, and technical mediation has not eliminated political participation and contestation entirely. Political conflict survives outside traditional channels and indeed, as Robert Bianchi (1989) noted, takes place within the very state-created institutions intended to channel and constrain demands. Legal limitation on formal participation in venues such as elections and political parties has fostered the politicization of social institutions.

This chapter examines how the Tunisian workers' union, the General Labor Union of Tunisia (UGTT), acts as an important arena of contestation within the Tunisian political sphere. Officially, the UGTT is the only Tunisian labor union, representing all workers' interests in all sectors in decisionmaking on labor laws and rights (particularly during the triennial and tripartite social negotiations with the state and the employers' union). At the same time, however, the UGTT is ingrained in the Tunisian political system as a forum for political expression, even for individuals who belong to illegal political parties (such as Islamists or left-wing extremists). Fieldwork in Tunisia shows that union activism is driven not only by social motives, but also by formal and informal networks that link union members—the elite rank and file—to other important political actors, including political parties.[8]

The chapter begins with a discussion of how struggles within corporatist institutions may present opportunities for political participation in Tunisia, followed by a discussion of the ways in which the state has attempted to constrain the union, and the tensions that remain, despite (or perhaps because of) state involvement. The chapter next posits that bureaucratization in Tunisia cannot be understood as merely depoliticization, and instead must be understood as having political motivations and contexts. The chapter then considers how the UGTT promotes political socialization at the individual level, and explores current dynamics and tensions between the UGTT and the state. Given its somewhat contradictory roles, as well as the conflicts existing both within the union and between the union and the state, the UGTT remains an important arena for contestation over the balance of power among actors, and indeed for contestation over the boundaries of the state.[9]

■ Internal Plural Expression in Authoritarian Regimes

The expectation that political mobilization in authoritarian regimes is weak has a long history. Juan Linz argued compellingly that authoritarian regimes require weak political mobilization efforts (2000: 159). If political elites mobilize their constituents to participate in government, they risk frightening other elements of the regime and forcing its evolution toward either totalitarianism or democracy. Thus, Linz argued, authoritarian regimes come to be characterized by the hesitance of party militants and the depoliticization of society.

Yet Linz focused on mobilization as a means of gaining access to political institutions, rather than on contestation within such institutions. This approach raises two objections. First, it assumes the field of political institutions to be unchanging, disregarding the power struggles that inform its organization. Second, it assumes that political institutions are monolithic, disregarding internal tensions, which are in fact political mobilization.

As the UGTT demonstrates, the ability of ruling Tunisian elites to retain a dominant and central position in distributing resources and establishing a balance of power does not eliminate contestation within institutions. The role of management becomes to control the externalization of political expressions, rather than to prevent their emergence. In that sense, the UGTT is an arena that offers competing actors a means to express themselves, to organize themselves, and to be heard.

■ The UGTT: Confined to Social and Economic Issues?

In 1962, the UGTT and the Tunisian Industry, Commerce, and Crafts Union (UTICA)—the employers' union—became the sole interlocutors for laborers and employers who were assigned to channel requests and objections to the authorities. Links between the unions and the state were reinforced by the appointment of labor union leaders to government ministries. Most notably, Ahmed Ben Salah, the former secretary-general of the Central Labor Union (1954–1956), was appointed to lead the Ministry of Economy by Habib Bourguiba. As minister of economy, Ben Salah introduced socialist practices into Tunisian economic policy through the use of cooperatives and planning programs (1960–1969), based on the economic report he presented to the sixth UGTT congress in 1956, when he served as secretary-general. Yet the relationship between the UGTT and the government is not entirely symbiotic. The merging of the UGTT with institutions of Tunisian corporatist pluralism can be seen as an attempt to bring the labor union to heel, affirming the now unique party's primacy over other organizations while providing party elites with options of change, conversion, and alliance. Indeed, Ahmed Ben Salah himself was pushed away from the UGTT leadership for fear that he would turn the UGTT into a true political opponent of the ruling party, New Destour.[10]

The ambiguous relationship between the UGTT and the state continued after the change of president in 1987. On the surface, the UGTT complied with the ensuing political and economic reforms, formally realigning itself with its partners in industry and adopting the new, liberal discourse that accompanied reform. Tunisian authorities also deepened and systematized the mechanisms aimed at formalizing the roles of the "social partners in industry": the state, UTICA, and the UGTT. The union's responsibilities in social matters were demonstrated by the inclusion of labor unions in economic and social decisionmaking processes (especially through the Economic and Social Council).

Most notably, the triennial, tripartite negotiations affirmed the social and economic importance of the unions. These negotiations brought together the UGTT, UTICA, and the state to set wages and other economic policies. Such agreements had existed since 1970, but they were not updated on a regular basis. In 1990, the state formalized this process, establishing the provision that the agreement be negotiated every three years based on collective agreements. This both integrated the union into the process of promoting economic reform and tied the UGTT's hands in demanding higher wages (as well as making other, more political demands). Now responsible for Tunisia's ability to meet the "requirements" of national competitiveness, the UGTT became a safeguard for existing rights. No longer could the UGTT extend demands for higher wages or broader political freedoms.

Thus, implicit understandings between the UGTT, UTICA, and the state have constrained the UGTT. Wage increases are granted in return for restraint in the UGTT's demands, limiting action to the defense of rights acquired through legislation, made for the most part at the firm—not sectoral—level. In this way, in the 1990s, the union committed itself, at times against the interests of its political base, to a policy of "social stability" in order to guarantee a balance in the distribution of the benefits of economic liberalization and social stability. Such agreements proscribe any actions from the UGTT for demands exceeding the terms of these conventions. In short, the union found itself in the position of managing the social impact of economic reform, hand in hand with employers and political actors. As Christopher Alexander pointed out, the aim of this strategy was to demonstrate that the UGTT was a responsible partner in reform. "In turn, they hope[d] that this moderation and commitment to dialogue [would] make the government and private owners more willing to accept a stronger institutionalized role for the UGTT at both the national and plan level" (1996: 275).

In concurrence with restricting union responsibilities, the state began to exercise more power over the leadership and structure of the UGTT. The Tunisian president now appoints the secretary-general of the UGTT, which gives the president heavy influence over the labor union. Similarly, members of the executive committee, such as union directors, are often appointed, then assigned by order of the president or of a minister, to public companies for which they do not hold an elective mandate.

The structure of the UGTT has become highly centralized. It is organized hierarchically in ten levels, from its national congress, which elects the secretary-general, to union locals. In the 1990s, the UGTT leadership reinforced its centralization and control of the movement by requiring the secretary-general's authorization for any strike action. "Peak leaders work to prevent federations from organizing sector- or region-wide strikes during collective bargaining for fear that politicized militants on the left or the right will try to use them for political ends" (Alexander 1996: 266).

In the face of these constraints, the UGTT has changed its methods of engagement. For the most part, labor conflicts are now managed at the firm level, where since 1994 elected employee representatives have participated on a joint advisory committee for companies of forty or more employees. Importantly, these conflicts are seldom picked up by the media. Socioeconomic confrontations and "class" conflicts therefore switched from being addressed collectively or publicly, to being addressed within individual channels and outside the media spotlight. In other words, the "consensus" on economic policy led effectively to political "neutralization."

These changes have significant consequences. The UGTT seeks to reinforce its role in economic and social institutions through a position that Riadh Zghal qualified as "managerial" (1998: 6–17). But this does not eliminate conflict. There are increased tensions within individual companies, which are affected by competitive pressures or privatization. There is also conflict at the very center of the labor movement over the role that the UGTT plays with regard to economic reform, leading to the proliferation of socioeconomic movements outside the purview of UGTT authorities (most notably evidenced in "wildcat" strikes).

Indeed, the UGTT has not transformed to reflect national changes in the economic structure, and this exacerbates tensions within the union. Public service employees remain overrepresented, provoking a concentration of union dissidents among certain sectors like the post office, telecommunications, and public education. The UGTT's inability to renew its membership, the reluctance of the private sector to accept unionization,[11] the limited reconfiguration of union to private sector, and the specificity of its labor claims all limit the UGTT's expertise and negotiating capacities, and thus its relative power.

On the other hand, the UGTT remains an active political force. Union representation in the public sector, which is known for its militancy and confrontational attitude toward union leaders and the political authorities, remains remarkable. Certain sectoral unions also exert significant influence, such as unions among the bank trades, which are today at the heart of the privatization movement and thus at the heart of the revival of the union action.

Thus, although hierarchical in nature, the UGTT is not unified, and internal disputes are often expressed through the union's formal structures. In this respect, the UGTT offers a forum for debate by tolerating and maintaining the expression of positions at its center, even of a political and social nature. Such "posturings," while not organized opposition per se, appear essentially through three types of channels: (1) branch unions, especially those representing the public sector, including elected public offices; (2) regional unions, which have historically been in dispute with the central authorities and are closely linked to regional economic infrastructure, such as specialized industrial zones (phosphates in Gafsa, or chemistry in Gabes, for example); and (3) structured internal movements, often in anticipation of union elections, conceived around historic labor personalities and texts (for example, the labor union "platform," and the contemporary listing of the outgoing UGTT secretary-general at the time of the 2002 Djerba congress).

Another important forum for opposition can be found in the relatively powerful general trade unions, which are capable of sustaining prolonged strike actions. Such unions use their mobilization powers to involve labor unionists and most of the affected personnel in the event of labor conflicts. These unions are generally found among the large public companies (Tunisair, and Tunisie Telecom, for example), but can also be found in the foreign companies targeted for their employment basins. In such cases, a strike threat is often used when a disagreement with the management arises, generally in relation to incomes (wages or promotions), or layoffs arising from privatization. If not moments of political participation themselves, the strikes demonstrate the mobilization power of the union. More important, such instances of collective action force UGTT authorities to condone strikers' actions in order to maintain internal legitimacy. Labor union leadership must constantly prove its capacity to defend employee rights without compromising its most active sectors and its relationship to the state.

In sum, despite the policies and strategies established to associate the UGTT with the public management of liberalization, the state cannot entirely control the union. Elements within and outside the UGTT constantly maneuver to challenge its place on the political chessboard. At all levels of the UGTT, there is a logic of action and mobilization, both political (with respect to the political power and to the internal power stakes within the union), and social (with respect to the defense of worker interests, the channeling of labor demands to the competent public and private authorities, and the coadministration and transformations of the economic sphere). For public authorities and trade unionists alike, there are multiple motives for action—economic, social, and political—and prioritization cannot be established *a priori* from a simple sectoral analysis to predict their actions.

■ Depoliticization Through Bureaucratization?

Many analyses of the UGTT examine it as an institution within the Tunisian government system, studying it as a bureaucratic structure. Based upon a political point of view *stricto sensu,* such analyses consider the union to be an organization functioning much like a political power. According to this view, the union creates its own conditions of social powerlessness by developing internal power issues, which then block any effective actions.

Both scholars and practitioners who consider the UGTT's role as a labor union may view it, at worst, as besieged by bureaucratic paralysis, or at best, as limited by the need to negotiate minor social advancements while maintaining power as an organization integrated into the Tunisian political system. Both views imply that the bureaucratization and nationalization of the UGTT bring it entirely under the state's control. Bureaucratization here both depoliticizes the labor union and withdraws it from broader social issues. This perspective offers a means to understand how institutions may function within the regime: by providing support for the regime, the union in turn is augmented by the regime. In this way, Salah Hamzaoui's clever analysis underlines the similarities between state organizations and labor union organizations, among which centralization, top-down legitimization, and corruption are dominant (2001: 369–380). He correctly points a finger at the internal blocking of "traditional" union activity as a paradoxical consequence of its bureaucratic development, and of its very foundation and power. He then shows how the UGTT itself becomes an object of power subject to internal fights. In this sense, the union as a formal institution may be seen as deviating from its original role of defending workers' interests, becoming instead a venue for personal interests, professional mobility, and personal conflicts. Whether or not one agrees entirely with Hamzaoui's argument, which essentially considers bureaucracy the cause of the UGTT's social lethargy, his theory helps explain how actors within the union may use social issues to position themselves at the center of the organization.

Indeed, in order to understand mobilizations within the UGTT, whether they be of members or branches or regional organizations, it is necessary to examine both the union's position on necessary social actions as well as its political vision for itself. For example, during the February 2002 congress, held in Djerba, the labor union "platform," which included a number of labor unionists known for their "historical" commitments,[12] presented its own candidates for the executive committee and articulated a program condemning the inaction of leaders on social issues as a consequence of their political corruption. In their analysis of the situation and criticism of the UGTT's administration, the unionists used the term "deviation" to describe what had happened to the basic values of the labor union, the ethics of labor unionism, and the social and political role of the UGTT.[13] They also brought up the need to "return to internal democracy" or risk having union pluralism prevail. Because no authorization is required to create a labor union, the threat of a split in the UGTT is a very real, legal scenario.

Here complications arise in the logic of state control. According to the party-state corporatism of Tunisian authoritarianism, it would make most sense for the state to only accept a single UGTT interlocutor and limit the emergence of multiple labor unions. However, not only is it legally uncomplicated to form another labor union, but keeping the union united is, paradoxically, a recurring slogan of union activists.

To leaders and "dissidents" alike (the latter are often former leaders), the threat of union pluralism is a reminder of the worst moments of tension between the UGTT and the government, in which the creation of alternate unions was encouraged to dismiss the political demands of UGTT elite.[14] Elites fear that the government could again interfere in the UGTT's internal affairs and therefore endanger the movement's autonomy. At the same time, they also fear that the UGTT's national role could be undermined. This explains why, despite the executive committee's limited tolerance for divergent views and use of government relations to limit dissent,[15] the majority of internal opponents, whatever their tendency, do not leave the UGTT to form new unions. In fact, the UGTT itself insists on the notion of autonomy and internal democracy as a guarantee to the unity of the labor unionists. If the bureaucratization of the UGTT can be considered to be the instrument and cause of its social inaction, it is also paradoxically a means for maintaining relative autonomy.

A simple bureaucratic analysis is therefore not sufficient. The UGTT, at all levels, and perhaps more so at intermediate and higher levels, is composed of people with activist backgrounds. Although members are frequently united, they periodically compete within the UGTT and within (sometimes unauthorized) political parties. The Djerba congress of February 2002 took place within such a context of internal tension. The UGTT had to redefine its position within the political arena, formulate new alliances, and explore new themes for social demands based on formerly friendly or enemy relations built up during the activist years (as is the case for a list of members presented by the "platform"). Similarly, internal "opponents" often use their former records and relations to position themselves with respect to leaders as a mark of personal legitimacy as well as a means to remain within the UGTT.

Political connections, or more accurately, connections to power, are not the only mark of legitimacy or means for the members of the executive committee to remain in place. These connections also rely on social demands tied to a history of political opposition, and on the historical position of the UGTT as the only vehicle to express disagreement with the regime. Social and political issues are therefore neither dissociated from each other, nor treated on a hierarchical basis, nor canceled out by one another. Rather, they are closely tied together by all the actors, whether individual or collective, who express themselves within the UGTT. This permanent tension between the union's political and social-economic function is precisely what characterizes both the unstable integration of the union within the Tunisian political system and also, perhaps paradoxically, its continuing position as a national labor union.

We must then assume that while a bureaucratic analysis partly explains the positioning of the labor union's actors, it does not wholly explain their motivations or alliances made between seemingly "strange bedfellows." Particularly in the case of alliances made with political parties in the legal opposition and with associations, authorized or prohibited, over specific (yet nationally relevant) political issues, a more nuanced explanation proves necessary. In order to understand these movements, we must take into account the activist backgrounds of UGTT members.

The UGTT's central bureau continues to risk occasional political confrontations with the authorities, both physically and rhetorically. For example, at the UGTT's national council in December 2001, which preceded the congress in Djerba, the issue of general amnesty was debated,[16] approved by vote, omitted from the official minutes, and then replaced by a somewhat sheepish, official explanation.[17] Even if we consider the decision of the UGTT's national council to put this issue on the agenda to have been against the recommendation of the secretary-general, acting as an internal protest against the alliance between the union leadership and the state, such an analysis remains incomplete, for several reasons. First, the members of the UGTT who are called to serve and express themselves during the course of the national council are themselves elected and recognized as such by the union's central bureau. Therefore, they are an integral part of the union's bureaucracy. Moreover, the general vote on the request for amnesty was favorable, implying that when this type of political issue is raised in an organized and collective manner within the UGTT, it becomes a legitimate topic for a debate.

In yet another example, several UGTT regional offices, admittedly known for their "dissenting" positions, organized and sponsored demonstrations against the US intervention in Iraq in March and April 2003. These actions took place despite the fact that demonstrations not organized by the UGTT's central bureau were de facto prohibited. The demonstrations were particularly surprising in Sfax and Gabès, where they were suppressed and where the police were occasionally forced to intervene even in local union offices. At the national level, the UGTT was able to organize a demonstration (this time officially) against the war in Iraq without help from the DCR.[18] Other organizations and political parties, both legal and illegal, also participated in the march; some joined the DCR's own gathering, and others took part in the March 24 demonstration (such as the Tunisian Communist Workers Party, an illegal party, the Tunisian League for Human Rights, and the Progressive Democratic Party). The March 24 demonstration, organized by the UGTT and controlled by police force, gathered the most people (between 5,000 and 10,000, depending on estimates). The police force intervened only at the end as the demonstration was breaking up.

The UGTT is indeed successful in rallying both members and outsiders over issues of a political nature. Its actions are considered legitimate even in the eyes of other organizations that more or less openly mobilize against the government. At the same time, the UGTT's status as a governing institution of Tunisia gives it a legal quasi-immunity, providing protection and even refuge to active dissidents.

Individuals and small groups often join forces on political issues and act within the UGTT, sometimes operating out of UGTT offices. Such was the case for a doctor in October 2005 who went on a hunger strike to support the protest of eight Tunisian civil society personalities who had been on a hunger strike since October 18, 2005, at the regional office of the UGTT in Sidi Bouzid.[19] Since this action was openly directed against the political authorities, the UGTT's secretary-general had to intervene and remove the doctor from his regional office. More general issues of a political nature often become grounds for direct confrontation between the UGTT hierarchy and the state apparatus (including more often than not the police force), who sometimes engage in a game of mutual provocation.

Direct confrontation became more intense during the winter and spring of 2005. For the first time since 1984, the UGTT produced a text that took a stand against a decision made by the president, who had extended a personal invitation to Ariel Sharon to hold the UN World Summit on the Information Society in November 2005 in Tunis. The president's action was officially justified by the fact that Israel is a member of the United Nations. This should have relieved him from a decisionmaking role in the invitation, but his action nevertheless gave opponents an opportunity to mobilize domestic rallies based on international political arguments. At first the UGTT and opposition parties condemned the decision through official statements.[20] Strikes, gatherings, and demonstrations rapidly ensued. A number of UGTT regional offices, supported by a number of trade unions, such as the Higher Education Union, and with the help of students, organized illegal gatherings and engaged in confrontation with the police force. The conflict escalated until associations and opposition parties attempted to mobilize a rally in the heart of Tunis on March 4, 2005. An overwhelming police presence prevented demonstrators from gathering and forced a number of them to take refuge within the UGTT offices, which were then encircled by the police force. Consequently, the demonstration was stopped.

These events illustrate a role that the UGTT and its members were once identified with—a shared image of the political power that the UGTT during its long tenure as the only organization through which opposition could be expressed, and the only organization that had the means to mobilize against, and sometimes even violently and openly confront, the regime.

Importantly, these events demonstrate that the UGTT's bureaucratization and participation in economic reform policies did not succeed in lowering the political expectations of union members.

▓ Political Socialization and Union Activism

The UGTT remains an essential place for political socialization and for the creation and maintenance of activist networks. There are several channels through which union members become politically involved. First, existing political activists are mobilized via the union structures. Second, new activists are socialized and trained within the union, both by providing a space for meetings, conferences, debates, and workshops, and by hosting and maintaining networks that extend outside the UGTT membership. Third, UGTT resources are used in political institutions outside the union, through membership in existing parties and even through the creation of new parties.

Conflicts with the government such as those mentioned previously reveal and rekindle former alliances and friendships between actors who may wear several hats within the UGTT, within the broader political sphere, and in their careers as activists. Most leaders or activists in the major trade unions are affiliated with opposition (particularly left-wing) parties, both legal and illegal. Even among the leaders of the UGTT, cleavages and affinities between members of the executive committee are likened to political affiliations ("Maoists" and "Nationalists").

Even among nonaffiliated union members, political feelings are often one of the main reasons for engagement in the UGTT. Partly, the role of the union as a space for political socialization is a generational effect. Many of today's union activists and leaders joined the UGTT at a time when opposition parties were prohibited and the union served as a space for political expression. Similarly, in interviews, younger union members also mentioned the importance of the UGTT as a "political landmark," which sets it apart from other organizations.

Logistically, internal debates and meetings play an essential part in political socialization. Organized by official legal structures, whether by the central bureau itself or by intermediate structures with relative autonomy from the UGTT's leadership, these meetings serve as a space for political engagement, in which conflicting positions are frequently expressed. More often than not, regardless of the topic of discussion, debates raise the issue of the role of the union and its position toward political power. During the conference "Democracy and Development: Which Union Responsibility?" (January 19, 2006, on the sixtieth anniversary of the UGTT), union accountability led to a polemic between the speaker and the secretary-general. The lecturer, a former minister of economy, declared that Habib Achour, secretary-general of the UGTT during its most intense period of political opposition, had intended to form a labor party and expressly convert his social activism into political involvement. As the meeting ended, the current secretary-general, a friend and self-proclaimed heir of Habib Achour, had to refute this statement for its implication of a confrontation with the current president of the republic, Habib Bourguiba. This immediate denial reveals a malaise that does not come from the union background alone, but is also indicative of the current room for maneuverability left to the UGTT. Even as the UGTT's political nature is deeply felt by its members, the debates that the UGTT is engaged in—and the political role of the UGTT—cannot be publicly discussed outside union walls.

The union's internal workshops are also occasions for debates over the history and current political role of the UGTT. Training sessions organized by the central bureau's youth division emphasize to young people that the most important terms one must associate with the UGTT are "activism," "independence" (from the political power, but also from other political parties), and (internal) "democracy." Under the supervision of the UGTT members responsible for youth programs, including the member of the executive committee who is responsible for youth, this training in union culture (wishfully unitary) initiates lively discussions among young UGTT members about each one of these terms. Beyond the arguments raised, the workshops make clear that true political discussion can take place within the UGTT, whereas elsewhere such unconstrained debates are close to impossible.

A final important component of political socialization in the labor union is learning about political constraints, including the limits of participation, political taboos, and the costs of repression. Whether police repression is exercised at demonstrations, strikes, or gatherings, it is part of the political learning process, as it has become a routine part of collective action.

■ Taking the Labor Union Seriously: Mobilization Through Labor Conflicts

The principal issue for the UGTT today is its adaptation to the private sector. In order to remain prominent, the UGTT must both attract private sector workers and be able to influence working conditions in this growing sector. In short, the UGTT must take seriously its role as a "labor union" and, in the most traditional sense of the term, defend workers' interests. This new consciousness, however late in developing, is also deeply ambiguous. On the one hand, supporting private sectors would enable the UGTT to oppose the political and economic orientations of the political authorities; on the other hand, it would limit the UGTT to its historical role as an agent for social change. In order to open itself to the private sector, and in particular to sectors with large, unskilled labor pools like the textile industry, the

UGTT would need to accept a transformation of the labor union culture and a weakening of its role in political socialization. Yet such a view partly misunderstands the political stakes inherent in social conflicts—it is these trades that most require union action, and that the UGTT, after long neglect, is finally beginning to address.

The position of the UGTT authorities is complicated further by the fact that it is precisely this new consciousness that is driving the debate over union capacity and power within the Tunisian political arena, both at the center and at the margins of its membership base. Recent strikes, which have been properly linked to labor conflicts, have been particularly revealing of the transformation in the ways workers express their interests, as well as of the renewed political activism of UGTT militants. These strikes are generally limited to a particular company,[21] and often to a specific legal issue, irrespective of the labor code, union rights, and collective bargaining agreements. More recently, strikes have proceeded irrespective of labor and staffing commitments made in the course of negotiating privatization agreements.

For the most part, strike actions have respected the framework established by the "social pact" for the presentation of grievances. However, opposition has been innovative in the use of media leverage (national and international, primarily via the militant networks), in the displacement of their grievances and corresponding actions (through sit-ins and factory occupations, but also hunger strikes—an action hitherto reserved for conflicts of a political nature), and in the mobilization of support from the rank-and-file employees directly concerned. The process is nothing short of a reinvention of the politics of social mobilization. More exactly, methods of social action have been reformulated for actors who are also politically organized, employing rhetoric of legitimation that has historically been used within the union.

Attempts at reorganizing strikes as "movements" with broader appeal can be attributed to actors who have been previously involved with sociopolitical mobilizations. In this context, UGTT leaders are more often summoned to intervene than they are themselves taking the initiative. Reasons for UGTT involvement vary; union leaders may be called by the political authority to contain conflict or to limit its duration, and they may be invited to mediate a conflict and to verify grievances or validate claims on behalf of the parties of a conflict.

In this respect, the December 2002 strike at Moknine is enlightening. It was initiated by the local union, without the agreement of the UGTT's central bureau, to demand that factory owners comply with previous agreements (in this case, guarantees given at the time of the privatization of ICAB (International Company of Ayadi Bittan), a textile factory, that were never respected). The strike action led to belated and hesitant interventions

by members of the UGTT's executive committee, and was ended by a negotiated agreement that went unsigned by the committee. It was followed by
other, localized but increasingly systematic strikes,[22] revealing more
changes in the management of labor conflicts. Indeed, the strikes led to
intervention from actors outside the UGTT, such as RAID-ATTAC Tunisia
and the Tunisian League for Human Rights, who staffed the support committee, ensured its (international) media coverage, and provided updated
information throughout the conflict.[23] A closer look at the members of these
organizations reveals that a number of them were also members of unions
related to their own professions (frequently public sector unions) and that
they belonged to associations, or even to illegal political parties.
Demonstrators were not therefore acting on behalf of a movement inside the
UGTT or even the local union; rather, union involvement gave them legitimacy within social conflicts. However, when demonstrators signed official
statements intended for the media to use in covering the support committees, they did so either on behalf of their profession, or by affirming their
political affiliation. Seldom did they sign as members of the UGTT.

While these movements remain within the legal limits prescribed by the
government and by agreements between social partners, they also are venues for both social and political forms of contest. More specifically, the
strikes present an opportunity for the UGTT leadership both to reassess the
social consequences of economic liberalization and to consider what it
means in terms of loss of power for the union. Members of the support committees condemn the attitude of the UGTT, criticize the local union leaders
who try to limit the extent of the strikes, and refuse the intervention of non-
union members, calling the position of the latter a "censure of the labor
union bureaucracy" and pointing out cases of corruption among union leaders (Ben Sedrine 2004). In that sense, the support committees mix social
issues and political issues, which may fuel each other or oppose each other
in a statement of what a labor union should be. Indeed, the criticism
addressed to the UGTT leadership for their lack of support for actions taken
against the consequences of privatization in these particular plants only
matches the criticism of the leadership's lethargy, or even resistance, in the
face of general changes brought on by the economic liberalization. Union
leaders are alternately criticized for their inability to acquire the resources
(in terms of members, expertise, and possibility of political autonomy and
internal reform) to weigh in on the three-way balance between the state,
UTICA, and the UGTT, and therefore their inability to play the part of a
social and political alternative.

However, while these occurrences may be the result of internal contestation, we cannot assume that they reveal a dichotomy between the base and
the leadership that would cause the UGTT to stagnate. Indeed, many members of the UGTT's executive committee have roots in political and activist

groups close to the current opposition, and are often left-wing. This was the case during the strike mentioned previously, when members of the executive committee known for their close ties to these dissidents,[24] and for their disaffection for the government, were the ones sent to negotiate with the strikers. Social tensions here become opportunities for internal negotiations, focusing more on the UGTT's role in the political scene than on the role of union leaders.

▓ Conclusion

There are numerous, and somewhat ambiguous, ways to understand the UGTT as a channel for political participation. As a governing "social institution," the UGTT and its members play a series of balancing games: between its central social position and its submission to the political power; between its capacity for political mobilization beyond its membership and its control of labor protest; between its symbolic political weight and its control of internal conflicts. In doing so, the UGTT seeks to maintain a political role, while ensuring its autonomy and therefore its power vis-à-vis the state authorities.

Considering the limited access to the political sphere and the weakness of the opposition political base, the labor union does not just fight for its own political force but also attempts to stretch political limits. Whether in support of increased political action or for the legitimacy of raising issues that have otherwise been excluded from political debate, this expansion is the result of a fight for political participation in an authoritarian regime that closely regulates the political arena.

Thus the Tunisian labor movement oscillates between the depoliticization of social issues through instrumentalization of the movement (social negotiations), and the repoliticization of these issues by extending social demands beyond corporatist or individual trade interests. Political participation then means building and managing the political, even controversial, motives for debate on the shaping of society. The 2006 creation of the Tunisian Social Forum by a number of protest organizations rooted in the UGTT testifies to the recognition by the latter of the political stakes of social issues and the force of political participation even within the tightly constrained authoritarian system.

▓ Notes

I thank Peter Gillespie for translating this text from French. I am deeply grateful to Ellen Lust-Okar, Saloua Zerhouni, and others for reviewing and commenting on the content of this chapter.

1. From 19 percent in 1993 to 20 percent by the general elections of 1999.
2. The 1999 general election introduced a plurality of candidates. The consti-

tutional reform, approved by referendum in May 2002 and introduced for the 2004 general elections, eased qualifying conditions.

3. President Ben Ali announced this change on November 7, 2003. On November 8, the first privately owned radio station with national coverage, Mosaïque FM, was launched. The opening of Mosaïque FM was followed by the launching of a privately owned national television station, Hannibal TV, in 2005.

4. The requirement for legal deposit prior to publication was removed by a presidential amendment to the press code on January 9, 2006, adopted by parliament. This administrative restriction on newspaper content gave rise at times to production delays that effectively blocked distribution, and was qualified as "censorship" by nongovernmental newspapers. On January 20, 2006, *El Maouqef,* the publication of the legal opposition party, the Parti Démocratique Progressiste (Progressive Democratic Party), filed a complaint that the Ministry of Interior, pursuant to Article 73 of the press code, had abused its right to "seize all copies of any edition whose publication would be of a nature to disturb the public order," seizing their issue number 342.

5. For an analysis of election outcomes within such limitations, see Geisser 2000.

6. For an interesting study of opposition political participation through elections, see Heumann and Abdelhaq 2000.

7. For an analogous development concerning the whole of the Tunisian political field, see Camau 1997.

8. This conclusion is mainly based on field research conducted in Tunisia between 2002 and 2006: writings from the UGTT, the internal unionist opposition, and the political parties were collected. I also attended demonstrations and public meetings organized by unionists, as well as internal workshops, especially those directed to the young unionists; and conducted interviews with former or present unionists, whether they were peak leaders —i.e., members or former members of the executive committee—or union activists. I deeply thank all of them, whom I cannot name for security reasons.

9. For a detailed development of the idea of state autonomy as a construct inherent to the relations of power and place, see Mitchell 1991.

10. The former name of the DCR.

11. The attitude of business owners in the private sector is not clear. It is generally known that business owners, under certain circumstances, prefer to deal with union representatives, with whom negotiation and accommodation are more easily achieved compared to unaffiliated and therefore unidentifiable employee representatives.

12. By "historical" I mean (using the language of the actors themselves) union activists who had held responsibilities at the heart of the UGTT during the period of greatest tension with the political authorities, essentially the 1970s through the early 1980s. For the most part, these individuals were subject, at one point or another, to imprisonment and torture for their union activism. "Historical" thus refers both to seniority in terms of their union commitment and electoral mandates, but also to their active role during a period of time considered the most glorious in the history of an independent Tunisia.

13. Unionist platform for the rehabilitation of the UGTT, authorized translation from Arabic to French, October 2001.

14. Habib Achour, secretary-general of the UGTT during the 1970s, was at times the instrument for, and at other times the victim of, the proliferation of alternative union movements by the political authorities.

15. As an example, there are reports from certain unionists who are at odds with the members of the executive committee, and by others promoting internal dissent, themselves frequently employees of the large public sector employers, of cases of leadership intercession, with the political authorities requesting professional favors: refusal of transfers, promotions, and professional "side-lining."

16. The debate over general amnesty, which is to say amnesty for prisoners considered to be political and even Islamist by members of the opposition, was launched several months earlier by the Ligue Tunisienne des Droits de l'Homme (Tunisian League for Human Rights). It was then taken up by unrecognized or non-tolerated civic groups, and by unrecognized but official opposition movements, notably via the Internet. Union management demanded that the question be debated in the UGTT's national council, and that this debate be reported in the minutes.

17. At a press conference, the secretary-general of the UGTT, Abdesselam Jrad, when asked to explain the failure to include the motion in the minutes of the union's national council, stated that the question was more of an "ongoing concern" than a "demand." This followed a senior ministerial declaration that the question was moot, since officially, in Tunisia, there were no political prisoners.

18. The demonstration was preceded on March 24 by an authorized demonstration organized by the nonparliamentary opposition, Ettajdid (formerly the Communist Party), civic associations (the Tunisian League for Human Rights), and organizations representing the legal profession (the Tunisian Bar and Young Lawyers Association). They were associated as the "National Committee for the Defense of Iraq," without support from the DCR, and monitored by the police. Recall that, unlike parties other than the DCR, the UGTT is recognized as a "national organization."

19. See http://www.tunisnews.net/31octobre05.htm.

20. The Progressive Democratic Party and the Democratic Forum for Work and Freedom, both recognized opposition parties; the Tunisian Communist Workers Party, forbidden; and the Tunisian League for Human Rights and the National Council for Freedom in Tunisia, not recognized.

21. Beginning with the UGTT's 1990 congress, the labor union tended to circumscribe activism, obstruct local trade actions, and block any national strike actions. To be legal, a union's strike action must be approved by the secretary-general.

22. For example, the Naasen strike (January 2004), the strike at the Hotrifa plant in Moknine (January 2004), and the strike at Fantasia in Tunis (July 2005).

23. RAID (Rally for an International Alternative to Development) is a nonlegalized organization affiliated with the alter-mondialist, international movement ATTAC (Association for the Taxation of Financial Transactions to Aid Citizens). See press releases from RAID-ATTAC Tunisia, dated December 8, 9, 10, 12, 2002. Also see *Echos Syndicaux* (Union Echoes), published by the "Unionist Democratic Mainstream at the Core of the UGTT" in November 2002, and based on the UGTT platform.

24. That is, previous members of the UGTT platform, now members of the UGTT's executive committee.

PART 4

Conclusion

13

Looking Forward

Saloua Zerhouni

Does political participation matter? In a context characterized by rapid growth and the rise of Islamist movements, violence, and terrorism, political participation factors heavily into the political and socioeconomic developments that might be undertaken in the Middle East and North Africa (MENA) in the coming years. The processes of political and socioeconomic reforms initiated by countries in the MENA region during the past decade have not in large part led to any meaningful political change. Most authoritarian regimes have maintained strict control over power, despite the enlargement of spaces for political participation in a number of countries, such as Morocco and Jordan. The transition paradigm has so far failed to explain and capture the "change in continuity" that has characterized the kind of political openings taking place in the region.

By exploring political participation beyond its relationship with real or supposed democratization processes, this volume works to expand our comprehension of the more elastic nature of authoritarianism. It also provides us with another perspective and in-depth understanding of the real obstacles to reform and change in the MENA region. The diversity in modes of participation analyzed, perspectives offered, and countries explored creates a space for identifying new areas of research.

Though the authoritarian nature of the MENA regimes may determine the extent of participation, it does not inhibit actors from participating. For instance, in Egypt, as noted by Nihad Gohar in Chapter 9, nongovernmental organizations (NGOs) are encouraged "only if their activities remain within the service provision sector, and only if those activities do not reflect any political stance or attempt at social transformation." Even if the impact of various actors on policymaking processes remains relatively limited, there are diverse spaces for participatory activities by a wide range of actors with varying degrees of influence.

Political participation is shaped to a substantial degree by political, social, and economic contexts. While the chapters in this volume bring to light the importance of participation in general, they simultaneously show that the dynamics of participation as well as its potential effectiveness vary from one country to the other. For instance, if NGOs in Morocco could become a potential force of change, the same is not the case for NGOs in Egypt. So if political participation in the MENA countries matters, what are the lessons learned, and how can we make them more substantive?

■ Lessons Learned

The examination of political participation *as it exists* reveals much about the complexity of the politics of authoritarianism in the MENA countries. As contributors to this volume demonstrate, both formal and informal channels of participation play significant roles in shoring up authoritarian regimes. Instead of being a means of introducing change, instruments and institutions of participation such as elections, parliaments, and civil society actors often serve authoritarian regimes to develop new mechanisms of endurance. In most of the cases, liberalization measures are part of the regime's "conscious survival strategy," to use Daniel Brumberg's expression (see Brynen, Korany, and Noble 1998).

The formal channels of participation play a different role and have a different function in MENA countries than in Western democracies; they are often instrumentalized in struggles over political power and state resources (Bahrain, Iran). While parliaments in Western democracies are independent legislative bodies whose main role is often lawmaking and government oversight, in many MENA countries they are used for managing intra-elite conflicts, containing the opposition, lobbying for specific interests, and ensuring the stability of the regime (Morocco, Bahrain). The impact of these channels on policymaking therefore remains insignificant. Formal institutions, as they play out in these regimes, constitute vehicles for voicing the demands of the elites rather than spaces for defending public interests and defining policies.

The ambivalent role that formal institutions tend to play in the region is a major factor that inhibits effective political participation. Most of the case studies in this volume show how the same channels of participation are used by different actors—whether the ruling elite, the opposition, or the public— to achieve divergent objectives and agendas (i.e., the General Labor Union of Tunisia). The same applies to actors participating in electoral processes. Voters in countries such as Jordan and Iran are predominantly concerned with the tangible benefits they will obtain through the act of voting (whether personal services or a stamp on an identification card).

Another important barrier to effective participation is the gap between the official (artificial) discourse about the necessity of political participation and the reality of participation in MENA countries. The discourse about democracy that most Arab leaders and regimes undertake is mainly a response to international pressure. The public opening of spaces of political participation is in fact often accompanied by a series of measures that inhibit its impact on decisionmaking processes. The leadership's lack of both a political will to give up power and a commitment to meaningful political reforms presents another obstacle to the effectiveness of political participation in the region.

Clearly, this ambiguous and dual discourse serves the interests of the ruling elites in the MENA region. But for how long will the ambivalence that characterizes the role of institutions and the hypocrisy of the discourse on democratization continue to be effective? Will the renewal of the discourse on political participation lead to its own demise?

What is important to recognize in all of the case studies is that the array of institutions and actors reflects the complex interactions between "traditional" and "modern" forms of participation. On the one hand, there are parliaments, political parties, trade unions, and civil society organizations; on the other hand, tribes, guilds, *majalis,* and *ma'atim* still play important roles. If "modern" channels have a limited role, in many cases they are also used by the regimes to maintain power and to project the image of a democratic state. The coexistence of formal and informal mechanisms of participation characterizes and affects decisionmaking processes and political outcomes. The permeability of formal institutions and the reproduction of the traditional structures of power within these institutions reinforce their weaknesses and further limit their impact.

Modern and formal modes of participation have gradually become outdated, whereas traditional modes of participation and informal networks are effective and still hold a strong legitimacy. The weakness of formal institutions of participation resides not in their compatibility with the societal and cultural contexts of the MENA countries, but rather in the politically pragmatic and opportunistic ways in which they have been instrumentalized by various actors.

Implications for Scholarship

For the field of comparative politics, the MENA has remained one of the regions in the world where democracy is deficient and the least present. Whether this democratic deficit is explained through simplistic culturalist arguments, structural-economic and social problems, or simply the region's "exceptionalism," the focus has often been on the obstacles to democratization, which vary from the weakness of civil society and social-class formations, to the power of the states to dominate their societies, to the more recent arguments that democratic reforms might lead to the rise of Islamic groups that threaten liberal democracy. But often missing from these arguments is the fact that different potentials of political participation do exist under authoritarianism, such as parliaments, civil society organizations, and trade unions. Even if we quickly assume that all the political actors within these institutions are directly under the hegemonic power of autocratic rulers, it should not preclude us from analyzing the politics and internal dynamics of these actors as they interact with or relate to the authoritarian state.

For too long, observers and political scientists have privileged the states and political elites of the MENA region as a way of uncovering the complex layers of authoritarianism and the obstacles to democratic transition. Perhaps what is needed at this juncture is a new agenda for research and a new way of thinking about the "the politics of the people" in MENA countries. We need to start moving away from wishful and abstract thinking and instead concern ourselves with what is feasible in order for the people to participate and contribute to advancing democracy. In the face of entrenched authoritarianism, it is time to ask less about the basis of its endurance and more about the social and political forces that can undermine it.

Looking at the question of endurance of authoritarianism in the MENA region, the big player absent from political analysis has often been the people. We must begin to ask a question that has been long disregarded: Will change possibly come from the people? More research needs to be done on the agency of various social actors when faced with structural constraints. From a scholarly perspective, the search for the limits, extent, autonomy, and power of various political actors vis-à-vis authoritarian structures of rule can provide us with new insights into the potential forces of change. In the context of the MENA region, this entails excavating an emerging and expanding political arena as well as uncovering and listening to local and autonomous democratic voices who have started to speak the language of change and claim a role in the decisionmaking process.

The debate about reform in MENA countries has often been seen as triangular, comprising the elites, the international community, and scholars. The masses and their aspirations have often been excluded by all three. What kind of state do the Tunisian, Moroccan, Egyptian, Jordanian, or Iranian masses want? In defining the mechanisms of change and developing programs for reform, the expectations of the people are most often not taken into consideration.

The ideals of human rights, rule of the law, transparency, and equality are all part of the political discourse, and authoritarian regimes cannot ignore them. Such ideals are currently spoken of and debated in ways that may challenge the MENA regimes. Political scientists can embark further on studies about the actors and mechanisms for the diffusion and impact of these ideals. For example, how exactly are the ideals of good governance, transparency, gender, and equality being used by various actors to press for local change? To what extent does the transnational transfer of ideas, funds, knowledge, and technical know-how affect the nature of political participation of various actors and translate into a challenge for authoritarianism? To what extent are these changes or the processes of economic liberalization creating new dynamics or divisions within seemingly opaque authoritarian regimes?

Researchers should attempt to investigate areas such as the systems of citizen representation in MENA countries, and ask new questions about the kind of institutions that people best identify with. People in the MENA region are confronting new challenges and new demographic, economic, social, and cultural changes. They are facing the power of globalization and international media, which affect their behavior and value systems in significant ways. Yet few sociological studies have been conducted on the attitudes, behaviors, and perceptions of MENA citizens toward state institutions and electoral participation, or the visions citizens have about the regimes they want. More comparative studies on the sociology of electoral bodies are needed. Comparative studies on the attitudes and perceptions of the masses could provide us with interesting insights into the gap that separates the people from their outdated authoritarian rulers.

◼ Prospects of Reforms

Making political participation more substantive is very much related to the potential of introducing serious political and social reforms in MENA countries. There is no "quick recipe" for reform; it is a long process in which various actors play critical and specific roles. For example, reformation of legal and regulatory arrangements factors into the performance of various institutions and processes of participation. In Egypt, Jordan, and Morocco, the preeminence of the executive power is within constitutional prerogatives. Moreover, the legal framework is instrumentalized by those regimes to constrain political institutions and control their participation in a way that won't challenge the system. Thus the constitutional powers and capacities of formal institutions should be revised.

The frontiers between formal and informal venues of participation should be defined according to a set of formal rules. The criteria of good governance could be reached by revisiting traditional channels and introducing democratic rules to make them more effective institutions. This might also affect the functioning of formal institutions and make them less permeable to informal channels. In other words, establishing the rule of law can influence the role and functions of these institutions, and political outcomes more generally.

The weaknesses of formal institutions and processes should be overcome not only by the establishment of rules, but also by the enhancement of public awareness about the importance of these institutions and their roles. Political activists should strive to overcome their fragmentation and avoid principled and legalistic viewpoints that inhibit dialogue. Voters should be aware of the importance of their vote, and the state should play a more active role in providing services to the citizenry. Elections should be governed by strict laws, and awareness campaigns need to promote the basis of a democratic culture for both the masses and the elites.

The complex realities of formal and informal participation should then be taken into account more seriously by scholars, political actors, and international donors. As Laila Alhamad states in Chapter 3, "It is about understanding how an effective social movement can turn into a political party and gain popular support. Certainly, such a shift requires a greater disposition to pose difficult questions and undertake the necessary research and thinking that a task as massive as bringing democratization into the Middle East and North Africa necessitates."

Transparent decisionmaking processes constitute another sine qua non condition for making political participation more effective. The ambiguity of decisionmaking processes is a major obstacle to reform. Legal rules are often disregarded. Moreover, the functions and prerogatives of various political actors are not well defined, and if they are, there is often a distinction between what is formal and what is de facto.

Ruling elites need to be pressured to give up some of their powers and to engage more seriously in reforms. One of the important obstacles to meaningful reforms in most MENA countries is that the incumbent elites have taken a more quiescent stance because they "find their interests better served by not rocking the boat" (Volker 2004: 307). Only through a stronger commitment on the part of ruling elites to pressure for and introduce new measures of change can a more meaningful participatory society thrive.

Political parties and parliaments must concurrently address the ways authoritarianism is reproduced within their institutions. They must demonstrate the values of democratic participation through internal structures and processes—delineating and organizing the dividing lines between the formal and the informal political spheres and insisting on the principle of accountability in the decisionmaking process. The fact that a wide range of actors and institutions intervene in politics without defining their prerogatives and demarking their boundaries is a major obstacle to a more favorable context for participation.

The role of international donors should also be rethought. Developmental programs should take into account the local specificities in order to avoid "carbon copy" formulas. Short-term financial and technical support from international donors is of limited impact. In conceptualizing and implementing their programs, international donors must take a more participatory approach that includes affected local actors. Affected citizens need be identified and consulted about potential solutions to specific problems. Without the inclusion of these actors in the process, these programs might suffer a lack of legitimacy, making their implementation more difficult if not impossible.

While international donors assist developing countries in reinforcing their institutions, they often do so by introducing practices, such as the concentration of decisionmaking processes, abusive budgetary constraints, or rigid bureaucratic machinery, that seem to defeat the purpose of their goals. In addition, international donors may hold dual discourses and reproduce in ironic ways the same bureaucratic problems, practices, clientelist system, and alliances with local authoritarian elites that they are supposed to reform. International donors are also not immune to the authoritarian system; the creation of mechanisms that keep international actors independent becomes equally important.

In addition, the ways in which Europe and the United States are willing to exercise their economic and political influence in the MENA region will influence future prospects for democracy. Support for more democratic participation could play an important role in the creation of a dynamic for change. In the long run, what will make political institutions more effective is not "revolutionary change," which has become outmoded, but a persistent and consistent support for the creation of institutionalized local participative democracy that has the potential to attract more local and grassroots political actors.

Progress toward increased democracy in the MENA region has been minimal in part because of the continuous support of authoritarian regimes by Europe and the United States. Such efforts have been at the expense of the social forces and political actors who have started to call for more democratic political participation, as illustrated by civil society organizations in Morocco and Egypt, and by the Islamists in the Palestinian Authority and Lebanon. If there is a serious Western concern for the promotion of democracy in the MENA region, then support for institutions and instruments of effective political participation that challenge the authoritarian structures of the state is of essence.

Democratization in the MENA region should be conceived in a way that increases the potential for political participation and challenges and eventually weakens the structural basis of authoritarianism. Constitutional reform, separating the branches of governments, increasing the powers of parliaments, encouraging the role of independent civil society actors, and

Bibliography

Abbour, Sameh Said. 2005. "Wage Workers in the Private Sector and Political Transformations in Egypt." November 11. http://www.elbosla.com/default.aspx?tabid=63.

'Abd al-Nasir, Jabbi. 1998. *Al-intikhabat: al-dawlah wa-al-mujtama'*. Algiers: Dar al-Qasabah lil-Nashr.

'Abdallah, Ahmad. 1990. *Al-intikhabat al-barlamaniyah fi Misr: dars intikhabat—1987*. Cairo: Markaz al-Buhhuth al-'Arabbiya.

Abdnoudy, Ateyyat. 1998. *Days of Democracy: Egyptian Women in Elections*. Cairo: Kassem.

"About NDI: The Work of the National Democratic Institute." 2006. Washington, D.C.: National Democratic Institute for International Affairs, November 24. http://www.ndi.org/about/about.asp.

Abukhalil, As'ad. 1997. "Change and Democratisation in the Arab World: The Role of Political Parties." *Third World Quarterly* 18 (1): 149–163.

Abu-Amr, Ziyad. 1996. "Pluralism and the Palestinians." *Journal of Democracy* 7 (3): 83–87.

Akhavi, S. 1987. "Elite Factionalism in the Islamic Republic of Iran." *Middle East Journal* 41: 181–202.

al-Azm, Sadik J. 2000. "The View From Damascus." *New York Review of Books*, June 15.

al-Amin, Hazem. 2006. "Jordan's Muslim Brotherhood on the Verge of a New Phase: Interview with Salem Falahat: The General Regulator of the Muslim Brotherhood in Jordan." *Al-Hayat*, April 25. http://english.daralhayat.com/spec/04-2006/article-20060425-d15eac7d-c0a8-10ed-01d1-b9b7566f0f98/story.html.

al-Khalifa, Shaikh Khalid bin Khalifa. 2005. "At-takwin ath-thuna'i al-mutawazin li's-sulta at-tashri'iyya." Paper presented at the workshop "Aliyat wa quwam wa salahiyyat majlis ash-Shura." Manama, May 5.

al-Khawaja, Abdulhadi. 2004. "Seminar on Poverty." Manama: 'Uruba Club, September 24.

———. 2003. "Discrimination in Bahrain: The Unwritten Law." Paper presented at a House of Lords seminar. London, December 16.

al-Minoufi, Kamal (ed.). 1995. *Intikhabat Maglis al-Shaab: 1995.* Cairo: Cairo University, Faculty of Economics and Political Science, and Friedrich Ebert Stiftung.

al-Missioui, Abdelaziz. 2000. "The Censure Motion." In *Moultamass Arrikaba.* Rabat: Imprimerie Impériale.

al-Nahhas, Mona. 2005. "Candidates Aplenty." *Al-Ahram Weekly,* November 2.

———. 2004. "Tomorrow's Party Today." *Al-Ahram Weekly,* November 10.

al-Rifa'i, Yehia. 2005. "The State of the Egyptian Judicial Surprise." *Al-Jazeera,* May 17. http://www.aljazeera.net/nr/exeres/a65f2542-ff63-48e4-ae7 ea2c7b0f27159.htm.

al-Sawi, Ali (ed.). 2004. *Al-shabab am al-nuwab.* Cairo: Cairo University, Faculty of Economics and Political Science, and Parliamentary Program.

al-Sayyid, Mustapha Kamel. 2000. "Clash of Values: U.S. Civil Society Aid and Islam in Egypt." In Marina Ottoway and Thomas Carothers (eds.), *Funding Virtue: Civil Society Aid and Democracy Promotion.* Washington, D.C.: Carnegie Endowment for International Peace.

Al-Urdun al-Jadid Research Center. 1995. "Post-Election Seminar: A Discussion of Jordan's 1993 Parliamentary Election." Amman.

Al-Wifaq. 2005. *Min agli al-Bahrain: istratijiyyat 'amal 2005 li-jamiyya'at Al-Wifaq al-Islami al-watani.* Manama.

Al-'Alam, Sawfat. 2005. *Al-Itisal al-Siyassi wa al-Da'aya al-Intikhabiyya.* Cairo: Dar al-Nahda al-Arabiyya.

Albrecht, Holger. 2005. "How Can Opposition Support Authoritarianism? Lessons from Egypt." *Democratization* 12 (3): 378–397.

Albrecht, Holger, and Oliver Schlumberger. 2004. "'Waiting for Godot': Regime Change Without Democratization in the Middle East." *International Political Science Review* 25 (4): 371–392.

Alexander, Christopher. 2000. "Opportunities, Organizations, and Ideas: Islamists and Workers in Tunisia and Algeria." *International Journal of Middle East Studies* 32: 465–490.

———. 1996. "Between Accommodation and Confrontation: State, Labor, and Development in Algeria and Tunisia." PhD diss., Durham, N.C., Duke University.

Amawi, Abla. 2001. *Against All Odds: Jordanian Women, Elections, and Political Empowerment.* Amman: Konrad Adenauer.

Amin, Galal. 2001. *Whatever Happened to the Egyptians? Changes in Egyptian Society from 1950 to the Present.* Cairo: American University of Cairo Press.

Amnesty International. 2005. "Bahrain: Amnesty International." http://web .amnesty.org/report2005/bhr-summary-eng.

an-Naim, Abdullah. 2002. "Religion and Global Civil Society." In *Global Civil Society Yearbook, 2002.* New York: Oxford University Press.

Anderson, Lisa, 1991. "Absolutism and the Resilience of Monarchy in the Middle East." *Political Science Quarterly* 106 (Spring): 1–15.

Antara, Mohamed, 2007. "Al-maihad al-malaki li-atakafa al-amazighia, siyak al-nacha, al-adah wa takyim." *Wijhat Nathar* 31 (Winter): 40–47.

Arjomand, S. A. 2002. "The Reform Movement and the Debate on Modernity and Tradition in Contemporary Iran." *International Journal of Middle Eastern Studies* 34: 719–731.

———. 1988. *The Turban for the Crown.* New York: Oxford University Press.

as-Sayyid, Jalila. 2003. "At-Tamyis: Ru'iyya qanuniyya." Paper presented at a seminar on discrimination organized by the Bahrain Center for Human Rights. Manama, October 16.

Ayubi, Nazih. 1995. *Over-Stating the Arab State: Politics and Society in the Middle East.* London: Tauris.

Azimi, F. 1999. "Iranian Parliaments from Beginning up to Present." *Negahe Now* 42: 13–47.

Baaklini, Abdo, Guilain Denœux, and Robert Springborg. 1999. *Legislative Politics in the Arab World: The Resurgence of Democratic Institutions.* Boulder: Lynne Rienner.

Bahrain Monetary Agency. 2004. *Economic Indicators, June 2004.* Manama: Economic Research Directorate.

Bahrain Transparency Society. 2002. *More Transparency for Enhanced Election Integrity.* Manama.

Baker, Joharah. 2005. "Assassinations, Rockets, and Postponed Elections." *Palestine Report,* June 8.

Bakhash, Shaul. 2000. "How the Good Guys Won in Iran." *Washington Post,* February 27.

Baktiari, B. 1996. *Parliamentary Politics in Revolutionary Iran: The Institutionalization of Factional Politics.* Gainesville: University of Florida Press.

Bamyeh, Mohamed. 2005. "Civil Society and the Islamic Experience." *ISIM Review* (Spring). http://www.isim.nl/files/review_15/review_15-40.pdf.

Banegas, Richard. 1993. "Action collective et transition politique en Afrique: la conference nationale du Bénin." *Cultures et Conflits* 17: 137–175.

Batatu, Hanna. 1993. "Of the Diversity of Iraqis, the Incohesiveness of Their Society, and Their Progress in the Monarchic Period Toward a Consolidated Political Structure." In A. Hourani, P. Khoury, and M. Wilson (eds.), *The Modern Middle East.* London: Tauris.

Baumgarten, Helga. 2006. *Hamas: der politische Islam in Palästina.* Munich: Diederichs.

Bayat, Asef. 2002. "Activism and Social Development in the Middle East." *International Journal of Middle East Studies* 34: 1–28.

———. 1997. *Street Politics: Poor People's Movements in Iran.* New York: Columbia University Press.

———. 1996. "Cairo's Poor: Dilemmas of Survival and Solidarity." *Middle East* (202): 2–12.

Baylis, Thomas A. 1978. "The Faces of Participation: A Comparative Perspective." In John A. Booth and Mitchell A. Seligson (eds.), *Political Participation in Latin America.* New York: Holmes and Meier.

Bellin, Eva. 2004. "The Robustness of Authoritarianism in the Middle East: A Comparative Perspective." *Comparative Politics* 36 (2): 139–158.

———. 2000. "Contingent Democrats: Industrialists, Labor, and Democratization in Late-Developing Countries." *World Politics* 52 (January): 175–205.

———. 1995a. "Civil Society in Formation." In August R. Norton (ed.), *Civil Society in the Middle East.* Boston: Brill Academic.

———. 1995b. "Les industriels Tunisiens et l'état." In William I. Zartman (comp.), *Tunisie: la politique économique de la reforme.* Tunis: Les editions de la Méditerranée.

Ben-Dor, Gabriel. 1975. "Civilianization of Military Regimes in the Arab World." In Henry Bienen and David Morell (eds.), *Political Participation Under Military Regimes.* London: Sage.

Ben Nefissa, Sarah (ed.). 2002. *Pouvoir et associations dans le Monde Arabe.* Paris: CNRS.

Ben Salah, Hafedh, and Henri Roussilon. 1995. "La représentation des intérêts professionnels en Tunisie." Tunis: Faculté de Droit et des Sciences Politiques de Tunis, Presses de l'IEP de Toulouse.

Ben Sedrine, Sihem. 2004. "Strike at the 'Prestige' Factory, Naasen." *Kalima* (January).

Bennani-Chraibi, Mounia, Myriam Catusse, and Jean-Claude Santucci. 2004. *Scènes et coulisses de l'èlection au Maroc.* Paris: Éditions Karthala.

Bennani-Chraibi, Mounia, and Olivier Fillieule (eds.). 2003. *Résistances et protestations dans les societes musulmanes.* Paris: Presse de Sciences Po.

Bianchi, Robert. 1989. *Unruly Corporatism: Associational Life in Twentieth-Century Egypt.* New York: Oxford University Press.

Bienen, Henry, and David Morell (eds.). 1976. *Political Participation Under Military Regimes.* London: Sage.

Bill, James A., and Robert Springborg. 1990. *Politics in the Middle East.* New York: HarperCollins.

Bin Nafisa, Sara, and Alaa al-Din Arafat. 2005. *Al-intikhabat wa al-zabaniyya al-siyassaya fi Misr.* Cairo: Cairo Center for the Study of Human Rights.

Booth, John A., and Mitchell A. Seligson. 1978a. "Images of Political Participation in Latin America." In John A. Booth and Mitchell A. Seligson (eds.), *Political Participation in Latin America.* New York: Holmes and Meier.

——— (eds.). 1978b. *Political Participation in Latin America.* New York: Holmes and Meier.

Bouandel, Youcef. 1999. "Human Rights in the Maghreb." In Yahya Zoubir (ed.), *North Africa in Transition: State, Society, and Economic Transformations in the 1990's.* Gainseville: University of Florida Press.

Boussard, Caroline. 2005. *Crafting Democracy: Civil Society in Post-Transition Honduras.* Political Series no. 127. Lund, Sweden: Lund University, Department of Political Science. http://www.svet.lu.se/fulltext/caroline _boussard.pdf.

Bras, Jean-Philippe. 1996. "Tunisie: Ben Ali et Sa Classe Moyenne." *Pôles* (April–June).

Bratton, Michael, and Nicolas van de Walle. 1997. *Democratic Experiments in Africa.* New York: Cambridge University Press.

———. 1994. "Neopatrimonial Regimes and Political Transitions in Africa." *World Politics* 46 (July): 453–489.

Brown, Nathan. 2002. *Constitutions in a Nonconstitutional World: Arab Basic Laws and the Prospects for Accountable Government.* Albany: State University of New York Press.

———. 1997. *The Rule of Law in the Arab World: Courts in Egypt and the Gulf.* Cambridge: Cambridge University Press.

Brownlee, Jason. 2004. "Ruling Parties and Durable Authoritarianism." Paper presented at the annual meeting of the American Political Science Association. Chicago, September 2–5.

Brumberg, Daniel. 2005. "Liberalization Versus Democracy." In Thomas Carothers and Marina Ottaway (eds.), *Uncharted Journey: Promoting Democracy in the Middle East.* Washington, D.C.: Carnegie Endowment for International Peace.

———. 2002. "Democratization in the Arab World? The Trap of Liberalized Autocracy." *Journal of Democracy* 13 (4): 56–86.

———. 2001. *Reinventing Khomeini: The Struggle for Reform in Iran.* Chicago: University of Chicago Press.

Brynen, Rex. 1995. "The Neopatrimonial Dimension of Palestinian Politics." *Journal of Palestine Studies* 25 (1): 23–36.

Brynen, Rex, Bahgat Korany, and Paul Noble (eds.). 1998. *Political Liberalization and Democratization in the Arab World.* Vol. 2. Boulder: Lynne Rienner.

——— (eds.). 1995. *Political Liberalization and Democratization in the Arab World.* Vol. 1. Boulder: Lynne Rienner.

Buchta, Wilfried. 2000. *Who Rules Iran? The Structure of Power in the Islamic Republic.* Washington, D.C.: Washington Institute for Near East Policy.

Bunce, V. 2000. "Comparative Democratization: Big and Bounded Generalizations." *Journal of Democracy* 33: 703–734.

Camau, Michel. 2001. "La transitologie à l'épreuve du Moyen-Orient et de l'Afrique du Nord." In *Annuaire de l'Afrique du Nord, 1999.* Paris: CNRS.

———. 2000. "NGOs, INGOs, GO-NGOs, and DO-NGOs: Making Sense of Non-Governmental Institutions." *Middle East Report* 30 (1): 12–15.

———. 1997. "D'une republique à l'autre: refondation politique et aléas de la transition libérale." *Monde Arabe–Maghreb-Machrek* 157 (July–September): 3–16.

Camau, Michel, and Vincent Geisser. 2003. *Le syndrome autoritaire: politique en Tunisie de Bourguiba à Ben Ali.* Paris: Presses de Sciences Po.

Carapico, Sheila. 2000. "NGOs, INGOs, GO-NGOs and DO-NGOs. Making Sense of Non-Governmental Institutions." *Middle East Report* 30 (1): 12–15.

———. 1998. *Civil Society in Yemen: The Political Economy of Activism in Modern Arabia.* Cambridge: Cambridge University Press.

Cardenas, Sonia, and Andrew Flibbert. 2005. "National Human Rights Institutions in the Middle East." *Middle East Journal* 59 (3): 411–436.

Carothers, Thomas. 2004. "Democracy's Sobering State." *Current History: The World* (special edition) (December): 412–416.

———. 2002. "The End of the Transition Paradigm." *Journal of Democracy* 13 (1): 5–21.

Cassarino, Jean-Pierre. 2000. *Tunisian New Entrepreneurs and Their Past Experiences of Migration in Europe: Resource Mobilization, Networks, and Hidden Disaffection.* Aldershot: Ashgate.

Cavatorta, Francesco. 2005. "The International Context of Morocco's Stalled Democratization." *Democratization* 12 (4): 548–566.

———. 2001. "Geopolitical Challenges to the Success of Democracy in North Africa: Algeria, Tunisia, and Morocco." *Democratization* 8 (4): 175–194.

Center for Strategic Studies. 1998. *Istatla'a al-ra'i hawl al-dimuqratiyya fi-l-Urdunn, 1998.* Markaz al-Dirasat al-Istratajiyya, al-Jami'at al-Urdun.

Central Intelligence Agency. 2006. "Bahrain." In *The World Factbook, 2006.* November 2. https://cia.gov/cia/publications/factbook/geos/ba.html.

Chehabi, H. E. 2001. "The Political Regime of the Islamic Republic of Iran in Comparative Perspective." *Government and Opposition* 36: 48–70.

Chehabi, H. E., and Juan Linz (eds.). 1998. *Sultanistic Regimes.* Baltimore: Johns Hopkins University Press.

Chourou, Bechir. 2002. "The Challenge of Democracy in North Africa." *Democratization* 9 (1): 17–39.

Claisse, Alain. 1985. "Le parlement imaginaire." In *L'expérience parlementaire au Maroc.* Casablanca: Editions Toubkal.

Clark, Janine. 2004. "Social Movement Theory and Patron Clientelism: Islamic Social Institutions and the Middle Class in Egypt, Jordan, and Yemen." *Comparative Political Studies* 37 (October): 941–968.

———. 2003. *Islam, Charity, and Activism: Middle-Class Networks and Social Welfare in Egypt, Jordan, and Yemen.* Bloomington: Indiana University Press.

Collier, David, and Steven Levitsky. 1997. "Democracy with Adjectives." *World Politics* 49: 430–451.

Conge, Patrick J. 1988. "The Concept of Political Participation. Toward a Definition." *Comparative Politics* 20 (2): 241–249.

Cox, Gary W. 1997. *Making Votes Count: Strategic Coordination in the World's Electoral Systems.* Cambridge: Cambridge University Press.

Cunningham, Robert, and Yasin Sarayrah. 1993. *Wasta: The Hidden Force in Middle Eastern Society.* Westport: Praeger.

Dahl, Robert A. 1989. *Democracy and Its Critics.* New Haven: Yale University Press.

———. 1971. *Polyarchy: Participation and Opposition.* New Haven: Yale University Press.

Denœux, Guilain. 1999. "La Tunisie de Ben Ali et ses paradoxes." *Monde Arabe–Maghreb–Machrek* 166 (October–December): 32–52.

———. 1993. *Urban Unrest in the Middle East.* Albany: State University of New York Press.

Denœux, Guilain, and Abdeslam Maghraoui. 1998. "The Political Economy of Structural Adjustment in Morocco." In Azzedine Layachi (ed.), *Economic Crisis and Political Change in North Africa.* New York: Praeger.

Desrues, Thiery, and Edwardo Moyano. 2001. "Social Change and Political Transition in Morocco." *Mediterranean Politics* 6: 21–47.

Diamond, Larry. 2002. "Thinking About Hybrid Regimes." *Journal of Democracy* 13 (2): 23–35.

Diamond, Larry, Marc F. Plattner, and Daniel Brumberg (eds.). 2003. *Islam and Democracy in the Middle East.* Baltimore: Johns Hopkins University Press.

Dillman, Bradford. 2000. "Parliamentary Elections and the Prospects for Pluralism in North Africa." *Government and Opposition* 35 (2): 211–236.

Dobry, Michel. 2000. "Les voies incertaines de la transitologie: choix stratégiques, séquences historiques, bifurcations et processus de path dependence." *Revue Française de Science Politique* 50 (August–October): 585–614.

Dresch, Paul. 1989. *Tribes, Government, and History in Yemen.* Oxford: Clarendon.

Ehteshami, Anoushiravan. 2004. "Islam, Muslim Polities, and Democracy." *Democratization* 11 (4): 90–110.

———. 2003. "Reform from Above: The Politics of Participation in the Oil Monarchies." *International Affairs* 79 (1): 53–75.

———. 1999. "Is the Middle East Democratizing?" *British Journal of Middle Eastern Studies* 26 (2): 217.

Ehteshami, Anoushiravan, and Emma Murphy. 1996. "Transformation of the Corporatist State in the Middle East." *Third World Quarterly* 17 (4): 753–772.

el-Gawhary, Krista Masonis. 2000. "Egyptian Advocacy NGOs: Catalysts for Social and Political Change." *Middle East Report* (214): 38–41.

el-Mikawy, Noha. 1999. *The Building of Consensus in Egypt's Transition Process.* Cairo: American University of Cairo Press.

el-Mikawy, Noha, and Marsha Pripstein Posusney. 2000. "Labor Representation in the Age of Globalization: Trends and Issues in Non-Oil-Based Arab Countries." Paper presented at the third Mediterranean Forum. Cairo, March 5–8.

el-Nahhas, Mona. 2005a. "Candidates Aplenty." *Al-Ahram Weekly,* October 27, 2005.

———. 2005b. "Opposition Cries Foul." *Al-Ahram Weekly,* June 8..

———. 2004. 14. "Tomorrow's Party Today." *Al-Ahram Weekly,* November 10, 2004.

el-Shubki, Amr. 1997. "Transformation of the Political Environment in Egypt: From Ideological Co-optation to Social Confrontation." Paper presented at the conference "Reform of the Election System." September 23–24.

Erguder, Ustun, and Richard Hofferbert. 1987. "Restoration of Democracy in Turkey? Political Reforms and the Elections of 1983." In Linda Layne (ed.), *Elections in the Middle East: Implications of Recent Trends.* Boulder: Westview.

Esfahani, H. S., and F. Taheripour. 2002. "Hidden Public Expenditures and the Economy in Iran." *International Journal of Middle Eastern Studies* 34: 691–718.

Esfandiari, Haleh. 2003. "Is Iran Democratizing? Observations on Election Day." In Larry Diamond, Marc F. Plattner, and Daniel Brumberg (eds.), *Islam and Democracy in the Middle East.* Baltimore: Johns Hopkins University Press.

Essam el-Din, Gamal. 2005. "The Silent Majority." *Al-Ahram Weekly,* December 26.

———. 2002. "Corruption Shockwaves." *Al-Ahram Weekly,* August 8.

———. 2000a. "Corruption Stigma Haunts NDP." *Al-Ahram Weekly,* July 6.

———. 2000b. "Corrupt MPs Suffer Court Fury." *Al Ahram Weekly,* June 29.

Fairbanks, S. C. 1998. "Theocracy Versus Democracy: Iran Considers Political Parties." *Middle East Journal* 52: 17–31.

Farouk-Sluglett, Marion, and Peter Sluglett. 1987. *Iraq Since 1958: From Revolution to Dictatorship.* London: Routledge.

Gallissot, René. 1985. "Interrogation critique sur la centralité du mouvement ouvrier au Maghreb." In Noureddine Sraieb (comp.), *Le mouvement ouvrier Maghrébin.* Paris: CNRS.

Gamblin, Sandrine. 1997. *Contours et détours du politique en Egypte: les élections législatives de 1995.* Paris: L'Harmattan.

Gandhi, Jennifer, and Adam Przeworski. 2001. "Dictatorial institutions and the survival of dictators." Paper presented at the annual meeting of the American Political Science Association. San Francisco.

Gandhi, Jennifer, and James Vreeland. 2004. "Political Institutions and Civil War: Unpacking Anocracy." Unpublished manuscript.

Gasiorowski, M. J. 1987. "The 1953 Coup d'Etat in Iran." *International Journal of Middle East Studies* 19: 261–286.

Geddes, Barbara. 1999. "Authoritarian Breakdown: Empirical Test of a Game Theoretic Argument." Paper presented at the annual meeting of the American Political Science Association. Atlanta, September.

———. 1991. "A Game Theoretic Model of Reform in Latin American Democracies." *American Political Science Review* 85 (2): 371–392.

Geisser, Vincent. 2000. "Tunisie: des élections pourquoi faire? enjeux et 'sens' du fait électoral de Bourguiba à Ben Ali." *Monde Arabe–Maghreb-Machrek* 2 (April–June): 168.

Gellner, E. 1994. *The Conditions of Liberty: Civil Society and Its Rivals.* London: Penguin.

Gheissari, A., and V. Nasr. 2006. *Democracy in Iran.* New York: Oxford University Press.

Glosemeyer, Iris. 1993. "The First Yemeni Parliamentary Elections in 1993: Practising Democracy." *Orient* 34 (3): 439–451.

Golder, Matthew. 2003. "Democratic Electoral Systems Around the World, 1946–2000." November. http://homepages.nyu.edu/~mrg217/electoralsystems1.pdf.

Guilhot, Nicolas, and Philippe C. Schmitter. 2000. "De la transition à la consolidation: une lecture rétrospective des democratization studies." *Revue Française de Science Politique* 50 (August–October): 615–631.

"Gunmen Release Gaza Police Chief." 2004. *BBC News,* July 16. http://news.bbc.co.uk/1/hi/world/middle_east/3900649.stm.

Hadenius, Axel, and Jan Teorell. 2005. "Authoritarian Regimes 1972–2003: Patterns of Stability and Change." Paper presented at the conference "Authoritarian Regimes: Conditions of Stability and Change." Istanbul, May 29–31.

Hafez, Muhammad. 2003. *Why Muslims Rebel: Repression and Resistance in the Islamic World.* Boulder: Lynne Rienner.

Hale, H. E. 2005. "Regime Cycles: Democracy, Autocracy, and Revolution in Post-Soviet Eurasia." *World Politics* 58: 133–165.

Halpern, Manfred. 1962. "Middle Eastern Armies and the New Middle Class." In J. J. Johnson (ed.), *The Role of the Military in Underdeveloped Countries.* Princeton: Princeton University Press.

Hamad, Ghazi. 2005. "Controversy in Rafah." *Palestine Report,* May 11.

Hamdy, Iman A. (ed.). 2004. *Elections in the Middle East: What Do They Mean?* Cairo Papers in Social Science. Cairo: American University of Cairo Press.

Hammami, Rema. 2000. "Palestinian NGOs Since Oslo: From NGO Politics to Social Movements?" *Middle East Report* (214): 16–48.

Hamzaoui, Salah. 2001. "Champ politique et syndicalisme en Tunisie." *Annuaire de l'Afrique du Nord, 1999.* Paris: CNRS.

Hamzawy, Amr. 2005. *The Continued Costs of Political Stagnation in Egypt: Policy Outlook.* Washington, D.C.: Carnegie Endowment for International Peace. http://www.carnegieendowment.org/files/hamzawy-final.pdf.

Harb, Imad. 2003. "The Egyptian Military in Politics: Disengagement or Accommodation?" *Middle East Journal* 57 (2): 269–290.

Harik, Iliya. 1980. "Lebanon." In Jacob Landau, Ergun Ozbudun, and Frank Tachau (eds.), *Electoral Politics in the Middle East.* Stanford: Croom Helm.

Harik, Iliya, and Denis Sullivan (eds.). 1992. *Privatization and Liberalization in the Middle East.* Bloomington: Indiana University Press.

Hartlyn, Jonathan, Jennifer McCoy, and Thomas Mustillo. 2003. "The 'Quality of Elections' in Contemporary Latin America: Issues in Measurement and Explanation." Paper prepared for 2003 international congress of the Latin American Studies Association. Dallas, March 27–29.

Hawthorne, Amy. 2004. "Middle East Democracy: Is Civil Society the Answer?" *Carnegie Papers* 44.

Henry, Clement M., and Robert Springborg. 2001. *Globalization and the Politics of Development in the Middle East.* Cambridge: Cambridge University Press.

Heper, Metin, and Ahmet Evin (eds.). 1994. *Politics in the Third Turkish Republic.* Boulder: Westview.

Herb, Michael. 2004. "Princes and Parliaments in the Arab World." *Middle East Journal* 58 (3): 367–384.

———. 1999. *All in the Family.* Albany: State University of New York Press.

Herbert, David. 2003. *Religion and Civil Society: Rethinking Public Religion in the Contemporary World.* Religion, Culture, and Society Series. Aldershot: Ashgate.

Hermet, Guy, Richard Rose, and Alain Rouquié (eds.). 1978. *Elections Without Choice.* New York: Wiley.

Hertog, Steffen. 2006. "The New Corporatism in Saudi Arabia: Limits of Formal Politics." In Abdulhadi Khalaf and Giacomo Luciani (eds.), *Constitutional Reform and Political Participation in the Gulf.* Dubai: Gulf Research Center.

Heumann, Bernard, and Mohamed Abdelhaq. 2000. "Opposition et élections en Tunisie." *Monde Arabe–Maghreb-Machrek* 2 (April–June): 168.

Hibou, Béatrice. 1999. "Les marges de manœuvre d'un 'bon élève' économique: la Tunisie de Ben Ali." *Les Etudes du CERI* (December).

Hilal, Reda. 2003. "The Elections of the Egyptian Press Syndicate: Democratic Change or Suicide?" *Al-Ahram,* March 8, 2003. http://www.apfw.org /indexarabic.asp?fname=articles%5carabic%5cara1012.htm.

Hinnebusch, Raymond. 1985. *Egyptian Politics Under Sadat: The Post-Populist Development of an Authoritarian-Modernizing State.* London: Cambridge University Press.

Hirschman, Albert O. 1970. *Exit, Voice, and Loyalty: Responses to Decline in Firms, Organizations, and States.* Cambridge: Harvard University Press.

Hourani, Hani. 1994. "Intikhabat 1993 al-urdunniyyah: qira'ah fi khalfiyyatiha, tharoufiha, wa nitaja'iha." *Al-Urdunn al-Jadid* 4 (2): 7–31.

Hourani, Hani, et al. 2004. *Who's Who in the Jordanian Parliament: 2003–2007.* Amman: Dar Sindbad lil-Nashr.

———. 2002. *Dirrassat fi al-intikhabat al-niyyabiyah al-urdunniyah: 1997.* Amman: Dar Sindbad lil-Nashr.

———. 1998. *Who's Who in the Jordanian Parliament: 1997–2001.* Amman: Al-Urdunn al-Jadid Research Center.

Hudson, Michael. 1997. *Arab Politics and the Search for Legitimacy.* New Haven: Yale University Press.

Human Rights Watch. 1997. *Routine Abuse, Routine Denial: Civil Rights and the Political Crisis in Bahrain.* New York.

Huntington, Samuel P. 1968. *Political Order in Changing Societies.* New Haven: Yale University Press.

Huntington, Samuel, and Joan Nelson (eds.). 1976. *No Easy Choice: Political Participation in Developing Countries.* Cambridge: Harvard University Press.

Hyden, Goran, Julius Court, and Ken Mease. 2003. "Political Society and Governance in Sixteen Developing Countries." *World Governance Survey* (July).

Ibrahim, S. 1997. "From Taliban to Erbakan: The Case of Islam, Civil Society, and Democracy." In E. Ozdalga and S. Persson (eds.), *Civil Society and Democracy in the Muslim World.* Istanbul: Swedish Research Institute.

Idrissi, Hachimi. 1995. "Le grand cirque." *Maroc-Hebdo,* May 5.

Ishiyama, John. 1997. "The Sickle or the Rose? Previous Regime Types and the Evolution of the Ex-Communist Parties in Post-Communist Polities." *Comparative Political Studies* 30 (3): 299–330.

Jibril, Mohamed. 2005. "Le syndicalisme en crise." *La Gazette du Maroc,* April 4.

Jonasson, Ann-Kristin. 2004. *At the Command of God? On the Political Linkage of Islamist Parties.* Göteborg: Göteborg University Press.

Karl, Terry Lynn, and Philippe C. Schmitter. 1991. "Modes of Transition in Latin America, Southern and Eastern Europe." *International Social Science Journal* 128: 269–284.

Khalaf, Samir G. 1980. "Lebanon." In Jacob Landau, Ergun Ozbudun, and Frank Tachau (eds.), *Electoral Politics in the Middle East.* London: Croom Helm.

Khalafallah, Ahmed Taha. 2001. *Tahawulat al-democratiya fi Misr.* Cairo.

Khaldouni, M'barek. 1984. "La troisième expérience parlementaire marocaine (1977–1983)." PhD thesis, Rabat, Mohamed V University.

Khiari, Sadri. 2000. "Reclassements et recompositions au sein de la bureaucratie syndicale depuis l'indépendance: la place de l'UGTT dans le système politique tunisien." In Béatrice Hibou, *La Tunisie sous Ben Ali.* http://www.ceri-sciencespo.com/cerifr/dessus.htm.

Khomeini, R. 1981. *Islam and Revolution I: Writings and Declarations of Imam Khomeini.* Annotated and translated by Hamid Algar. Berkeley: Mizan.

Khouri, Philip S. 1984. "Syrian Urban Politics in Transition: The Quarters of Damascus During the French Mandate." *International Journal of Middle East Studies* 16: 507–540.

Khouri, Rami. 2003. "Jordan: A Constitutional Tribal Monarchy in Transformation—Background Paper." In *Better Governance for Development in the Middle East and North Africa: Enhancing Inclusiveness and Accountability.* Washington, D.C.: World Bank.

Khuri, Fuad I. 1980. *Tribe and State in Bahrain: The Transformation of Social and Political Authority in an Arab State.* Chicago: University of Chicago Press.

Kilani, Sa'eda, and Basem Sakijha. 2002. *Wasta: The Declared Secret.* Amman: Jordan Press.

Kimmerling, Baruch, and Joel S. Migdal. 2003. *The Palestinian People: A History.* Cambridge: Harvard University Press.

Kostiner, Joseph (ed.). 2000. *Middle East Monarchies: The Challenge of Modernity.* Boulder: Lynne Rienner.

Kratochwil, Gabi, and Abderrahman Lakhbassi. 2004. "Associations culturelles amazighhes." In Maria-Angels Roque (ed.), *La société civile au Maroc.* Paris: L'Harmattan.

LaGroye, Jacques. 2003. *La politisation.* Paris: Belin.

Landau, Jacob, Ergun Ozbudun, and Frank Tachau (eds.). 1980. *Electoral Politics in the Middle East.* London: Croom Helm.

Langohr, Vicky. 2004. "Too Much Civil Society, Too Little Politics: Egypt and Liberalizing Arab Regimes." *Comparative Politics* 36 (2): 181–204.

Layachi, Azzedine. 2001. "Algeria Flooding and Muddied State-Society Relations." *Middle East Report Press Information Report 79.*

Layne, Linda (ed.). 1987. *Elections in the Middle East: Implications of Recent Trends.* Boulder: Westview.

Leca, Jean. "La democratisation dans le monde arabe: incertitude, vulnérabilité et légitimité." *Démocratie sans Démocrates.* Ghassan Salame. 35–93.

Levitsky, Steven, and Lucan Way. 2003. "Autocracy by Democratic Rules: The Dynamics of Competitive Authoritarianism in the Post–Cold War Era." (Revised version of paper prepared for the annual meeting of the American Political Science Association. Boston, August 28–31.) Presented at the Columbia University conference "Mapping the Great Zone: Clientelism and the Boundary Between Democratic and Democratizing."

———. 2002a. "Autocracy by Democratic Rules: The Dynamics of Competitive Authoritarianism in the Post–Cold War Era." Paper presented at the annual meeting of the American Political Science Association. Boston, August 28–31.

———. 2002b. "The Rise of Competitive Authoritarianism." *Journal of Democracy* 13 (2): 51–65.

Lindberg, Staffan. 2005. "Consequences of Electoral Systems in Africa: A Preliminary Study." *Electoral Studies* 24 (1): 41–64.

———. 2004. "When Do Opposition Parties Boycott Elections?" Paper prepared for the international conference "Democratization by Elections? The Dynamics of Electoral Authoritarianism." CIDE, Mexico, April 2–3. http://www.svet .lu.se/staff/personal_pages/staffan_lindberg/when_do_opposition5.pdf.

Lindholm, Charles. 2002. *The Islamic Middle East. Tradition and Change.* Oxford: Blackwell.

Linz, Juan J. 2000. *Totalitarian and Authoritarian Regimes*. Boulder: Lynne Rienner.

Linz, Juan J., and A. Stepan. 1996. *Problems of Democratic Transition and Consolidation*. Baltimore: Johns Hopkins University Press.

Longuenesse, Elisabeth. 1998. "Maroc, Tunisie, Egypte: transition libérale et recompositions syndicales." *Monde Arabe–Maghreb-Machrek* 162 (October–December): 3–56.

Lopez Garcia, Bernabé. 1989. *Política y movimientos sociales en el Magreb*. Madrid: Centro de Investigaciones Sociologicas.

Lucas, Russell. 2005. *Institutions and the Politics of Survival in Jordan: Domestic Responses to External Challenges, 1988–2001*. Albany: State University of New York Press.

———. 2003. "Press Laws as a Survival Strategy in Jordan: 1989–1999." *Middle Eastern Studies* 39 (4): 81–98.

Lust-Okar, Ellen. 2006. "Elections Under Authoritarianism: Preliminary Lessons from Jordan." *Democratization* 13 (3): 455–470.

———. 2005a. "Democracy in Jordan: Opportunities Lost." Paper presented at the US Institute of Peace workshop "Beyond Liberalized Autocracy? New Options for Promoting Democracy in the Arab World." Washington, D.C., July 18–19.

———. 2005b. *Structuring Conflict in the Arab World: Incumbents, Opponents, and Institutions*. Cambridge: Cambridge University Press.

———. 2001. "The Decline of Jordanian Political Parties: Myth or Reality?" *International Journal of Middle East Studies* 33 (4): 545–570.

Lust-Okar, Ellen, and Amaney Jamal. 2002. "Rulers and Rules: Reassessing Electoral Laws and Political Liberalization in the Middle East." *Comparative Political Studies* 35 (3): 337–366.

Mackow, Jerzy. 2000. "Autoritarismen oder 'Demokratien mit Adjektiven'? Überlegungen zu Systemen der gescheiterten Demokratisierung." *Zeitschrift für Politikwissenschaft* 10 (4): 1471–1500.

Madjid, Nurcholish. 1998. "The Necessity of Renewing Islamic Thought and Reinvigorating Religious Understanding." In C. Kurzman (ed.), *Liberal Islam*. New York: Oxford University Press.

Maghraoui, Abdeslam. 2002. "Democratization in the Arab World: Depoliticization in Morocco." *Journal of Democracy* 13 (4): 24–32.

Mahoney, James. 2000. "Path Dependence in Historical Sociology." *Theory and Society* 29 (4): 507–548.

Mandaville, P. 2001. *Transnational Muslim Politics: Reimagining the Umma*. New York: Routledge.

March, James, and Johan Olsen. 1989. *Rediscovering Institutions*. New York: Free Press.

Marzouk, Mohsen. 1997. "Associative Phenomenon in the Arab World: Engine of Democratisation or Witness to the Crisis?" In David Hulme and Michael Edwards (eds.), *NGOs, States, and Donors: Too Close for Comfort?* New York: St. Martin's.

McCann, Paul. 2002. "Ten Killed in Gaza, Including Two UNRWA Staff." United Nations Relief and Works Agency for Palestine Refugees in the Near East, December 6. http://www.reliefweb.int/rw/rwb.nsf/alldocsbyunid/3c74b0acd 9085fc385256c8700539476.

McFaul, M. 2005. "Chinese Dreams, Persian Realities." *Journal of Democracy* 16: 74–82.

Meinel, Ute Devika. 2002. "Die Intifada im Ölscheichtum Bahrain: Hintergründe des Aufbegehrens von 1994–98." Münster: Lit-Verlag.

Merkel, Wolfgang, and Aurel Croissant. 2000. "Formale und informale Institutionen in defekten Demokratien." *Politische Vierteljahresschrift* 41: 3–30.

Milani, M. M. 2001. "Reform and Resistance in the Islamic Republic of Iran." In John L. Esposito and R. K. Ramazani (eds.), *Iran at the Crossroads.* New York: Palgrave.

———. 1993. "The Evolution of the Iranian Presidency: From Bani Sadr to Rafsanjani." *British Journal of Middle Eastern Studies* 20: 83–97.

Milbrath, Lester W. 1971. *Political Participation: How and Why Do People Get Involved in Politics?* Chicago: Rand McNally.

Mineesy, Ahmed, and Manal Lutfi. 2001. "Intikhabat Maglis al-Shaab: 'anasir al-thibat wa al-tahawul." *Ahwal Masriyya* 2: 150–157.

Mitchell, Timothy. 1991. "The Limits of the State: Beyond Statist Approaches and Their Critics." *American Political Science Review* 85 (1): 77–94.

Moench, Richard U. 1987. "The May 1984 Elections in Egypt and the Question of Egypt's Stability." In Linda Layne (ed.), *Elections in the Middle East.* Boulder: Westview.

Mohammadi-Nejad, H. 1977. "The Iranian Parliamentary Elections of 1975." *International Journal of Middle East* 8: 107–108.

Moslem, M. 2002. *Factional Politics in Post-Khomeini Iran.* Syracuse: Syracuse University Press.

Mouaquit, Mohamed, 2004. "Le movement des droits humains au Maroc." In Maria-Angels Roque (ed.), *La société civile au Maroc.* Paris: L'Harmattan.

Moustafa, Hala (ed.). 2001. *Intikhabat Maglis al-Shaab, 2000.* Cairo: Al-Ahram Center for Political and Strategic Studies.

———. 1995. *Al-intikhabat al-barlimanaya fi Misr.* Cairo: Al-Ahram Center for Political and Strategic Studies.

Mozaffar, Shaheen. 2002. "Patterns of Electoral Governance in Africa's Emerging Democracies." *International Political Science Review* 23 (1): 85–101.

Mozaffar, Shaheen, and Andreas Schedler. 2002. "The Comparative Study of Electoral Governance: Introduction." *International Political Science Review* 23 (1): 5–27.

Munck, Gerardo and Richard Snyder. 2004. "Mapping Political Regimes: How the Concepts We Use and the Way We Measure Them Shape the World We See." Paper prepared for 2004 annual meeting of the American Political Science Association. Chicago, September 2–5.

Murphy, Emma. 1999. *Economic and Political Change in Tunisia: From Bourguiba to Ben Ali.* London: Macmillan.

Mustafá, Hala. 2001. *Intikhabat Majlis al-Sh'ab 2000.* Cairo: Markaz al-Dirrassat al-Siyyassiyah wa al-Istirratijjiyah.

Mustafá, Muhammad. 1990. *Al-dimuqrattiyah wa-al-intikhabat.* Cairo: Dar al-Ma'arif.

Naciri, Khalid. 1985. "Le parlement sur le créneau de la production législative quantitative." In *L'expérience parlementaire au Maroc.* Casablanca: Les Editions Toubkal.

———. 1984. "Le droit politique dans l'ordonnancement constitutionnel: essai d'interprétation du système de gouvernement au Maroc." PhD thesis, Paris, Paris II Unviersity.

Niblock, Tim, and Emma Murphy. 1993. *Economic and Political Liberalization in the Middle East.* London: British Academic Press.

North, Douglas. 1990. *Institutions, Institutional Change, and Economic Performance.* Cambridge: Cambridge University Press.

Norton, August Richard (ed.). 1996. *Civil Society in the Middle East (Parts 1 and 2).* Netherlands: Brill.

Nourbakhsh, A. A. 2005. "Iran's Next President: What Is the Likely Outcome of 17 June?" *Iran Focus* 18: 6.

O'Donnell, Guillermo. 1993. "Delegative Democracy." In Larry Diamond and Marc F. Plattner (eds.), *The Global Resurgence of Democracy.* Baltimore: Johns Hopkins University Press.

O'Donnell, Guillermo, Philippe C. Schmitter, and Laurence Whitehead (eds.). 1986. *Transitions from Authoritarian Rule: Prospects for Democracy.* 5 vols. Baltimore: Johns Hopkins University Press.

Ottaway, Marina. 2003. *Democracy Challenged: The Rise of Semi-Authoritarianism.* Washington, D.C.: Carnegie Endowment for International Peace.

Pappe, Ilan. 2004. *A History of Modern Palestine: One Land, Two Peoples.* New York: Cambridge University Press.

Parker, Christopher. 1999. *Resignation or Revolt? Socio-Political Development and the Challenges of Peace in Palestine.* London: Tauris.

Parliamentary Human Rights Group–London. 1996. *Bahrain: A Brickwall—Correspondence Between Lord Avebury and the Foreign and Commonwealth Office of the British Government on the Human Rights Situation in Bahrain.*

Perthes, Volker. 2004. "Politics and Elite Change in the Arab World." In Volker Perthes (ed.), *Arab Elites: Negotiating the Politics of Change.* Boulder: Lynne Rienner.

Posusney, Marsha Pripstein. 2002. "Multi-Party Elections in the Arab World: Institutional Engineering and Oppositional Strategies." *Studies in Comparative International Development* 36 (4): 34–62.

———. 1998. "Behind the Ballot Box: Electoral Engineering in the Arab World." *Middle East Report* (209): 12–16.

Posusney, Marsha Pripstein, and Michele Penner Angrist (eds.). 2005. *Authoritarianism in the Middle East: Regimes and Resistance.* Boulder: Lynne Rienner Publishers.

Pretty, Jules. 1995. "The Many Interpretations of Participation." *Focus* 16: 4–5.

Przeworski, Adam. 1991. *Democracy and the Market: Political and Economic Reforms in Eastern Europe and Latin America. Studies in Rationality and Social Change.* Cambridge: Cambridge University Press.

Przeworski, Adam, Michael Alvarez, Jose Cheibub, and Fernando Limongi. 2000. *Democracy and Development: Political Institutions and Material Well-Being in the World.* Cambridge: Cambridge University Press.

Qasamil, Ahmad. 1991. *Intikhabat Majlis al-Sha'b 90 wa-azmat al-dimmuqrattiyah fi Misr.* Cairo: Al-'Arabbi lil-Nashr wa al-Tawzzi.

Razi, G. H. 1987. "The Nexus of Legitimacy and Performance: The Lessons of the Iranian Revolution." *Comparative Politics* 19: 453–469.

Regular, Arnon. 2005a. "Fatah Takes Most Councils; Hamas Wins Larger Towns." *Ha'aretz,* May 8.

———. 2005b. "Hamas Gunmen Open Fire on Fatah Command Center, Home of Senior Official in Gaza." *Ha'aretz,* July 20.

———. 2005c. "Hamas Leader Says Group Rejects Ruling on Gaza Election Results." *Ha'aretz,* May 20.

———. 2005d. "Hamas Warns of Flare-Up Due to Fatah's Election Antics." *Ha'aretz,* May 9.

"Representatives Win with Services . . . and Apologies to the Constitution." 2006. *Al-Misry al-Yawm* 15 (January): 5.

Reuters. 2005. "In a Blow to Hamas, Palestinian Court Nullified Local Election Results." May 18.

Richards, Alan, and John Waterbury. 1998. *A Political Economy of the Middle East.* Boulder: Westview.

———. 1991. *A Political Economy of the Middle East: State, Class, and Economic Development.* Cairo: American University of Cairo Press.

Robinson, Glen. 1997. *Building a Palestinian State: The Incomplete Revolution.* Bloomington: University of Indiana Press.

Roy, O. 1999. "The Crisis of Religious Legitimacy in Iran." *Middle East Journal* 53: 201–217.

Rubin, Barry. 2001. "The Military in Contemporary Middle East Politics." *Middle East Review of International Affairs* 5 (1): 47–63.

Rustow, Dankwart. 1985. "Elections and Legitimacy in the Middle East." *Annals of the American Academy of Political and Social Science* 482 (November): 122–146.

Sadiki, Larbi. 2002. "Political Liberalization in Bin Ali's Tunisia: Façade Democracy." *Democratization* 9 (4): 122–141.

Saeed Ali, Abdel Monem. 2003. "Governance in Egypt: Background Paper." In *Better Governance for Development in the Middle East and North Africa: Enhancing Inclusiveness and Accountability.* Washington, D.C.: World Bank.

Saffari, S. 1993. "The Legitimation of the Clergy's Right to Rule in the Iranian Constitution of 1979." *British Journal of Middle Eastern Studies* 20: 64–82.

Salame, Ghassan. 1994. *Démocraties sans démocrates: politiques d'ouvertures dans le monde arabe et islamique.* Paris: Fayard.

———. 1991. "Sur la causalité d'un manque: pourquoi le monde arabe n'est-il donc pas démocratique?" *Revue Française de Science Politique* 41 (3): 307–341.

Salamon, Lester. 2004. *Global Civil Society: Dimensions of the Non-Profit Sector.* Vol. 2. Bloomfield, Conn.: Kumarian.

Samii, A. W. 2005. "The Changing Landscape of Party Politics in Iran: A Case Study." *Journal of the European Society for Iranian Studies* 1: 53–62.

———. 2004. "Dissent in Iranian Elections: Reasons and Implications." *Middle East Journal* 58: 403–423.

———. 2001. "Iran's Guardians Council as an Obstacle to Democracy." *Middle East Journal* 55: 642–663.

———. 2000. "Iran's 2000 Elections." *Middle East Review of International Affairs* 4: 1–15.

Sato, Tsugitaka (ed.). 1997. *Islamic Urbanism in Human History: Political Power and Social Networks.* London: Kegan Paul.

Sayigh, Yezid. 1997. *Armed Struggle and the Search for State: The Palestinian National Movement, 1949–1993.* Oxford: Oxford University Press.

Scaff, Lawrence A. 1975. "Two Concepts of Political Participation." *Western Political Quarterly* (September): 447–462.

Scaff, Lawrence A., and Edward J. Williams. 1978. "Participation and the Primacy of Politics in Developmental Theory." In John A. Booth and Mitchell A. Seligson (eds.), *Political Participation in Latin America.* New York: Holmes and Meier.

Schedler, Andreas (ed.). 2006. *Electoral Authoritarianism: The Dynamics of Unfree Competition.* Boulder: Lynne Rienner.

———. 2002a. "The Menu of Manipulation." *Journal of Democracy* 13 (2): 36–50.

————. 2002b. "The Nested Game of Democratization by Elections." *International Political Science Review* 23 (1): 103–122.

Scheper-Hughes, Nancy, and Philippe Bourgois. 2005. "Introduction: Making Sense of Violence." In Nancy Scheper-Hughes and Philippe Bourgois (eds.), *Violence in War and Peace: An Anthology.* Oxford: Blackwell.

Schirazi, A. 1998. *The Constitution of Iran: Politics and the State in the Islamic Republic.* Translated by John O'Kane. London: Tauris.

Schlumberger, Oliver (ed.). 2007. *Debating Arab Authoritarianism: Dynamics and Durability in Nondemocratic Regimes.* Stanford: Stanford University Press.

Schmitter, Philippe C. 2001. "Se déplaçant au Moyen-Orient et en Afrique du Nord: 'transitologues' et 'consolidologues' sont-ils toujours assurés de voyager en toute sécurité?" In *Annuaire de l'Afrique du Nord, 1999.* Paris: CNRS.

————. 1979. "Still the Century of Corporatism?" In Philippe C. Schmitter and Gerhard Lehmbruch (eds.), *Trends Toward Corporatist Intermediation.* London: Sage.

Schulz, Donald E., and Jan S. Adams (eds.). 1981. *Political Participation in Communist Systems.* New York: Pergamon.

Schwedler, Jillian, and Laryssa Chomiak. 2006. "And the Winner Is . . . Authoritarian Elections in the Arab World." *Middle East Report* (238): 12–19.

Schwedler, Jillian, and Samir Fayyaz. 2006. "Disciplining Dissent: Toward a Legal Geography of Protest in Jordan." Paper presented at the Seventh Mediterranean Social and Political Research Meeting, Florence and Montecatini Terme, March 22–26.

Sehimi, Mustapha. 1979. *Juin 1977: étude des élections législatives au Maroc.* Casablanca: Somaded.

Seifzadeh, H. S. 2003. "The Landscape of Factional Politics in Iran." *Middle East Journal* 57: 57–75.

Shafiq, Amina. 2001. "Imra' amila fi al-intikhaba." In *Kitab al–Ahali.* Cairo: Al Ahali Foundation.

Sharabi, Hisham. 1988. *Neopatriarchy: A Theory of Distorted Change in Arab Society.* New York: Oxford University Press.

Shehab, Shaden. 2006. "Gomaa's Last Stand." *Al-Ahram Weekly,* April 6.

————. 2005. "Party at the Crossroads." *Al-Ahram Weekly,* December 15.

Shehata, Samer 2003. "In the Basha's House: The Organizational Culture of Egyptian Public-Sector Enterprises." *International Journal of Middle East Studies* 35: 103–132.

Shi, Tianjian. 1999. "Voting and Nonvoting in China: Voting Behavior in Plebiscitary and Limited-Choice Elections." *Journal of Politics* 61(4): 1115–1139.

Singerman, Diane. 1997a. *Avenues of Participation: Family, Politics, and Networks in Urban Quarters of Cairo.* Princeton: Princeton University Press.

————. 1997b. "Informal Networks: The Construction of Politics in Urban Egypt." In Tsugitaka Sato (ed.), *Islamic Urbanism in Human History.* London: Kegan Paul.

————. 1995. *Avenues of Participation: Family, Politics, and Networks in Urban Quarters of Cairo.* Princeton: Princeton University Press.

Slymovics, Susan. 2001. "A Truth Commission for Morocco." *Middle East Report* (218): 18–21.

Snyder, Richard, and James Mahoney. 1999. "The Missing Variable: Institutions and the Study of Regime Change." *Comparative Politics* (October): 103–122.

Soeffner, Hans-Georg. 1992. *Die Ordnung der Rituale*. Frankfurt am Main: Suhrkamp.

Springborg, Robert. 1978. "Professional Syndicates in Egyptian Politics, 1952–1970." *International Journal of Middle East Studies* 19: 275–295.

Stacher, Joshua A. 2001. "A Democracy with Fangs and Claws and Its Effects on Egyptian Political Culture." *Arab Studies Quarterly* (Summer): 4.

Stark, David, and Laszlo Bruszt. 1998. *Postsocialist Pathways: Transforming Politics and Property in East Central Europe*. Cambridge: Cambridge University Press.

Steinmo, Sven, Kathleen Thelen, and Frank Longstreth (eds.). 1992. *Structuring Politics: Historical Institutionalism in Comparative Analysis*. Cambridge: Cambridge University Press.

Swedenburg, Ted. 1995. *Memories of Revolt: The 1936 Rebellion and the Palestinian National Past*. Minneapolis: University of Minnesota Press.

Tabari, K. 2003. "The Rule of Law and the Politics of Reform in Iran." *International Sociology* 18: 96–113.

Tamadonfar, Mehran. 2001. "Islam, Law, and Political Control in Contemporary Iran." *Journal for the Scientific Study of Religion* 40 (2): 205–220.

Testas, Abdelaziz. 2002. "Political Repression, Democratization, and Civil Conflict in Algeria." *Democratization* 9(4): 106–121.

Tétreault, Mary Ann. 2000. *Stories of Democracy: Politics and Society in Contemporary Kuwait*. New York: Columbia University Press.

Tezcür, Güneş Murat, and Taghi Azadarmaki. 2008. "Religiosity and Islamic Rule in Iran." *Journal for the Scientific Study of Religion* 47 (2).

Tezcür, Güneş Murat, Taghi Azadarmaki, and Bahar Mehri. 2006. "Religious Participation Among Muslims: Iranian Exceptionalism." *Critique: Critical Middle Eastern Studies* 15(3): 217–232.

Thelen, Kathleen. 1999. "Historical Institutionalism in Comparative Politics." *Annual Review of Political Science* 2: 369–404.

Tilly, Charles. 2007. *Democracy*. New York: Cambridge University Press.

Tozy, Mohamed. 2000. "Political Changes in the Maghreb." *CODESRIA Bulletin* 1.

Trimberger, Ellen. 1978. *Revolution from Above: Military Bureaucrats and Development in Japan, Turkey, Egypt, and Peru*. New Brunswick, N.J.: Transaction.

Turan, Ilter. 1994. "Evolution of the Electoral Process." In Metin Heper and Ahmet Evin (eds.), *Politics in the Third Turkish Republic*. Boulder: Westview.

Usher, Graham. 2005. "The New Hamas: Between Resistance and Participation." *Middle East Report Online*, August 21.

Valenzuela, J. Samuel. 1989. "Labour Movements in Transitions to Democracy: A Framework for Analysis." *Comparative Politics* 21 (4): 445–472.

Vandewalle, Dirk. 1998. *Libya Since Independence: Oil and State Building*. Ithaca: Cornell University Press.

Verba, Sidney, and Norman Nie. 1972. *Participation in America: Political Democracy and Social Equality*. New York: Harper and Row.

Volker, Perthes. 2004. "Elite Change and System Maintenance." In Perthes Volker (ed.), *Arab Elites: Negotiating the Politics of Change*. Boulder: Lynne Rienner.

Vollan, Kåre, and Nils Butenschøn. 1996. *Interim Democracy: Report on the Palestinian Elections, January*. Oslo: Norwegian Institute of Human Rights.

Waltz, Susan. 1991. "Making Waves: The Political Impact of Human Rights Groups in North Africa." *Journal of Modern African Studies* 29 (September): 3.

Waterbury, John. 1997. "From Social Contracts to Extraction Contracts: The

Political Economy of Authoritarianism and Democracy." In John P. Entelis (ed.), *Islam, Democracy, and the State in North Africa.* Indianapolis: University of Indiana Press.

Wedeen, Lisa. 2003. "Seeing Like a Citizen, Acting Like a State: Exemplary Events in Unified Yemen." *Comparative Studies in Society and History* 45 (4): 680–713.

———. 1999. *Ambiguities of Domination.* Chicago: University of Chicago Press.

Weiner, Myron. 1971. "Political Participation: Crisis of the Political Process." In Leonard Binder et al. (eds.), *Crises and Sequences in Political Development.* Princeton: Princeton University Press.

Weiner, Myron, and Samuel P. Huntington (eds.). 1987. *Understanding Political Development.* Boston: Little, Brown.

Wickham, Carry R. 2002. *Mobilizing Islam: Religion, Activism, and Political Change in Egypt.* New York: Columbia University Press.

Wiktorowicz, Quintan (ed.). 2004. *Islamic Activism: A Social Movement Theory Approach.* Bloomington: University of Indiana Press.

———. 2000a. "Civil Society as Social Control: State Power in Jordan." *Comparative Politics* 33: 43–61.

———. 2000b. "The Salafi Movement in Jordan." *International Journal of Middle East Studies* 32: 219–240.

Wiktorowicz, Quintan, and Suha Taji Farouki. 2000. "Islamic NGOs and Muslim Politics: A Case from Jordan." *Third World Quarterly* 21: 685–699.

Williamson, Peter J. 1989. *Corporatism in Perspective.* London: Sage.

Willis, Michael, 1999. "After Hassan: A New Monarch in Morocco." *Mediterranean Politics* 5(3): 115–128.

World Bank, 2001. "Kingdom of Morocco: Poverty Update." Report No. 21506-MOR, March 30.

"Zahrat tawrith al-maqa'ed fi Maglis al-Shaab." 2006. *Al-Misry al-Yawm,* January 1.

Zartman, I. William. 1995. *Tunisie: La politique économique de la réforme.* Tunis: Alif–Les Editions de la Méditerranée.

Zeghal, Malika. 1999. "Religion and Politics in Egypt: The Ulema of Al-Azhar, Radical Islam, and the State (1952–94)." *International Journal of Middle East Studies* 31: 371–399.

Zghal, Riadh. 1998. "Nouvelles orientations du syndicalisme tunisien." *Monde Arabe–Maghreb–Machrek* 162 (October–December): 6–17.

Zoubir, Yahia, and Daniel Volman (eds.). 1993. *International Dimensions of the Western Sahara Conflict.* Westport: Praeger.

The Contributors

Holger Albrecht is a postdoctoral research fellow at the Center for the Study of Democracy of the University of Lüneburg, Germany. He has published numerous articles on authoritarianism and regime change; his recent focus has been the relationship between authoritarian regimes and political opposition in Egypt and elsewhere in the Middle East and North Africa.

Laila Alhamad is a social development specialist with the World Bank. Her research interests include governance, participation, and gender, with a focus on the Middle East and North Africa.

Delphine Cavallo is a PhD student in political science at the Political Science Institute of Aix-en-Provence in France. She was a scholar at the Institut de Recherche sur la Maghreb Contemporain in Tunis between 2002 and 2006. Her PhD dissertation is on the social aspects of authoritarianism in Tunisia.

Nihad Gohar is a child protection officer at UNICEF (Egypt). She previously served as senior program officer at the International Labour Organization. Her PhD dissertation focused on global civil society and the role of parallel summits in promoting the causes of the developing world. Her research interests include civil society and political participation.

Ellen Lust-Okar is associate professor of political science and chair of the Council on Middle East Studies at Yale University. Her first book, *Structuring Conflict in the Arab World* (2005), examines how authoritarian elites manage political opposition. Her current work focuses on elections in the Arab world.

Driss Maghraoui is assistant professor of history at Al-Akhawayn University in Ifrane, Morocco. He received his PhD in history from the University of California–Santa Cruz. His research examines colonial history, memory, and subaltern studies, with a focus on Algeria and Morocco. He has published in international academic journals and edited volumes, and is currently working on a book titled *History, Memory, and the Culture of French Colonialism.*

Güneş Murat Tezcür is assistant professor of political science at Loyola University. His research interests include Islam and politics in Iran and Turkey, and Kurdish nationalism. He received his PhD from the University of Michigan in 2005.

Katja Niethammer is currently a postdoctoral fellow at the Center for International and Regional Studies, Georgetown University School of Foreign Service in Qatar. She previously served as a researcher on the Middle East and Africa at the German Institute for International and Security Affairs (Stiftung Wissenschaft und Politik). Her PhD dissertation focused on the reform process in Bahrain, and her other work deals with Islam and democratization in the Gulf states.

Samer Shehata is assistant professor of Arab politics at the Center for Contemporary Arab Studies in the Edmund A. Walsh School of Foreign Service at Georgetown University. He has published numerous articles on Egyptian politics, the Muslim Brotherhood, and US foreign policy toward the Middle East.

Dag Tuastad is a lecturer in Middle Eastern studies in the Department of Oriental Languages and Cultural Studies at the University of Oslo. His PhD, on social anthropology, is a comparative study of the role of kinship in Palestinian politics, based on fieldwork in Galilee and Gaza.

Saloua Zerhouni is assistant professor of political science at Mohammed V University, Rabat, Morocco. She has undertaken extensive work on elites as agents of change, theories of political transformation, Islamist movements, and political parties in Morocco. She is currently revising a manuscript titled *Elite and Democratic Transition in Morocco: The Parliamentarians of the 1997–2002 Legislature.*

Index

Abbas, Mahmoud, 125, 133
Abdelnour, Mounir Fakhry: campaign behavior, 99–100; campaign poet, 119(n32); ejection from Wafd party, 99; election fraud and the defeat of, 97–98; political background, 96–97; political discourse, 107–112; religion as political issue, 119(n28); residence and representation, 107, 119(n26)
Abdi, Abbas, 62
Accountability: Abdelnour on the role and function of parliament, 108–112; civil society groups, 39–40; constitutional monarchy, 235(n6); Iran's power structure, 56; political participation in authoritarian regimes, 16
Achour, Habib, 249–250
Activism, defensive nature of, 17; defining, 17; reactive, 17; social, 19, 250; types of, 29(n4)
Administrative bodies: Bahrain, 150–151
Agadir, Morocco, 211
Agadir Chart, 211
Agrarian reforms, Morocco's, 221
Ahmadinejad, Mahmoud, 67–68, 71(fig.)
Algeria: Amazigh culture, 202, 211; liberalization as response to economic austerity, 37–38; quality of union participation, 17–18; repression of civil society organizations, 198

al-'Amal al-Islami (Bahrain), 154–158
al-'Amal al-Watani ad-Dimuqrati (Bahrain), 154–158
Amazigh culture, 5, 194, 202, 211–214
Amazigh Network for Citizenship (RAC), 202, 213–214
Amnesty, 146, 163(n16), 247
Anbarloui, Mohammed, 64
Anticolonial institutions, 37
Arab Socialist Union (Egypt), 173, 175
Arafat, Yasser, 125
Arbitration panel, Morocco's, 206
Aref, Galal, 182
Arhmouch, Ahmed, 213–214
Ash-Shirazi, Muhammad, 158–159
Assembly of Experts (Iran), 51–52
As-Sistani, Ali, 150
Association Marocaine des Droits Humains (AMDH), 198–199
Association of Judges (Egypt), 177–178
Authoritarian regimes: endurance of, 1–2; Gaza's neopatrimonial authoritarianism, 137(n1); international forces influencing participation, 10; Morocco's civil society organizations conferring legitimacy, 194; paradox of participation and, 16–21; political liberalization and, 24–25
Awad, Yusef, 132
al-Awwa, Selim, 180
Ayubi, Nazih, 42–43
al-Azhar, 26

Badrawi, Hosam, 112–113
Bahrain: deadlock between parliamentarians and opposition, 151–153; formal and informal institutions shaping participation, 9; human rights violations, 163(n12); institutions mobilizing civil society, 8–9; opposition's constitutional reform campaign, 154–158; political decisionmaking, 149–151; political history and context, 144–148; radical opposition through NGOs, 158–161; societal fragmentation driving political strategies, 5; venues of political participation, 148–149
Bahrain Center for Human Rights (BCHR), 158–161, 168(n106)
Banisadr, Abdolhasan, 60
al-Banna, Hassan, 179
Banzakour, Abdelaziz, 209
Basri, Driss, 196
Ben Salah, Ahmed, 241
Benzekri, Driss, 208
Berber Manifesto, 211
Bicameral parliament: Bahrain, 146–147; Morocco, 220–221, 225–226
Bora'i, Negad, 187
Bouderka, Mbarek, 209
Boukouss, Ahmed, 213
Bourguiba, Habib, 241, 250
Boutrus Ghali, Yousef, 116(n3)
Boycotts: Bahrainis resuming participation, 162(n7); Bahrain's deadlock between parliament and opposition, 151–153; Bahrain's election boycotting coalition, 143, 147, 162(n1); Bahrain's opposition campaign for constitutional reform, 154; Egypt's judges boycotting the 2005 elections, 177–178; Egypt's Tagammu party, 176; Iran's elections, 68–69; Morocco's opposition, 221–222
Buraq, Najaf, 41
Bureij. *See* Gaza

Cairo Agreement, 133–134
Cairo Center for Human Rights Studies, 186
Camp David Accords, 175
Campaign spending, 59, 78, 117(n11)

Campaigns, elections: Abdelnour's campaign behavior, 99–100, 104–107; Abdelnour's discourse on the role and function of parliament, 108–112; Abdelnour's victory, 97; attracting Iranian voters, 67–68; Egyptian voter behavior, 112–113; Egypt's abundance of candidates, 118(n21); Egypt's fiscal motivation for running, 100–102; Egypt's residence and representation, 119(n26); Gaza's nonpolitical local elections, 126–127; Iran under Pahlavi rule, 54; Jordan's candidate behavior, 85–88; poets, 119(n32)
Candidate behavior: Fatah's controversial candidate list, 126–127; Iran under Pahlavi rule, 54; Jordan's candidate behavior, 85–88; Tunisia's government-selected opposition, 239
Caravanes de la vérité (truth caravans), 208–209
Caucuses, 230–233
Censorship: Iran, 72; Tunisia, 254(n4)
Center for Strategic Studies, 81–84
Centralization of power, Morocco's, 222–223
Chafik, Mohamed, 211, 213
Citizenship Forum, 199–200
Citizenship issues, 199–200
Citizenship Network (REC), 201
Civil conflict: Bahraini intifada, 145; elections fueling Iran's interfactional conflict, 52; stability of, 77–78
Civil society: and conservative groups, 39; Bahrain's liberalization, 148; Egypt's civil society organizations, 178–179; Egypt's funding limitations restricting participation, 187–188; expanding political participation and political space, 35–36; limited role in Middle East participation, 27–28; means of participation, 21–22; Morocco's Amazigh cultural institutions, 211–214; Morocco's co-optation of, 205–207; Morocco's creation and participation of civil society organizations, 198–203, 206–208; Morocco's inclusion policy, 193; Morocco's liberalization under Hassan II and Mohammed VI,

196–198; Morocco's public service delivery, 197; Morocco's truth and reconciliation commissions, 208–210; objectives of participation, 3; parliaments as tools for legitimacy, 219; political participation in authoritarian regimes, 16–17; state participation in, 31(n18); Western attempts to strengthen, 33–34, 47(n4)

Classical channels, 15–16. *See also* Civil society; Parties, political

Clerical rule: Bahrain's election boycott, 143; Islamic Republic of Iran, 55–56; Pahlavi Iran, 72. *See also* Islamism

Clientelism: intermediation mechanisms, 31(n21); Jordan's competitive clientelism, 4, 75, 81, 92–93; Palestinian Authority as neopatrimonial authoritarian regime, 121–125. *See also* Patronage

Clubs, in Bahrain, 148–149

Coalition building, Bahrain, 143

Collective action: history of the Middle East's informal institutions, 41. *See also* Union labor

Colonialism: Amazigh culture and, 202; history of civil society organizations, 37

Commercial networks, 41–42

Committee for Coordination of Union Rights and Liberties (Egypt), 183

Competition: elections as legitimating and elections as democracy promoting, 77–78

Conference des presidents (Morocco), 231

Conflict. *See* Civil conflict

Congress (NGO), 202–203

Constitutional monarchy: accountability, 235(n6); Iran under Pahlavi regime, 52–54; Moroccan king's function, 235(n8); Morocco under Mohammed VI, 206–207. *See also* Morocco

Constitutional reform: Bahrain, 146–147, 154–158; Morocco, 221, 223–228

Copts, 97, 116(n3), 119(n28), 180. *See also* Abdelnour, Mounir Fakhry

Corporatism: defining, 30(n13); Middle East, 26–28; mobilized and autonomous participation, 20–21; UGTT merging with Tunisia's formal institutions, 241; unionism, 17–18

Corruption: Abdelnour on, 111; Egypt's legal immunity for parliamentarians, 102, 117(n13)–117(n14); UGTT mirroring state organizations, 245

Council of Guardians (Iran), 66–70

Crony capitalism: elections as arena for competition over state resources, 80–81; political participation intertwining with economic structures, 19

Cultural rights, 211–212

Dana Mall rally, 157, 168(n99)

Daoud, Diauddin, 174–175

Democracy: appearance of election drivers, 7–8; Bahraini executive power, 162(n8); democratization expanding the significance of participation, 1–2; Egypt's Nasserists, 175; Egypt's NPUP, 189; Egypt's professional syndicates, 181–182; Iran's leftist reformists, 61–65; Khomeini's view of, 73(n10); long-term prospects for MENA reforms, 265–266; Mohammed VI's advance toward and retreat from, 206–207; Morocco's citizenship education programs, 200

Democracy polls, Jordan, 78–81, 79(fig.), 81–84, 94(nn4,5,7)

Democracy promotion, elections as, 76–78

Democratic Constitutional Rally (DCR; Tunisia), 239

Democratic Forces Front (FFD; Morocco), 229

Democratic rule, participation and, 16

Demonstrations: Bahraini opposition, 147–148; Bahrain's constitutional reform campaign, 156–157, 168(n99); Egypt's labor unions, 182–184; imprisonment of BCHR's al-Khawaja, 159; Muhammad cartoons, 21; opposition to Egypt's restrictions on participation, 185; response to Bahrain's liberalization, 150; UGTT protesting US intervention in Iraq, 247–248; UGTT's quasi-immunity allowing, 248

Destabilizing, elections and, 77
Developers Council (Iran), 67
Development, economic, Morocco's co-optation of civil society, 207
Diaspora participation, Morocco's, 202
al-Din, Ali Diab, 131
Disabled individuals, 136–137
Disqualification of election candidates in Iran, 57–61, 64–65
Districting, 89
Diwaniyya (advisory council), 44–45
Djerba congress, 246
Dughmush family, 123–124
Durability, regime, 77–78
Dynasties, political, 116(n5)

East Bank: Jordanian voter behavior, 82–83
Economic activism defining political participation, 19
Economics: Bahrain's liberalization, 145; economic importance of Tunisia's labor unions, 242; employment, 109; foreign investment, 110–111, 197; and housing issues, 110; lower-income classes, 22–23, 31(n19); middle classes, 22; poverty, 197; structural adjustment programs, 196; upper-middle class, 22
Education: on citizenship issues, 199–201; Moroccan parliamentarians and, 234(n1), 236(nn29,30)
Egypt: Abdelnour on the role and function of parliament, 108–112; ballot design, 118(n23); campaign spending, 117(n11); candidate behavior, 100–102, 117(nn12,13,14); civil society organizations, 178–179; co-optation of religion institutions, 16; Coptic parliamentarians, 116(n3); election drivers, 4; formal restrictions on political participation, 184–186; funding limitations restricting participation, 187–188; institution building, 21–22; internal party practices, 188–190; international forces influencing participation, 10; judiciary, 176–178; Khalil and Badrawi campaigns, 112–113; labor unions, 17–18, 182–184; NDP's internal conflict, 119(n37);

parliamentary election schedule, 2005, 103(table); parties, 172–176; political dynasties, 116(n5); populism experiment, 26; professional syndicates, 181–182; regime type determining the role of elections, 76–77; role of elections and parliament, 78–79; societal obstacles to participation, 186–187; societal organizations, 31(n18); voter turnout, 29–30(n5)
Egyptian Trade Union Federation (ETUF), 183–184
Election fraud: Egypt, 97–98, 116(n7); Fatah's refusal to accept defeat, 129–132
Elections: independent candidates in, 98, 101, 122; political drivers for, 3–4, 7; role and function of, 78–81; two opposing views of, 76–78; and resource access, 4, 80–81 *See also* Boycotts; Campaign spending; Campaigns
Elections, Egypt: ballot design, 118(n23); candidate behavior, 117(n12); controversial defeat of Abdelnour, 97–98, 116(n7); election season, 104–105, 118(n22); NDP's 2000 electoral defeat, 173–174; parliamentary election schedule, 2005, 103(table); press syndicate, 182; service representatives, 120(n40); and socioeconomic factors, 114–115; voter behavior, 95, 113–115; worker/farmer representation, 98–99, 116(n6), 118(n23)Elections, Gaza, 125–128
Elections, Iran: election characteristics, 57–61; elections and distribution of power, 55–57; hard-liners' victory, 66–70; municipal, 51–52; popular election types, 51–52; turnout and vote for Ahmadinejad, 71(fig.)
Elections, Jordan: competitive clientelism, 75; electoral rule manipulation, 89–92; elite manipulation of, 88–92; seat gains under 2003 electoral law, 91(table); voter behavior, 81–85
Elections, Morocco: *gouvernement d'alternance,* 225; Mohammed VI's sup-

port of, 206; transitional government, 196; transparency of, 218
Electoral law, Bahrain, 147
Electoral reform: Morocco, 218; Tunisia, 239
El-Haiba, Mahjoub, 209
Elite interest: long-term prospects for MENA reforms, 264
Elite interests: Bahrain's social institutions, 148–149; co-opting civil society groups, 39–40; diverse motivations for participation, 6–7; driving Iran's elections, 4; Jordanian candidate behavior, 85–88; Jordan's candidate behavior, 88; Jordan's electoral rule manipulation, 89–92; Palestinian leaders marginalizing antielitist structures, 122–124; participation in Middle Eastern countries, 25; political participation challenging incumbency, 16–17; role of elections in identification and mobilization of, 80; Tunisia's intrainstitutional contestation, 240–241; undermining Gaza's election results, 121. *See also* Civil society
Emergency law, 187, 221, 235(n7)
Equity and Reconciliation Commission (Morocco), 5, 194, 208–210, 235(n4)
Ethnicity defining Bahraini society, 145
Ethnographic research, 102–104
Executive power: Bahrain, 149–151, 162(n8); Egypt's NDP, 172–174; Islamic Republic of Iran, 55–56; Morocco's IRCAM, 212–213; restricting Egypt's political participation, 184–186
Expediency Council (Iran), 56
Ezz, Ahmed, 113

Factionalization: Egypt's Nasserists, 175; Gaza's familism, 124–125; Gaza's Fatah Party, 126; Gaza's local elections, 128–129; Gaza's party reform, 134–135; Gaza's postelection violence, 129–132; Iran's distribution of power, 55–57; Iran's elections as factional conflict, 70–73; Iran's hard-liners' election victory, 66–70; Iran's reform movement, 61–66; UGTT's disempowering

internal conflict, 245, 249–250; UGTT's internal conflict, 243–244; UGTT's labor strikes, 250–253
Fallacy of electoralism, 76–77
Familism, Gaza's, 122–125, 136, 138(n3)
Family code reform, Morocco's, 227–228
Faqih (judicial expert), 55
Fatah (Palestine): Hamas victory, 128–129; local elections, 125–127; nullification of Hamas election victory, 132–134; Palestinian leaders marginalizing antielitist structures, 122; push for party reform, 134–135; refusal to accept defeat, 129–132
Formal institutions: ambivalent role, 260–261; Egypt's venues for participation, 171; government control of Tunisia's, 239–240; informal institutions and, 2, 46, 143–144; limits of, 36–40; means of participation, 21–24; shaping participation, 9; Tunisia's UGTT as a government institution, 244–245. *See also* Elections; Parliament; Parties, political
Forum de la Citoyenneté (Citizenship Forum), 199–200
Forum des Alternatives Maroc (FAM), 200–201
Fouad, Ahmed, 97, 118(n24); Shireen Ahmed, 97, 98(table)
Fragmentation: Bahraini society, 145; neopatrimonialism in Palestine, 136, 137(n1)
Free Officers Movement, 179
Funeral houses, Bahrain's, 148–149

Gaza: election drivers, 4; Fatah defeat, 128–129; Fatah's refusal to accept defeat, 129–132; nullification of Hamas election victory, 132–134; party reform, 134–135
General Labor Union of Tunisia (UGTT), 5–6, 240; autonomy of, 246; as a governing social institution, 253; conflict resolution within, 243; labor conflicts mobilizing, 250–251; nationalization, 245; pluralism in, 246; political socialization, 249–250;

union pluralism, 245–246
Geography defining Bahraini society, 145
Ghad Party (Egypt), 31(n18), 176, 189
Gomaa, No'man, 99, 116(n8)
Gouvernement d'alternance (Morocco's opposition government), 206, 225, 236(nn20,21,23)
Governance: antilegal nature of informal institutions, 45
Grass-roots structures, Gaza's, 125–128
Greater Middle East Initiative, 185
Group for Democratic Development, 187
Group participation. *See* Mobilized participation
Group/professional representation, Egypt's, 98, 116(nn6,7), 118(n23)
Guardian Council (Iran), 55, 57–61, 67
Guilds, 42

Hajjarian, Saeed, 62
Hamas (Palestine), 4; election victory, 128–129; Fatah's refusal to accept defeat, 129–132; illegal local election participation, 125–127; nullification of election victory, 132–134; party reform, 134
Hard-liners, Iran's, 63–64, 66–70, 73(n2)
Hassan II, 234(n3); Amazigh culture preservation, 211–212; human rights response to, 198–199; political repression, 195–196
Heyba, Hassan, 105–106, 118(n24)
Higher Election Committee (Palestine), 130, 133
Hoveyda, Amir Abbas, 54
al-Hudaybi, Hassan, 179
Human rights organizations: Bahrain's radical opposition through BCHR, 158–161; Morocco's AMDM and OMDH, 198–199; Morocco's truth and reconciliation commissions, 208–210
Human rights violations: Bahrain, 145, 163(nn12,16); Egypt's restriction on participation, 186; Morocco, 210, 234(n2)
Human trafficking, 197
Hunger strikes, 248
Hybrid regimes, 76–78, 207

Identity politics, 212
al-'Ikri, Abdunnabi, 156
Immunity, legal, 102, 117(nn13,14)
Independence, institutional, 176–177
Informal institutions: Bahrain's mediation, 152; Bahrain's social institutions, 148–149; circumspect political space giving rise to participation through, 35–36; Egypt's venues for participation, 171; formal institutions and, 2, 143–144; historical context of, 40–42; kinship networks, 81–84, 82(fig.), 86–87; MENA civil society organizations, 36–40; Middle Eastern social networks, 28; modern persistence of, 42–45; permeating formal institutions, 46; shaping participation, 9; strengthening civil society groups towards democratization, 33–34. *See also* Union labor
Institutional structures: institutionalization of Morocco's royal powers, 206–207; Jordanian elites' manipulation of elections, 88–92; means of participation, 21–23; as venue for raising political demands, 8. *See also* Formal institutions; Informal institutions
Interest politics: corporatism, 30(n13); Morocco's parliament preserving, 229–230; UGTT mirroring state organizations, 245. *See also* Elite interests
Intermediation mechanisms, 22–23
International Company of Ayadi Bittan (ICAB), 251–252
International forces: impact on local political participation, 9–10; long-term prospects for MENA reforms, 265–266; opposition to Egypt's restrictions on participation, 185
International Monetary Fund (IMF), 196
Internet, 147
Intifada, 125, 145
Iran, Islamic Republic of: election characteristics, 57–61; election drivers, 4, 7; elections and distribution of power, 55–57; elections as factional conflict, 70–74; elite manipulation of elections, 88; hard-liners' election victory, 66–70; rise and fall of the

reform movement, 61–66; turnout
and vote for Ahmadinejad, 71(fig.);
voter turnout, 7–8
Iraq: elections without democracy, 79;
US intervention in, 247–248
Islamic Action Front (Jordan), 84–85,
92
Islamic Iran Participation Front, 63–64
Islamic Platform (Bahrain), 151–153
Islamism: autonomous and mobilized
participation, 21; Bahrain's shift,
145–146; Egypt's state co-optation
of religious institutions, 26; elections
and distribution of power in Iran,
55–57; Gaza's nonpolitical local
elections, 125–126; Jordan's Salafis,
44; labor union participation, 17–18;
Morocco's inclusion policy, 193;
Morocco's representation, 226–229;
oppositional institutions, 28; roots of
Iran's leftist reform movement,
62–63; social movement organizations, 23; as threat to civil society
groups, 39; US as external mediator
in Bahrain, 152–153
Israel: Jordan's IAF opposition to,
89–90; UGTT opposition to Sharon
visit, 248
Istiqlal Party (Morocco), 221, 223–224,
229
Iznasni, Mustapha, 209

Jabali, Ghazi, 135
Jabber, Nasser, 134–135
al-Jamri, Mansur, 147, 156
Jbabdi, Latifa, 209
Jenin Martyrs Brigades, 135
Jettou, Driss, 206
Jibrin, Hassan, 129, 134–135
Johns Hopkins Comparative Nonprofit
Sector project, 198
Jom'a, Noaman, 176
Jordan: candidate behavior, 85–88; districting and malapportionment, 89;
election drivers, 4, 7; elite manipulation of elections, 88–92; formal and
informal institutions shaping participation, 9; international forces influencing participation, 10; liberalization as response to economic
austerity, 38; perceived effectiveness

of parliament, 79(fig.), 80; proportional representation, 90(table); role
of elections and parliament, 78–81;
Salafi Islamist network, 44; seat
gains under 2003 electoral law,
91(table); voter behavior, 81–85,
82(fig.)
Judiciary: Egypt, 176–178; promoting
participation in Middle Eastern countries, 25–26; supporting authoritarian
regimes, 32(n27)
Juleid, Fawz, 152

Karroubi, Mehdi, 62–63, 68
Kefaya (Enough) Movement (Egypt),
185
al-Khalifa, Hamad bin Isa, 144–145,
150, 152; Khalifa bin Salman al
Khalifa, 150, 159; Mohammed bin
Atiyatallah, 148
Khalil, Hisham Mustapha, 112–113,
120(nn38,39)
Khamenei, Ali, 60–61; Hadi, 62–63
Khatami, Mohammed, 62–67
al-Khawaja, Abdulhadi, 158–160,
168(n106)
Khomeini, Ruhollah, 55–56, 63, 73(n10)
Kinship networks, 81–84, 82(fig.),
86–87
Koutla al-Democratiya (Democratic
Bloc; Morocco), 223–224, 235(n16)
Kuwait, 22

Labor unions. *See* Union labor
Language and culture, 211–212
Lebanon, 156
Leftist movements: history of civil soci-
ety organizations, 37; Iran's
reformist movement, 61–67, 72,
150–151. *See also* Reforms
Legislative Politics in the Arab World
(Baaklini, Denoeux, and
Springborg), 217
Legislatures. *See entries beginning with
Parliament*
Legitimacy: elections legitimating
authoritarian regimes, 75–81; Iran's
Pahlavi regime, 52; Islamic Republic
of Iran, 55–56; labor strikes, 252;
Morocco's civil society organiza-
tions conferring, 194; parliaments as

tools for, 219; UGTT's political connections, 246–247; voter turnout conferring, 29–30(n5)

Liberalization, economic, 193, 197–198

Liberalization, political: Bahrain, 144–148; elections without democracy, 79–80; Gulf states, 32(n25); maintaining authoritarianism in the face of, 24–25; Morocco under Mohammed VI, 206–208; response to Bahrain's, 149–151; as response to economic austerity, 37–38; Tunisia, 239

Liberalized autocracy, 197, 208

Local elections: Fatah defeat, 128–129; Fatah's refusal to accept defeat, 129–132; Gaza's Bureij referendum campaign, 125–128; nullification of Hamas victory, 132–134

Ma'atim (funeral house), 149

Madi, Abul Ela, 180

Majalis (private gatherings), 149, 154

Malapportionment, 89

Mass-integration parties, 155, 167(n80)

Media: Bahrain's use of alternative media, 147; Egypt's opposition parties, 118(n20); Egypt's press syndicate elections, 182; Iran's election campaigns, 59; Iran's suppression of, 72; leveraging UGTT strikes, 251–252; Morocco's Amazigh culture, 212; Tunisian government's repression of, 239; Tunisia's private sector media, 254(n3); Tunisia's suppression of, 254(n4)

Mediation, Bahrain's, 152

Mediterranean Institute, 201

MENA. *See* Middle East; *specific countries*

Middle East: informal methods of individual participation, 23–26; institutional role in political participation, 27–28. *See also specific countries*

Military forces: co-opting Palestinian Authority police, 136; defining political participation, 18; participation of Middle Eastern middle classes, 25

al-Minbar at-Taqaddumi (Bahrain), 151–153

Ministères de souveraineté (sovereign ministries), 224

Mohajerani, Ata'ollah, 62

Mohammad Reza Pahlavi, 53

Mohammed VI: Equity and Reconciliation Commission, 235(n4); political liberalization with monarchical control, 194, 196, 206–208, 218–219; reorganizing the ACHR, 209

Mohyiddin, Khaled, 175, 189

Moin, Mostafa, 67–68

Moroccan Alternatives Forum (FAM), 200–201

Moroccan Forum for Truth and Justice (MFTJ), 208–210

Moroccan Human Rights Association (AMDH), 198–199

Moroccan Human Rights Organization (OMDH), 199

Moroccan Research and Cultural Exchange Association (AMREC), 211

Morocco: Amazigh cultural organizations, 211–214; artificial and official discourses of participation, 218–220; civil society occupying political space, 194–196; creation and participation of civil society organizations, 198–203; democracy strategies, 228–229; Equity and Reconciliation Commission, 208–210; *gouvernement d'alternance*, 206, 225, 236(nn20,21,23); informal institutions, 5; Islamist representation, 226–228; king's function, 235(n8); labor unions channeling Middle East participation, 26; liberalization as response to economic austerity, 38, 234(n2); Mohammed VI's adherence to authoritarian structures, 206–208; parliamentarians' educational demographics, 234(n1); parliamentary caucuses and committees, 230–233; promoting local and professional interests, 229–230; quality of union participation, 17–18; repression of civil society groups, 39; role and function of parliament, 220–222

Mosaddeq, Mohammed, 53

Mubarak, Gamal, 119(n37), 173–174, 185; Hosni, 116(n3), 173, 185

Mukhtar institution, 9, 122–123, 138(n3)

Multi-member majority vote, 122
Musavi, Mir Hossein, 61
Musavi-Khoeniha, Mohammed, 62
Muslim Brotherhood (Egypt): alliance with New Wafd, 174; campaign spending, 101; fear of Islamism, 185; Gaza's Fatah, 126; history and function of, 179–180; internal party practices, 189–190; 2003 election victory, 182; Wasat Party tensions, 180–181
Muslim Brotherhood (Jordan), 84–85

Nabaheen, Yusef, 123
Nadawat (campaign meetings), 104–105
Nashaar, Issa, 131
Nashabat, Mahmoud, 129, 135–136
Nasserism, 26, 31(n18)
Nasserist Democratic Arab Party (Egypt), 174–175, 182, 189
National Action Charter (Bahrain), 146–147
National Council on Human Rights, 186
National Democratic Institute (NDI), 9–10, 152
National Democratic Party (NDP; Egypt): Abdelnour's election loss, 97; campaign spending, 101; Coptic candidates, 116(n3); Egypt's restrictions on participation, 185–186; election ballot design, 118(n23); history and function of, 172–174; internal party practices, 119(n37), 188–189
National Party (Iran), 53
National Progressive Unionist Party (Tagammu: Egypt), 102, 175–176
National representatives, Egypt's, 120(n40)
National Resurrection Party (Iran), 54
National Union of Popular Forces (UNFP; Morocco), 221
Nationalism: Egypt's Nasserists, 175; Morocco's' Amazigh culture, 211–212
Neopatrimonialism. *See* Clientelism
Networks, kinship (Jordan), 23, 81–84, 82(fig.), 86–87
New Destour party (Tunisia), 241
New Iran Party, 53
New Wafd Party (Egypt), 174, 189
News media. *See* Media

No-confidence vote, 221, 223
Nongovernmental organizations (NGOs): Bahrain's liberalization, 148; Bahrain's radical opposition through, 158–161; Egyptian civil society's lack of power, 178–179, 259–260; Egypt's funding limitations restricting participation, 187–188; means of participation, 21; Morocco's increasing, 193; Morocco's informal institutions, 5; Morocco's public service delivery, 197
Nour, Ayman, 176
Nouri, Abdollah, 62, 73(n17); Nateq, 64

Obeid, Makram, 176
Obol, Aziz, 154, 167(n79), 168(n105)
Omar Effendi department store, 106, 119(n26)
Opposition groups: Bahrain's constitutional reform campaign, 154–158; Egypt, 31(n18); Egypt's difficulty in forming, 172; Egypt's Muslim Brotherhood, 189–190; Egypt's Wafd party, 174; Iran's reformists, 61–67, 72, 150–151; Middle Eastern oppositional institutions, 28; modern informal institutions of resistance, 42–45; Morocco's constitutional reform, 223–228; Morocco's increasing opposition participation, 223; Morocco's king's tense relations with, 235(n12); Morocco's no-confidence vote, 221; Morocco's tension between liberalization and authoritarianism, 218; Tunisia's provision for, 239; UGTT's political and social functions, 246–247
Organisation Marocaines des Droits Humains (OMDH), 199
Oslo Agreement, 89–90
Oversight: role and function of Morocco's parliament, 219–221
Oversight of the Democratic Transition in Morocco, 200

Pahlavi regime (Iran), 52–54
Palestine: accountability of civil society groups, 39–40; election drivers, 4, 7; formal and informal institutions shaping participation, 9; Jordanian

voter behavior, 82–83; Jordan's elites manipulating elections through malapportionment, 89; voter turnout, 31(n21)

Palestine Liberation Organization (PLO), 121

Palestinian Authority, 121–125, 129

Palestinian Legislative Council, 130

Parallel institutions, 35

Parliament, Bahrain: deadlock with opposition, 151–153; National Action Charter, 146–147; political strategies, 144

Parliament, Egypt: Abdelnour's discourse on the role and function of, 108–112; candidate behavior, 100–102; Coptic members, 116(n3); Egypt's parliamentary election schedule, 2005, 103(table); Muslim Brotherhood representation in, 179–180; and service delivery, 114

Parliament, Iran: first parliament under the Pahlavi regime, 52–54; hardliners' election sweep, 66–70; popular election types, 51–52; reform movement, 64

Parliament, Jordan: perceived effectiveness, 79(fig.); proportional representation, 90(table); seat gains under 2003 electoral law, 91(table); voter behavior, 81–82; voters' perception of, 85, 86(fig.)

Parliament, Morocco, 5; artificial and official discourses of participation, 218–220; caucus and committee participation, 230–233; constitutional reform, 223–228; democracy strategies, 228–229; educational demographics, 234(n1); Islamist representation, 226–228; promoting local and professional interests, 229–230; regime stability from 1977–1992, 222–223; role and function of, 220–222

Parliament, Tunisia: legal provision for opposition, 239

Parliamentary elections: boycott of Bahrain's, 147; Egypt's internal party practices, 188–190; postponing Gaza's, 133–134

Parliaments: durability of elected parliamentarian regimes, 77–78; role of elections and parliaments in legislation and policy, 78–81. *See also* Elections

Participation, autonomous, 19-20; and citizenship, 16-17; content of, 21–22; defining, 6, 17, 19, 171, 193; and intent, 6, 30(n6); local level participation, 230; and manipulation, 195–196; means of, 21–22; mobilized, 19–20, 26–27; motivations for, 7; passive, 196; political nature of, 18–19, 75; quality of, 17–18; societal obstacles to, 186–187; society-driven, 20–21; state-mobilized participation, 20–21, 26–27

Parties, political: Bahrain's active and inactive societies, 164(n27); Bahrain's deadlock between parliament and opposition, 151–153; Bahrain's opposition campaign for constitutional reform, 154–158; Bahrain's political societies, 162(n4); civil society groups as alternatives to, 38; Egypt's internal party practices, 188–190; Egypt's parties, 172–176; Egypt's societal obstacles to participation, 186–187; Iran under Pahlavi rule, 53–54; Jordan's candidate behavior, 87–88; Jordan's voter behavior, 83–85; long-term prospects for MENA reforms, 264; Morocco's caucuses and committees, 231–232; motivation for participation, 219; nascent nature of Iran's, 72; revolutionary, 175; role of Egypt's, 8; Tunisia's UGTT representation, 240, 247; unionism and, 17

Party for Progress and Socialism (PPS; Morocco), 229

Patronage, 7; electoral rules affected by, 92; Gaza, 121–125, 136, 137(n1); informal networks permeating formal institutions, 46; Jordan's candidate behavior, 86–87; Jordan's voter behavior, 83–84. *See also* Clientelism

People's Assembly (Egypt). *See* Parliament, Egypt

People's Party (Iran), 53

Police forces, 135–136, 248

Political socialization, 249–250
Popular Front for the Liberation of
Palestine (PFLP), 123
Populism, 20–21, 26–28, 30(n12)
Positive Action for Women's Rights in
the Maghreb (APDFM), 201–202
Power, Gaza's conflicting sources of,
121
Presidential elections, 71(fig.); Egypt's
Ghad victory, 176; Iran, 51–52,
59–61, 67
Presidentialism, Iran's, 55–56
Pretty, Jules, 195
Prime minister: Bahrain, 150–151, 159;
Morocco, 206
Prisoners, political, 180, 234(n2)
Private voluntary associations (PVAs),
21–22
Privatization: Morocco, 207; Tunisia,
252
Professional societies and syndicates,
252; Bahrain, 148–149; Egypt,
181–182
Professionals, political, 19
Progressive National Unionist Party
(Egypt), 189
Proportional representation, Jordan's,
90(table)
Protests. *See* Demonstrations
Public services. *See* Service delivery
Public sphere. *See* Civil society
"Purity" party (Bahrain), 151–153

Qajar dynasty, 53
Qalibaf, Mohammed, 67–68
Qassim, Isa, 143, 158, 167(n86)
Qutb, Sayyed, 179

Radhi, Hassan, 146
Radical groups: Bahrain's BCHR,
158–161
Rafsanjani, Ali Akbar, 60–62, 64, 67–68
Raissouni, Mohamed Mustapha, 209
Rashed, Al-Sayyid, 183
Reconciliation commissions, 208–210
Reformist movement, Iran's: elimination
from legislative and executive branch-
es, 72; increasing voter apathy, 66–67;
response to Bahrain's liberalization,
150–151; rise and fall of, 61–66
Reforms: Bahraini opposition's constitu-

tional reform campaign, 146–147,
154–158; civil society organizations
demanding, 33–34; Egypt's NDP
party reform, 173–174; long-term
prospects for, 263–266; Morocco
under Mohammed VI, 196;
Morocco's family code reform,
227–228; underestimating the influence of, 1–2
Refugee, Committee (Gaza), 134–135;
refugee situation, 123–125
Regime type: determining the role of
elections by, 76–77; source, channels, aims, and types of participation,
28–29
Regulatory frameworks as tool to control civil society groups, 39
Religion and religious groups:
Abdelnour's political discourse, 107;
Bahrain's shift, 145; Bahrain's social
institutions, 149; as channel for participation, 32(n28); Egypt's civil
society organizations, 179–181;
Egypt's difficulty in forming opposition parties, 172; Egypt's professional syndicates, 181; historical context
of informal institutions, 40–42;
Iran's Islamism, 55–56; parallel
institutions, 35; as political issue in
Egypt, 119(n28); promoting partici-
pation in Middle Eastern countries,
26. *See also* Islamism
Representation, proportional, Jordan,
90(table)
Repression, government: Jordan's dis-
tricting and malapportionment, 89;
stifling civil society groups, 38–39
Republicanism, 63
Réseau Amazigh pour la Citoyenneté
(RAC), 202
Revolutionary Guard (Iran), 55, 64
Revolutionary movements, 25
Reza Shah, 53
Rezai, Mohsen, 67
Rideina, Nabil Abu, 133
Rousseau, Jean-Jacques, 207
Royal Institute for Amazigh Culture
(IRCAM; Morocco), 5, 194, 211–214

Sadat, Anwar, 173, 179
Safi, Khaled, 126–127, 129–130

Safiyah, Usama Abu, 132
al-Said, Rif'at, 189
Salafis, 44
Salman, Abdunnabi, 153; Ali, 152, 157–158
Sectarianism, Bahrain, 149, 151–153, 158–160
Security apparatus defining political participation, 18–19
Sedki, Ali, 211
Serageddin, Fouad, 174
Serrafi, Mohamed, 111–112
Service delivery: Abdelnour's discourse on the role and function of parliament, 108–112; affecting voter behavior, 95, 260–261; driving elections, 4; Egyptian parliament subsidizing, 112–113; Egypt's public and individual services, 114; Morocco, 197; political liberalization as response to economic austerity, 38
Shafiq, Amina, 115–116(n1)
Shaheen, Fawzi, 98
Shamala, Abu, 134
Sharon, Ariel, 248
al-Shawiye family, 124
Sh'lan, Abdelhamid, 98, 116(n7)
Shukri, Ibrahim, 173
Shura Council, in Bahrain, 146–147, 168(n104); in Egypt, 172
Single-party regimes: Iran under Pahlavi rule, 53–54; Tunisia, 239
Sitra Island rally, 157, 168(n99)
Skalli, Badia, 224
Smires-Bennani, Latifa, 224
Social movement theory, 23
Social movements, 251–252
Social networks, 28
Socialist Union of Popular Forces (USFP; Morocco), 226
Socialization, political, 249–250
Societal factors. *See* Civil society; Liberalization, political
Societal organizations, 31(n18). *See also* Civil society
Societies, political, 147. *See also* Parties, political
Soroush, Abdolkerim, 62
State-society relations, 15
Sufi brotherhoods, 41

Sunni-Shia conflict, Bahrain, 145, 151–158
Syria: election candidate behavior, 86; elections without democracy, 79; history of civil society organizations, 37; history of informal institutions, 41–42

al-Tagammu' al-Qawmi (Bahrain), 154–158
Tagammu Party (National Progressive Unionist Party; Egypt), 102, 175–176
al-Taha, Muhammed, 126, 134
Technologies of control, 208
Term limits, Morocco's, 235(nn13,15)
Territorial dispute, Morocco's, 235(n12)
Terrorist activities, 227
Textile industry, 251–252
Tribal networks, 44–45
Truth commissions, 208–210
Tunisia: civil associations, 198; labor unions channeling Middle East participation, 26; quality of union participation, 17–18; UGTT's ambivalent role, 5–6. *See also* General Labor Union of Tunisia
Tunisian Industry, Commerce, and Crafts Union, 241
Turkey: judicial support for authoritarianism, 32(n27); Middle East occupation, 40–42
Turnout. *See* Voter turnout

UGTT. *See* General Labor Union of Tunisia
Ukraine, 156
Ummah (Muslim community), 40–42
Underground organizations, 23
Unemployment Committee (Bahrain), 160
Union labor: as bureaucratic institutions, 244–245; channeling Middle East participation, 26; Egypt, 182–184; General Labor Union of Tunisia, 5–6, 240, 245–246, 249–251, 253; Morocco's unions' loss of political stamina, 197; parties and, 31(n19); political participation intertwining with economic structures, 19; quality of participatory

activities, 17–18; unions as alternative venue for political voice, 8; strikes, 184, 250–253. *See also* General Labor Union of Tunisia
United Kingdom: Iranian coup, 53
United National Front for Change (Egypt), 116(n3)
United Nations Development Programme (UNDP), 187
United Nations Relief and Works Agency (UNRWA), 123
United States: Bahrain's external mediation, 152–153; Iranian coup, 53; Iraq intervention, 247–248; Islamic democracy, 63–64; strengthening civil society organizations, 47(n4)
Urban poor, 22, 31(n19)

Violence: Bahraini intifada, 145; Egypt's religious civil society organizations, 179–181; Gaza's postelection violence, 129–130, 133–134; Iran's reformist victory, 65; response to Bahrain's liberalization, 150
Voice option, 29(n3)
Voter behavior: Jordan, 81–85; service delivery influencing, 95
Voter registration: Fatah's lack of preparation, 130; Iran under Pahlavi rule, 54
Voter turnout: Bahrain's constitutional reform, 167(n91); Egypt, 114–115, 186; Iran, 7–8, 58–61; Iran under Pahlavi rule, 54; Iran's reform movement's increasing apathy, 66–67; Iran's reformist victory, 65; Jordanian voter behavior, 82–83;

Middle Eastern low turnout, 24; relevance of, 29–30(n5); turnout and vote for Iran's Ahmadinejad, 71(fig.)

Wafd Party (Egypt), 31(n18), 96–97, 103, 118(n20), 174
Wasat Party (Egypt), 180–181
Wasta (intermediation mechanism), 22–23, 31(n21), 80–81
al-Wifaq (Bahrain), 154–158, 162(n7), 167(nn79,80,81)
Women: Bahrain's social institutions, 149; civil society groups addressing the needs of, 38; Egyptian civil society's lack of power, 178–179; exclusion from political institutions, 45; Moroccan parliamentarians, 224; Morocco's family code reform, 227–228; restrictions on Egyptian NGO participation, 188
Workers Democratic Confederation (Morocco), 229
World Bank, 196

Yazdi, Mohammed Mesbah, 63–64
Yemen: popular activism, 32(n24); tribal networks, 44–45; voter turnout, 31(n21)
Youssoufi, Abderrahman, 196, 225, 235(n4)
Youth: Egypt's Ghad party, 176; Egypt's Wasat party, 180; Morocco's Citizenship Forum, 199–200

Zahar, Mahmod, 132–134
Zaverei, Reza, 67
Zuhri, Abu, 132

About the Book

Political participation in authoritarian regimes is usually considered insignificant, or important only insofar as it promotes democracy. Turning this common wisdom on its head, *Political Participation in the Middle East* demonstrates the vitality, variety, and significance of political activism across the Middle East and North Africa.

Through an in-depth exploration of seven countries, the authors address how formal and informal political institutions create opportunities for participation in venues as varied as trade unions, civic associations, political parties, and elections. And, without losing sight of the fact that authoritarian regimes manipulate participation to reinforce their rule, they reveal ways in which citizens do benefit—by influencing decisionmaking, for example, or obtaining state resources. An engaging read for scholars and students, this work vividly illustrates how citizens matter in the politics of authoritarian regimes.

Ellen Lust-Okar is associate professor of political science and chair of the Council on Middle East Studies at Yale University. She is author of *Structuring Conflict in the Arab World*. **Saloua Zerhouni** is assistant professor of political science at Mohammed V University in Morocco.